Coastal Carolinas
Tales and Truths

By Pulitzer Prize Winning Journalist
W. Horace Carter
and
Scott Burleson

A Three Section Book

1 – Pirates, Bootleggers and Others

2 – Fishing, Hunting and Outdoor Stories

3 – Places To Go and Things To See In The Coastal Carolinas

INTRODUCTION

Stretching in and out of wetlands, sloughs, bays and tributaries from the southern border of Virginia to the northern extremity of Georgia near Savannah, lie more than 400 miles of shoreline of the Carolinas. Once a dismal, undeveloped jungle where pirates, poachers and bootleggers flourished, it has grown along with the rest of the United States, and cities and vacation resorts make it one of the most desirable places to live in the world.

It once was marked with violence as pirates seized upon the villages that dotted the coastline to hold up and harass helpless ships and crews while bloodsucking the money from land-based commerce as well.

In later years, moonshine whiskey makers circumvented the law and taxes by turning out discount-priced white lightning that was shipped to distant points and marketed illegally while cunning, hard-to-apprehend bootleggers kept the still fires burning in the dismal swamplands.

Pirates and moonshiners have disappeared from the coastal Carolinas. It remains a Utopia in many respects today as it is among the last frontiers for fresh and saltwater fishing, quail and deer hunting, among other outdoor delights.

This book is about those early days in the coastal Carolinas and the people of the area today who live and enjoy making a living off the land and the water as their ancestors did. There's emphasis here upon fantastic fishing and hunting with advice to help the reader acquire the techniques and expertise necessary to make your outdoor excursions successful adventures in our time. There are three sections to this book that offer something for every reader.

WHC

FOREWORD

The first section of this book is filled with stories about the coastal people of the Carolinas centuries ago when notorious pirates roamed the Atlantic and the low country villages. It was a vicious era in history where might seemed to make right and the lawless preyed upon the helpless with little compassion. Pirates punctuated history in that time period and romance and intrigue remain a fascination to students of the period.

Bootlegging illegal whiskey was rampant along these coasts after the heyday of the pirates and their cunning techniques and brazen lifestyles that flouted the tax laws well into the 19th century are legendary. Some of the largest moonshine liquor operations thrived in the swamplands of the Carolinas.

Perhaps not as thrilling for today's readers as pirates and bootlegging operations, the second section of this book notes the many places, people and things that are historic and attract visitors from around the world.

The final or third section is written for the outdoorsmen of today. It's about hunting and fishing along the near wilderness coastlines where saltwater species of fish continue to feed families while bringing a myriad of thrills and excitement to fishermen young and old, tourists and natives. Then there are chapters highlighting the great freshwater fishing in coastal rivers and lakes that remain productive for both the meat angler and the sportsman in quest of outdoor excitement.

Finally, there are stories of hunting for a variety of wildlife that still thrive in the desolate woodlands and remote farms. It's a bastion for deer, bear, quail, fox, rabbit, squirrel and duck hunters.

Stories here are generally true, although the place, time and outdoorsmen involved may have been changed to protect surviving relatives of some bygone years.

There's something for every reader of this book from the history buff to the cottontail rabbit hunter and cane pole fisherman. Hopefully, someone will enjoy reading it as much as I have enjoyed writing it.

WHC

ABOUT THE AUTHORS

W. Horace Carter is a native of Stanly County, North Carolina, who has lived in Florida part of the years since 1974. He has a home at Cross Creek in Alachua County and one at Yankeetown on the Withlacoochee River. He is a life-long hunter, fisherman and outdoorsman who realized his love for nature as a Boy Scout, earned his Eagle Badge and later served as a scoutmaster.

After graduating from Endy High School in Stanly County, he earned his degree in journalism at the University of North Carolina in Chapel Hill where he worked his way through school at the University News Bureau. He also edited the student newspaper, the *Tar Heel*.

After serving four years in the Navy during World War II, he founded the *Tabor City* (N.C.) *Tribune*, a weekly newspaper, in 1946, and as editor-publisher of that newspaper he won the Pulitzer Prize for Meritorious Public Service crusading against the Ku Klux Klan in 1953. He was the first weekly newspaper editor ever to win that pulitzer.

He and a partner eventually owned and operated seven weekly newspapers in the Carolinas.

He turned his publishing company over to his son in 1974 and since that time he has written 22 books and more than 2,000 magazine articles. Most of his books have been about the out-of-doors, but one is a history of golf at Myrtle beach, South Carolina, and another the story of how he won the Pulitzer Prize with his three-year editorial fight against the Ku Klux Klan. That book, *Virus of Fear* is now being considered for a movie or television series.

He loves to write about people and creatures in rural America through out the world. He has traveled in 51 foreign countries.

This book researches the activities of everyday Americans who lived extraordinary lives along the North Carolina-South Carolina coast.

Scott Burleson, my oldest grandson and an avid outdoorsman, contributed to the research and writing of this book. He began hunting and fishing with his father, Dr. Rowell Burleson, of Lumberton, North Carolina, when he was still in elementary school. He graduated from North Carolina State University and now works with the marketing division of John Deere in Raleigh, North Carolina.

Coastal Carolinas
Tales and Truths

Pirates, Bootleggers and Others

HOW COASTAL NAMES WERE BORN

Legends vary and the truth is evasive, but the strange names of North Carolina coastal communities intrigue the curious and challenge historians. Whether truth or tale, the folklore stories of how early American Tar Heel towns were named is fascinating.

None is more uncertain than Nags Head along the Outer Banks where offshore rocks and reefs once destroyed sailing vessels and earned the ocean there the dubious distinction of "Graveyard of the Atlantic." Hundreds of ships from Europe disintegrated in the rocky shallows, sending crews to their graves and wealth to the ocean floor. Often this destruction was the work of unscrupulous land pirates with villainous hearts saturated with greed who stooped to murder and deceit for nothing more than the waterlogged bounty that washed ashore from shattered merchant ships that they led astray and onto the rocky destruction.

Among the most prevalent stories of the source of the name "Nags Head" is the one that condemns early American settlers in the age of Blackbeard the pirate. Often suffering from hunger and poverty, they devised a plan to entice ship's crews onto the reefs. Shipwrecked and battered asunder, supplies and materials from the shattered crafts floated or washed ashore to the land pirate scavengers who dragged the bounty to wives and families.

These desperate sea robbers lured the richly-laden ships that swept up and down the coast between Charleston, South Carolina, and points north to their graves on mean stormy nights when they knew the crews were having trouble knowing their exact positions on dark, starless nights.

Long before the era of sophisticated electronic navigation when only the stars, moon and planets helped establish ships' positions in the coastal Atlantic, and when they were blacked

1

out on stormy, cloudy nights, desperate land robbers tied a lighted lantern around the neck of a nag, a wild Banker pony that lived among the sand dunes and roamed the marshes. They led the pony to roaming along the beach with the lantern swinging slowly with each step. Lookouts aboard lost ships, desperately seeking a sign that would establish their location and possibly lead them to a safe haven out of the storm, construed the slow-swinging lantern as a lighted signal from a ship that had found refuge and safety in a snug harbor. Many changed course to join what they believed to be another ship anchored safely and avoiding the threat of disaster on the stormy sea.

It was a cruel ruse! Ships quickly found they were engulfed by ferocious waves and shoreline breakers. They crashed on the beaches or inshore reefs. Crews were drowned and their cargoes sank in the shallow waters or washed up on the strand. Pilfering thieves reaped the easy harvest that they carried home or sold to unsuspecting buyers. The trick brought the demise of many fine early American ships, but mariners learned about the piracy and soon avoided the Carolina coast on stormy nights.

And that, say folklorists, is how Nag's Head got its name, notwithstanding, other researchers contend it was so named because the shoreline sand dunes resembled the head of a horse. Still others say it was named from an English pub behind the Royal Opera House in London with that same name. Others say a tiny stream in Devon, England was named Nags Head Creek and settlers from that community between Exeter and Cullompton who settled on he Carolina coast stole that moniker. Other early settlers came from Cornwall on the Isle of Scilly where a rock formation juts out into the sea and roughly resembles the shape of a horse's head.

Yet, the most intriguing origin of the name of Nag's head is that of the lantern around the pony's neck on stormy nights.

OCRACOKE ISLAND

Winds howled, giant waves pounded the beach, sand chattered against the ships' portholes in the wee hours of a blustery winter morning in 1718. Anchored on a 16-mile-long island off the North Carolina coast with the ominous skull and crossbones flag fluttering violently overhead, the infamous pirate Blackbeard nervously paced the deck. He cursed the night that was delaying the dawn. Soon his cutthroat crew would face a hand-to-hand battle with hearty seamen from Virginia sent to this lonely haven to get a notorious criminal of the Atlantic who pilfered and plundered ship after ship unlucky enough to encounter the murdering scoundrel without a conscience.

Fingering his curved sword that dangled from his belt and looking to the east where the first signs of daylight were nowhere to be seen, Blackbeard angrily muttered, "O cry cock!" It was his way of wishing for dawn when the last fight of his lawless life would begin and his ugly bearded head would roll.

Those words of Blackbeard, urging the rooster's wakeup call for the new day, named the Outer Banks island where his ship lurched and swayed. It sounded like "Ocracoke" and that is the name by which the historic island on the Pamlico Sound at the southernmost tip of the Outer Banks of North Carolina is known today.

Whether the naming is fact or fiction, truth or tale, will never be documented. It's as good a story of the origin of Ocracoke's name as any other. And as the Ocracoke Civic and Business Association says, "Ocracoke has always been a special place, etched in history and blessed with natural beauty.

When the first Europeans arrived on Ocracoke in the 1500's, the island was inhabited by Indians. In 1715 the North Carolina Colonial Assembly recognized a settlement established by seafaring pilots who guided vessels through Ocracoke Inlet and officially appointed Ocracoke a town in 1753.

Ocracoke was a favorite haunt of Edward Teach, the infamous pirate Blackbeard, In 1718 he was killed off Ocracoke in a hand-to-hand battle and then beheaded.

In 1990 the village of Ocracoke was listed on the National Register of Historic Places. The Historic District includes the 1823 Ocracoke Lighthouse, the 1942 Coast Guard Station, several historic commercial buildings and over 100 homes.

Ocracoke Village (pop. 700) is situated near the southern sound side of the island. Homes, hotels, restaurants, cottages and stores are scattered around the harbor where boats of all sizes seek haven. Ocracoke offers comfortable accommodations for visitors who like a friendly, small-town atmosphere by the water.

With access only by ferry, private boat or plane, Ocracoke is truly a place to get away . . a place to relax and take life easy. One of the barrier islands of the "Outer Banks" of North Carolina, Ocracoke is 16 miles long, and is washed by the Pamlico Sound on one side and the Atlantic Ocean on the other.

STEDE BONNET: THE GENTLEMAN PIRATE

An eerie calm filled the spirit of the Charles Towne harbor as Captain Stede Bonnet's body swung from a live oak tree for the fourth day. The town officials decided to leave him there for four days after his hanging to send a message to other pirates.

The wind rocked him back and forth like a macabre pendulum. It carried the smell of death across the peninsula.

With hands in pockets, a child watched the corpse with interest. Fifty yards away, laborers busied themselves digging a grave in the salt marsh.

- - -

The *Dolphin* was a small tavern near the harbor on the north sound of Barbados. Major Stede Bonnet swallowed a slug of rum and gazed out the glassless window. Major Bonnet was a wealthy plantation owner. His ascension to wealth and power had left him with no more worlds to conquer. He spent most of his days in the Dolphin, listening to old salts tell tales of the sea. He drank heavily and embellished some stories of his own. A young woman, not a day older than eighteen, massaged his shoulders lightly. She had long jet-black hair and a dark, tanned complexion. Bonnet stared at her. The girl understood and took his glass back to the barmaid for a refill. Ships of all sizes and purposes rested solemnly in the harbor. Bonnet studied one particular craft. It was anchored less than one hundred yards from the loading docks. Rum, sugar, indigo, rice and cotton were shipped from these docks in large quantities every day. In the fading moonlight he could just barely make out the name of this ship, the *Ancient Mariner*. The young woman brought him another glass of rum. Bonnet took the glass and drank it without even removing his focus from the *Mariner*. Oh, what freedom to sail the seas! To travel from port to port! To not be tied down with obligations of family and business! Major Bonnet gave the girl a single gold coin and staggered out the door. He boarded a rowboat and slipped off towards the craft. He grabbed the anchor rope off the bow. Bonnet imagined that he was a pirate, sneaking on board a rich privateer's craft. Slay the captain and take the riches! Then onward to greater pleasures!

Bonnet sat upon the deck of the *Ancient Mariner.* The crew was apparently absent. They were enjoying their leave in Barbados. The *Mariner* was a grand old vessel. Red paint accented the outer rim of the bow. It was carved to look like the head of a dragon. The ears of the dragon were slicked back, as if from too much wind.

"We call 'er Elizabeth," came a voice, "and she don't like strangers snoopin' around on her deck."

Bonnet turned around. A short, round, balding man stood before him. Even though he was only a few steps away, Bonnet hadn't heard him approach. "I'm sorry, sir, I am very sorry. I wasn't trying to snoop. I was merely . . . " Bonnet's words faded as he noticed the cutlass which hung on the round fellow's belt.

"Well, you were snoopin' and so now you should leave. But first, what's your name? Where do you live?"

Bonnet barely heard him. As if the man were calling him from miles away. Stede could not take his eyes off the cutlass. He glanced up to look into the short fellow's eyes. But he *felt* himself *not looking* at the cutlass. It danced in his peripheral vision. The sheath of the great blade was old and worn. The leather was painted black. The opening was stretched from hundreds of plunges of the blade. Stede thought he imagined a tint of blood on the man's pants. "Oh, my name is Major Stede Bonnet."

The short fellow's eyebrows met in a thoughtful pause. "Bonnet! Major Bonnet! Ah, I am a customer of your sugar and rum plantations. Ahem."

He cleared his throat and wiped his hands and forehead with a towel. "Mr. Bonnet, ah, Major Bonnet, please accept my apologies. My name is Israel Morton. Welcome aboard the *Mariner.* Our captain perished with a ah, well, a strange illness in the colonies. We traditionally transported rum there. But this ship is old and is in desperate need of repair. So our owner wishes to hold it here for awhile. Major Bonnet, would you like some rum?"

Major Stede Bonnet, wealthy and bored plantation owner of Barbados, and Quartermaster Israel Morton, leader of a crew without a ship, commenced drinking large quantities of rum together. Bonnet confided that he had recently bought a ship, the *Revenge*, and had spent considerable money reconditioning it. Morton proposed that they inspect it together and that if it were in good enough shape, they could go into the rum business together. He slipped below decks for a moment. Bonnet heard a scurrying of activity below. When Morton came back on deck he was adorned with two pistols on either side of his belt.

They began rowing towards the location of Bonnet's ship. On the backstroke, Stede caught the glimpse of a dagger hidden in Morton's belt under his jacket. Bonnet thought to himself that he should have been worried, but curiously, he wasn't. It was the most excitement he had known in years. As they moved around the southwest tip of the island, Stede could see the black shadow of the *Mariner* pivot. It was following them.

The *Revenge* was anchored in a shallow harbor. Upon boarding, Morton ran all about, knocking on boards, checking the steering wheel, observing the new cloth in the sails. A quick inspection left Morton with his mouth watering.

"You've done a good job with this, Major Bonnet. If I didn't know better, I would've thought that you were just waiting for my crew and me to come along." Bonnet saw Israel's hand reach in his belt for his dagger. He could also see the *Ancient Mariner* approaching.

Israel's tone changed to a darker, deeper one. "Mr. Bonnet, I have a confession to make. Our crew, well, we're are an independent lot. We don't like to work for any one person for very long. Because, you see, after a while, the owner of the ship starts to think that he owns you, and not just the ship."

"I don't believe that I follow you, Miss-sster Morton," Bonnet said. He smiled because he knew he was tempting fate. Israel''s face tensed. "We, sir, are pirates. And I have a proposition for you. We'll elect you captain of the *Revenge*. Then we will proceed to fulfill all of those dreams you mentioned. The ocean will be your home, just as you have fantasized. Your family and business will no longer be worries to you. And we will all be rich beyond comprehension."

"You can release your dagger, Mr. Morton, because I accept."

The crew, a rough lot, boarded with the arrival of the *Mariner*. They had followed Morton and Bonnet. Morton had planned to take the vessel with or without Bonnet's consent. But Major Bonnet was pleased, for he was now *Captain* Stede Bonnet, dreaded Caribbean pirate.

The *Revenge*, equipped with an experienced crew and an ambitious captain, began terrorizing ships from the Caribbean all the way up to the northern colonies. Bonnet paid particular attention to his dress. He wore a black cape, black hat and a scarlet shirt that looked like fire when the wind breathed through it. Like a child with a new toy on Christmas morning, he was often seen practicing with his sword on the ship's bow stabbing at a barrel. He enjoyed looking through the maps and plotting the next move. And his reputation as a ruthless pirate grew.

When he captured the *Turbet* off the coast of Virginia, he burned the ship and its inhabitants to the waterline. He made prisoners walk the plank. He tied his disobedient crew members to the mast. According to legend, he buried large amounts of captured treasure in the swamps of islands in the mouth of the Cape Fear River. It was also rumored that he hid treasure on North Carolina's barrier islands, in the mouth of the Chesapeake, and on islands off the South Carolina coast between Charleston and Hilton Head Island.

As part of his quartermaster duties, Morton updated the maps with information about the buried treasure.

"Captain Bonnet," Morton began, "I have a suggestion for you sir. But you're going to have to trust me. I want to sail to a small island off the Spanish Main."

"Do you think that we've gotten too predictable?" asked Bonnet.

"Ah, yeah, that's it. Definitely too predictable. But also there's somebody I want you to meet. We need to be there by the next full moon."

Bonnet nodded. "You haven't led me wrong so far. Let us go there. Yes, I will order it effective immediately. Ahem. Quartermaster Morton, please inform the men that we will turn around immediately and sail for the southern continent. Is this command understood?"

Morton smiled. "Yes sir. Immediately, sir."

The *Revenge* arrived on location off the modern coast of Colombia exactly two days before the full moon. Morton spent his time in the crow's nest looking at the horizon through an eyepiece. He looked like a hawk searching for the direction of the wind from the treetops.

Finally, a convoy of ships came upon them. Under orders from the quartermaster, a pirate gunner fired three consecutive shots from the bow. Three shots rang out from the other ships. The smoke from the shots had not even cleared the air when Bonnet saw a bantam craft coming from them with a lone rower. The visitor was adorned in an outfit of black. His long black curly beard reached down to his waist. Captain Bonnet's heart skipped a beat as he prepared to meet Captain Blackbeard (Edward Teach).

Once Blackbeard was aboard, he, Morton and Bonnet went to the captain's quarters. "Captain Bonnet, your reputation precedes you! Please tell me that you won't maroon me or tie me to your mast."

"Of course not Mister, ah, Captain Teach," replied Stede. Blackbeard laughed at this remark. The two captains proceeded to drink huge quantities of rum. While inebriated, Bonnet agreed that the two captains should combine forces. He then agreed to stay in the luxury of Blackbeard's cabin. Blackbeard appointed one of his own, a Lieutenant Turner, to helm the *Revenge*.

At first Bonnet enjoyed the deal. The pirates were highly effective at surrounding trading vessels and quickly taking their loot. But a visit to Charles Towne curbed Bonnet's appetite for piracy. Blackbeard captured a ship traveling from Charles Towne to England, the *Crowley*. He took all of the passengers hostage. These were well-to-do citizens. Children were also aboard.

Blackbeard sent word back to Charles Towne that if they

did not send medicines immediately, he would start killing the hostages. An envoy of pirates and Charles Towne citizens rowed into the harbor to give the message. They eventually returned with the required goods. However, it took several days. In this interval, Blackbeard ran about the ship like a wild animal shouting his threats to kill his new "passengers." Perhaps these up-scale folks reminded Bonnet of his own family. Maybe his lack of responsibility gave him time to reflect upon his recent sins. For whatever reason, Captain Bonnet felt badly about what was going on. As this successful mission was accomplished, and Charles Towne harbor was left behind in the salty wake of the *Revenge*, he wondered how he could ever get back home to Barbados and his family without being known as a criminal.

Bonnet quit drinking rum. He quit sleeping all day. He spent his time leaning over the stern rail of the ship watching the horizon. Bonnet looked like he was searching for something. Blackbeard grew weary of Bonnet's moping. "Captain Bonnet, am I correct in assuming that you did not approve of the manner in which I obtained these medicines?"

"No sir, not exactly," replied Bonnet.

"What do you mean 'exactly'?" asked Blackbeard.

Bonnet shrugged his shoulders and looked back to the horizon. "Stede, I have a suggestion. We're running awfully heavy. We'll take you to Bath Towne in the Carolina colony. You ask Governor Eden for a pardon. I'll hide the loot and return there to ask for a pardon myself. Then we'll grab the loot, split it, and go our separate ways."

Stede considered this! He remembered all of the other loot he had hidden. But to obtain it he would have to steal Morton's maps. But with a pardon, he could return to Barbados and his family with enough treasure to prove his success as a pirate.

"Captain Teach! Onward to Bath Towne!" he said with more enthusiasm than he had known since the beginning of his venture.

The infamous Captain Stede Bonnet received his pardon in Bath Towne. But he would never see Blackbeard or his loot again. As badly as he wanted to return to Barbados as a pardoned citizen, he couldn't dare go back without physical evidence of his travels. Or with the humiliation that Blackbeard had given him.

He called Morton into his chambers to plot his final objective. "Quartermaster Morton, I have had enough."

"Well, Captain Bonnet, I *assumed that* since you asked for a pardon. How about if we take you back to Barbados and we'll keep your ship. You wouldn't want it reminding you of all this," said Israel.

"But Mr. Morton, what about all the treasure we hid? I would like may share you know, which should be 75%."

"I see. I was counting on you not taking so much."

Bonnet grasped the handle of his sword. "Mr. Morton, may I remind you who is captain of this vessel?"

"No sir, of course not. However, might I ask a favor of you?"

"You may," said Bonnet.

"You can't let Blackbeard make a fool of you. Let's attack a couple more ships. We'll call you a false name so folks will not think that you have broken the agreement of your pardon. Also, the 25% of all the treasure that the crew and I get will be bigger. I think they'll be happier that way. Besides, they've been getting restless lately."

"Excellent Quartermaster Morton! Call me Captain, ah, *Captain Thomas*. Yes, that's a good name. And it is now mine. Also, we cannot call this the *Revenge* any longer, for it is well known as a pirate ship. It is now the *Royal James*."

A cold, thoughtful smile shown from Morton's face like the sail of a blockade runner through the fog. "By the way, Captain Thomas, I suggest that after we load up one last time that we 'clean our heels' in the Cape Fear River. Then we can more swiftly transport your 75% of the loot to Barbados. And after that, I'll be no more than a faint memory to you," said Morton.

"Another excellent suggestion! I shall announce it to our men immediately!" said Bonnet. By "cleaning our heels," Morton referred to repairs and maintenance of the ship. This was necessary about once a month.

The sea hardly stirred on that fateful night. Bonnet, masquerading as Captain Thomas, slowly walked about the deck in the moonlight. The shadows of the golden moon lay still about the deck of the ship. They watched Bonnet walk and reminisce about his career in piracy. And they laughed at his dreams of home. As Bonnet turned to go to his quarters, he noticed that a rowboat was missing.

Over the following weeks, the *Royal James* efficiently disabled and robbed several ships off the Virginia coast. Bonnet was finally ready for his return voyage. Within a few days, they were careening in the mouth of the Cape Fear River, between Southport and Wilmington, North Carolina.

- - -

Colonel William Rhett pulled a handkerchief out of his pocket. He wiped the brass handle of the steering wheel of his warship, the *Sea Nymph.* He admired the perfect shine of the full moon's face on the glassy surface of the brass. His men scurried about the ship busily. An important-looking man in military dress approached him.

"Lieutenant Peters! Please report to me the status of our vessel!" commanded Rhett.

"Colonel Rhett, sir, all of the ammunition has been stored by each cannon and gun, sir. All knives and swords have been sharpened and are wielded by each man. All are eating supper now, sir, so they will have plenty of energy for our attack. We should reach them at 4:00 a.m., sir," replied Lieutenant Peters.

"Lieutenant, do you speak of just our ship, or our other vessel, the *Henry*?"

"Both ships, sir. Also, I should add that the men are extremely excited. As in all of Charles Towne, we thirst for the blood of all pirates, especially that bastard Charles Vane. Vane has robbed our city of more than gold and silver, for he has taken our pride as well. Blackbeard, Captain Bonnet, our city is tired of bowing to the whims of such trash. The emotional advantage will be ours in this battle. With our firepower it should not take long," said the Lieutenant.

"Now Mr. Peters you should caution the men about one thing. Regardless of how much emotion the men have, these pirate suspects are to be taken alive if possible. We are not a barbaric mob. If we were, sir, we would be little better than the pirates themselves. We are a civilized military force that will apprehend the suspects and take them to a fair trial before the citizens of Charles Towne. Do you understand?" said Rhett.

"Yes sir, Colonel Rhett."

"By the way, how is the pirate's traitor doing?"

"Sir?'

Colonel Rhett shook his head, "Not traitor, I meant our *informer.* What is he doing?"

"He is a despicable fellow. Right now he is drunk and passed out on my cabin floor. Do you have his list of demands?"

"You mean besides all the rum he could drink? Yes, I have it. One of his comrades is to meet us at the opening of the channel. The two of them will be pardoned in exchange for their cooperation and testimony."

"Yes, sir," said Lieutenant Peters

"Lieutenant," Rhett began, "wake the fool when you detect the Bald Head Island lighthouse with your spyglass. In case his friend doesn't show up, we'll need his help to find Vane's ship."

"Yes, sir."

- - -

When the good captain saw two warships sailing up the channel, his mahogany pipe dropped out of his mouth. The conscience of the entire crew felt the enemy presence at once. All could hear the pipe slide down the deck.

In a scramble, the pirates attended their battle stations. But they moved too quickly. When the sail slid up the mast, the *Royal James* traversed into a sand bar. The ship quit moving forward and spun around, burying the keel deeper. Bonnet sat on the deck and pulled a whiskey bottle from his vest. The *Henry* and the *Sea Nymph* ran aground on either side of Bonnet's *Royal James*. The Charles Towne cannons began pummeling the *James.*

The good pirate captain finished his whiskey and climbed into the crow's nest. He tore off his white shirt and waved it into the air, gesturing his surrender.

Captain Bonnet, the "gentleman pirate," enjoyed a relatively luxurious prison life prior to his trial. Colonel Rhett was so overwhelmed that it was not Charles Vane whom he captured that he agreed to let Bonnet reside in the marshal's home rather than in jail. In Charles Towne, Bonnet was treated like a celebrity. Young boys battled each other in the streets with toy swords, each pretending to be Stede Bonnet. Young ladies batted their eyelashes at him. They whispered among themselves about how good looking he was and about his brave adventures. The general consensus of the town was that he would not receive the death penalty.

Older ladies in the town stopped by the marshal's house with cakes and tea for the good captain. As a man raised in a wealthy home, Bonnet accepted the attention graciously, But more than ever, it made him miss his home in Barbados. He missed his family. He knew that if he were convicted of piracy he could never return home. Never.

He sweet-talked a young maiden into bringing him some women's clothes. Then, dressed as a woman, he escaped. In a stolen craft, he traveled directly into a storm. The violent winds washed him onto nearby Sullivans Island.

He begged the citizens for forgiveness. He begged the governor for forgiveness. He cried at the thought of being hung. But at the conclusion of the trail, he was found guilty. Alone in jail. Alone as death. The jail was as black as the bottom of the ocean.

A mob greeted him on his day of execution. They taunted him as his death cart was paraded around modern day Meeting Street in downtown Charleston. The festival of people surrounding him took Bonnet to the end of Charles Towne known today as the "Battery."

"Any last wishes?" asked the executioner.

Bonnet looked down at himself. Sitting on a horse backwards. Noose around his neck. Acres of curious people. "Let me face the ocean. And then bury me in this marsh."

The executioner considered this request and nodded. As he turned the horse so that Stede could face the ocean, Stede saw Morton on the front row—*smiling*. Morton waved at him with a scroll. ". . . the maps," Stede whispered to himself. He looked across the ocean and inhaled a deep breath. The horizon beckoned him again for another adventure. An instant before the whip cracked on the horse, Captain Bonnet noticed that the wind was coming from the northwest. He whispered, "It'll be rough out there."

The town left Captain Stede Bonnet's body hanging from the oak tree for four days. The spot of his execution was marked with a block of marble. He was buried in the marsh as he requested. Later, the marsh was filled in with dirt and protected with concrete—forever sealing the pirate's body into the Charleston Battery.

Today the oldest house in Charleston is the home of Colonel William Rhett. A marker on the Rhett house reads, "William Rhett House—built in 1713 by William Rhett—Colonel in the militia, and vice-admiral of the province. In 1706, he repulsed a French-Spanish naval attack and in 1718 captured Stede Bonnet, pirate."

WILLIAM, THE PASTOR & BLACKBEARD

During a renovation of a Charleston plantation home, a book written by Will Eporantez was found. Eporantez was a wealthy planter during pre-Revolutionary War times. The book documented one particularly interesting rendezvous with the most notorious sailor along the historic Carolina coast.

— — —

The story of how much money I have acquired from my plantation is not nearly as exciting as the story of how I originally acquired my riches. During this episode, I met Blackbeard the Pirate. This fellow is every bit as treacherous as legends have made him out to be. His woolly appearance petrified sailors. His hair was black as death. His beard was long and braided like a hideous mask. Blackbeard laughed at men who dared to stand before him. His enemies were more likely to retreat than attack.

I had an interesting partner back then. His name was James Tacker. It was assumed by the general populace that Tacker was an idiot. He did funny things like repeat phrases under his breath. He repeated them over and over again. He ignored everyone. Some folks around Charles Towne said he did well in school as a child, but he just never developed any social skills. We both lived on Johns Island, near Charles Towne.

People called him "the Pastor." Tacker got the name "Pastor" because he always carried a Bible with him. *Always.* And more than that, he read from it constantly. He copied pages of Ecclesiastes over and over and over. He did other strange things too, and boy, did he bother old Blackbeard.

Pastor Tacker and I both worked on the docks in Charles Towne. When our adventure began, I was 18 and he was 28. The people in Charles Towne didn't like Tacker. He spoke in riddles from one book of the Bible, Ecclesiastes. Tacker was a sorry excuse for a worker. During his work hours, he copied Ecclesiastes verses out of his old leather-bound Bible onto paper, or boards, or anything his pencil marks would stay on.

Tacker's mother, Martha, was sick and couldn't take care of him anymore. I had planned a trip to England and she asked me if I would take him with me. She had a nephew in London who was a monk. Considering "Pastor" Tacker's daily habit of copying Ecclesiastes over and over again, the nephew thought that he could put Tacker to some productive Christian work.

I remember when Tacker and I worked the docks for the last time. He rambled aloud as usual.

"As a dream comes when there are many cares, so the speech of a fool when there are many words," he said.

"Tacker, my friend," I said, "we are going to be together for a long time on this voyage. If you want to copy your Bible pages, then fine. But I really don't want to hear about it right now."

Tacker said, "Two are better than one, because they have a good return for their work: If one falls down, his friend can help him up."

"All right. Fine. Do what you want to do, fool," I said.

He said, "One falls down . . . another can help . . . one falls down . . . another can help. But pity the man who falls and has no one to help him up! Though one may be overpowered, two can defend themselves. A cord of three strands is not quickly broken."

"OK, I see your point. Was that part of your Bible verse?"

Tacker said, "Yes."

I waited for him to give some explanation, but all he said was "Yes." He was indeed a strange fellow. He continued to mutter, "One falls down. . . another can help . . . one falls down . . ."

In May 1718, we began our voyage on our ship, the Matthew. Under the bright eye of the sun, the *Matthew* battled the currents of Charles Towne harbor. It was a wooden monster that plowed along persistently. All the passengers were on deck, taking in the newness of being at sea.

The sky was bright blue, almost shiny. The wind whipped our sails. They popped them back and forth. I felt the money in my pocket. I had a bad habit of continuously checking to see if I had lost it.

It felt good to be at sea. The wind cooled my face. The sea gulls chirped and followed along behind. Normally I considered their sounds to be disruptive noise. Today it was music celebrating our departure.

Tacker sat on the deck. He lightly bumped his head on the mast as he whittled something into it. There was no doubt that whatever words he made were from Ecclesiastes. The Bible was opened before his eyes. His lips mumbled in an indiscernible language.

The other passengers took in the sights. The ocean was a novelty to them. Children threw stones into the sea. Husbands held their wives and pointed to the horizon. Doubtless all were excited about going to England. Little did we know that not all of us would make it there.

For it was then that we saw the beast. A large galleon with dozens of gun barrels. Metal-plated armor. A flag with a grotesque picture of a skeleton flew atop the mast. Barnacles clung to the evil sides. Under the heat of the sun, I thought I saw the crew dancing in circles. Before us was Blackbeard's ship, the *"Queen Anne's Revenge."* Two other ships split from behind the eclipse of the *Queen Anne's Revenge.* I could have sworn that the damn thing had just multiplied—like an amoeba. These were two other ships of the bearded one. They were the *Revenge* and the *Adventure.*

Standing at the bow of the *Matthew*, Blackbeard waved two pistols in the air. In a panic our captain waved back with two white flags. He waved one so violently that he accidentally threw it into the air.

Within minutes Blackbeard boarded our ship—alone. He was obviously confident in our inability to harm him. A single bead of sweat rolled down my cheek. I dared not move to wipe it. The crew and passengers were assembled on deck.

"Fair citizens of Charles Towne, this is the luckiest day in your life! Normally we should relieve you of your heavy cargo, (that is, your gold coins) but today our vessels are full. And since we are not greedy, *we would like to borrow* some of your medicines."

The way he said the word "borrow" made my toes cringe. Obviously he was stealing the goods. His implication of a false friendship mocked our weakness. It made the whole event seem even more sinister. His words had barely left his forked tongue when our captain placed a wooden crate before him. "That's all we have, sir," he said.

The passengers were wonderfully terrified. Scared, and yet, they were in awe of the presence of such a celebrity.

Poor ol' Tacker never even seemed to notice the intrusion. He sat with his back to the mast. His hands were hastily copying pages. He appeared to be finishing his homework just before class.

The pirate was satisfied that we had given him all we had. The fear on our faces was all the proof he needed. Blackbeard tipped his hat and turned to leave. The alignment of my fate with pirates should have ended right there. But it was not to be. Tacker walked over to Blackbeard. He marched until he was inches from Blackbeard's face. He stared into the cold eyes of the pirate. Tacker was clearly amused. He tugged at the long black beard. He giggled. His mouth opened wide. My heart sank. I had a fatalistic desire to plunge into the ocean and take my chances of swimming back to Johns Island.

Tacker said, "I saw the tears of the oppressed—and they have no comforter; p*ower was on the side of their oppressors*—and they have no comforter. And I declared that the dead, who had already died, are happier than the living, who are still alive. But better than both is he who has not yet been, who has not seen the evil that is done under the sun."

When he said "power," missiles of saliva assaulted the pirate's face. Tacker smiled. His grin was childlike. Time stopped. The face of the Blackbeard progressed from apathy to anger. He was not amused. "What did you say? Just what did you say?" The silence in the idiot's face was deafening.

Tacker sat down. He sat down by Blackbeard's feet. He proceeded copying pages as if the whole event had not happened. As if he were by himself on the docks of Charles Towne.

"Boy! Get up! Why do you talk nonsense in the face of your death?"

I felt my survival instincts trying to silence my mouth. But my mind was not as quick as my foolish tongue. "He is an idiot," I said. "He can't help it. Mr. Blackbeard, please pay him no mind, he really can't help it."

Tacker looked at me. He said, *"The fool folds his hands and ruins himself."* He pointed to the leg of the intruder.

Blackbeard needed no more justification. He gripped Tacker's hair and tugged him to his feet. Tacker held his papers tightly. He squeezed his Bible inside his jacket. His legs drew up into a fetal position.

"Please stop!" I said. "Really, he *is* an idiot."

That was my last memory. I don't remember anyone hitting me, but I came to consciousness below deck on board Blackbeard's ship. It was dark. The odor of rotten fish tickled my nose. The floor was sticky beneath my seat. I could hear the sound of Tacker's pencil scribbling away. My shirt collar was soaking wet. As I touched the back of my neck, I felt the sticky goo of my own blood.

"Tacker? Where are you? Are you all right?" I asked.

He didn't answer, but his scribbling picked up pace. I was tempted to scold him, but what good would it have done? He didn't know any better. "Come on, Tack, I'm not mad at you. Are you all right?"

"Will?" called Tacker.

"Yes, I'm here."

"I . . . am . . . all . . . right," he said. He pronounced each word crisply as if it meant something by itself.

He began whispering more scripture. The words reverberated through the empty corridor like music. "There is a time for everything, and a season for every activity under heaven: a time to be born and a time to die, a time to plant and a time to uproot, a time to kill and a time to heal, a time to tear down and a time to build, a time weep and a time to laugh, a time to mourn and a time to dance, a time to scatter stones and a time to gather stones, a time to embrace and a time to refrain, a time to search and a time to give up, a time to keep and a time to throw away, a time to tear and a time to mend, a time to be silent and a time to speak, a time to love and a time to hate, a time for war and a time for peace. Will, it is time for one of these things *now*," said Tacker.

"Well," I began, "which *thing* is it the time for?"

His scribbling stopped. In the darkness, I could see his glance turn to the void of the darkness. "I don't know."

I said, "You don't know what?"

"Yes. I don't know," he said.

I could hear him whispering, ". . . time for everything . . . time for everything, time for every season; born . . . *die* . . . plant . . . uproot . . . kill . . . heal . . . *tear down* and build, yes tear down and then build . . . weep and then laugh . . . *mourn* . . . dance . . . . "

H repeated the passage with emphasis on certain words. "No, Mr. Will, I don't know."

"Tacker, quit it with your verses! What do you expect? To figure out what time now is supposed to be for?"

He quit whispering and looked up. "I don't know. If I repeat them, then I might figure out what we are supposed to be doing now. But if I do figure it out, by that time it will probably be time to do something else and so then I'll have to figure that out. So it's really all meaningless."

I said, "If it's meaningless, then why don't you just be quiet!"

"Meaningless! Meaningless! Utterly meaningless! Everything is meaningless," Tacker said.

"You are truly a nut," I said. I lay back down onto the sticky deck. I fell asleep.

I dreamed that Tacker was in the crow's nest of the ship. The moon whirled around and around his head. The pirates did their normal chores without even noticing him. He was shouting, "Meaningless! Meaning—less! Everything is meaningless!

Meaningless!"

I was shouting back, "Shut up! Shut up, you idiot! Be quiet." But he kept on, "Everything is meaningless without..."

I was awakened by a pirate. I wasn't sure which parts of this adventure I had dreamed and which parts were real. He pulled me with one hand and Tacker with his other. This pirate was the dirtiest, grimiest, smelliest person that ever touched me. His smell was a vile combination of body odor, rum, and fish. His skin was brown leather. His clothes of fine quality, though filthy, were obviously stolen.

He brought us up to the deck. The brightness of the white sun consumed me. Pirates scrambled about tending to their duties. They argued a little and sang a little, but they were mostly too busy to do anything except work. Our pirate threw us each a small towel, a bucket of water, and a bar of soap. "Bathe," he said. So we did. This was obviously not the time for modesty and after lying in that filthy hold, it felt good to wash. As I scrubbed the wound on the back of my head, round clumps of clotted blood fell to the deck. The pirate emptied our pockets. He put our belongings in a pile. He handed us each a change of clothes. The clothes were very comfortable. They were loose and were made of cotton.

"Follow me," he said. And we did. We descended into another cabin. I was afraid that we were going back into our dungeon. He brought us into a narrow room. It had numerous benches and tables. "Sit," he said. And we did.

He brought us both a piece of stale bread, an apple, a small bowl of rice, a piece of smoked fish, and a cup of water. Among these folks, there was no doubt that this must have been a feast. Of course, this kindness was confusing. Tacker did not question it. He appeared perfectly at home as he devoured his meal. We finished in only a few minutes.

Our guide said, "Follow me now." And we did.

He tugged us up some stairs and then back down stairs. I sensed that we were toward the stern of the ship. I felt better after the nourishment. I figured we were about to become slaves to assemble ammunition or something. Through a narrow corridor, the pirate stopped at a large oaken door. He knocked three steady times with the bottom of his fist: boom . . . boom. . . boom. I don't know why, but I was hoping that door would never open. I had an anxious feeling about what predatory evil might lurk in the echo behind it.

If nobody answered the door, I fantasized that our pirate might say, "Ah, the heck with it. You guys take our little schooner and head back to Charles Towne." But instead, he pushed us in front of him.

The door opened. We entered. It was a large room. Bright red and purple tapestries lined the walls. Half-empty bottles of wine were scattered about. A cabinet contained several dozen pistols beautifully black and clean. The other wall was lined with swords and knives of all dimensions. Double-edged daggers, seven foot broadswords, throwing knives with two blades, ivory handles, ebony trim, every possible combination was there. Two large oaken beams divided the room into thirds. To the right, I could see a small bedroom through an open doorway. To the left there was a rectangular table. A pleasant lady sat on a bench on the far side of the table. Behind her was the outer hull of the ship. She had fair skin and light red hair. She was petite. A sweet feminine island amongst these hooligans. She smiled.

Blackbeard sat at the head of the table. He was not wearing his blood-red hat or coat. His yellow teeth split through his beard as he smiled. Another fellow sat to Blackbeard's left. He was dressed like a banker from London. He wore a suit and he even had his cane and cap leaning next to him. Playing cards were distributed across the table. Inventories of gold coins were before each person.

Blackbeard said, "Excellent! Excellent! Mary, if you would leave us; and Robert, you too, please. I have some business to discuss with our passengers."

The banker popped up immediately and placed his cap perfectly on his head. He did not even look at us as he walked out. Tacker whispered in my ear, "All *his days he eats in darkness, with great frustration, affliction and anger.*" I looked at him sternly. He was going to get us killed yet.

The lady disappeared behind the bedroom door. Her light steps didn't even seem to touch the floor as she hovered across the room. The door slowly closed behind her.

Our escort departed. The large oaken door closed. We were alone with him. We were alone with Blackbeard.

"Greetings, gentlemen, and welcome on board my ship. My name is Edward Teach, also known in your beloved Carolina as Blackbeard. I am a privateer. Some would say I am a pirate. It really doesn't matter. Please, won't you both sit here at my table," he said.

Tacker's Bible was open. His eyes focused intently upon the pages. He mouthed the words quickly. I tugged at his shirt sleeve and we both sat on the bench where the lady had been. Once we sat down, Tacker pulled out his notebook and started copying verses. He mouthed the words as he wrote them.

Blackbeard, the same person who was enraged at Tacker's comments earlier, seemed not to even notice his eccentricities. now.

"Thank you, gentlemen. Originally I captured you two because of your disrespect to me upon your ship. But I have had a change of heart. You see, I have a special job for each of you. I am concerned about how the colonial people think of me. I do have some important friends, but most people are afraid. I can tell that each of you has had a decent amount of education. Don't ask me how I know. I just do. I need two scribes. Mr. William Eporantez, I will dictate to you a brief history of my adventures. I need you to write it down perfectly. And when you finish, you will spend one year with me. You will document our further adventures and in your spare time you will make copies of these books. I am sure we will make you as comfortable as possible. Is this acceptable?"

"Ohm," I heard myself say, "I guess, ohm, I accept." I couldn't believe I had said those words. Hell no, I didn't want to stay on this ship one more second than I needed to. But what choice did I have?

Blackbeard said, "Excellent! And Mr. Tacker, you have an important job indeed. You are to reproduce my treasure maps! Many men have died searching for my treasure. You are the only person I will ever provide this information to. If you share it with anyone, especially your associate Mr. Eporantez, I will kill you. But I know that we don't have to worry about that, now do we? Mr. Tacker, will you perform this service?"

Tacker quit scribbling. He closed his Bible. He glared at the old pirate. With one solemn motion, he nodded his head.

"Excellent! It is settled. There is nothing to wait for. You two have rested, bathed and eaten. I want to start immediately. He hurried into his bedroom and closed the door. He returned immediately with a large ceramic jar.

"Mr. Tacker," he said, "These are the maps. Go into my bedroom. My wife will show you a secret room adjacent to it. Inside there are all the pencils and paper you will ever need. You will lock the door behind you every time you leave. And you are to never, ever remove a copy of a map from that room. If I ever find you with one, the sharks will feast on your liver that evening. Do you understand?"

Again, Tacker responded with an affirmative single nod. He gathered his Bible and papers and briskly disappeared into the bedroom.

"Now, Mr. Eporantez, if I ever find you anywhere near my map room, my bedroom, in this room without my permission, or anywhere at all with one of my maps, you can't imagine the death that will take you."

I looked around the room at all the robes and weapons. It occurred to me that all of these things had belonged to people. People who were probably part of the oceanic biosystem now. *They were all dead.* What did these people have in common? They were all at the wrong place at the wrong time when ol' Mr. Edward Teach crossed their paths.

"Please, Mr. Eporantez, forgive my harsh nature. Most people I have known on the sea would have gladly placed one of my own daggers in my back if I gave them the opportunity. Don't be scared off by my warnings. I just want to make sure that you understand me. You will not get a second chance for breaking a rule. Now, let us put these unpleasantries behind us. Lots of people would love to be in your place; to hear the story of Blackbeard from his own mouth. This really will be fun. If you ever need anything on our voyages, ask and I will provide it if I can. I will share some of our loot with you also. One year from now, I will drop you off at Charles Towne and you will be a wealthy man. In addition, you will have the manuscript of a book that the bookmakers will beg for the right to publish. You have fallen into good fortune!"

I said, "Was it good fortune that struck my head?"

Blackbeard laughed. He clutched his sides as he chuckled. "Yes, your humor will serve you well on this voyage. Here. You need a real pirate's hat. He took his own red hat and placed it on my head. It was too big. The front dropped over my eyes. I had a feeling that maybe I belonged here. Anyhow, I must admit, I liked wearing the hat.

"And here, you are a pirate now. You must wear a sword."

He took a three-foot-long broadsword off the wall and handed it to me. The blade was silver and beautiful. Like a child on Christmas morning, I strapped it on quickly.

"And now, Will Eporantez, dreaded pirate of the Atlantic, let us begin our story together, shall we?"

Everything he said seemed to make sense. In the past 30 minutes, my emotions had gone from terrified to content. I was almost excited about writing Blackbeard's story.

Let's get started," I said.

Blackbeard said, "This is how I want to do this. We are on course for Ocracoke Island. I do not anticipate intercepting any ships for awhile. I will tell you a summary of my adventures, and once settled at Ocracoke, we must replenish our supplies, clean the sides of the ship and perform some repairs. Next we will leave for Boston—lots of silver shipments have been heading that way. You will get to observe our assault techniques. Anyhow, after we leave Ocracoke, I will fill you in on the details of my story. Is this acceptable?"

"Yes," I said.

He placed a neat stack of papers on the table. He gave me a shiny black pencil from his shirt pocket.

"Good. My name is Edward Teach. I'm from Bristol, England. I spent my childhood days at the docks, watching the ships come in. I quickly made friends with the mates who came ashore after their months at sea. They were rougher than I. Much like you, I had to go to school. The soft lifestyle of a schoolboy didn't suit me very well. I wanted to be tough as the seamen.

"I finally convinced the best pirate of the Atlantic, Captain Hornigold (his first name was Ben), to let me be his cabin boy. But as soon as we were at sea, I proved worthy as a regular member of his crew. Captain Hornigold was a tough man. And he was brilliant. He shared his strategies with me. I studied them and witnessed their perfect execution many times.

"Hornigold liked to accumulate ships. This way, he could ambush the merchants like a real navy. When the merchants saw us coming, they usually surrendered without a fight. This is the ultimate victory—the kind where your opponent surrenders without any defense. I convinced him to let me be the captain of one of his ships, the *Serpent*.

"He was immediately impressed. But at that stage in my career, I knew everything Hornigold knew, so I took the *Serpent*, and her crew and struck out on my own. We plundered many vessels. It was unbelievably fun. I used to know all of our victims' names, but I can't remember any more. There have been so many.

"My favorite endeavor was when I alone held your precious city of Charles Towne, indeed the whole province of Carolina, hostage. I captured some prominent citizens. For instance, I held that coward, Samuel Wragg in this very vessel. All I asked for was medicines. That's why I asked for medicines from your ship, to relive those sweet memories. I held all the bastards captive until they gave me the goods I wanted.

"I guess you think these things make me a bad person. Once I felt guilty for these crimes, if you call them that, and I asked Governor Eden for a pardon. He is a friend of mine, so he did. I decided I would be a farmer or some such nonsense and live in North Carolina. I married a local girl. She was sweet as the morning.

"But all my life had been at sea. I couldn't just stop. I started trading again on my ship the *Adventure*. My friend, trading and pirating are just not the same. I missed the thrill of the ambush of an unsuspecting vessel. I missed the fear in the eyes of the merchants. I missed the chanting and shouting of my own victorious men.

"So we started attacking ships again. But now I had a certificate of pardon from the governor! I have hidden treasure in a hundred places around the Outer Banks. My maps are in terrible condition and I don't have the time to recopy them. That is why I'm letting your idiot friend do it. I noticed that he had enough smarts to copy those pages of the Bible, but he obviously is (like you said) an idiot. That's exactly the type of fool I need to copy my maps.

"Anyhow, that's basically how I've gotten to where I am. I wish the general land-living public thought higher of me. That's your purpose. I want you to scribe my history—exactly as I tell you so that it will increase my popularity. Otherwise, some scoundrel will eventually send his blasted warships after me. I know that they won't give me this free reign forever. Am I going too fast for you, son?"

I looked at my note pad. I had scribbled every phrase. I had captured every idea. I was rather impressed with myself. "No sir, I have everything."

For the next several days, I spent a few hours daily with Blackbeard. Every morning Tacker and I were awakened by a grunt pirate who led us to his captain. Then Blackbeard told me stories and I documented them. Tacker spent those same hours by himself copying maps. Before Tacker entered the map room, Blackbeard himself would use his key, the only key, and let him in. Every time Tacker left the map room, he searched the poor fellow from head to toe for any sign of a map.

Tacker openly resented these searches. While he said nothing, he jerked his arms away when Blackbeard touched them. Through these searches, he even tossed his Bible aside. Blackbeard ignored Tacker's protests. I suppose he just assumed that it was part of the fellow's weirdness.

I was awakened one morning by cannon fire from our ship. The thunder of the pirates scurrying up on the deck concerned me. Something was wrong. These were not the sounds of the boasting crew which overtook our vessel from Charles Towne.

Tacker rolled off his hammock onto the floor. He knelt and prayed, "O Lord, deliver us today. O Lord, deliver us today. O

Lord deliver us today. Amen."

"Will?" he called.

"Yes," I answered.

"Whoever loves money never has money enough; whoever loves wealth is never satisfied with his income. This too is meaningless. Will, repeat what I said back to me."

I could hardly believe my ears. First, Tacker rarely addressed me by name. Second, he had conviction in his voice that I had never heard. I heard gunfire from the distance. The cannons topside fired again.

"Tack, something is going on out there, it sounds like there may be a battle. I really think we should hide down here somewhere," I said.

"Will, listen to me. Repeat after me: Whoever loves money never has money enough," he said.

I was startled by Tacker's tone of voice and I was frightened by the battle up on the deck. It seemed insane to have a Bible lesson now. "Tacker! We need to hide."

"Will, repeat after me: Whoever loves money never has money enough."

"Whoever loves money never has money enough," I said.

He grabbed my arm. "Whoever loves wealth is never satisfied with his income. This too is meaningless."

"Who loves wealth isn't satisfied with his income. This is meaningless too," I said.

"Good," said Tacker. He grabbed his Bible and ran to the stairs. He turned and pointed at me. "Wait," he said. He ran upstairs and disappeared.

I surely wasn't going anywhere. Tacker returned in a few minutes. "Come," he said.

What else could I do? I followed him up the stairs. The sounds of screaming pirates on the deck suddenly got louder.

Two warships were about 200 yards away. I searched the horizon for Blackbeard's other vessels, but they were gone. The guns of the warships roared at us. Our guns roared right back. Blackbeard was arguing with his pilot. His angry shouts dominated all other sounds.

Tacker started pushing a lifeboat over the side. It was secured to two large timbers with thick hemp ropes. Tacker pulled a knife out of his belt and cut the ropes. The boat fell into the sea.

"Jump! Now!" he said.

This I was glad to do. I jumped as far out as I could. The last thing I saw before I hit the water were the large barnacles along the bottom edge of Blackbeard's ship. The water was thick and cold. It seemed that I sank a long way before I rose back up like a cork. Even though I had jumped first, Tacker was already in the boat.

I climbed in. We had no oars. We could do little now but float and watch the battle. By a stroke of luck, the currents spun our rowboat away.

"Tacker, look over there. Blackbeard's ship is turning in circles! I don't understand. Those pirates are excellent navigators."

Tacker smiled. He reached into his jacket and pulled out a wadded mass of cable. "They could steer better before I removed this," he said.

"Tacker, you are acting strange. I mean, you're acting *normal*. Normally you say nothing but Bible verses. Tell me why."

"Will, there is a time to tear down and a time to build, a time to weep and a time to laugh, a time to mourn and a time to dance. All of these things are true. But the most important thing you need to know is that everything is meaningless," he said.

"I don't understand," I said, "but who cares? I never have before, either! Look, Tack, something's happened over there."

The sounds from the battle stopped. A few small boats from the attacking warships paddled towards Blackbeard's ship. It appeared that Blackbeard might not be faring well.

I said, "Think about this. If they burn Blackbeard's ship! Those treasure maps will be lost forever."

"Will, there is a time to scatter stones and a time to gather them," said Tacker.

"So are you trying to tell me something or are you just rambling again?" I asked.

He handed me his Bible. "You should study what is inside."

I opened it and by some natural instinct I turned to Ecclesiastes. Maps were drawn on top of the text. *Treasure maps.*

He smiled and stretched out on the floor of our boat " . . . a time to scatter stones and a *time to gather them.*"

"CALICO JACK" RACKHAM

"You'll pay for this, Rackham, you'll pay for it! Nobody crosses Captain Charles Vane!"

Calico Jack Rackham, so-called because of the colored calico shirt he always wore, laughed insanely. Only moments before he was only the quartermaster for the infamous pirate, Charles Vane.

His coup was simple. In the middle of the night Jack broke the steering shaft of Vane's primary attack ship. All of the loot was on a recently captured ship, the *Kingston*. At dawn, Rackham took the *Kingston* and escaped. Vane ran about the deck in his underwear, "Fool! Fool! You've betrayed me! Traitor! Take the bloody treasure! May it curse you for the rest of your days, which won't be many!"

Jack considered these threats. He hurried to the ship's cargo bay and returned with handfuls of gold watches. He didn't say a word, but held them high for Vane to see. Captain Vane pulled his sword from its sheath, broke it over his knee and threw it into the ocean. Jack lowered his arms and smiled.

As the crew of the *Kingston* searched for ships to rob, Jack found himself searching the horizon for Vane. He was terrified of an ambush. Pete Lumter was his quartermaster. The two often stood in the crow's nest to watch the horizon for an evil presence. Their individual fears of Vane fed off each other. Jack and Pete's only memories of Vane seemed to be his vicious killing tactics.

"I don't know, Jack. I really don't know. If he sees us, he'll kill us," said Pete.

"That's only if he can catch us," said Jack.

"Are you kidding? With all this treasure?" The water level is past my deck window. At this weight, they can take us easily."

Jack considered this. "What are you proposing? That we throw the treasure overboard?"

Pete said, "No. Of course not."

"Well, good."

"But I do have a suggestion. We could fill one of our smaller craft with loot and leave it behind. Even his black heart can't sail past free loot like that."

Jack said, "Leave our loot behind? Leave our bloody loot behind? Let's analyze this. First, why in hell are we robbing other ships anyway, if we just decide to leave gold behind—to just *give* it away?"

"Well, because . . . "

"And secondly, it could appear that we are bribing him to leave us alone? I won't do it! I will not do it! That treasure is mine! Mine! He can't have it!"

Pete nodded slowly. "Perhaps you are right, Captain."

The days passed slowly. All of the crew imagined that Vane was always just out of their sight, following them. Waiting until they pulled into a harbor. Waiting to trap them against the shoals. When Vane caught them, they would all die slow deaths. Or they would be bloodied—to attract sharks—and thrown overboard. They had all witnessed it many times. With the anxiety of the crew increasing exponentially every day, Jack decided to make an announcement about their future.

"My good men, we have all profited well from our privateering ventures. It is time for a change in strategy. We are going to return to the island of Providence. (Fitting is it not?) There we will receive pardons from the governor. Also, we will keep our loot and I, your captain, will keep this ship. Any questions?"

The relief of the men blew across the deck like a warm southerly wind.

The governor of Providence happily granted the pardons in exchange for a termination of piracy crimes. Jack and Pete established a legitimate business buying the supplies off ships and distributing them to retail outlets. Jack's fear of Vane kept his desires for the open sea subdued.

Most every day, Jack searched for incoming ships. He walked the docks and studied the horizon. Once, he saw a woman with long hair sitting on the pier dangling her feet over the side. The bottoms of her shoes just barely glanced over the surface of the water. Jack admired her tiny frame. Her hair was long and brown with a tint of redness from the sunshine. Captain Jack decided to approach. He walked slowly until he was standing right behind her.

Her skin looked tough and leathery, with a dark brown hue. Sensing his presence, she slowly turned her head. It was a slow and feminine turn. Jack felt as awkward as a child before his teacher. Life on the sea had deprived him of exposure to females. Everything about his life was hard, coarse and cruel. This lady's presence was pushing cerebral buttons that had long been dormant.

Her eyes were green as the middle of the deep, crystal ocean. The very movement of the waves pulsed in her glance. Although this moment was only that, a moment. It seemed to Jack as if she stared at him for days.

"Hello," said the lady.

"Hello, I am Calico Jack Rackham."

"Oh, so you're Calico Jack. I've heard a lot about you."

"For instance . . . ."

The lady said, "Why everyone has heard about the great Captain Calico Jack Rackham, who so recently decided to retire upon receipt of a pardon to our little isle of Providence. You're quite a local celebrity."

"That so?" asked Jack.

"It is. See, my name is Anne Bonny. My husband, James, is a pardoned pirate as well."

"I know your husband. He'd sell his soul if the price was right. He has sold the heads of many privateers to your precious governor," said Jack.

Anne smiled. "And so what of it? The governor's gold is just as good as the gold you are now getting for *peddling*."

"I'm not peddling," Jack said. He opened up his mouth

again to explain his position, but nothing came out. His eyebrows met. His teeth clenched together. But he could think of nothing to say.

"Well, Jack, that's o.k. Don't get so huffy. I've got to go anyway. I have an *appointment*. I do hope that I see you around some more."

Still speechless and angry, Jack watched her walk away. She seemed to hover over the pier with silent steps.

After that, Jack saw Anne Bonny on the docks often. She was socially bounced from ship to ship as if the harbor were one big festival. As much as she irritated him, Jack always looked forward to seeing her. He always stopped to talk. He was always subdued by her feminine nuances. But he was also usually angry when they parted. She had the strange talent of knowing exactly where a person's tender spots were. And she enjoyed prodding them liberally to get a rise.

But Jack appreciated the attention nonetheless. Something about her attracted him like a pirate to a gluttonous hoard of gold. He began to give her extravagant gifts that he came across in his trading. He gave her a gold necklace laced with heavy emeralds and diamonds. But she asked him if he had access to weapons. Jack found this to be a strange request, but he confided that he had access to anything.

So one day he gave her a sword. A shiny blade that was thinner and lighter than most. Anne was more excited about the sword than the diamonds and emeralds. Jack found this peculiar, yet intriguing. He eventually brought her several pistols, a rifle, plenty of ammo and black powder and a chain-mail armored vest.

While enjoying a glass of rum in a pub called *Thor's Cave*, Jack was approached by a huge man. His fat belly poked out from under his shirt. His unshaven face could not conceal the hideous scars on his nose and forehead. The man took Jack's glass and smashed it onto the table immediately below Jack's chin. The liquor exploded all over both men. Blood poured from the man's hand where glass shards were still hanging in the flesh.

"Sir, my name is James Bonny. I believe you know my wife, Anne. I thought you might like to know something. Because of my wife's disobedience to me and her newfound love in you, she will be beaten publicly in two weeks. It's legal and everything. If you will excuse me, I don't care to listen to your comments."

Jack wiped the stinging liquor from his eyes as he heard the door slam behind Bonny. With a solemn face, he whispered, "She loves *me*?"

The next morning, Jack waited on the docks for Anne to appear. As predictable as the morning sun, she came walking along. She bounced as she moved. Something about her seemed more like a wild animal than a gentle woman.

"Gu-morning, Captain Jack!" said Anne.

"Anne, my dear, is there something you want to tell me?" asked Jack.

"No, *dear*, there's not," replied Anne.

Jack grabbed her arm firmly. "Well then, can you explain for me a conversation I had with your husband?"

"O yeah, that. I guess I should have told you about it. Why Mr. Rackham, are you going to save your lady in distress?" asked Anne. She grinned with a taunting smirk.

"I may be a pirate. But I am also a gentleman. Now I have a plan. . . "

"Wait, Mr. Gentleman, *I* have a plan," said Anne.

Jack wanted to take her and his considerable riches and travel westward to begin a new life, perhaps farming. Anne would have no part in a life away from the sea. Since Jack could not stand to listen to Anne's bickering, he gave in to her plan.

A ship christened the *Chance* was being repaired in the harbor. It was a narrow vessel. It was not meant to contain large stores, but it was extremely fast. Anne made a point to visit it more often than usual. She quickly learned the times that the ship was totally empty. Jack rounded up his old crew. He hid his treasure. On the midnight before the day that Anne was to be beaten, she sneaked out of her house and met Jack at the *Chance*. His crew had already scared away the remnants of the *Chance*'s crew.

Jack and Anne were alone at last upon the seas. Anne was ecstatic at being a pirate. Jack slowly became bitter, having given up his legitimate business. With a vengeance, Jack's ship preyed upon all the vessels they could see. Local governments even prohibited their warships from going after Calico Jack because of his reputation for cruelty. Jack no longer feared Vane, he actually looked for him. During the battles, Anne raved about the crew, shouting commands. Jack listened to her and the rest of the crew followed his lead.

Jack became increasingly withdrawn. He drank rum all night and slept in his quarters all day. He looked forward to nothing except the plunder of more ships. He discussed the gory details for hours with any of his crew who would listen.

After they had been at sea for three months, they found themselves in the midst of a dry spell. Not dry as in weather, but dry as in the number of ships to attack. They went a full month without seeing one.

"Jack, you're not as fun as you used to be," said Anne.

Jack ignored her, as did all of the crew members. He pulled a double-edged dagger from his pocket and stabbed it into the deck.

"Jack, did you hear me? You're not any fun anymore."

Jack smiled. "Good! Great! Fantastic! What shall I do, a jig for you? I don't believe I will." Jack tightened his fists. He felt the leather from his gloves pull across the back of his sunburnt right hand.

"Well, I might as well come out and say it. Jack, I'm pregnant."

Jack inhaled deeply. "I see," he said.

He stood up to strike her. Jack slowly moved his right arm to the left, adding drama to his preparation, when *THUMP*, an oar pounded his head. He fell to the deck. He grabbed his head, only to feel the blood oozing from the fresh wound. Jack turned around to face his attacker when *THUMP*, the oar smashed his right temple. He lay on the ground, afraid to try to get up. Jack reached into his pocket and pulled out a flask of rum. He poured a healthy swallow into his mouth. Most of it overflowed onto the dry, salty deck. Blood caressed his head all over as it traveled like small purple-red glaciers. He drifted off to sleep.

In the early morning darkness, Jack rose to see a familiar crew member standing over him with a sword. "Martin, is that you?" asked Jack.

"Well, sort of," came Martin's voice. Martin, who, oddly, was always clean shaven, removed his cap to reveal long black hair.

Anne appeared from behind Martin. "You see, Jack, Martin is actually Mary. She is a woman, not a man."

"Martin, you're in my crew and you're a woman? And I didn't know?"

"No sir, Mr. Rackham, I don't suppose you did," said Mary.

"Well, did the rest o' the crew know?"

"Some did," said Mary.

"You hit me, didn't you? You hit me and left me to die!" said Jack.

"I feel bad about it. But you were going to strike Annie, and I had to protect her," said Mary.

Jack tossed his rum flask into the ocean. He stood tall and faced both women. For once in their lives, these masculine females were afraid. Both of their heads turned to the deck to avoid Jack's stare.

Jack went below deck and tapped all of the whiskey kegs. All of the crew, save the women, began to drink heavily.

Mary and Anne returned to the deck. They were laughing and giggling about their victory over the men. They talked for an hour. They danced and had mock sword fights. As the early morning sun peeped its revealing eye above the horizon, the women got a surprise. A British warship was a mere two hundred yards away.

They manned the sails. The *Chance* was equaled by no vessel anywhere in speed. With a crew working properly, they would have had no problem outrunning the warship. But the two women could not do all of the work themselves. In their panic to get the sails up, they forgot to lock down the rudder.

The *Chance* proceeded to move in a half-circle, then go backwards, then spin around, then go in a half-circle in the other direction. They shouted to the men below. "Warship! Get up here! Warship! Help us. Please help! Please come up! We're serious. There is a warship right here!"

The men shouted obscenities and continued drinking. The women said later that they even heard them dancing below while the cannon balls of the warship smashed holes in the deck. While hysterically pleading for assistance, Mary and Anne manned the guns themselves. The battle was indeed not a long nor a memorable one. It ended in miserable defeat.

Sentenced to death for piracy, Jack pressed his forehead against the bars of his jail cell. He would hang at daylight. For his last request, he asked that Anne be brought before him.

Anne walked into the cell and kissed his forehead with mock affection.

"You ole salty dog. If you had had courage enough to fight, you wouldn't be hanging tomorrow," said Anne.

Jack laughed. "Oh, I had courage alright. Ole Calico Jack showed more courage in that battle than in his whole life."

Fire burned in Anne's eyes. She said, "Are you really the idiot you seem to be? What are you talking about?"

He reached through the bars and kissed her hand.

He said, "I'm finally free."

Anne ran from the cell, crying. Jack picked up his infamous calico shirt and lay upon his bed. He was smiling when he heard the jingle of keys that unlocked his cell door, and he glanced toward the sea through the misty dawn for the very last time!

THE TALE OF THEODOSIA'S PORTRAIT

On a cold November morning a deathly white fog hovered over the inlet. These waters were normally turbulent. The slightest wind could anger them into a tempest. But there was no wind today. With the sails drawn and the steering wheel unattended, the *Patriot* drifted against the outgoing tide, stubbornly going into port.

Moses D'Abrams was a fisherman. He was setting his nets on the smooth ocean when he first saw the *Patriot*. It was a fine ship. Sturdy. Colored with brass accessories. Glowing with red-painted details. A proud, aristocratic vessel. It looked alive, as if it had decided to come into the inlet on its own. The grand ship moved slowly and deliberately. Moses wiped his brow and squinted. He could not see anyone on board! He thought, "It looks abandoned. But it can't be. An abandoned ship never would have found its way around Pompano Shoals." Moses tied off his nets. He rowed to the opposite side of the nets to pull them in. But he could not shake the image of the *Patriot*. So proud. So, so strange.

Moses was the epitome of the old salt. His neatly cut white beard hid his face perfectly. His eyes were wrinkled from years of looking to the east every morning for thirty years as he collected his nets. He wore no cap. The skin on his ears was worn and beaten. His clothes were faded, although neatly tucked in. Hours passed! He pulled his nets in only to find a meager catch of spots and croakers, among a hoard of junk fish. He couldn't take his mind off the image of the *Patriot*, last seen heading northward through the sound. "Too curious for my own good," he thought. Moses started rowing back home.

The market at Nag's Head didn't pay good prices that day. But sorry prices were better than no prices. The lady who always bought his fish, referred to as "Miss Clam" (it was assumed that this nickname was somehow derived from her profession) was not even at the dock where he met her every day. Boats lined these docks to sell shrimp, crabs and fish. But on this day, the people were gone. Further down the coastline, Moses saw why.

The *Patriot* was docked at the quarantine station. A dozen Nag's Head residents observed the ship from the pier. Moses approached.

Men watched with curiosity as the ship sat deathly still. A few women gathered in the background, their hands covering the fear caught in their mouths. "What's the problem here?" asked Moses.

"This ship floated right here to the docks. The old quarantine man walked on board like he always does, thinking that the crew was below decks. But he got scared an' ran off. Now nobody want to go inta' there," replied a child. The boy was right in front of Moses, but the old seaman hadn't even noticed him until he spoke.

"Thanks, son," he said.

Moses tossed his bow rope to the boy. The old salt grabbed a dangling line from the stern of the *Patriot* and started climbing. The callused surface of his hands and his muscular forearms provided a smooth ascension.

The deck was clean and glossy. The sails were neatly tied away. His old heart pounded as he walked towards the stairs which led to the monster's belly. It was quite abandoned. He couldn't figure out what could have scared the quarantine man. Every room was empty. Finally, he walked to the captain's quarters.

A full meal for two was set upon the table. The food was unspoiled. Then he saw *it*. A portrait of the prettiest woman he had ever seen. It was on the wall between two brass candle holders. She was elegant, feminine and gentle. The image was as lovely as the red sky which greeted him each morning—and it looked just as far away. In his world, life was tough and hot. The days tested his rugged soul. They dared him to return again. Not so with this princess. He fell in love with the picture instantly. Moses gently touched the frame—half expecting her to sigh—and took it off the wall.

42

Moses lived in a shack on a small island in the Albemarle Sound. It was too small to actually even be anyone's property. Who would buy a piece of land that might be buried by a modest storm? His house was a one-room cabin composed of odd boards. You could tell that some of them used to be billboards because they were decorated with the colors of advertisements. The pipe of an iron stove pointed out of the roof. There was a window on each of the four sides of the house. They contained no glass, only a cloth barrier. He had two chairs, a box for a table and another box for provisions. A few articles of clothing hung on wall pegs.

He hung the picture on the east wall. He smiled at the heavenly, female image. It added a presence to his home. It instantly became a warmer place. From that day forward Moses talked to his "friend" while at his house. He always felt that she could hear him. Sometimes Moses listened to himself and thought that he must be mad. But "What does it really matter?" he would always conclude. As the days retired, he watched the last rays of dusk on her fair skin. She seemed to go to sleep as the light faded from her eyes.

The years passed on and Moses died right in that house. A local elderly woman, known only as "Miss Mann" found old Moses deceased and lying on the floor. He had died in his sleep. Miss Mann arranged for his funeral.

In going through his things, she could not help but notice the beautiful picture on the wall. Moses was gone and had no known kin, so she took the picture and hung it on her own wall. Miss Mann caught herself talking to the picture from time to time. She thought it was strange for her to be doing so. Eventually, she developed a paranoia. Miss Mann thought she heard the painting whispering *about her* when she wasn't facing it. If she observed it through her peripheral vision, the lady appeared to move. The painted beauty turned her head and twisted her hands. But when Miss Mann turned to face the picture, the lovely creature was always back in her original pose, without a sign that she had ever moved. Miss Mann finally sold it to a local mercantile store. She found that her peace of mind was returned to her in exchange for the painting. Her delusions ceased and she lived a relatively normal life again.

A doctor from Morehead City, Dr. Pool, was awestruck by the beauty of the picture. A bachelor, he had just bought a new house. He would put the picture in his study.

Years later, Dr. Pool was reading a magazine article on the disappearance of Theodosia Burr Alston. She was the wife of Joseph Alston, a former governor of South Carolina. She was also a well-known socialite of the large Northeast cities. Theodosia's father was Aaron Burr, the former Vice President of the United States. Aaron killed the great statesman Alexander Hamilton in a duel.

The article showed a picture of the Burr family. When Dr. Pool observed the fair Theodosia, his eyes widened so much that his spectacles fell onto his chest. She looked exactly like the woman in the portrait. The smile was the same. The wrinkles on her forehead were identical, as was the hairstyle. The style of dress was the same.

The article detailed the mysterious disappearance of Theodosia. She was traveling on a small ship, the *Patriot*, from Georgetown, South Carolina, to New York. The vessel was never seen again. The article went on to document an interesting turn of events. Before two pirates were executed in Norfolk, Virginia, they confessed to having robbed a ship off Nag's Head. They claimed that they had forced all of the passengers to walk the plank.

They asserted that this ship was the *Patriot*. One of the criminals cried for peace. He claimed that the "dark eyes of a princess" placed a curse on him as she walked the plank. Her lovely vision haunted him still, even up to his own death.

Dr. Pool closed the magazine. He looked at the portrait. He half-expected her to smile or talk. But she didn't. He left the room, feeling her stare all the way.

Legend of the Bleeding Arch

On vacation, nine-year-old Peter runs around the tomb-stones in Cedar Grove Cemetery in New Bern, North Carolina. His parents are studying the old markers, some of them over 250 years old. He walks under the arched entryway and looks up. Red drops of something are precipitating in the arch's rocks.

His father walks over to him. "Come on, Son, I've had about enough of your mother's history lesson today."

"Look, Daddy! It looks like that rock is bleedin'."

"Right," said the father, not even looking up.

"Now come here, Son, you are filthy. Your mom will kill us both if . . . . "

He was interrupted by a drop of something wet and sticky in his hair. "Darn birds . . . " he began. He pulled a handkerchief from his pocket and wiped the mess in his hair.

A blank expression fell over him as he examined the dark red splotch on the handkerchief. He looked up at the arch. Another red drop was forming . . . . Drip . . . Drip.

- - -

Richard Dobbs Speight was a politician from New Bern. Like most politicians, he was also a lawyer. As governor of North Carolina, Richard found some good ole' hometown competi-tion with another New Bern lawyer, John Stanley. A member of the state legislature, John loved to speak at the podium. He not only loved to speak, but he thrived on debate. He taunted his rivals. He jousted sarcastically with them. John was known to throw papers and then laugh heartily to get his point across.

Richard was a quiet fellow. A good listener, he usually slowly nodded his head in agreement, while the speaker was often more animated. He walked with large slow steps. He smiled and laughed a lot. It was easy to see why the town of New Bern and the State of North Carolina loved him.

John was aggressive. His large gut twisted in time as he hurriedly walked to wherever he went. John argued right up in people's faces. He loved to be visited by his opponents in his office in New Bern. He would make them wait a long time before seeing them. When they were finally admitted, John let it be known that he was too busy for their trivial issues. He loved his own importance, and he resented Richard's popularity.

Richard associated with the common man of New Bern. He spent time with the fishermen, the millers, the shoemakers, the farmers and the blacksmiths. The people loved his humor. Richard was serious about using his office of governor to help the citizens, his friends.

John's face turned red just at the thought of Richard and the townspeople. John thought, "After all, they were only regular people, right? Not great statesmen or scientists. Why does the idiot Richard listen to them so?" He was terribly envious.

John and Richard were destined for a political collision. In 1825, their paths malevolently crossed. General Lafayette was planning a trip to the United States. It was important to John that the general be impressed with North Carolina. He drafted a bill to allot a significant portion of the budget to provide grand social events for the general.

As the debate started, it was clear that the consensus was against the measure. Richard thought it was ridiculous. "Spend our people's money for this? How will this help them. I won't stand for it."

Others in the legislature expressed similar sentiment. John's face turned red. He could feel his heart pounding harder and harder. His hate for Richard squeezed through the small openings in his arteries. He had to wait a full hour before he could defend his measure. Beads of perspiration swelled on his forehead.

When he finally got to speak, he said, "This is a most important dignitary. It is our responsibility to ensure that he is impressed with our fine region. He probably thinks of us as savages. We must prove the other case. We will prove the other case. And I formally dare any of you to stand in the path of this measure!"

Silence consumed the chamber. John tore up his notes and threw them to the floor. They could not believe the firmness of his words. After the vote, guess who still opposed John? "The good King" Richard. John immediately challenged Richard to a duel. John's lower jaw popped open. He heard himself say, "I accept." In the early 1800's, he really had no choice. To not accept the duel was to surrender his honor.

John was a firearm fanatic. His collection of guns was enormous. Richard, on the other hand, had never touched one. In the days before the duel, Richard practiced loading and shooting muzzle-loading pistols, but he was scared to death of what was about to transpire.

John insisted that the duel take place at the gates of Cedar Grove Cemetery. He knew the implied death of this site would torture Richard's mind. On September 5, at dawn, the two New Bern lawyers and North Carolina politicians showed up at the cemetery in their best clothes. The whole town was there, eerily watching and waiting for the event.

Children hid behind their mothers. Ten-year-old boys conducted faux duels using sticks as pistols. The young boys' "seconds" or assistants opened an imaginary box with the "pistols." A pretend marshal counted the boys off 20 steps. They turned to each other and yelled, "Bang! Bang!" Both kids fell dead in perfectly dramatic form while several girls ran to them in pretend horror. The drama of the children was a dark play to the adults who knew that real bloodshed was not far away.

John and Richard faced each other. Richard was shaking so violently that he could barely grasp the firearm. The seconds presented the pistols. They marched off their 20 steps. "Fire!" shouted the marshal. Both pistols fired. The townspeople watched in dismay at the black cloud which covered the duelists. But when the smoke cleared, both were still standing. They had both missed!

The seconds reloaded the pistols and the ritual was repeated. "Fire!" shouted the marshal. When the smoke cleared again, both men were still standing again. The kids playing thought this was great. They modified their own ritual to include both boys shooting and missing.

The seconds once more reloaded the pistols. This time the duelists were only allowed to walk ten steps. The marshal informed them that if both men missed this time, the duel would be called off and both men could walk away with no loss of honor. At this announcement, it was later said that Richard winked at John and John smiled back. "Fire!" the marshal shouted. What happened next was never quite agreed upon by the witnesses. John's shot went straight through Richard's chest—a fatal wound. Richard's shot went up in the air way over John's head. Some witnesses said that Richard's shot was so off its aim because he flinched as he was hit. Others claimed that Richard purposely aimed high, hoping that both men would walk away from the duel.

Fulfilling his duty, John placed Richard in a casket. He proceeded to wipe the blood which incidentally got on his hand on the arch over the cemetery. Blood dripped onto the ground from the spot where John wiped it. As Richard's body was hauled away, blood continued to drip from the stones.

To let the bad publicity he received from the death of Richard Speight subside, John visited Washington, D.C. for a month. When his trip was over, he decided to ride alone back to New Bern to maintain his low profile. It rained the last two hours of his ride. Soaking wet, he stopped by the cemetery on his way home. Under the arch, he saw a red circle bubbling in the ground. He looked up at the arch. Drops of blood were swelling and dropping. Drip. Drip. Drip.

To this day, a few drops of a red fluid ooze from the stones. Some speculate that maybe an old mason left a nail in the center of the stone, and as it rusts, the red fluid drips out.

Locals say it is the blood of Richard, forever soiling the ground. Forever reminding the town of his fatal duel long ago. . . . The mystery lives on.

TALE OR TRUTH–YOU BE THE JUDGE

There is no documentation for this story, but it was widely circulated on the South Carolina side of the Savannah River a few decades ago. To say the least, it is a bizarre incident that hopefully will not befall anyone in our time.

A middle-aged widow lived alone in a modest house on the Savannah River, and for protection she had a huge German shepherd that was devoted to her. The big canine stayed in her house, and was a comfort both day and night.

One hot summer day, the widow had to go into town to get groceries. It was so hot that she decided against taking the dog with her. He would suffer in the car when she was inside the store, so she left him in the house.

An hour later, the widow returned. Her beloved dog was suffering with convulsions, wallowing on the den floor. He was kicking, gasping for breath and his eyes were rolled back as if he were begging for help. The widow dragged the big dog to the car and rushed him to the vet's office a few miles away.

The veterinarian had another animal sedated and was performing surgery when she arrived. He quickly glanced at the shepherd, told the anguished widow her dog would be fine, and said he could not attend to him until he completed surgery on the other animal.

"Just leave him with me. Go home, and as soon as I finish this operation, I'll take care of your dog and call you," the veterinarian suggested, "He's not dying as it appears."

The lady drove back home, worried and frustrated that her dog was suffering with a strange affliction. When she drove up in her yard, she could hear the telephone ringing. She ran to it and said, "Hello."

"Ma'am!" an excited voice on the line almost yelled, "This is the vet. Quietly hang up the phone, go outside and close your door. I have called the sheriff. He'll be there in a couple of minutes. When he leaves, you can come and get your dog. He's fine. He just had two fingers of a man's right hand in his throat and they were choking him. I got them out."

The widow was horrified, but she hung up, walked outside and closed her front door. The sheriff's car screeched to a halt in her driveway almost at the same moment. The uniformed officer pulled his revolver and quickly went inside while the widow, paralyzed by fear and anxiety, waited beside the car.

Moments later, the sheriff appeared at the door half-dragging a man by the arm who was holding a bleeding right hand with two missing fingers. He had lost a lot of blood and was near death. The man had been found in a closet where he had hidden when he heard the widow come back from the grocery store. The man obviously had intended to rob the widow, but her dog had objected. Biting two fingers off was a cruel, but effective deterrent which landed the would-be thief directly in the penitentiary.

CAROLINA'S POACHING CAPER

Three shots shattered the silence and splintered the front door of the old mobile home on the river bank. A scared John Kennedy hardly dared to breathe and Cindy Delaney rushed into the room from the back of the trailer half expecting to see the bleeding, prostrate body of her partner sprawled lifeless on the floor. A hefty, drunken fish poacher reeled around the room with the smoking rifle in his hand and muttering that it really wasn't loaded, was it?

Kennedy was a veteran of the North Carolina Wildlife Service. They were paying a little drop-in visit on a onetime convicted murderer whom they suspected of illegally selling freshwater fish. Only this time they were pretending interest in an old antique sewing machine the poacher's wife had for sale.

The untimely rifle shots disrupted the buying of a bag of freshwater fish at $2.00 a pound from the ex-con on that occasion, but this young pair of unlikely-looking law enforcement officers had already documented his illicit dealing in wildlife. They caught him red-handed again and again in the weeks ahead. He was one small part of a lengthy, combined effort of the state and federal authorities to catch a horde of fish and game thieves in the Carolinas by working from the inside.

Before this handsome man and good-looking girl completed this caper under the guise of being from Chapel Hill and in the area searching for Indian arrowheads and other relics, they pinned arrests on 33 North Carolinians with 106 different wildlife charges. They took a few days of their time to cross over into South Carolina for seven more arrests on ten charges of poaching. Twenty-six of the arrests in the Tar Heel State led to convictions for freshwater fish poaching. This inside operation obviously was near foolproof.

While catching game and fish poachers with a uniform is possible, the success is multiplied many times when working from the inside as Delaney and Kennedy did.

One enforcement agent put it aptly when he said, "Catching these fish poachers with your uniform on is kind of like trying to put butter up a wildcat's hind end with a red-hot awl. It has its moments of danger, but catching them from the inside is much easier and convictions are not as difficult."

Kennedy said the fish poachers normally make their catches at night with unweighted gill nets or by placing traps in narrow, fast-water channels in the river. They hold the captured fish in wire boxes under water and retrieve them only when they make a sale. At least one of the illegal fish marketers had an artesian flow that fed a hidden holding enclosure where he easily kept his fish alive, usually about 125 pounds at a time.

One wholesale fish poacher was caught numerous times. He disposed of about 700 pounds of bass and bluegills every week. He was such a volume poacher that he got only about $1.00 a pound, but he sold them to a few selected friends with whom he had been doing business for years. He escaped the Delaney-Kennedy dragnet.

"There's no maximum limit on the number of bluegills you can have in your possession in North Carolina. This makes it difficult to catch many poachers and impossible unless we go undercover. This one big-timer can catch his 700 pounds in a couple of days and pocket his $700 quickly. It's all tax-free, of course, and he had a profitable illegal business going," Kennedy says.

Working undercover had its moments of fear. Kennedy caught many of the poachers in his home district where he had been known for years. A lot of these people that Cindy and John caught had seen him many times in uniform. But when he donned plain clothes, a $25.00 wig and sunglasses, he easily passed for a visiting collegian in a hurry to find Indian relics. But he was constantly expecting to be recognized and that would have meant the jig was up.

"Commercial fish and game poachers can be dangerous. These people are often involved with other illegal activities, whiskey bootlegging, gambling, and all sorts of game violations. They are bullies and clannish. They tend to stick together and the good people who live near them are often scared to squeal on them. They are a pretty scummy bunch of characters and there is certainly no love/hate, fox and hound relationship between wildlife agents and professional poachers," Kennedy said.

While some poachers wholesale their freshwater fish for about $1.00 a pound, John and Cindy bought most of their evidence for about $1.50 a pound. Under pretense of needing 125 pounds for a Myrtle Beach, South Carolina, fish fry for 70 people, they were able to get them for $1.00 a pound from a poacher named "Jake." This verbose fish thief said, "Fish sell like hotcakes and I can hardly catch enough to keep up with the demand."

Another poacher among the convicted from John and Cindy's caper thought he had worked out all the angles.

"All the wardens are dumb," he told Kennedy. "They don't have a chance of catching me. When I plan to go gill netting on the lake or river, I just have a friend call up the wildlife enforcement officers in the area and tip them off that someone is night hunting deer in some distant swamp. By the time they check that out, I'm back at home with my fish safely in the holding tank." He must have wanted to eat those words when Kennedy testified against him in the courtroom.

One of the poachers ran a store in the country near a lake and when the long-haired man with sunglasses stopped in with the pretty girl for a cold drink, he seemed to immediately like them. He was even friendlier after they bought a couple of wooden bread trays from his handicraft counter and asked him about canoeing down the river. They inquired about buying some fish that they could fry on the river bank, but he said they would have to get them from a neighbor across the road. He didn't sell 'em, he said. They bought some from the neighbor. He figured if there was anything wrong here, he would let his competition suffer.

But the pretty blond doll and bespectacled long-haired visitors were back in a few days and showed considerable interest in the dugout canoes the man had for sale. Again they bought cold drinks and asked about some fish. He figured it must be safe. His neighbor hadn't heard anything from his sale. John and Cindy bought the fish and returned time after time for additional purchases. By this time, Cindy was so at home that she was constantly snapping pictures of the beautiful landscape, the dugout canoes, and even the fish and money changing hands. The case was airtight.

Some of these sellers of fish are outlets for others who do the catching. Some are gill netted and brought to the marketers and others are legally caught with hook and line and then illegally sold. Many of these fish catchers are given money or liquor for their catch. Some are just bums who don't work, collect welfare money and fish for recreation and supplemental income.

Don Curtis, chief of the North Carolina Wildlife Commission on Enforcement Division at the time, said, "For years, (illegal) commercialization of game and fish has been prevalent. When the price of beef rose dramatically and the unemployment rate went up, people turned to wild game for food. All illegally killed deer carcasses usually sell for about $35.00 and this figures out to about 35 or 40 cents per pound. With illegal fish, the situation is different. Bluegills and bass sell for up to $2.00 a pound dressed, while people can buy commercially taken saltwater fish for much less. Still, the popularity of buying and selling game fish is still on the rise." (Poached deer sells for about $70.00 and freshwater fish undressed at about $1.25 per pound.)

The North Carolina Wildlife Resources Commission Enforcement Division makes hundreds of arrests each year for night deer hunting, and the number of arrests increases each year.

Although game fish and deer were the prime targets of the undercover caper of Delaney and Kennedy, many other animals were discovered that were illegally taken by the poachers. Beaver, alligator skins and wild turkeys succumbed to the illicit trade.

Kennedy says, "This was the first large-scale undercover operation we've tried and it worked well. The uniformed wildlife officer has his place, but there is no way he can get to the heart of a market hunting operation. To do that, you have to work from the inside. After it was over, a lot of sportsmen and court officials congratulated us. These sportsmen said they knew commercial poaching was going on, but felt helpless to do anything about it. They just didn't complain or report the poaching. I don't think they need to feel helpless anymore."

This collegiate-looking team put some poachers out of business and their undercover work is worthy of the movies. It's the kind of success that breeds other success and sportsmen and wildlife officers everywhere may have picked up some pointers that will be a real deterrent to the meat hunters intent upon fast profits at the expense of the species.

Author's Note: Bassmaster magazine and the author appreciate the assistance of Mark Taylor of *Wildlife in North Carolina* and John Kennedy, a wildlife enforcement supervisor, for their co-operation in gathering the facts of this undercover detective story.

. . . Best Laid Plans, etc.

Smith Ward lived about as far in the back woods as you can live in the Alligator Creek section along the Tar Heel Coast. After World War II ended, he came home from the service and went into the hog business. He not only raised the hogs that you could see roaming around in his muddy lot on his backwoods acres, he barbecued hams and shoulders and sold them to the general public. That factor accounted for the constant smoke that curled from his backyard smokehouse every day in the week, puffed skyward and curled over the jungle tree line. The smoke marked his place of abode and site of his livelihood.

Ward had to keep a hickory wood fire going night and day to properly smoke-cure the hams and shoulders that were in great demand. He was constantly slaughtering porkers and curing them in his old smokehouse, or so he told the neighbors in the desolate community.

His ham business also accounted for the several cars that frequently bounced down the old washboardy road on Friday afternoons and Saturdays. That was when the townspeople came to Ward to buy his meat. Again, that was what he said. And it all made good sense. His customers came to him and he didn't have the expense of peddling his meat.

One day it was obvious that the ham curing had gotten out of hand. Flames shot up above treetop level from Ward's place and neighbors surmised his house was afire. They rushed down the road to see if they could be of any assistance in that era when there were no rural fire dpartments. Normally, fire departments can at least save the brick or rock chimney and metal posts that hold up the porch and the neighbors thought they could do that.

The fire was not coming from his residence, but from his smokehouse and by the time the neighbors arrived, it had burned to the ground. A few hams did indeed sizzle in the ashes, but the most unexpected discovery was the automobile radiator, smoldering staves from several barrels, some twisted copper pipe and a 40-gallon stainless steel kettle that had surely been used to boil mash at this camouflaged smokehouse distillery.

His ham-curing business had been a good camouflage for years, but his moonshining days were over. Soon he was thrown out of church for his sinful ways and he moved away, probably to someplace where he could again go in to the business of curing hams and resume the dual use of his smokehouse.

If history was any indication, it would take his new neighbors a long time to discover his camouflaged still. His illicit distillery was a secret that he easily concealed from inquisitive revenue agents and even his neighbors. He was never heard of again in that remote wilderness.

A Mad 'Gator

There are many native and tourist anglers who fish from the banks of rivers, lakes and creeks along the Carolinas because: 1) they don't have a boat; or 2) they like the serenity and peacefulness of fishing from the shoreline. These fishermen need to be aware that many of these marshy swampland banks are homes of the American alligator and they choose to rest, sleep and nest on the mucky knolls.

Not normally a threat to man, the giants are not friendly when stepped upon or when their young appear endangered. They are not harmless when cornered or their nest threatened by man, their only predator.

An avid bass fisherman climbed into his small plywood boat to cast for bass after he had walked upon an old mama 'gator sunning with her brood of newborn babies on a shoreline mudbank at Town Creek at Winnabow. As he neared her territory in his boat, he dropped his paddle and cast a topwater lure near the bank where the old mama 'gator was protecting her young family. She just grunted. He cast again and the 'gator snarled, opened her mouth and challenged the invader. The third time he cast, the mama 'gator got really mad. She plunged into the river and headed straight for his homemade boat. She raised her long, tough tail and slammed it across the fisherman's boat. The plywood splintered and the angler found himself neck-deep in the clear river with the mad mama 'gator staring him in the face.

"I forgot about my rod, reel and tacklebox. They sank to the bottom. I only thought about being eaten alive by that big old 'gator. I lit out for the distant shoreline 60 feet away, and I was swimming for my life. The 'gator was in hot pursuit, but I climbed out just ahead of her and didn't look back as I ran the fastest 100-yard dash of my life through the swamp. I could hear that old 'gator lumbering over the bushes behind me. She finally gave up and I stopped to get my breath. Amazingly, I discovered that I was wet on only one side. I must have swum that river so fast my body was only half in the water," the scared and thankful angler later reminisced.

JEALOUSY ENDED CAREERS

Jake Lattimer, like a lot of bootleggers, was jealous of his neighbor, Stick Carothers, who had a larger still than he did, thus producing more illicit whiskey for the trade than he could. Likewise, Carothers had the usual greed of moonshiners and resented Lattimer, envying his business, though it was humble compared with his own. With Lattimer out of business, then Carothers would have had a near-monopoly on the stumphole traffic in the Brunswick-Columbus County section of eastern North Carolina

This selfishness and antagonism between the two bootleggers led to self-destruction in a strange and dangerous turn of events. Sheriff Willie Locklear got caught right in the middle, but tough old bastard that he was, he came out the winner in a struggle that could have easily meant his demise.

It all began when Lattimer conjured up a scheme for selling his whiskey in broad daylight in Shallotte and elsewhere along the Carolinas coast. Lattimer had a local printer make him some labels reading "Pure Apple Cider." Then each time he made a run of white lightning, he stored it in glass jugs and added a touch of brown cake coloring. It turned the booze cider-colored during this era when all moonshine whiskey was clear as tap water. The imbibers were used to their whiskey being clear, not colored like the legal, government-taxed store-bought whiskey. But when Lattimer hit upon this idea of camouflaging his product and labeling it "cider," he transported it in his pickup truck boldly and peddled it all over the neighborhoods and his customers soon learned that the brownish fire-water was just as potent as the clear stuff. For a time, Lattimer did a booming liquor business openly.

Then Carothers learned about the deception. It angered him more than just somewhat that his competitor was getting away with a scheme he wished he had thought of. He went to the sheriff and tipped him off about the phony cider.

The next Saturday afternoon when Lattimer came to town with his usual load of booze and started down the street with a gallon of the brown whiskey in each hand, the sheriff confronted him as he started across the main street in Southport. Suspecting that his secret was out from the look in the sheriff's eyes, Lattimer instinctively dropped both jugs. They shattered on the concrete and the evidence quickly disappeared. Locklear didn't like that.

"Damn you, Jake! I had you in my grasp and let you destroy the evidence. But at least the jig is up with your cider scheme. You'll not get away with hauling it all around here like it was legal any more. Stick Carothers told me the cider was phony and that it was really liquor that you made in the swamp. I didn't believe it at first, but now I see it was obviously true," Sheriff Locklear snarled, angry that he had been hoodwinked for weeks by this near moron with a sneaky idea that worked.

Jake was thankful that those were the last two jugs he had with him that day and that he had had the foresight to break them before the sheriff could seize the evidence. But he was understandably chagrined that his secret was out. He drove off toward his home at Supply muttering and cursing about his misfortune.

He slowly rehashed in his fumbling mind what the sheriff had said. He stopped when he got to the part where the sheriff said, "Carothers told me." Instantly, he was mad enough to kill. That damned neighbor of his had given his secret to the sheriff.

Jake mulled over his misfortune for a week. He didn't even run his still. He was too busy hating Carothers for squealing on him. Getting him out of business would be great.

"That bastard ain't going to get away with it. I'm going to turn his ass in," Lattimer muttered to himself, picked up his old straw hat and headed for his pickup. He drove straight to Sheriff Locklear's office and walked in just like he was the most respected citizen of the community seeking to be a good citizen by doing his duty.

"Sheriff, you want to catch Carothers and his hands at a

big still?" he asked, squirming and looking around to make sure they were alone.

"Yeah, sure I do. I know he is turning out a lot of that rot-gut stuff up there in the river swamp somewhere, but there's far too much territory for me to find it. If you want to give me some good dope about that still, I'll sure see that he is put out of business soon," the sheriff promised. And he always kept his promises.

Those words delighted Lattimer. He wanted to get Carothers caught. It would leave a bigger slice of the booze market for him and at the same time he would be getting revenge for Carothers squealing about this phony cider.

"I know exactly where his still is at Lockwood Folly. I'll tell you about it," Lattimer said anxiously.

"Not on your life! There's far too many sloughs at Lockwood Folly for me to try to find a still without some help from someone who really knows that wilderness. You'll have to go along with us. You've already said you know where it is. I'm deputizing you right now. I'll call the ATU agents who have been trying to catch Carothers for several months. They'll be here Friday at noon. You be here too. We'll all go get that still and catch old Stick in the act. That'll make the ATU boys happy and me and you too," Sheriff Locklear said with a crafty smile. He knew that a big still bust would help him at election time.

Lattimer was not all that happy. Informants seldom are overjoyed when they put the finger on another lawbreaker. They are acutely aware that they lurk in a dangerous shadow, and life or death often hangs in the balance. He wanted to see his competitor caught red-handed and he was still mad about the cider secret that Carothers had leaked to the sheriff, but Carothers was as mean as a cottonmouth moccasin. Lattimer sure didn't want Carothers to know he had fingered him or his life wouldn't be worth a plugged nickel. Both bootleggers were so untrustworthy that they would have to be muzzled in a barrel of bear guts. Surely, Lattimer was caught in a bind. He had to go along on the raid. The sheriff had made that clear. If he refused now, Locklear would make it rough on him the rest of his life. He would probably never be able to make moonshine anywhere in this territory again.

Lattimer was at the sheriff's office at noon Friday as he had been directed. He walked in and two uniformed, young ATU agents shook his hand. They looked agile and capable of making a still raid in the jungle where they were going.

"These are the federal agents I told you that we would take along with us to the still. This is Agent Long and Agent Anderson. Now let's get going," Locklear was ready to go.

"We'll have to go into Lockwood River by boat. It's down the river and there are no roads. I've got a homemade 20-foot cypress boat that's big enough to carry us. It has an outboard kicker on it that's old, but I think it will get us near the area where the still is, then we will walk to the still yard that Lattimer says is operating close by," the sheriff took control of the raiding party.

They crawled in the leaky old boat that natives had used for crabbing and clamming in the distant past and shoved it off into the scenic river that laced through the dismal swampland. The raiding party was on its way.

"This is tidal water and that's why I asked you to be here at noon. We can't just motor to the area without spooking Carothers. He would hear the motor. So we'll launch the boat at the bridge and motor down the river a few miles, then cut the engine and let the outgoing tide drift us to Lockwood Folly on the south side of the river. It will take us about an hour to get there," the sheriff-turned-boat-captain continued to talk.

"By the time we catch the bootleggers, cut down the still and get back to the boat, the tide will have turned and the current will help us get back to the highway and our cars," Sheriff Locklear made sure everyone understood how knowledgeable he was about bootleg raiding and the river. After all, at that point in time there were so many bootleggers that they had to wear badges to identify themselves.

At exactly 3 o'clock, and well past Shallotte, Lattimer pointed to an uprooted sweetgum tree that had fallen into the river along the south shoreline.

"We'll tie up the boat against that tree and slip into the woods from there," Lattimer whispered so quietly that the sheriff had to repeat it to the agents. But the coincidence of the decade unfolded before the officers a moment later when the boat eased against the fallen tree and stopped.

At that very instant, Carothers and one of his hired still hands, pushed through the dense undergrowth to the river bank, no more than 50 yards downstream. Carothers yelled and pointed at the boat, obviously recognizing the uniformed ATU officers as revenuers and perhaps seeing Sheriff Locklear as well. Lattimer tried to flatten himself on the deck, hoping that they would not recognize him. He was a reluctant participant in this raid to begin with, and scared stiff to boot.

Both moonshiners, obviously coming to the river for water needed at the still, dropped the buckets they had in hand. Carothers disappeared into the woods and his hired hand was close behind. No more than 30 second passed as the officers tried to tie up the boat and disembark. Before they could do that, however, Carothers yelled from his hiding place in the swamp: "Turn that damned boat around and get out of here right now or all of you will be crabmeat before night!" A 30-30 bullet buried itself in the sweetgum log near where the boat was tied. Shots rang out every few seconds as it was now clear that both men were armed and determined that no one else would set foot on the Lockwood shoreline that afternoon.

"Lattimer, you son-of-a-bitch, I see that old straw hat of yours. I would know it anywhere. You'll have to come out from behind that log sooner or later and I'll get you along with the rest of the bastards in that boat!" the moonshiner yelled, knowing he had been betrayed and that his still was endangered.

A steady barrage of bullets pinned down the officers. It was a precarious position that the sheriff and his posse found themselves in.

"Anderson, can you get a shot at him from the bow of the boat?" Locklear screamed at the ATU agent.

"Hell, I could shoot from now until doomsday and not hit him. I can't see either of the snipers and in that jungle, firing my revolver into the undergrowth would be like firing at a piss ant in the Pacific," Anderson was emphatic. It was nearly impossible to hit anything that was so well covered in that wilderness.

Only the big sweetgum log and the thick cypress lumber the boat was built of kept them from being sitting ducks. There were enough limbs on the tree to partially hide them and the freeboard on the boat let them hover down with a little safety. There was no way they could climb out and get to the hill without getting shot.

While they were disadvantaged and pinned down tight, the gunmen were also in a quandary. If they left their hiding places and tried to slip closer or get an open shot, they ran the risk of being seen and the sheriff and ATU agents were anxious to use their pistols if anything moved within range. And the gunmen certainly were in easy range.

"What can we do?" Lattimer nervously asked the sheriff.

"Not a damn thing. Just sit tight and wait 'em out. They don't dare leave their cover and we can't get out of the boat. We'll just have to wait," Locklear said decisively.

The wait continued hour after hour, with an occasional burst of rifle fire assuring the pinned-down officers that the stalkers were still there.

The tide changed and darkness descended upon the river. Locklear silently untied the boat and gave it a little shove out into the current. It moved away silently without alerting the bootleggers that the boat was making a getaway. Three or four minutes elapsed before anyone in the boat dared sit up and look around. The boat had drifted a hundred yards or more down the river when Locklear yanked on the outboard starter rope and Lattimer and the agents heard that wonderful sound of the kicker firing that would get them out of this hell hole. Shots rang out and bullets ricocheted off the water around the boat, but on a moonless night in a fast current, and pushed along by even an ancient outboard, the boat quickly outdistanced the bootlegging gunners on the shoreline. The officers made it to the highway, tied the boat to a tree, rushed to their cars and dashed back to town. They could get the boat later.

Back at the sheriff's office, the officers were enraged and frustrated. They had been the hunted instead of the hunters and it was not supposed to be like that. Lattimer was scared to death and asked if it was all right for him to go home. The sheriff motioned him to go ahead. He jumped in his pickup and headed toward Supply.

Neighbors later told the sheriff that Lattimer came home for only a few minutes. He packed a few things in an old trunk, got back in his vehicle and sped away. He was never seen again in Supply. His bootlegging days were over. Relatives said he lived the last ten years of his life in a crude camp miles inside the dense Green swamp of North Carolina.

After the sheriff's posse escaped, Carothers and his hired hands moved the still deeper into the swampland and left only ashes and residue at the old still site for federal agents to find later. Carothers had escaped the clutches of the law again, as he had many times previously. As a matter of fact, he was never arrested for bootlegging. After that gun-firing episode, he became a respected commercial fisherman the remainder of his life.

And why the conversion?

The morning after being pinned down in the river, Sheriff Locklear and the ATU agents went back to the landing on the highway to get the boat. It had been chopped to splinters during the night and was a total wreck.

Locklear, a full-blooded American Indian, turned the color of red that means you are mad as hell. Not only had his life been threatened the day before, now his cherished old boat had been vandalized too. He looked at the agents a moment before he spoke.

"There's something I have to do. Can I leave you at the fish camp here for an hour or so? I'll be back to get you by midday," he promised. He got in his car, turned off the highway and drove west toward Carothers' shack in the swamp.

There's no record of what transpired when the sheriff knocked on Carothers' door. The generally accepted version in the Supply area now is that Carothers opened the door and Locklear grabbed him by the throat and beat hell out of him right there on his front porch. Then he said something like this:

"Carothers you have been a bootlegging, no-good bastard for years. That is over. You tried to kill me yesterday and then cut up my boat last night. I am giving you a chance that you didn't give us yesterday. You can destroy that still and never fire up another one or I am going to kill you right here and now. I can easily claim you tried to shoot me on the porch when I came to arrest you for attempted murder for firing on us yesterday in the boat and every juror in this county will believe me. Now what will it be? Are you out of bootlegging or would you rather I shoot you between the eyes?" Sheriff Locklear asked, as he menacingly pulled his revolver from its holster.

"I'll give up bootlegging. Just give me a chance. I'll be straight from now on," Carothers whimpered as he was sure Locklear meant exactly what he had said.

The sheriff picked up the agents at the fish camp and drove back to town.

"You don't need to worry about bootlegging around here anymore for awhile. Carothers is out of the business and I don't think Lattimer will be around anymore," Locklear said, almost nonchalantly.

The agents looked at each other quizzically. Neither bothered to ask anything. They were glad to be able to leave this wilderness alive, especially now that the bootleggers were no longer a problem.

Sheriff Locklear was often heard repeating some advice he heard from his father: "Never do anything bad, but if you do, do it alone and keep your mouth shut."

Note: *All names in this chapter have been changed to protect living members of the families who still live along the Carolina Coast.*

Shall We Gather at the River . . .

A believe-it-or-not event happened in the Carolina swamp-lands on the Lumber River one winter day in the 1950's. Reports of a moonshine operation on the river a few miles from Fair Bluff kept filtering into the district ATF office two or three times every year. A memorable report came near Easter when a Baptist pastor called the ATF office and more or less pinpointed the location of a still that he particularly wanted shut down.

As the story goes, moonshiners were operating in a desolate spot and hadn't moved their still site for years. It was tough to reach and even harder to find if you didn't know those dense jungle acres like the natives did. It was easy to leave the reports on a back burner for a more appropriate time—perhaps in the spring or sometime other than now.

But the preacher was adamant. He wanted something done about the free-flowing booze that was corrupting the community. And he noted the specific case of Josh Shuford, a pitiful alcoholic, who was certainly going to hell if his white lightning supply didn't soon dry up.

"Shuford is so addicted to alcohol that he drinks shaving lotion, shoe polish, canned heat and on one occasion, shampoo. He thought it was shaving lotion, and after holding his nose and downing the whole bottle, he came out of his house bubbling, his mouth foaming so that neighbors thought he had gone made with rabies. It made him sick and he hasn't tried the shampoo since.

"He gets so desperate for a drink that he will steal or do almost anything else to get his hands on a bottle of booze. His father runs a general store. Josh was doing some cleaning for his dad in the store recently and went upstairs, presumably to sweep and tidy up the storeroom a bit.

"But Josh had other ideas. He was broke and needed whiskey. He began throwing out boxes of shoes, overalls, gun shells and a number of other items from the back room's upstairs window. Finally he came downstairs and hung around until after dark. Then he returned to the rear of the store, picked up the loot he had stolen from his dad and sold it so he could buy another bottle or two of moonshine. You see what this liquor is leading to in my community?" the distraught minister made his point. "Josh is never going to get any better if we don't shut down the moonshiners around here."

The preacher-informant circled a spot on a map of the Lumber River wilderness where he said the still causing most of the trouble was located on a tiny stream.

"You've got to catch those moonshiners and tear up that still if you want the people in this community to have any respect for the ATF," this man of God challenged.

Despite the rain and cool weather, the three agents nodded their agreement, and on Easter morning they stopped their car on an old sawmill road a mile off the beaten path and trudged along the shoreline of the river toward the reported still—which was still two long country miles or more away. Every slippery step over muck and through dense undergrowth in the blowing rain was difficult and challenging. After walking an hour, with fatigue setting in and their hands and feet wet and cold, they decided the tip wasn't accurate. The preacher had given them bad directions or he was misinformed. They would give up this wild goose chase and return to the comfort of home, or at least to a nearby motel room where they could rest and thaw out.

They agreed on the logic of retreating and started backtracking. But wait! The loud and not-so-harmonious strains of a well-known hymn echoed up and down the swamp. Someone was happy, and if he was a moonshiner, he certainly wasn't aware that his nemesis, ATF officers, were stalking him in the nearby wings.

"Hey, we're in luck! The still must be right around the next bend and the moonshiners are so confident that they are celebrating Easter.

"Let's go get 'em," the ATF leader challenged, and minutes later they walked right into the still yard where the fires were burning and a tiny stream of white lightning was pouring from the radiator-condenser into a jug that was spilling over. The booze trickled down on the ground and puddled into the tiny creek.

Only one man could be seen. He wasn't making moonshine or doing any work at all. He was just sitting on a log near the fire with a half-gallon Mason jar of whiskey in his hands and singing at the top of his intoxicated lungs. Strains of the old hymn, "Shall We Gather at the river. . . " echoed in the forest.

The agents were somewhat amused even while being disappointed. This didn't look like a real still operator in the condition he was in. They could not make the bust they had anticipated. But maybe they should arrest this lone vocalist. He was at the site and the still was running, even if the end product was pouring into the ground.

"Mister, what's your name?" one of the exhausted federal officers asked. "And what are you doing here?"

"I'm Josh Shuford and I'm celebrating Easter; can't you see?" the drunk sputtered. I couldn't find no whiskey down in town, so I walked here where I heard they were making some. But them two fellers who was here heard me coming through the bushes and skedaddled before I got here. But that's O.K. They left this thing a-runnin' and I been having a time drinking it about as fast as it comes out of that spout," the old reprobate confessed.

It was obvious that Shuford knew the moonshiners and had been here before, fighting his way to this desolate spot in his desperation to find a drink. He was not a moonshiner.

The officers chopped up the still, and with Shuford in tow, they headed toward the river and on to their car and civilization. Shuford was a pain in the ass every stumbling step of the way, but he continued to be happy with the normal serenity of the river every time they stopped for a breather. It gave him another chance to take a swig from his half-empty jar.

While the officers made no arrests, they reasoned the Baptist minister-informant would be happy to know that they had not only destroyed the troublesome still, they had rescued the alcoholic member of his beleaguered flock. He had taken up temporary residence at the still site that the preacher had reported. The moonshiners had fled in disarray in the nick of time to avoid arrest and imprisonment.

There was poetic justice for the bootleggers in having avoided these unpleasantries by the narrowest of margins because one overzealous customer thrashed through the swamp looking for their merchandise and then couldn't refrain from joyfully singing the Christian song of eternal salvation—"Shall We Gather at the River. . . " They mistook his noisy approach for stalking revenuers and escaped. It was their salvation that Easter morning, be it ever so temporary.

Postscript to the Shuford Story

As unbelievable as this story of Josh Shuford sounds, it is based on a true incident and only the names have been changed to avoid embarrassing close relatives who still live along the river swamp. And there is a postscript to the story:

Shortly after the still was destroyed, the Baptist preacher who had tipped off the ATF of the location of the bootlegging operation was delivering a fiery Sunday sermon on the evils of alcohol, as many did in the mid-century years in that region. As he neared the conclusion of his remarks he said:

"I only wish that I had within my grasp all the whiskey in the world. I would take it right down here on the banks of the river and pour it all out. It would make this a better world, free from alcoholism and its evils."

Closing his Bible the minister nodded to several "amens" and then turned to the congregation.

"What shall we sing for our closing hymn?" he asked.

From a pew near the back of the sanctuary, Josh Shuford held up his hand, "Preacher, let's sing 'Shall We Gather at the River.'"

A Converted Moonshiner

It was August and there was no wind in the wilderness along the coastline near Georgetown. The temperature hung around the century mark and even the young squirts with the Treasury Department's bevy of hot-to-trot revenue agents were reluctant to stalk swampland bootleggers until the heat wave subsided. Hot and humid weather put the moonshiners to work after dark when the temperature was a little more bearable, but the no-see-'ums and mosquitoes were terrible. When illicit liquor distillers fired up their stills, the smoke helped discourage some of the pesky insects. They turned out their white lightning by the barrel for drinkers in Charleston and even Columbia and beyond when prohibition curtailed legal availability and for years after the law was repealed.

Many of the swamp's salty veteran moonshiners could find their way through the dense swamplands blindfolded, even when they had to wade water ankle deep. But there were very few ATF agents anxious to traipse through these wilderness woodlands in the dark and tempt the cottonmouths, rattlesnakes and alligators. So the heat favored the moonshiners in the daytime and the darkness curtailed distillery hunting at night. The wilderness along the river seemed custom-made for unmolested bootlegging.

The revenue agents destroyed a few upland stills regularly and hoped that would satisfy the regional office as well as the churchgoing society that strongly advocated elimination of alcohol in all forms in their neighborhoods. They kept the pressure on the agents to do a better job and to stamp out the illicit liquor business in the church communities. Church men rightly blamed much of the violence and lawlessness along the coastal community on the drunks. And those imbibers wouldn't be drunk if the bootleggers didn't supply them with stumphole alcohol.

Liquor continued to be plentiful on the coast, a quart Mason jar full of these spirits was going for four dollars. Dozens of bootleggers continued to make a living brewing corn whiskey on the dunes in the swamps where a labyrinth of creeks, spring runs and dense undergrowth made their sites virtually impossible to locate, even if officers dared enter these no-man's lands. Moonshiners continued in the lucrative business for years with a minimum of interference from state or federal officers. Few arrests were ever made in the wilderness, but some peddlers of the whiskey were picked up in town from time to time. They were always just flunkies and the boss moonshiners quickly paid the fines and got the hired still hands back on the job in a day or two.

Some of the young and serious ATF agents were disillusioned. They wanted to do a good job. They wanted to catch and convict the big moonshiners, some of whom were getting rich, but they were helpless and frustrated.

Moonshining was illegal because the product made at the stills did not have government tax stamps. The illicit distillers could not buy state and federal stamps because the manufacture of the product without government permission was illegal and they could not stamp the liquor. In that it did not bear the costly stamps, bootleggers could undersell the so-called bonded liquor when prohibition was repealed and they continued to thrive selling their discount alcohol. Crime did pay in that era.

The bottled-in-bond whiskey was the recreation vehicle of the sophisticated and the affluent and the stumphole variety generally went to the hard-hat Americans on weekends and the alcoholics seven days a week.

Bootleggers knocked the legal, bonded whiskey, noting that "It is so dingy that you can't see through it." The non-taxed liquor from the moonshiners was always as clear as tap water and that was considered a mark of quality not found in the high-priced bourbon in the liquor stores. It was a phony assumption, but one used by the moonshiners. Certainly the non-tax-paid variety destroyed marriages, wrecked homes, prompted spouse and child abuse and caused deaths on the highways just like the tax-paid alcohol did.

Mogul bootleggers remained free and prosperous, often boasting that they would never be caught by a bunch of raw kids who worked for the Alcohol and Tobacco Tax Unit of the Treasury Department who were not dry behind the ears. Unfortunately, they were right more often than not about being apprehended. And that situation is what made agents sit up and take notice when they apparently got an unexpected break.

Their lack of distillery destruction and apprehension of the most notorious of the liquor makers in the area is what prompted a visitor from the local Baptist church to barge into the ATU office one Monday afternoon. The man obviously was high-strung and certainly he was more than just somewhat irritated. He was mad and totally lacking in diplomacy.

"You one of them revenooers?" the bespectacled middle-aged gentleman asked, eyeballing the uniformed agent he expected to answer his question.

"Yes sir, I am," the agent responded. "What can I do for you Mr. . . . ?"

"Vanderford. W. T. Vanderford. I'm the pastor of the Baptist Church in Georgetown and I have some information that I want to give to somebody if I have your promise to do something about it. If I don't have that promise, I'm going to some higher-ups. I'm getting plenty tired of coming up here and reporting the location of liquor stills in my community and then nothing being done about it. This is my third time to go out of my way to pass along information about a big liquor still. It's my last trip to this ATU office," the reverend said, with obvious frustration.

"The bootleggers are ruining our community and I want them caught now. I realize that they will burn me out or kill me if they find out that I am squealing on them, but I am ready to take that chance. I want the big boys in the liquor business caught. And the biggest of them all is Hank Whitley. I know all of you have heard about him."

Indeed the agents had heard. He compared with North Carolina's Percy Flowers among bootlegging legends. He was a real bastard who had one or more big stills going in the swamps the year 'round. Agents had caught some of his lieutenants who either collected for him or delivered the stumphole alcohol. When these cohorts were arrested, it didn't even faze them. They just laughed and made it clear they would be free in a few hours.

"The boss will get us out of jail before you get to sleep and no court has ever convicted one of the Whitley boys," they bragged. And, unfortunately for the agents, that was true.

"If you don't destroy Whitley's still and catch him this time, I'm going to Washington and see if I can get you fellows all fired. Do you want my information based on that promise?" Reverend Vanderford asked, and he looked at the agent expectantly. "Let me point out that this still is operated by Whitley, but he has financial backing from several local businessmen with big political clout. If you can catch him at the still and destroy that huge operation, you'll also be sending a message to those financial backers. They'll be slow to put other bootleggers in business in our community.

"Whitley farms but he is the biggest bootlegger in this part of the Carolinas. He has been in the liquor business all of his life. And he has never been arrested. He farms for a front. You may find this hard to believe, but he is in my congregation and is one of my most liberal contributors. But he is destroying a lot of homes and making drunks out of husbands and fathers, even teenagers. I can't approve of such evil. I learned about his still location from one of my flock and I know it is accurate. My informer saw it with his own eyes when he was 'coon hunting two nights ago," the preacher confided.

This sanctimonious old codger was sincere and the agents understood how he felt. They wanted to cooperate. There are some good people in the world and perhaps Vanderford was one of them. Certainly he talked a good Christian fight. He deserved the attention of the agents.

"Preacher, I am new here," the senior agent answered, "I don't know whom you have told about a liquor still in the past, but I can assure you that all of us are interested in catching Mr. Whitley. He is the most notorious moonshiner in this part of South Carolina and we will do almost anything to catch him. We have not been able to get information from informants and have never had the evidence to arrest him. If you have an accurate location of his operating still, I can guarantee you that we will catch him. If we don't, we will understand that you are reporting us for incompetence and perhaps collusion. We indeed might lose our jobs," the agent in charge made an instant contract with the minister across the desk. He didn't know at that point how hard it would be to keep his word. Later he wondered if he had spoken too soon.

Reverend Vanderford seemed convinced that the agents were serious and would make every effort to catch the liquor mogul. This man was a giant in the illicit liquor business in the area, but so was Percy Flowers in North Carolina, and he was eventually put out of business. Whitley had to fall too.

The preacher made a pretty good plea for help, knowing he was sticking his neck out a mile. Agents got the feeling that he was willing to make personal sacrifices to put Whitley out of business, but he could do it only with ATU help.

Always interested in building a reputation as a firebrand type of agent, the senior officer knew that if he made a case against this liquor-making daddy rabbit of the Carolinas, it would be a pretty feather in his cap, as well as in his associates'. They were human. They wanted to be recognized for outstanding efforts and success. They wanted to catch Whitley.

"We'll catch the bootlegger. Just tell me where the still is," the agent firmly and convincingly said to Reverend Vanderford.

The minister pulled a wrinkled road map with a sheet of ruled notebook paper attached to it from his breast pocket. It looked like something he had torn out of a school child's notebook. But it was specific. Vanderford, either for religious or personal reasons, had an ax to grind with Whitley. He pointed out exactly where a big still was operating off Highway 17 in a far corner of the swampland.

"To catch Whitley at this still, you'll have to leave your cars on this country road and go by foot through the swamp. It's about three miles. The still is not far from an old sawmill road on the west side, but you can never get to the still from that direction without being seen. There are open farm fields all along the swamp fringe. But Whitley has no guards up on the swamp side. He feels he is perfectly safe from that direction. He can see for half a mile on the field side. He has operated safely in that location for months and he thinks he can get away with it forever," Vanderford revealed his vital information.

"When you move through the swamp toward his operation, you will find that Whitley has black sewing thread strung around the still. He inspects that string before he fires up to make a run. Generally, if he finds the string is broken, he assumes the location has been discovered, might be under surveillance, and his better judgment tells him to get out of there for a few days. But if you find the black thread when you are going in is broken, don't tie it back together. Sometimes he breaks the string on purpose. He theorizes that a deer or other wild animal might break the thread, but only a revenuer is going to tie it back together. So if you find it broken, leave it that way," Vanderford further advised.

The agents were amused at the detailed information the preacher had on this bootlegger and his still. The things he was relating were mostly old hat to the veteran revenue officers, but few laymen would have any knowledge of the broken sewing thread trick. It had alerted many a moonshiner.

"Preacher, how did you learn where this still was located and in particular, how did you hear the story about the thread around the still site?" The agent inquired of Vanderford as he turned to leave.

"I have a member of my congregation who worked for Whitley at that still until a few weeks ago. Whitley only paid him starvation wages and he got tired of running all the risks and not making enough to support his family. He is trying to get away from bootlegging and be a better citizen. He thinks the liquor from the still is making his son-in-law an alcoholic and it has addicted many other youngsters. He wants to get it stopped if he can without getting killed. That's the confidential information I have passed along to you. Whitley would probably have us both killed if he got word of this meeting," Vanderford was as serious as he could be.

"I'm going now. Remember, if you foul up this raid, I'll be convinced Whitley is paying you fellows off and I'll see that this charge is heard by your superiors. Don't mess it up. Catch him and destroy that big still quickly while he is personally running it," the reverend implored, and he left without smiling. Informing on a major liquor manufacturer is a serious, sometimes deadly, business. Many informers met untimely deaths all over the South during the moonshining heyday as they did in Chicago, New York and other big cities where gangster bosses controlled illegal bootlegging shenanigans for decades.

The senior officer grinned at his associates. He knew he had first-class inside information on one of the state's leading liquor law violators. He had a chance at a big bust that would get a lot of media coverage and make ATU look like it was doing its job well. This challenge was too good to miss.

"Fellows, today is Friday. Let's go after that still Monday night. The preacher thinks it was fired up and going earlier this week. Maybe Whitley will be making a new run by Monday. We'll leave the office in time to reach that spot at the swamp about three o'clock in the afternoon. We should be able to make our way three miles through the swamp and reach the still before dark. Then we'll stake out the still and wait for brother Whitley to show up and get the run going. Then we'll nab him." The officer planned the raid on the spot and later got permission from his superiors to lead the raiding party of three.

They parked their car in a sawmill road on the edge of the swamp in mid afternoon on Monday. It was the hottest day of the year. There was not a leaf stirring and the sun blazed down on the wilderness on a cloudless day. The agents pulled on their boots and drab clothing and pushed into the dense undergrowth for the long trek through the swamp. Quickly the sweltering revenue agents were soaked with sweat. Already they were beginning to wish Vanderford hadn't given them this inside dope on Whitley's distillery. It was not going to be a cake walk.

"Fellows, remember when we get close to the still, we are splitting up and we will take positions that will keep us concealed until dark in case Whitley makes a tour of his string to see if anyone has been nosing around. And most important of all, keep in mind that we cannot fail to make an arrest. If Whitley gets away, we will certainly hear something from the higher-ups. Vanderford will sure as hell report us and contend that we purposely let Whitley get away. We don't want to lose our jobs by failing on this bust," cautioned the agent in charge.

For hours they crawled, pulled, pushed and fought their way through a dense maze of bushes, briers and vines. Never had any of the agents been so totally fatigued before as the hot, humid weather took a toll every inch of the three swampy miles. It was pure torture.

At last, panting and drenched, they could see the setting sun on the horizon on the western edge of the swamp. A few steps further and they could see the giant distillery just as Reverend Vanderford had described it. The smell of fermenting mash swept over the jungle, even on the calm afternoon. Hundreds of barrels and hogsheads were scattered under a huge hammock of trees that was no more than three or four hundred feet from a corn field on the western border of the swamp.

Obviously there was no one at the still when the agents came within sight of it. They hadn't expected Whitley to be there in the daytime. They split up according to their plan and soon were buried under gallberry bushes, bramble briers and assorted prickly weeds and then began the wait in the torturous heat. They felt certain Whitley would show up at dusk, but when darkness settled over the wilderness, not a soul appeared. Only the eerie call of a hoot owl and a few tree frogs disturbed the spooky silence. About nine o'clock when they had been almost eaten alive by mosquitoes, the agent in charge called to the others to come out.

"Let's take a careful look at the distillery and the mash. Obviously Whitley isn't going to make a run tonight. Let's look around, but don"t leave any footprints or touch anything. We surely don't want him to find out we have been here," he instructed. Softly, almost like they expected the devil to jump out from behind the nearest tree, they eased onto the still site, keeping several yards between themselves and the still so there would be no footprints in the soft, muddy earth. They carefully surveyed the project.

"Stay here!" the boss agent told the others. "I want to look at the mash." And he tiptoed to the nearest hogshead and looked at the ugly, bubbling, brown mash that moved like it was alive.

Flies, mosquitoes, dragonflies and other assorted insects were drowned on the surface. They would be strained off when the mash was cooked and if you didn't know about the flies, the liquor would be as tasty as if it were brewed under the most sanitary conditions. What drinkers didn't know wouldn't hurt them was the general consensus among moonshiners, but there are numerous documented accounts of stumphole whiskey being lethal. It poisoned and killed many imbibers.

The agents had raided scores of stills over the years and could easily tell what stage the mash was in by looking and smelling. Experiences teaches revenue agents how ripe mash is and when the operation will be fired up for the next run.

"This mash isn't ready to run. It's going to need three or four more days before it has fermented enough. That's why Whitley didn't show up. He will be back when the mash is ready, and right now that looks like Friday night to me. Let's ease our way out of here to the field and find that country road. We'll call the sheriff or catch a ride back to our car. We can't fight our way back through that swamp again tonight. But," he hesitated reluctantly, "we'll have to fight our way through it again Friday afternoon," he said, not surprised to hear the other agents groan. "We can't risk being seen crossing that corn field."

Friday afternoon they pulled their car into the same sawmill pig-path road where they had parked previously and slowly climbed out into a sweltering oven, even hotter and more humid than it had been on Monday. They looked at each other. Would they punish their bodies again by trudging through three miles of this godforsaken jungle? Reluctantly, they pulled on their boots and fatigue clothing. They were getting more uncomfortable by the minute.

"Men, we can't hack it though this damned swamp again this afternoon. Let's drive over to the county road and belly-crawl through the corn patch to the edge of the swamp. We can scatter out and watch the still from the west side without the unbearable punishment of going through the swamp. I know that Reverend Vanderford wouldn't approve. He said we could not go in from the corn field side, but I'm in favor of trying it. What do you think?" the senior agent asked for their input.

All the agents were yes-men at the moment. They dreaded fighting through that swamp again like Daniel would had he been thrown into the lion's den twice. Besides, he was the boss. They would have followed him to hell and back if he had asked. But the swamp route was just too much on such a burning hot afternoon.

"We can make it without being seen if we leave our car a mile or so away and then crawl on our bellies across that corn field that's next to the still. Once we get to the edge of the swamp, we can hide in the brush and wait for Whitley. He probably won't show up until dark anyway. Not many moonshiners go to their stills in the daylight even to test the mash," The agent rationalized his decision to approach the still the easy way, as man is always prone to do.

The agents found a seldom-used dirt road that was a safe distance from the corn field near where the still was located. They parked and walked through the high and dry woodland until they were near the still site, then sneaked across the road and flattened out between the rows of knee-high corn. The corn had been cultivated once, but some crab grass was growing between the rows. The stalks and leaves provided pretty good cover when the agents lay flat on the ground. They were convinced that no one at the still could see them in the unlikely event that there was a watchman. They began snaking across a couple of hundred yards of growing corn.

They were no more than a dozen rows into the corn patch when they heard a gruff voice say "Whoa." That was mule language for stop, and they knew that meant trouble. At the far end of the field, a powerfully built farmer with a bushy red beard was unhitching a bay mule from a ground sled on which there was a one-horse cultivator.

"My God, it's Whitley," the senior agent whispered, trying to get under the ground to avoid being seen. The agent knew Whitley farmed, or that at least he used farming as a front, but he didn't think he would be out here plowing with a mule on such a hot day. He would ordinarily leave that to his hired hands. He must not own a tractor.

"We surely cannot get up and run. Whitley would see us

for sure and he would never go back to that still," the agent whispered to his associates.

"Let's ease on over a couple of rows and maybe he will go by without seeing us," he suggested, all the while knowing that the chance of staying undetected in the short corn was very slim.

He reasoned that maybe Whitley was here, not to cultivate his corn, but maybe this was his sneaky way of taking a peek at the still site to make sure all was clear for the night's liquor run. He could do that in apparent innocence in case the still operation was staked out. Whitley was no fool. He had escaped the law for years by outfoxing agents with the best laid plans. But then he could also be here just to get the grass out of his corn. In either case, he had the agents over a barrel and they envisioned Whitley spotting them and never returning to his still. Reverend Vanderford would surely go to Washington to get all three agents fired for conspiring with the notorious moonshiner. That's what he had promised to do.

With his mule burdened by the cultivator, Whitley headed toward the agents, scratching out the crab grass in the corn middles. He would pass within ten steps or so. The leader silently, and uncharacteristically, prayed that he would not look up from his work and see the three revenue agents trying to bury themselves between his rows of corn. It would be hard to explain such a presence if he caught them, as he almost surely would. At that moment the agents knew that only an act of God would save them from detection and from a total strike-out of their goal to catch the bootlegger at his still. They supposed they would lose their jobs. Maybe their wives and kids would go hungry.

One of the agents in the corn patch had been an entertainer in college. He had appeared in night clubs and fancy restaurants and used his ability as a ventriloquist to fascinate his audiences. And he was good at it.

He slowly turned his head toward Whitley as he approached, getting ever closer. Softly he asked for permission to try a brazen trick that he hoped would work.

"Let me try to confuse him. Let me throw my voice when he gets even with us."

The senior agent figured they had nothing to lose. They were caught for sure now.

"Why not!" he whispered, "We are going to get fired anyway."

When Whitley and his mule were almost breathing down their necks, the young agent cupped his hand over his mouth, and in a mysterious, almost ghostly voice, groaned out the words, "Go ye and preach the gospel."

Whitley's head snapped up and he looked around in every direction for a long moment. The agents were petrified and expecting the worst. But he did not stop his mule. He plowed on to the end of the row, made a U-turn and started back in the direction of the officers, who had managed to crawl a few rows deeper into the corn while Whitley's back was turned to them.

As Whitley again approached the agents, intently watching the dirt as it turned over under the cultivator, the amateur ventriloquist repeated his previous command, "Go ye and preach the gospel." Again Whitley peered around, looking particularly expectantly toward the sky. He saw nothing, and miraculously, again failed to see the federal agents trying to bury themselves in the dirt of that Carolina cornfield.

The agents couldn't believe that he had passed them twice without seeing them. But he had.

Again they moved a couple of rows toward the swamp as Whitley continued on to the end of the row, made his turn and started back toward the agents for the third time.

"I'm going to try to confuse him before he gets even with us this time," the agent-ventriloquist whispered. Again he cupped his hands over his mouth and in a weird voice he almost yelled his message when Whitley was about 50 yards away: "Go ye and preach the gospel."

This time the old bootlegger was visibly shaken. He looked around as he had the two previous times and saw nothing. He was ghostly white and pulled on the old mule's reins as he said, "Whoa." The mule stopped quickly. He immediately unhitched his beast from the cultivator in the middle of the field, left it standing there, and walked back to the end of the rows, leading the mule. He hooked the mule to the ground sled, stepped aboard and headed down the road toward his home at the edge of the swamp, coaxing the old mule into a fast trot.

The agents looked up with open mouths. A "what is going on?" look came over all their faces. The agents were dumbfounded. Whitely was almost upon them and then he had suddenly quit cultivating in the middle of a row and headed for home.

Had he seen the agents and was just trying to be coy about it? That seemed reasonable and they shuddered, realizing they might have lost their last chance to catch him. And might have lost their jobs, too.

"We might as well go on into the swamp and stake the still out. If Whitley saw us he won't be coming near that still, but if he didn't, he may be back about dark and we need to have the area surrounded so he can't get away. Maybe we haven't lost our chance to nab him yet," the agent said, and they slipped on into the jungle and took up positions about 100 feet from the mash and the still yard. Quietly they kept the area under surveillance until midnight. Not a soul appeared. Again they checked the mash. It was definitely ripe for boiling, but for some reason, Whitley had decided not to fire it up that night. The agents were more concerned than ever. He must have seen them and pretended not to. They would surely be in a bind when Vanderford learned they had once again failed to catch this super bootlegger. He seemed to have outfoxed the law again.

"Let's just leave everything as it is. It's getting late. We'll come back tomorrow afternoon and dynamite the still and the mash. It's going to take quite an arsenal to blow all this stuff up. I'm too tired to tackle it tonight," the senior agent said to his cohorts, and they walked out of the swamp to their car and headed for home. They were downcast. In an effort to avoid the discomfort of fighting their way through the swamp, they had lost their chance to catch the big-time moonshiner. What a shame! They had blown a great opportunity.

Around mid-day on Saturday they drove back to the corn field, took a case of dynamite from the car trunk and with an ax and crowbar in hand, walked across the field to the still, fully intending to blow everything to kingdom come, so it could never be used again. At least Whitley would have the expense of getting a new still made and buying a new supply of barrels and jars.

The sight that greeted them was unbelievable! When they walked up to the still, there was destruction everywhere they looked. The still had been chopped to bits with an ax, and perhaps a sledge hammer. Every barrel of mash had been chopped to splinters and the smelly stuff covered the ground everywhere. Nothing had been spared and nothing could be salvaged here to start another liquor operation somewhere else. someone had done the job for ATU and done it well.

"Fellows, I believe the sheriff's force or some of the state officers found this still and beat us to it. They have sure done one helluva good job tearing it up. I am glad they did, but I'm still concerned that we let Whitley get away.

"You know, we sometimes are able to make a case with circumstantial evidence. There's a clear path leading from this still. We might follow it and if it winds up at Whitley's house, we might still be able to make a case against him that would hold up in the courts. That would sure get Vanderford off our necks," the officer was grasping at straws, hoping for a miracle.

They followed the path, and sure enough, it led right to the back door of Whitley's home, a half-mile away. They knocked on the door and a chubby lady wearing a floury apron moved from the kitchen and asked, "Whatta you want?"

"Ma'am, we are looking for Hank Whitley. Does he live here and is he home?" the agent asked in his most courteous voice, remembering that his own mother often wore an apron and worked in the kitchen just as this lady did.

"Yes sir, he does, or did, live here, and no sir, he ain't home. I'm his wife, but I think he has lost his mind or something and I don't have any idea where he is. He came in here yesterday afternoon from plowing his corn and he was as white as a bedsheet. He said he had been called to preach and he was accepting the challenge. This morning he picked up his ax and hammer and went into the swamp and came back two hours later, dirty and sweaty from head to foot. He smelled like corn mash. He said he had chopped his still all to pieces and that he would never again be in the liquor business. He was really all stirred up and he said he was going to be a preacher. He packed a few things, got in his pickup and drove away, finally telling me he would call in a few days.

"He said he was going to Columbia to see if he could enroll in a Bible school so he could learn everything about the scriptures. He wanted to go and preach the gospel like he said he had been called to do. That's all I know about him. After being married for over 30 years, I still don't understand that man, but my heart's with him if he wants to preach." Mrs. Whitley's story was almost unbelievable.

The story could end with the remarks from Mrs. Whitley as the agents thanked her, returned to the car and headed back to the office without a case against her bootlegging husband. But there is more to the story.

Whitley did enroll in a short Bible course in Columbia, and six months later he returned home to his wife with whom he had kept in contact by telephone during his absence. He looked like a stranger. He was well-dressed, his beard carefully trimmed and his hair cut short. Under his arm he carried a huge King James Version of the Bible.

He told his wife he was withdrawing their savings from the bank and buying a big tent. He was setting out to evangelize the world and he would hold tent meetings all over the South. He wanted his wife to go with him. She did, and they traveled from town to town conducting tent meetings through all the remaining days of his life.

And he was not content with just preaching. He hired a painter to make hundreds of one-line signs with a variety of biblical commands and he nailed them to trees along every major highway. Some of them still stand and are legible. some of his signs read: "Jesus is coming soon," "Remember the golden rule," and "Love Thy Neighbor." But the most fascinating of those signs, at least to the ATU agents, were the ones that said, "Go ye and preach the gospel."

Hand of God

Swan Quarter, a village barely above sea level, sprouted along the northern shoreline of Pamlico Sound two centuries ago. It's still only a village, but there are those who believe the face of God smiled upon the fishing hamlet in 1876 in a unique but definite manner that can easily be interpreted as a miracle. Indeed, it can scarcely be anything else.

Early in the 1870's the Methodist congregation at Swan Quarter decided to build a church and a committee found a site that was the highest elevation in the community. They went to the owner of the vacant property and asked him to set a price on the lot for the new church. He refused, saying he had other plans for the site and would not consider selling it to them at any price.

Disappointed, but facing reality, the Methodists proceeded to build their little frame church near the waterfront on a less desirable lot. In September of 1876, the church was nearing completion when a powerful hurricane hit the coast and flooded Swan Quarter with more than five feet of water. On the second day of the violent storm, and with the village looking like a lake, the church gently floated off its foundation. With frightened members of the church looking on from windows and housetops, the building sailed down the watery street almost like it was being piloted. It passed houses and stores and made a 180-degree turn to the right at an intersection. Gently it moved on to the vacant lot the building committee had selected the first time. Slowly it maneuvered around to face the street and settled to the ground almost as if by magic.

The property owner watched this strange event with mouth open in disbelief. Before the day was done, he stepped into his fishing boat and paddled to the house of the church building committee chairman. Understandably nervous, the property owner told the committee chairman to meet him at the courthouse the next day if the water receded. It did, and the meeting was held despite the mud and sludge of the flooded village and courthouse. The site owner anxiously signed a deed donating the site to the Methodist Church. He seemed to be relieved.

The church builders set the structure on a new foundation and it was soon completed.

Proudly the church still stands today and is aptly named "Providence Church." Remembering the miracle of Swan Quarter, a sign tells the story: "The church moved by the hand of God." And so it was!

A Narrow Escape

ATF agents knew that a lot of non-tax-paid whiskey was being made in Brunswick County by a moonshiner named Saul Grainger and several other big-time bootleggers. They moved the whiskey to market late at night and in the wee hours of the morning and agents had not been able to apprehend any of the liquor law violators with a sizeable quantity of the stuff.

Then the law got a break. A hunter in the river wilderness section had been run off of one of the bootlegger's farms, apparently when he got too close to a distillery. In that he had 'coon hunted on the farm all of his life without being harassed, he was irritated. No, it was more than that, he was fighting mad. He turned informant and notified the ATF of the suspected illicit liquor operation. It was his way of retaliating for being run off "his" hunting land.

"Is this the ATF office?" a caller inquired one Saturday morning.

"Yes it is. I'm the local agent in charge. What can I do for you?" the agent asked expectantly.

"You want to catch them sons-of-bitches that are making liquor up here along the river in Brunswick County?" came the voice of an obviously angry man.

"Yes, of course I do. What can you tell us that will help catch the bastards?" the agent asked.

"I know that tonight they are hauling a trunk full of whiskey out of the dirt road that runs through the swamp east of the Old Tusk Lake and enters Highway 904.

"I think it will be loaded on a black, souped-up Chevrolet with a Georgia license plate. The load is bound for Savannah. I want you to catch that bastard that will be driving. Will you do it?" the caller insisted on an answer. He was pushy and sounded angry. He wanted to be positive the ATF would catch the liquor lord who had spoiled his 'coon hunt.

"Well, I can't guarantee anything, But you can bet your bottom dollar that we will be looking for that car. We want to catch him as much as you do," the agent promised, thanking the caller and hanging up.

About dark that evening the agents drove down the pig path road where they expected the load of liquor to come from and hid their car in some popashe bushes. The young agent was full of piss and vinegar and the leader was a seasoned veteran who seldom over-reacted to any challenge.

Nervous over the prospects of making his first arrest since joining the ATF, a boyish-faced agent fiddled with his sidearm. You couldn't help comparing him to some of the old Wild West marshals awaiting a showdown with Billy the Kid or some other equally notorious bad man.

"James, you hide here and watch for the car. Stop it if you can when it gets here. If you can't, fire a couple of shots in the air and that will warn me that the load of liquor is coming toward me. I'll be up the road about a half mile. You got that straight?" the leader asked, knowing he was talking to a brash young pup who was easily excited. He was also scared, and anticipating an adventure that he had only dreamed of.

"Yeah, sure I got it straight. I'm going to stop the car right here and arrest anybody in it. If I don't do that, I'll shoot a couple of times and you'll know they are coming," he paraphrased the instructions almost to a T.

Three tiresome hours later, on the darkest night of the year, a black pickup came bouncing up that old washboardy road. Tall trees lined both sides of the rough old road, and even if there had been a moon, it would have been difficult to see anything or anyone in the truck. The agent stepped out of the bushes, waving his arms for the pickup to stop. Thinking about it today, you can understand how any driver would have been reluctant to stop in those deep woods in the middle of the night when confronted by a husky man waving a revolver and hollering "Stop! Stop, or I'll shoot!"

The pickup slowed down for just an instant and then the frightened driver put the pedal to the metal and roared away at a much faster clip than anyone had ever driven over that mudhole-pocked road before.

Excited beyond reason, the young agent fired two quick shots, not in the air as he had been instructed, but at the back of the fast-disappearing pickup. Then he jumped in the ATF car and was in hot pursuit, firing several more wild shots as he went.

The leader knew the plan had gone astray and was prepared for such an eventuality. Quickly he dragged a dead treetop across the narrow road. He had chosen this spot with the dead tree to wait and hide. It was his ace in the hole if the first agent failed down the road. And he had certainly failed, as shots continued to ring out through the swamp and the roar of automobile engines shattered the normal stillness of the fall midnight. They came closer and closer.

The dead treetop was a substantial barricade. The agent knew no driver could bounce his car over that log and maintain control on such a pig-path road in the dark of night. The road was the pits, in today's jargon, full of potholes and standing water.

Bright headlights bounced toward the barricade. Then the truck stopped with the hood in the treetop. The trailing agent came to a sliding halt seconds later. The veteran agent stepped toward the driver's side of the truck with his handgun drawn.

"Don't shoot! Don't shoot! I'm gettin' out. Some man is trying to kill us and I was tryin' to get away!" the screaming voice of a black man was heard. He stepped out with his hands up. Screams were still coming from inside the vehicle.

"Tell everyone else in the truck to come on out with their hands up," the agent demanded. It was too dark to see much, but by the lights on the agent's car in the rear, you could see shadowy movements. There was a lot of moaning and crying.

The doors burst open and five small black children poured out of the truck, along with a middle-aged woman tightly cradling an infant in her arms.

"Mister, we ain't done nothin'. We was visiting down yon-

der with my Uncle Josh. We talked and talked until it was getting' late and we started home when this man here started shooting at us and coming after us in his car. I sure thought he was
going to kill us all!" the scared black lady babbled.

It didn't take a Sherlock Holmes to see that the ATF agent
had made a serious mistake. But just in case this family was
being used for cover and the car was loaded with whiskey, the
agents made a fast search. It was clean. The people indeed had
been visiting and were on their way home when the novice mistook them for the liquor car and began shooting.

There wasn't much the agents could say. In the middle of
these woods at midnight, no one would have stopped if a man
in the road was waving a revolver and yelling.

"I'm sorry, sir. We are federal revenue agents. We had a
report that a load of whiskey was being hauled over this road
tonight in a black truck. When you came along, we thought it
was the liquor car. We made a mistake," the ATF leader tried to
apologize. The agents pulled the tree out of the road and the
family headed for home after a traumatic, hair-raising experience.

As soon as they were out of sight, the leader jumped on
the young revenuer and gave him a verbal lashing.

"What in the hell do you think you were doing? You must
have shot a half dozen times at that car. You could easily have
killed one of those kids, and you could have gone to prison for
manslaughter."

"Oh, I was shooting at the tires. I wasn't shooting at the
driver," the young revenuer tried to justify his action.

"When a car is speeding over a rough, bouncy dirt road
like this, there is no such thing as shooting at the tires. You are
just as likely to hit the roof as the tires," the leader pointed out
the error in his judgment.

It was not the end of the adventure. Two days later the
Brunswick County sheriff called ATF regional office.

"You got agents in trouble. You better come up here and
let's talk about it," he said, without further explanation.

The agents had an idea that it had something to do with

that midnight chase. They drove to the sheriff's office and went inside, kind of dragging their tails behind them.

"Let's drive down the road a-piece," the sheriff invited the agent in charge, whom he had known a long time. He obviously wanted to get away from an audience.

A few miles down the road he stopped.

"What do you know about your officers shooting up the pickup of a black family down on the old river road last Saturday night?" he asked seriously, while fingering something in his hand.

The agent told the sheriff the whole story, finishing with, "My rookie agent made a very serious mistake. He could have easily killed somebody, but he is young and was nervous and excited. He said he was aiming for the back tires," he revealed truthfully.

"The family in that truck is one of the most respected black families around here. They have filed a charge against you and the ATF for the shooting. They brought their truck in and we dug this bullet out of the front seat directly behind the driver. How it missed those five kids piled in the truck and stopped short of the driver's back I'll never know," the sheriff said. His sympathies lay with the harassed family.

"My agent surely made the mistake, but I hope it doesn't go to court. It could really hurt the ATF," the revenuer grimly remarked, eyeing the bullet, real ironclad evidence.

"Roll down the window," the sheriff ordered.

The agent obliged and the sheriff threw the bullet into a huge growth of honeysuckle vines in the edge of the woods.

"No evidence, no case," the sheriff said, smiling, as he made a U-turn and headed back to Southport. The agent drove to the district office in Wilmington and told the sordid story. It ended there. But today it would have gone much further—and rightly so.

COMING BACK WAS OPTIONAL

Painted on a faded poster at the U.S. Coast Guard Station at Hatteras Island on the Outer Banks is this prophetic message that members of the U.S. Life Saving Service, forerunner to the Coast Guard, lived and died by for many years:

"The rule book says you've got to go out, it doesn't say nothing about coming back."

The historic message referred to a gallant troop of men who lived in the Coast Guard station or nearby who had the responsibility of rowing out into stormy seas at all hours of the night and day to rescue endangered crews wrecked along the reefs of the Graveyard of the Atlantic barrier islands. Many lost their lives in daring attempts to save lives, thus the message on the wall rings of danger, intrigue and even tragic death.

The record shows that in 1876 a whole rescue crew drowned in a valiant but vain attempt to save the helpless sailors aboard the "James Hill" that went aground off Hatteras. They didn't have to come back.

But generally the Life Saving Service compiled a miraculously enviable record in an era when there were no outboard motors and sophisticated boats. Of the 178,000 seamen stranded on wrecked ships between 1877 and 1915 when the Life Saving Service went by the rule book and rowed into rough seas in an effort to rescue the sailors, knowing their own lives were at risk, 177,000 were brought to shore alive.

The rescuers never knew whether they would return to dry land again when they shoved the old wooden boats into the dangerous Atlantic waves. They only knew they had to go and they didn't have to come back. Many didn't!

SAWMILL MOONSHINE

Long before today's expression "moonlighting," referring to those who hold two jobs, often of necessity to make ends meet, was coined, bootleggers were called "moonshiners" and their product "moonshine whiskey" because they normally made the illegal product at night when their stills were far less likely to be discovered. Stills had to be fired to boil the corn mash and the smoke was a dead giveaway in the daylight hours, but much less likely to attract attention in the dark, even when the moon was full.

Originally mash was boiled over wood fires. This obviously left a trail of smoke that you could see for miles in daylight. Later, sophistication caught up with the bootleggers. They shifted to propane and natural gas that produced almost no smoke, making it possible to operate 24 hours a day—if you had the market for that much illegal booze. Finding the wilderness stills then became much more difficult. Fewer and fewer informants came in to tell about seeing or smelling smoke drifting out of the river swamps and dense woodlands. Neighborhood informants often helped catch liquor law violators. But the bootleggers continued to run their illicit operations mostly at night, leaving their legitimate farming and sawmill operations for the daytime. This was the situation with Cyrus Almond who lived on what was then a very remote farm adjacent to a dense swamp. He was a known bootlegger who had never been apprehended and he was a substantial commercial fisherman and sawmiller as well. He was truly a "moonlighter" by today's jargon.

Almond had never been under surveillance by the sheriff or the ATF. He was so far in the backwoods that officers had never been pressured to catch him by the good church-going people of the community, so he had generally been left alone.

He ran his still and sold his stumphole stuff virtually unmolested for years, primarily because no disturbances were reported as a result of his lawless concoction.

One winter morning he came into Charleston, stopped at the service station-garage, and asked that they send a mechanic to his farm to get his old Fordson cranked. Fordsons at that time had to be cranked by hand and they were damned cantankerous as long as they were made by Ford. If spark plugs, carburetor, and other ignition paraphernalia weren't just right, you could wear yourself out getting one cranked. Often they backfired, forcing the crank to reverse its direction in one fast, violent "kick" that broke many a farmer's arm, bringing chagrin and pain to the breadwinner and his family, who suffered through the misfortune that "kicked" the victim out of action for weeks.

The garage manager promised to send a mechanic to Almond's farm the next morning. And he did.

The foreman instructed his only mechanic to get the tractor started the next morning before he reported to the shop. The veteran mechanic was an expert at cranking Fordsons. He had had his arm broken three times cranking these mean old machines. But if anyone could outlast a cantankerous Fordson, the Charleston mechanic could.

Never late for anything, the mechanic left for the Almond farm before daylight that morning and drove his old A-Model Ford up into the yard at the crack of dawn. There were no lights in the house. He blew his horn a time or two and nothing happened. Then he went to the front door and banged away, trying to wake someone. Still, all was quiet. He wondered if they had left home for some emergency, forgetting that he had been summoned to be here bright and early.

Always impetuous and totally devoid of patience, the mechanic went back to his car, cussing at having made the trip for nothing. He was in the process of turning around to leave when he saw the front door crack open ever so slightly. He cut off his engine and stepped to the ground.

"What you want, mister?" came a squeaky lady's voice from the door, where he could see nothing but a little stringy hair and one eye.

"I'm the mechanic your husband wanted to get his tractor cranked. He came by the garage in town yesterday and we promised to have someone here this morning. Is he awake? Or can you tell me where the tractor is?" he asked, with his usual impatience and unusual politeness.

There was a long pause. Then the small voice muttered, "He ain't here. He's sawmilling up there in the woods. Take the old road that runs past the barn and when you get to the woods, cross a creek and you'll find the tractor on the right at the sawmill. Cyrus is up there now. You'll have to walk. That road ain't fittin' for cars," the squeaky voice passed along the needed information. The door closed slowly and the apparent lady of the house disappeared.

The mechanic cussed some more under his breath. He would have to carry his heavy tool box God knew how far to the tractor in the jungle. In that era sawmills were erected in the woods, usually by big lumber companies, but occasionally by landowners with a lot of standing timber. Today the woods (as logs) are hauled to the mills near town. But it was different then. He grunted as he dragged the heavy toolbox out of his trunk and headed toward the distant wilderness. He trudged up a long muddy road that was not much more than a pig path.

About a half-mile into the woods, he smelled the stringent odor of boiling corn mash. He knew it was coming from a liquor still somewhere in the area, but he remained focused on his job of getting the whimsical tractor started and struggled on across the branch, up a little hill and there he saw the tractor at the edge of a giant sawdust pile with pine slabs scattered all over the place. Indeed, there had been some work going on at this sawmill. But not this morning.

He tinkered with the tractor's carburetor for half an hour and miraculously it fired and was hitting on all fours quicker than he had expected. There wasn't really much wrong with it.

He put his tools back in the box, cut the switch on the tractor and headed back toward the house.

Again he smelled the strong odor from the still, and peeking through the thick stand of palms, he could see a flicker of flame and smoke no more than a hundred yards away. Maybe he should look in on Cyrus and let him know the Fordson was O.K. He set his toolbox down and walked toward the fire.

In the mechanic's own words, "I walked right up on this little old still that was running. A tiny stream of white liquor about the size of a broomstraw was trickling out into some jugs Almond had on the ground. I do believe I could have drunk the liquor as fast as he was making it, but he did have a few jars and jugs that he had filled during the night. Cyrus had heard the tractor running so he was not surprised when I walked up. He just grinned and said, 'Hi, you want a snort of this good whiskey?' I was never much of a drinker, but I drank a few swallows from an old tin cup. I thanked Cyrus, told him I had the tractor going, and headed back to the pig-path road and on to the Almond farmhouse.

"As I was getting in my car, the front door slowly cracked open again and the same squeaky female voice attracted my attention. 'Did you find Cyrus at the sawmill?' she asked.

"Yeah, he is sawing away. He had already sawed a couple of gallons when I got there," the mechanic said with his usual dry wit. He got in his car and drove back to his job in Charleston. He had a sort of sly grin on his face.

That would have been the end of the story except for a quirk of luck that brought disaster to Almond's liquor business. A couple of U.S. Treasury agents had been sent to Charleston to make a general sweep of the area for stills. Some "good Samaritan" had reported that it was a mecca of bootlegging, and the ATF boss in the regional office had dispatched a pair of his energetic revenuers to make a search. Just two days after the mechanic stumbled on the still, the agents found it. It was not in operation, but it had been recently. They chopped and dynamited it into oblivion.

Almond never rebuilt. His bootlegging days came to an abrupt stop. But he was angry. He was sure the mechanic had reported the still and was responsible for its demise. He never confronted him with the belief, but around the community he let it be known that the mechanic would never fix any more tractors for him. It was fine with the tractor repairman. He didn't want to lug a toolbox a mile through the woods again just to see how many gallons of stumphole whiskey was being sawed.

It's odd, but illegal activities have a way of catching up with the perpetrators sometime, often as if by Providential guidance. That mechanic would never have squealed on Almond and his still. By coincidence Almond lost his liquor-making machinery at a time when an innocent mechanic had made his unexpected visit. It was only natural that Almond put two and two together and came up with four. But in that case, his math was in error.

He went back to sawmilling, fishing and farming and this shortcut to justice actually resulted in making him a well-to-do, honest citizen of the community for the rest of his life.

SHIPS' GRAVEYARD

The treacherous waters that lie off the coast of the Outer Banks bear the name Graveyard of the Atlantic. It is a grim, but fitting, epithet, for here more than 600 ships have wrecked, victims of shallow shoals, storms and war. Diamond Shoals, a bank of shifting sand ridges hidden beneath a turbulent sea off Cape Hatteras, has never promised safe passage for any ship. But seafarers often risked the shoals to take advantage of north or south-flowing currents that passed nearby. Many never reached their destination. Fierce winter nor'easters and tropical-born hurricanes drove many ships aground.

Ships were lost in wars. During World War II German submarines sank so many Allied tankers and cargo ships that these waters earned a second sobering name—Torpedo Junction. In the past 400 years the graveyard has claimed hundreds of lives. But many were saved by island villagers. As early as the 1870s villagers served as members of the U.S. Life Saving Service. Others manned lighthouses built to guide mariners. Later, when the U.S. Coast Guard became the guardian of the nation's shores, residents joined its ranks. When rescue attempts failed, villagers buried the dead and salvaged shipwreck remains. Today few ships wreck, but storms still uncover the ruins of old wrecks that lie along the beaches of the Outer Banks.

Nineteenth century island rescue crews returned shipwreck survivors to safety in small oar-powered boats. Today the U.S. Coast Guard patrols the Outer Banks with helicopters and other modern equipment. The Gold Lifesaving Medal, the highest peacetime honor for saving a life, has been awarded to many Hatteras rescuers for their extraordinary heroic deeds.

BLACK RIVER MOONSHINER

Simon Spivey drove into Burgaw one August day in the 1940's in an old 2 1/2-ton flatbed truck loaded with pigs. The woman with him in the front seat was presumably his wife. They went into the hardware store, bought some hog wire, nails and posthole diggers and left town headed for the Black River swamplands.

Simon, who was infrequently seen in town, soon had fenced in a hog lot in an oxbow in the river on the desolate west bank. Not long after that he built a two-room shack on the property, finally getting out of the tent he had called home since arriving from some unknown place the previous year.

Treasury agents assigned to the area to discourage the bootlegging that was rampant all along the desolate river swamp, received several reports from informants that Spivey was doing more than raising hogs. He was making moonshine whiskey. Some of the alcoholics in the neighborhood were known to visit the river oxbow frequently and they always came back stoned.

Several times the ATF agents went into the wilderness area and made a halfhearted effort to locate his distillery operation. They found nothing. Complaints continued to come in and they decided maybe their best plan was to hide out in sight of the Spivey shack and keep him under surveillance over a weekend when he had most of his company.

One Friday afternoon, two of the agents boated down the river to within a half mile or so of Simon's pig farm. They tied the boat to a cypress knee and quietly headed through the jungle toward the shack on the river bank. There was sweltering heat, high humidity and the mosquitoes, deer flies and no-see-'ums were ferocious. But finally they could see the pig farm through the palmettos and gallberry bushes. They flattened out on the ground in dense brush and focused on the front door about a hundred yards away.

Just before sunset, Simon came out of the house, walked into the woods and thicket and headed down river. He walked past his pig pens and disappeared in the wilderness. Ten minutes later he walked out of the woods carrying a half-gallon Mason jar in his right hand.

"He's got a jar of moonshine. He must have it stashed down the river and he goes and gets a jar or two at the time on weekends when he expects some business from town. Let's make our bust right now before he has a chance to hide that whiskey," one of the agents said, and they jumped from cover and ran to the door of the shack. they knocked. Almost instantly, the door opened and Simon stared at the uniformed agents on his steps.

"Whatcha want?" he asked innocently.

"Mr. Spivey, we saw you come out of the woods with a jar full of something. We believe it was moonshine whiskey and we are going to search the premises," one agent answered.

"Come right on in. Ain't no whiskey here, but you can see for yourselves," he politely invited the officers.

It was an humble two-room shack, with no ceiling. There was no place you could hide a half-gallon jar from trained revenuers. They were certain they could find the illicit liquor momentarily and they began the search.

Two hours later they were frustrated. They had looked under the bed, in the flour bin, in the firebox of the old wood-fired cooking stove, hunted for loose planks in the floor where a jar could have been stashed, plundered through dresser drawers and clothes closets and everywhere else. Even if it had been a needle in a haystack they believed they would have found it. But no luck! They didn't even find an empty half-gallon jar, assuming Simon had been able to dump his liquor. They didn't think he had had time for that before he met them at the door.

Finally, they gave up.

"We know you had a jar of liquor, but we can't prove it. We'll have to try again some other time," one exasperated ATF officer muttered as they left and headed back to their boat on the river.

A year later, the sheriff, who had been amused at Spivey's

outsmarting the ATF and laughed at the young revenuers time after time when they related their failure on the river, met Simon as he came out of the general store.

"Simon," the sheriff said quietly as he cornered the old hog farmer on the street corner, "Tell me how you outfoxed them young squirt federal officers when they saw you go in the house with the jar of moonshine. I'm not going to arrest you or anything. I just want to know how you hoodwinked them eager beavers," the sheriff grinned and Spivey knew he was sincere.

"I'll tell you, Sheriff, but don't ever tell them revenuers. You been in my place at hog killing time for tenderloin, ribs and pigs feet. You know we stay there in the kitchen around the old Majestic wood cook stove. We cook and eat there. You remember seeing that big old 5-gallon slop bucket beside the stove? We throw the scraps in the bucket and my wife pours the dishwater in it. When it's full, we feed it to the hogs.

"When I came in from the woods with that jar, I saw them revenuers hiding in the bushes. I didn't let them know I saw 'em, but walked right on in the house. That slop bucket was about two-thirds full of water and table scraps. I set that jar right in the slop bucket and the dirty water completely covered it. They looked everywhere, but never thought about the jar being under the slop," Spivey smiled and you could see his satisfaction at having hoodwinked his adversaries.

"Anyhow, I'm not in the moonshine business anymore. I got nothing to hide. But I'd just as soon you let them revenuers keep right on scratching their heads and wondering what I did with the jar of moonshine that Saturday morning," Simon said as he walked to his old flatbed truck and headed back to the oxbow in the Black River wilderness.

TRICKERY FAILED

A report was received in the ATF regional office that one of the long-time bootleggers was operating a still a few hundred yards from the river bank in a wilderness section along the Waccamaw River near the Carolinas border. This area had been dotted with illegal distilleries for two decades after World War II and long before. In this case, the informant said the still was operating in broad daylight. This was unusual in that moonshining was normally a nighttime operation.

Revenue agents knew the section. It was an area of blackjack oaks and cypress trees with a lot of vines and dense bush growth, with a few small patches of cleared ground on the wilderness fringe. The openings gave the moonshiners the distinct advantage of being able to see intruders some distance away. This made it difficult for the revenuers to slip up on the illicit liquor makers. But with this tip in hand, officers had to make an effort to catch the lawbreakers.

It was fine quail hunting territory. That played a part in the plan of attack the ATF agents outlined in their effort to apprehend the still operators.

Two of the young ATF agents decided that they would pose as bird hunters and catch the daylight moonshiners. They got their shotguns, borrowed a bird dog from a farmer friend at nearby Longwood, and set out on the unorthodox raid one Friday morning. They let the dog out of the trunk of the car and headed her into the woods where they were told the distillery was operating on a sandy knoll near a tiny stream.

Not more than 50 yards from the sawmill road the bird dog froze; she had pointed a covey of quail.

"What do we do now?" one agent asked.

The sensible thing would have been for the agents to circle the covey, call the dog off and ease on through the woods toward their quarry. Catching the moonshiners was their real mission. But they had gotten caught up in this quail hunt. Neither had shot a quail in years and the prospect of a good covey shot was tempting. They couldn't walk away with the dog so sure her nose was telling the truth.

The leader motioned his partner to ease into position and the birds flushed in a noisy flurry. The agents fumbled with the safeties on their automatic shotguns momentarily and then each fired three fast shots at the disappearing quail. It was blind shooting and they didn't cut a feather. They did clear a hole in a head-high pine sapling where the covey disappeared on their way toward a dense thicket in the center of the woods.

Flabbergasted and overwhelmed with surprise, the agents smiled and shook their heads in disbelief. Neither could hit the broad side of a barn.

They petted the dog to show their appreciation for her able assistance. She was really a great pointer. They were just out of hunting practice and didn't reward the dog by downing a quail as she had expected.

"Man what is all that shooting going to do to the men at the still? It can't be very far from here," one agent whispered, understandably quizzical.

"It might not have hurt a thing. Quail hunters are in this area all during the fall. Few of them ever report finding a still to the law. It's too dangerous. They might find their house afire the next night or their farm buildings dynamited if they squeal on the still operators. My guess is that the bootleggers have little fear of bird hunters and might stay right on the job despite the shooting," the other ATF agent reasoned, not nearly as confident as he tried to sound. Truly there was open season on informants in that era and in that part of the jungle coastal country.

Not more than five minutes later, the agents walked right up on a still not far from the clump of bushes where the quail covey had disappeared. The bootleggers had cleared a little spot about the size of a living room and they had a tiny fire burning under the mash. Even though it was in operation, there was not a soul in sight. The operation had been left hurriedly. The place was deserted.

The agents glanced around. On the fringe of the woods there was a small clearing. It appeared to have been a garden plot in the spring. Now only a few straggly stalks of collards rose above the weeds. Two men with hoes were chopping diligently around the collards. It didn't take a crystal ball gazer to know that these were the still operators. The garden work was their cover. The agents knew they would have a hard time convicting them if they arrested the "gardeners."

"We have stumbled across somebody's still. Let's get out of here, quick. These bootleggers have been known to burn houses and do informers a lot of damage when hunters report their operations. We better get out of here and stay out. We'll call the dog and go on back to Longwood to hunt," one agent hollered to his partner, loud enough that he was sure the "gardeners" would hear him and not suspect they were revenuers.

They walked away quickly, and when they reached their car, they loaded the bird dog and drove off noisily.

"What's the idea?" the other agent asked when they were well away from the apparently abandoned still.

"I wanted to make sure those fellows in the field believed we were hunters. We'll let them think that until tomorrow. Then we'll be back," the agent answered with a smirk.

The next morning, before daylight, the agents were back in those woods. One hid under an old clayroot that had succumbed to a hurricane in times past. It was close enough to the still to see it on two sides. The other agent was situated advantageously on the other side. They could see any movement into the thicket that hid the distillery equipment.

Not long after the first streaks of dawn swept over the savanna, two men clad in overalls walked across the woods and into the thicket. Minutes later the fire was going and the mash began to boil. The stench of fermenting meal swirled across the wooded bay. One agent signalled the other to move in. They walked into the thicket before the operators knew anyone was within miles. It was a total surprise.

"Hi, fellows, I see you decided to make liquor today instead of working the garden. Too bad! You're under arrest for manufacturing non-tax-paid whiskey," the ATF agent said with a real sense of accomplishment. You need to win these encounters once in awhile, and indeed, this time the ATF had won. They were happy. They had outfoxed the fox.

"What you talking about, gardening? We ain't done no gardening since June," one of the disheveled bootleggers seemed confused at the remark.

"When we came in here bird hunting yesterday, you two were digging in that old garden spot over there," the agent said, and he pointed to the tiny clearing on the fringe of the woods.

"Man, you're crazy. I ain't never been here before. I farm over yonder a' piece and I been having a hard time paying the bills. My neighbor Sam Atkins was over at my house after supper last night and said he had to go to Baltimore on business. He said he had this little still here and I could have whatever I could make off it until he got back in two weeks. So me and my son-in-law came in here this morning to fire it up. We don't know a damn thing about no gardening yesterday," the novice liquor maker said as agents put the handcuffs on him.

The ATF never did learn whether Atkins really went to Baltimore or if he simply was using this scheme to see if those really were bird hunters the day before that walked in while they were working the garden. And the agents hadn't been close enough to the gardeners to identify them from the day before.

The first-timers got probation. Atkins and his associate never went back to the still site where everything had been demolished. The moonshiners really had the last laugh. The ATF agents were not happy. In reality, they had been outsmarted again. It's difficult to trap a fox at his own game.

'GATORS—THEY LOOK LIKE VILLAINS

Tarzan movies, along with its naturally ferocious appearance, have made the American alligator feared and despised by millions of people around the country, many of whom are convinced that this reptile has a taste for people. Most of the populace clings to the mistaken notion that these ugly critters spend their time stalking humans. They quiver with fright when one is spotted lolling just under the surface of the water or along shorelines. It just ain't so. 'Gators generally are as anxious to avoid an encounter with man as other species of wildlife. But its menacing tooth-filled jaws and strong tail make it the villain of the wilds.

While alligators are naturally harmless, those living around people and taking handouts from the dinner table can be seriously regarded as dangerous. These possibly mistake swimmers for another free meal, and there are some documented stories that make you glad these critters are not your next-door neighbors as they are for many Carolinians who live on lakes and streams along the Carolinas coasts.

An aged fisherman was sitting on the end of his pier, nonchalantly casting a lure for anything that would bite near Lockwood Folly in Brunswick County, North Carolina. His little poodle was dashing about on the pier, which extended well out into the lake in the old gentleman's back yard. Suddenly there was a commotion near the shoreline and the angler turned around to see what was going on. Twenty feet behind him was a giant male alligator coming toward him with its mouth wide open. He threw down his rod and reel and jumped in the lake, quickly scampering to the shoreline and the safety of his house. He glanced back at the pier just in time to see the 'gator grab his little dog by the neck and swallow him as he yelped and cried for help. There was no help. The 'gator enjoyed his meal and then, with a splash, slid back into the water

Chagrined over the loss of his long-time friend and companion, the fisherman reported the devouring of his poodle by the marauding alligator to the North Carolina Wildlife Commission. An officer found the old reprobate half submerged in the saltgrass and killed him. Back at his home base at Morehead City, he dressed the 13-foot alligator and removed the dead poodle for its master who gave it a decent funeral. It was another case where crime did not pay.

The late Henry Crosby was a native of the historic little village of Davis on the Tar Heel coast. When he was a boy his father had let him tag along to a corn field where he was cultivating a crop along the rivers. Henry spotted a big female 'gator lying on top of a mud pile near the corn field and pointed it out to his father when the mule pulled the cultivator back to the end of the row.

"That is a mama alligator and she is lying on a bed. She either has eggs in that mud pile or little 'gators that have already hatched. You be sure to stay out of her way. She won't like it at all if you bother her," Henry's father cautioned.

But as the saying goes, "boys will be boys," and Henry's Dad had hardly gotten halfway down the next row before Henry began throwing sticks and stones at the old 'gator. At first she just snarled and turned to look at Crosby. Another stick fell on her back and she had had enough.

"I had no idea how fast a big 'gator could run, but she came right after me through the swamp. She didn't go around the bushes and stumps, she ran right over them and I know she would have caught up with me if I hadn't jumped in Dad's old pickup. She looked at that strange contraption and headed back for her nest. It taught me to leave mama 'gators alone," Henry said many years later. He never said whether he told his father or not. I kind of got the idea he purposely forgot to tell him about the alligator attack.

One of the most amusing near-misses, at least to bystanders, relating to alligators observed in recent years happened to a tourist fisherman in the Neuse River. It was on one of the first warm days of March and the trout were marauding around the cypress trees that grow along the shoreline. Ralph Medlin, an avid fisherman from one of the midwestern states, was flyrodding the cypress line, and wading in the knee-deep water, flipping a Mister-Twister grub into the shadows of overhanging limbs. He was so fascinated with his success that he didn't analyze the log he was stepping on to reach what looked like a fine trout haven. Medlin was standing with one foot on the muddy bottom and the other on top of the log, when suddenly it came to life. The log was a lolling 'gator more than 10-feet long and it was mad at being disturbed. It bellowed a warning that sent Medlin splashing on his back in the shallows, his flyrod and tackle flying in all directions. For one fleeting moment it appeared that the alligator would get revenge, maybe even a meal out of this episode. But it changed its mind and slowly eased off into the open water, its tail slowly propelling it away from the tree line and a thoroughly frightened fisherman. Again, you can't blame the 'gator for getting mad when someone carelessly stepped on him. As in most documented cases of near misses, the alligator was the villain, but only under circumstances that would have made any but the most docile creature unhappy.

Many of the best freshwater fishermen in the Carolinas look for alligators when searching for bass, speckled perch or even bluegills. The 'gators live primarily on fish and they are going to be found close to schools of fish. When you see a 'gator gliding gracefully along on the surface in the open water of a lake, it's a good bet that there are some crappie close by. For those fishermen who troll minnows and jigs in the open, finding a 'gator is often tantamount to locating schooling crappies. The alligator will dive and move out of your way if you choose to fish his spot. Just don't hit it with your prop. While they don't injure easily, they don't like to fight steel propellers. They must give them migraines. They slap their tails on the surface and send chills up the spines of the easy-to-frighten.

Some bass professionals use the alligator habitat as a tip-off to fish locations and cast the territory for largemouths. Often the 'gators have staked out claims on the same area as the lunker bass, perhaps because of the presence of forage fish. Both species know a good feeding ground when they find one and both may enjoy its bounty for awhile.

At a fishing tournament in Santee-Cooper a small alligator struck a big Rebel crankbait when it was cast under a bush near a half-submerged log. The angler didn't want to lose the lure. He reeled the three-foot critter to boat-side, took out a pair of pliers and yanked the plug out of the 'gator's mouth. Several young teeth came out with the lure, but the creature swam away, and was glad to lose only its teeth. Alligators grow their teeth back quickly, as a rattlesnake does its fangs.

Big alligators will eat some bass and the story is legend about the conservation-minded bass fisherman who kept two nice largemouths alive all afternoon on a stringer with the idea of releasing them at the end of the day, only to grimace when he watched a big 'gator yank both his fish off the line and swallow them. He was fit to be tied and that thieving alligator needed ear plugs for half an hour. When you make the statement that bass eat more alligators than alligators eat bass, that usually brings some quizzical stares. But that's the truth, as biologists have discovered. Bass like to eat little alligators when they are young and start swimming around for the first time. Many have been found in bass bellies all over Florida. But the 'gators eat each other too. They are cannibalistic, often eating their own young. In captivity, small 'gators are eaten by big adults even when they reach lengths of two and three feet.

No longer endangered, there has been a great population explosion of alligators over the last two decades, the lazy old reptile still throws fear into the hearts of many fishermen. But generally he only causes problems when he is mistreated, either deliberately or accidentally. Then with all his power, he becomes a threat to the offender. But there are no absolutes. The old man who watched his poodle disappear is not likely to find much good to say about any alligator. After all, he was just tending to his business when that old critter decided it was time to have poodle for dinner.

Shaw Helped Terrapins

A sleek, silvery, four-wheel drive vehicle was rolling down the eastern North Carolina highway in mid-morning pulling a bass boat toward the beckoning Chowan River. It was already late for launching a day's adventure in this semi-wilderness area for the largemouths that abound in the millions of acres of dark waters that flow from lowlands into Albemarle Sound and eventually on into the Atlantic. Suddenly the brakes were applied and the vehicle stopped. It was a straight stretch of black-top road and there wasn't another car in sight. The door opened on the driver's side and a man stepped out. He walked a few paces to his left and picked up a slow-moving terrapin that had just moved on the hard surface. He gently set the old shelled creature down on the other side of the road, got back in his car and moved on toward the Chowan.

"He may now decide to go back to the side he started from, but at least I got him across the road safely one time. There are so many people who deliberately run over and smash these old turtles when they are on the highway," so said the late Charles R. Shaw, then the executive vice president of the North Carolina Wildlife Federation.

This unusual act of compassion for one of nature's lowest creatures depicts accurately the unique character of this man from Raleigh, North Carolina, who felt a closeness to every species and diligently sought to protect and preserve them. That's one of the faces of Charles Shaw.

Earlier that same morning when the 46-year-old former home builder and land developer stopped in nearby Ahoskie, North Carolina, to pick up his fishing partner for the day, he had to first remove two big bags of garbage from the front seat and toss them in a county dumpster.

"Where did you get all that garbage?" Shaw was asked.

"I picked it up on the shoulder of the highway between

here and Raleigh. Someone had thrown out whole bags of trash and I thought I should haul it to one of these trash bins before it got scattered all over the countryside," Shaw said almost nonchalantly, as it it were normal to pick up the debris of the careless. That's another face of Charles Shaw.

After assuming the duties of executive vice president of the state's Wildlife Federation in 1974, after serving as president the previous year, Shaw introduced "environmental bass tournaments" in the Tar Heel State that were designed to promote litter-free waters and shorelines. The movement took hold, although it still needs greater participation. Inquiries from distant areas requested information for similar events.

The basic difference in the environmental bass tournaments started by Shaw and the North Carolina Wildlife Federation in 1978, and other tournaments, is the requirement that all contestants must bring in manmade litter by the garbage bag full in order to participate. They must actually pick up the cans, the paper, the bottles and anything else they see while they are casting for the largemouths. In the first three tourneys sponsored, more than two carloads of debris were brought in by the bass fishermen, totaling more than 15,000 pounds.

"Most of the litter that the fishermen bring in is cans, but at Kerr Lake, one boat brought in an upright deep freezer, a sink, a refrigerator and three big bags of litter. All of it was taken out of the water. This contestant went back again after unloading and came in with two more bags of litter," Shaw reported.

Shaw came up with the idea for these unique tournaments with special rules in 1977 and launched the program on Lake Gaston, March 4, 1978. The rules stipulated that every boat must gather at least a bag of litter to be eligible. Shaw also set other rules. All fish must be at least 14 inches long and there was a 2-ounce penalty for all dead bass and a 2-ounce bonus for all live bass brought to the weigh-in, a 4-ounce spread. In the first four tournaments the fishermen killed only three fish.

When daylight came that memorable morning that the tournaments began, the Lake Gaston area was covered with six inches of snow and the temperature was 22 degrees. Nevertheless, 33 teams showed up, and while they fell all over the ramp trying to keep their footing while launching boats, they gathered 109 bags of litter that cold day.

Fishing was incidental, but the winning angler received $1,050.00 for his 2-pound, 4-ounce bass, the only fish landed that day. "It was the world's most valuable 2-pound bass," Shaw said. Dollars from the $50.00 entry fees go to the winners in the form of cash prizes and trophies. They must qualify with a bag of litter in addition to the entry fee.

"We give prizes both to the winning team for fishing prowess and success and to the team winning the litter gathering competition. We haven't had a team win both the fishing and debris prizes at the same time, but one of our Kerr Lake tournaments had the litter winners coming in third with bass poundage.

"While we had 80 people, 40 teams, in one early Kerr Lake contest, we still do not have as much participation as we would like. We have spent about $3,000.00 promoting these events and trying to help our environment. It lets fishermen help their own image, too. People are glad to see them picking up some of the mess many of them helped make. I know some fishermen who once threw everything in the water are now among those who are cleaning up the water and shorelines. I've watched them change.

"People will pick up junk in their own yards, so why won't they pick it up when they are enjoying themselves, fishing, hunting, hiking or camping? Hunters and backpackers create a lot of litter, even in the national forests where people camp. It often looks like a junkyard. It's not just the fishermen who litter.

"I think there is more to going fishing than just sitting in a boat and casting. We have got to take care of our lakes and care for our natural resources. It only takes a second to think and not throw a bottle in the lake," Shaw opined.

"More people are using the water and woods than ever before. They have more free time to have fun. Education has not stopped people from littering. I have seen 'no littering' signs virtually obscured by a pile of cans and trash. We can stop the littering only with law enforcement and fines.

"The biggest problem with wildlife people is that the silent majority will not become involved with local or national issues. They won't get involved until the problem is in their own back yard. Then they go all to pieces and will finally get around to calling their congressman or attending a wildlife hearing.

"Progress is inevitable, but when any action is needed to protect environment and wildlife, objections should be raised early, in the initial stages of the planning, not after some enterprising industry or builder has spent thousands of dollars. If impact statements are needed on such a project, they should be requested early. There must be a reasonable approach to protecting the environment," said this environmentalist who once built housing developments.

"When I was building homes and developing communities, I always tried to save every tree possible. It was often costly, because after the project was complete, a tree here and there died and I had to pay for getting it removed. But later it was great to go back to some of those developments I started years ago and see the whole area enveloped, almost out of sight in trees," Shaw said with pride.

All of his life Shaw was an outdoorsman, beginning as a youth in the sandhill country of Overhill, North Carolina, where his father trained hunting dogs and horses for the John D. Rockefeller family. Bird dogs and fox hounds were trained, as well as horses used in the hunts.

There was a 200-acre lake located on that Overhills estate and from the time he was old enough to toddle, Charles fished for bream and perch there. Once when he was rigging up a cane pole and pine bark cork with a sewing thread line, several members of the Rockefeller clan drove up. One of the boys, probably the late Nelson Rockefeller, watched the youngster at work and smiled. A few weeks later when they returned for another hunt, he brought Charles a rod and reel, the first one he ever owned.

"I guess I eventually hare-lipped about all the bass in that lake. But one day when the weather was real bad, I picked up the rod and headed to the water. Dad didn't think much of my fishing such rainy bad weather and said, 'I'll eat all the fish you catch today, scales, guts and all.' Well, I went on fishing and put an old Florida Shiner lure, made by Barracuda, on my line. I remember it was bream-colored, heavy with triple hooks trailing and a spinner on both ends. I cast it a time or two and it seemed to me like the water exploded. I pulled, yanked, screamed and reeled and came in with a bass that weighed 9-pounds, 8-ounces. Naturally excited, I ran all the way to the house with that big fish and really gave my dad a ragging about promising to eat my fish scales and all.

"I had chores to do around the stables and the dog pens — Dad often had as many as 500 hounds in training at the same time. I often got off the school bus running to get my work done so I could get out there on that pond and fish. I mostly caught small bream with wasp nest larvae, earthworms and frogs for bait, but I eventually got around to fishing for bass with live bream baits. Then, after the Rockefellers gave me the rod and reel, a Bronson, I believe, I started using artificial lures when I could afford them," said the wildlife executive.

And except for the three years he spent in the army, Shaw put in his share of time fishing and hunting. He was a successful bass fisherman, having participated in 18 tournaments. He was rated among the top six in his local bass club in Raleigh for several years. He was a member of the state BASSMASTER team that competed in the national tournament in 1974 and 1975. "I fish every time I get a spare moment, but even if I qualify for some of the tournaments, I do not have time to fish any of the state or national events," Shaw said a few months prior to his death.

He organized the Raleigh Wildlife Club in 1960, was a member of the state endangered species committee, among many other positions. He was extremely proud of having participated with the National Wildlife Federation and the Natural Resources Defense Council in the eight-year lawsuit filed against the Soil Conservation Service that stopped the channelization of Chicod Creek in Pitt and Beaufort counties. The federal courts finally made a landmark decision that required the Soil Conservation Service to snap and clear only those trees that were about to fall in the water. And they had to be handled either by hand or with small tractors. The stream was saved and Shaw said it was a beautiful, natural creek that would have been turned into an unsightly ditch.

Charles and his wife, a science teacher in the Raleigh public schools, lived in a wooded area of Wake County where deer walked through the yard, 'coons ransacked the garbage cans, quail drank from water holes, and even wild turkeys came home to roost. While he dearly loved hunting and fishing, he also enjoyed watching these creatures in the habitat of the Shaw residence in Wake County.

"I really hope our environmental bass tournament idea will take hold and sweep across the land. It certainly would do a lot of good. Fishermen need the publicity of such a program. Many of them now have created a bad image by running their boats right past other fishermen, often stopped and fishing for panfish, at full speed without any courtesy whatsoever. Bass fishermen can improve this image by picking up litter and helping to improve our environment. These tournaments do a great deal toward promoting conservation and I want to see the movement grow," said the enthusiastic outdoorsman sincerely.

He knew the environmental tournaments needed publicity and was proud of the recognition given the movement by some of the manufacturers of various fishing equipment. He noted that even the U.S. Corps of Engineers in Mississippi has inquired about the details of the tournament. Other states expressed interest, too.

"There's litter everywhere on Kerr Lake and we are determined to do something about it," Charles R. Shaw said.

Providence Played a Hand

Small, desolate islands sprout just above sea level along the coasts of the Carolinas, some within eyesight of the shoreline. Some of them are unoccupied, and legal title to a few of them once was debatable. In times past, almost anyone who wanted to get away from it all and be a real loner could live on one of the spits of land and avoid society, whether he owned it or not, at least for awhile.

Half a century ago they were considered almost worthless. That brings to mind a trade by Sam O'Hara (not his real name), a native of Horry County, that today seems ludicrous and almost unbelievable. O'Hara had legal title to a tiny island in Cape Fear River. One of his children was born in the island's humble shack.

O'Hara was a commercial fisherman who was on the water with nets and fishing poles many nights. About the best light he ever had was a burning lightwood knot, a kerosene-soaked burning rag on the end of a stick, or at times, a lantern. Then, along came sophistication, after a fashion. The Coleman Company invented and began marketing a gasoline lantern that gave out many times more light than any of the old kerosene lanterns. O'Hara was fascinated with the gas light's brilliance.

Buster Elbert was also a fisherman in that era who lived up the river run with two of his grown sons. But they spent a lot of time on a tiny island just north of the river mouth. Elbert was among the first lucky anglers along the coast to buy one of the new-fangled lanterns. O'Hara saw it when he and Elbert were fishing the same area and he marveled at how its brightness lit up the water all around Elbert's boat. O'Hara was envious.

Obsessed with the lantern, O'Hara asked Elbert what he would take for the Coleman light.

"I ain't goin' to sell it," Elbert replied.

O'Hara had no money anyway, but he knew Elbert would really like to own the little river island where the O'Haras lived. He looked Elbert in the eye and made him an offer that today would seem asinine. But you must keep in mind that there were several islands, many with questionable ownership.

"I'll swap you my island with the house on it for the lantern," O'Hara propositioned Elbert.

"It's a deal," Elbert agreed, and he handed the two-mantled lantern to O'Hara. In a few days, the O'Haras moved off the island and later built a small home at Lockwood Folly. It was one of the strangest real estate deals in Carolina history—and there have been many unconventional, bizarre swaps along the Carolina Coast.

Time passed and the O'Hara family was living reasonably comfortably on the mainland. O'Hara loved his lantern and wasn't reluctant to tell acquaintances how he had procured it. "I swapped my island for it," he almost bragged. He obviously thought it was a good bargain, strange deal that it was.

In time the sheriff of the county heard about the lantern-for- an island swap and he began to wonder why Elbert wanted the O'Hara's desolate island. He and his boys fished nets, seines and cane poles for mullet, and occasionally he came into J.O. Dowdy's Fish House, a big two-story building on the river bank, to sell some fish, oysters or clams.

With the few bucks he got from commercial fishing efforts, he was able to buy the simple staple groceries his humble family required. They were frugal. Much of their food came from the sea and was caught with their own hands.

They built a small one-room shack with a tin roof on the island and an outhouse that was half-hidden under a palm tree at the west end of the island where there was a dense hammock of sweetgums, cypress and vines so thick you could hardly see through it. For drinking water they hung two giant porcelain bathtubs under the eaves of the shack's roof and caught all the rainwater they needed. For bathing and washing they diverted water from the river into two oak troughs on each side of the house. They were covered with screen wire to keep the mosquitoes from breeding in them.

The sheriff was not very popular and he had to knock out a liquor still now and then to keep the church people off his sorry back and to get their votes at election time. And that accounts for part of his interest in the Elberts. Why would they want to live in such desolation? He accidentally stumbled upon the answer when he watched the old man bring a box of crabs, a few oysters and a tow sack full of mullet to the seafood market. The dealer counted out what looked like better than normal pay for the seafood in a day when a dollar was worth a dollar. Elbert pushed it in a front pocket of his old Anvil overalls and walked away. He wasn't ready to head back to his island getaway yet.

Curious and naturally sneaky, the sheriff waited until the dealer had moved a few steps to buy a load of mullet from another fisherman. Then he rummaged through the box of oysters. The secret was out! In the bottom of the box, four quart jars of moonshine whiskey had been carefully concealed. It was no big cache, but it was enough for the sheriff. He could raid the island and make a show of his anti-liquor pledge. He would be a still-raiding sheriff.

The following morning the sheriff and two deputies met at the launching ramp and were preparing to make the run down river to Elbert's island where they knew it would be easy to find and destroy what was probably a tiny distillery. However tiny, it was, nevertheless, illegal and open season for the officers. And it would make a few headlines.

The sky was dark and ominous and the posse was a bit reluctant to shove off into what looked like a dangerous storm approaching. Another sheriff's car rushed into the fish house parking lot and the chief deputy jumped out.

"Sheriff, a radio message just came in from the weather bureau. A powerful hurricane is sweeping across Georgia and is expected to hit here around noon. They have suggested that we alert every resident along the coast that this is a dangerous storm and they must evacuate quickly. It's a killer storm," the obviously excited deputy blurted out. Hurricanes on the low-lying coasts are dangerous.

"O.K. You go up and down the highway alerting the

people. I'll run out to Elbert's island and tell them to evacuate. They'll have no chance if they stay out there," the sheriff said, and he showed some compassion for the loner family as he cranked the outboard and rushed down river. Maybe he could raid the still at the same time!

There was not a soul in the cabin when the sheriff arrived on the island. But the boat was tied up at the old broken-down dock. They had to be here and on an island no larger than a couple of acres, they could be found quickly, he conjectured. But it was not that simple.

The sheriff and deputies headed toward the thicket, half a football field away. It was the only place they could be. A tiny swirl of smoke streamed briskly eastward from the dense undergrowth as the storm's near gale-force winds approached. The deputies brushed back the bushes, and in a clearing no larger than a carport, stood a little still with a wood fire burning. It had been operating only minutes earlier. There was no one in sight.

"Elbert, this is the sheriff. I came out here to warn you that a dangerous hurricane is approaching. If you and your boys don't get out of here fast, you'll surely be drowned. We don't have time to hunt you. We have got to alert a lot of other people. Do you hear me? Evacuate and evacuate right now," the sheriff yelled. He knew the Elberts had to be within the sound of his voice if they were still on the tiny island.

"Come on! We've got to get out of here. Their boat is OK and we have warned them," the sheriff said to his deputies. They climbed in their boat and rushed back toward the dock. They hadn't seen the Elberts anywhere. And they didn't bother the still. The storm was too imminent.

As soon as the sheriff's boat was underway, all three Elberts spilled out from the one-seater outhouse. It looked like the old college fad of recent years when fraternities challenged each other to see how many people they could stack in a telephone booth.

Old man Elbert looked at the sky. He was no fool when it came to weather forecasting. He knew the storm was dangerously close.

"We're in for a big blow and the sheriff said we had to evaporate (he often mixed up his words). Let's string the fish nets on the wire to keep them from washing away and we'll get out of here." They had a strong wire cable stretched between two ancient live oaks that they used to dry their nets.

"If that sheriff is telling everyone to evaporate, this storm must really be a bad one," the elder Elbert remarked with concern in his voice, still confusing the words.

Elbert had ridden out many a hurricane, but no one had ever warned him to "evaporate" before. This blow must be something special, he reasoned.

They jumped in the boat and headed for the nearest shoreline, a deserted knoll near the mouth of the river. They tied up the old boat well above the high water mark, turned it over and climbed underneath. Huddled in the makeshift cover, they survived the worst hurricane the Carolina coast had ever endured. It lasted throughout that day and most of the night. High winds tugged at the old boat and waves almost reached their knoll, but not quite.

At dawn the sun peeked through the disappearing clouds. It was calm again. The Elberts shoved the boat in the water and motored back to their island. The shack was gone. The outhouse was gone, and, of course, the little still had been washed and blown away. There was no sign of it.

Papa Elbert walked to the wire line where they had strung out the fish nets. They were so entangled in the strong wire that they did not wash away even when five feet of water and hurricane-force winds rushed across the spit of land. The ancient oaks that held the cable had withstood the onslaught of the hurricane.

And then there was the miracle. Still flouncing in the nets were hundreds of fish. They had been forced across the island, snagged in the gill netting and were there for the Elberts to harvest. A few were dead, but none had spoiled. They were marketable.

"Boys, I think this is a sign that the Lord wants us to fish for a living. We have lost the still and everything else here, but let's gather these fish, haul them back to the fish house, get some money for them and come back home. We'll rebuild the cabin and from now on we'll be the best commercial fishermen in this part of the Carolinas. Christ had some favorites who were fishermen when He was here and He helped them. I believe He meant for us to be fishermen today," Elbert solemnly preached a message to his offspring.

Days passed. The sheriff visited the Elberts again, checking to see if maybe this time he could catch the moonshiners. There was no still. The Elberts were busy pulling seines and nets. They had indeed received a sign from the Almighty and no one ever suspected them of bootlegging again. They went straight, frequently even attending a mainland church when the weather was good.

It was a strange quirk of fate, but many residents of the area declare that it happened just like that. And who can say whether it was a miracle or an accident?

Tiny Boats a Bit Risky

Dr. Bill Berne, who built the first house on Bald Head Island, fishes locally for tarpon each fall and in the prolific water off Boca Grande Pass on the Florida Gulf coast as well. He notes that many of these big fish are landed by anglers from small boats who anchor in the tidal current, hang a fish and fight the tarpon for hours.

"I watched a young man standing in a 14-foot jonboat and pulling for all he was worth last year. The fish was about as strong and heavy as he was, and he rocked back and forth with the pull of the fish and the waves that tossed his boat around. I kept wondering if he would pull the fish to the boat or if the tarpon would get the best of the battle and pull him overboard. He outlasted the fish and eventually got it to the boat and then released it. But it was a long struggle," Dr. Berne says.

"My real apprehension began when I saw a giant 12-foot shark strike a tarpon within a few yards of his boat. It wasn't the one he had on the line, but another one and the tarpon was mutilated. I could just imagine what would have happened to the fisherman had he been pulled overboard," Dr. Berne recalls.

MINEOLA-LITTLE RIVER

Hard pressed against the North Carolina border on the northernmost fringes of Horry County is the ancient coastal village of Little River that the early Indians called "Mineola." Farmers hacked out marshland farms late in the 1600s and early in the next century and built shacks along the stream.

A safe refuge for pirates and survivors of shipwrecks, settlers were often forced to aid the lawless troublemakers who holed up for months awaiting repairs and another ship. At gun point the pirate faction squeezed food and lodging from the squatters who had little recourse in a land without organized law enforcement or government. Pirate names like Blackbeard, Captain Kidd, among several others, are a part of the Little River folklore today.

In 1740 the fiery Oxford Methodist, George Whitefield, visited the robust village and confirmed that it had been established before that era. President George Washington ate with James Cochran at Little River in April of 1791. As late as 1828, maps and material compiled by Robert Mills noted that there were only two villages in the county at the time. They were Little River and Conwayborough and swamplands were so dense that it was difficult for travelers to get from one to the other.

One of the most historic houses at Little River was the Thomas Randall home that was constructed in 1812. Known as the Randall-Vereen house, the burned-out framework swayed in the ocean breezes on a grassy sand dune near the water until it collapsed.

Captain Randall built three houses at Little River after the War of 1812 and the village was known in the area as "Yankee Town" because a number of residents were from northern states.

The shipping of lumber, turpentine and naval stores northward made Little River an important port for a time just before the Civil War. It prospered because of a sawmill payroll, port activity and a variety of trades that led to the building of retail stores, a school and one of the county's first banks. Several nice homes sprang up and a school was opened. A large factory turned out salt for the Confederacy. But progress was cut short when Union forces, using the scorched earth approach, burned virtually everything to the ground during the Civil War.

After the war, steamers made regular runs between Georgetown, Little River and Wilmington, transporting both cargo and passengers. Singer sewing machines were one of the items delivered by steamer. They were a novelty, much-needed at the time, and few homes were blessed with such sophistication. The machines created excitement among the women of the village and quilting parties and sewing bees were popular events. Women took turns peddling the early sewing machines.

Sea traffic continued in the Little River area until the 1920s when trucks, roads and railroads virtually eliminated the need for water routes along the Carolinas coasts. An area that had been home to pirates, smugglers and blockade runners, bootleggers and other violent men, disappeared.

Replacing the early Little River occupations were commercial fishermen, shrimpers, charter boat fishing captains and crabbers. Those occupations are the basis of the economy today, plus tourists who enjoy seafood caught and prepared within the sound of the breakers on the Atlantic Ocean beach.

Still unincorporated, Little River has about 4,000 residents in the area. It has a relatively new post office, golf courses, big schools, motels, condo complexes, and seafood—something that attracted even the Indians three hundred years ago.

COUNTRY DOCTOR

Before the middle of the century, country doctors in many areas made house calls. While many Carolina families never darkened the door of a hospital or medical facility, in dire emergencies, practitioners, at first in horse-drawn buggies and later in rattling automobiles, jostled over the coastal jungle pig paths to humble homes, their traditional black bags in hand. It was true of an Outer Banks physician, among others, decades ago.

One of those early house-calling MD's, accompanied by a companion, was on his way to deliver a baby in the wilderness near Buxton shortly after the Great Depression. It was nearing sunset as they bounced down the rough, winding road. They passed a shack with a neat stack of "stove wood," split pine wood about two feet long. For decades before electricity and propane gas was introduced in the rural South, such wood was burned in the cook stoves of Outer Banks families.

The good doctor looked at the neat pile of stove wood and turned to his companion, "The husband who lives in that house loves his wife," he said with confidence.

The companion simply grinned. He surmised that husbands who didn't love their wives left the wood splitting and stacking to the cook.

"Did I ever tell you the story about Aunt Sally Blotch whom we kept in the hospital for weeks before I got sorry for her and took her home?" the doctor inquired, trying to take both their minds off the bumpy ride.

"I don't recall having heard it," the companion replied expectantly.

Well, we had an old Negro lady I called Aunt Sally in the hospital for several weeks with serious ailments. She was old and wasn't going to live very long anyway. Her condition hadn't improved after a long stay in the hospital. One morning after I had been up all night delivering a baby, I passed her room and she was downcast, looking like she was going to burst into tears.

"What's wrong, Aunt Sally?" I inquired, turning on my best bedside manner.

"Doctor, I don't guess I'se never going to get home again. I just hates to die here," she whimpered pitifully.

Aware that here or at home she didn't have many days to live, I looked at her and said, 'So you want to go home! I tell you what. Get the nurse to get your things together. I'll run down to the office and have you discharged. You live on the road toward my house so I'll drop you off on my way," I told her, feeling really sorry for the old lady.

She was jubilant and immediately began getting up and trying to get ready to return home.

I got her discharge papers, came back to the room helped her into the back seat of my car and we chugged off toward home. She was silent for several miles.

"Aunt Sally, what you going to do when you get home?" I asked, simply trying to make conversation with the dejected old soul whom everyone loved.

"Doctor, the first thing I'se goin' do is get in my rocking chair on the porch and get me some lonesome. You just don't get no lonesome in a hospital," she said.

The companion grinned at the good doctor. There was a lot of philosophy in Aunt Sally's reason for wanting to get home. You don't enjoy much "lonesome" in a hospital.

FAITH TO MOVE MOUNTAINS

Everywhere people called him "Uncle Tom." He wasn't black and he didn't live in a cabin, but the humble home in rural Columbus County where he was born, raised and died was only slightly above the poverty level of the provocative fictional character of the last century. His humility, faith and absolute dedication to serving God were unswerving, and I have no doubt Christ would have chosen him as one of the dozen apostles had they walked the earth at the same time.

He lived close to nature like Peter, James and John. He fished, he farmed, he traveled over the poor roads of half a century ago, first by wagon, and later by Henry Ford's revolutionary T-Model cars. He prayed with such sincerity that the sick, the afflicted, the grieving and the disturbed of the Carolinas were constantly pleading for his services. They wanted him on his knees by their bedsides when death was near or catastrophe imminent. He always answered their calls.

I was just a child 65 years ago when he came to the rural church in Stanly County, North Carolina, 150 miles from his home, where my parents attended. He was no preacher. He had no formal education, but at revival times he was in demand. It seemed his very presence and his quiet, sincere talk with God when called upon to pray sent a feeling of divine presence through the audience. That's why he had been invited to Canton Baptist Church at the fall revival time.

But he was never content just to attend the formal services, pray, sing and amen the evangelist. He used the rest of the day to visit the sick, the depressed and the downtrodden. He knelt with them. He prayed and there was always a feeling his requests were heard. The prayer always seemed to get above the tree tops.

He seemed never to be alone in the world. He was never poor in his own mind. He was never without a smile, even in the most depressing situations. And he never felt that any request of God for human need was trivial, be it ever so unusual.

Followers of this man who walked with God recall a summer day 50 years ago when he walked along the banks of the picturesque Waccamaw River with its black waters winding through the muck of the Green Swamp not far from his tobacco-farm home. He carried a cane pole, hook and line in his hand. A glass jar of earthworms covered with the rich muck soil from his barnyard was in his hand.

He stopped along the river to chat with acquaintances.

"There's no use fishing today, Uncle Tom," they told him. "The fish have lockjaw or something. You can't buy a bite in this old river."

"Oh, I'll try anyway. I need a few bream for my family to eat. And we both know there are plenty of bream, warmouth perch and catfish out there somewhere," he said. "I'll just have to ask the Lord to help me like he did the apostles when they cast the nets on the other side," Uncle Tom said.

I wasn't there, but the story of the next few moments and the minutes after that have been relayed by eyewitnesses down through the decades. It is still being told with a twinkle of almost disbelief in the eyes of the listener today, nearly a half century after Uncle Tom passed away.

He took off his battered old hat. He knelt beside a cypress tree trunk on the river bank and he began his plea to God as he always did in church or out, at home or away.

"Lord this is your little boy Tommy Ward. I'm down here on the river bank as you can see and some of my friends here say the fish ain't biting today. But I need some fish to eat tonight and I'm asking for your help this morning. I don't need many, just a dozen or so for my family and I'd shore appreciate your helping them fish bite these worms I'm going to put on my hook in a few minutes. Won't you help me catch a mess? Thank you, God. Amen," were the words Uncle Tom said in a sober, audible voice that friends along the river heard as they sat silently and reverently.

He took his fishing pole in hand, baited it and began fishing. In less than an hour he had his mess of fish. Not another angler caught anything. He strung his bream and warmouth perch on a forked stick. Kneeling on the river bank, he thanked his Lord for the assistance and walked away from several amazed observers.

Tom Ward has been dead a long time. His life was so free of sin, his prayers so sincere, his existence so compassionate and he walked so humbly with his God, that he influenced everyone who knew him. He never asked for anything he didn't need and he needed so little. He influenced me. I'll go to my grave believing Tom Ward had God's hand on his shoulder. His influence brought hundreds into the church at a time when there was no television and mighty little radio. Travel was difficult and life was tough. He must have touched the hem of Christ's garment. He must have said often, "Here I am, send me." He always went and he made believers out of young and old.

There might have been a baker's dozen apostles had he walked the shores of Galilee in the era of Peter, James and John. Or Paul and Timothy might have had a third partner named Tom had he been born in their time.

Tom Ward walked humbly with his God and helped others.

THE MYSTERY OF THE MACO LIGHT

Tearing up the railroad and moving the tracks from the swampy terrain at the Brunswick County station at Maco in 1977 ended a ghostly scenario that began on a dark, rainy night in 1867. A tragic incident at the tiny station a few miles west of Wilmington became a legendary mystery of death and ghostly lights that baffled even the most learned skeptics of haunts. The mystery still remains, but the unexplained lights disappeared with the railroad track removal.

Joe Baldwin, a bored flagman, was riding in the caboose on a slow freight that fateful evening, when suddenly the train jerked, swayed and moved strangely. Moments later he was startled to find that the caboose was no longer coupled to the rest of the train that disappeared down the swampland tracks.

At the same moment that he made the frightening discover of being aboard a runaway caboose in the middle of the night, Joe saw the bright beam of a light on a fast passenger train rushing toward him and his powerless vehicle. He picked up his lighted lantern and frantically waved it from side to side, begging the onrushing steam engine to stop. He hoped his signal of imminent danger would warn the engineer before it was too late. He didn't succeed.

The short trestle over the swamp creek collapsed as the passenger train crashed into the lonely caboose. Joe Baldwin's bloody head was severed from his body and fell into the dark water on the opposite side of the track from his lantern. Workmen spent days clearing the damaged track before the trains could run again.

Baldwin's mangled body was recovered from the debris, but his head was never found. The body was buried without a head.

From that dreadful night on, Joe's headless ghost appeared regularly in misty, rainy weather at Maco, always with his lantern in hand. Observers standing at the rebuilt trestle first saw a faint flickering light that moved up and down the track. Then the beam moved quickly toward the observer, growing brighter and then much brighter. When it neared the trestle, it seemed to catch fire and burn brilliantly for an instant. Then the light backed down the track and faded into the night.

Folklorists with a passion for mystery surmise that the light was Joe's lantern and that he was still looking for his lost head. Others say he was still trying to warn the onrushing train.

The Maco light's tale attracted attention over a large part of the country. In 1889 President Grover Cleveland reportedly observed the mysterious light while touring the state on a political campaign. Throughout the years, hundreds of other reliable people saw the Maco light ghost. Then with the removal of the tracks, Joe's apparition disappeared, apparently forever. Joe must have given up on finding his head.

This North Carolina ghost story that was seen and curiously talked about for years until the track was removed two decades ago, has no reliable explanation. Who knows why Joe Baldwin continued to look for his head long after his body was buried?

COTTONMOUTH PROBLEM

It was one of those beautiful spring mornings when all of God's artistry was on display. Osprey squawked overhead and dived for minnows off the west bank of White Lake in Bladen County, North Carolina. A couple of cawing crows winged overhead and settled in a cypress tree. A lone limpkin pecked at insects in the bulrushes. Redwing blackbirds hung on the sawgrass and chirped at the boattail grackles that were hopping from one spatterdock lily to another. There were a few splashes that disrupted the calm surface as some yearling bass and a crappie or two hustled after the gambusia that were schooling along the shoreline. A stoic big blue heron and a smaller white egret posed motionless, like statues with long necks, watching ever so carefully for small fish that would make a breakfast morsel. Indeed, it was a day to remember with only a wisp or two of cirrus clouds in the sky. But all this serenity was not to last.

Lindy Evans teaches youngsters how to fish in a Valdosta, Georgia, middle school and he had driven from Georgia to catch bluegills that were bedding in the open water a few yards from the shoreline. We had shoved off from the public access ramp at about 7:30 in the morning.

Soon we anchored in six feet of water and baited No. 10 TruTurn hooks with live red worms. We had light lines with no cork and no lead. The system was proven years ago, and a few minutes after we put the hooks in the water, we began pulling bream over the gunnels. It kept us rather busy, but not too occupied to see the mean head and eyes of a cottonmouth moccasin that was swimming toward the boat from the hill. He seemed on a charted course for our bass boat, but a few licks with a heavy paddle convinced the poisonous reptile to submerge. We expected that noisy attack against the critter to end the disruption of our memorable morning. How wrong we were!

Minutes later, the same snaky eyes popped up on the starboard side. Again, the moccasin headed straight for the boat as if he were on a mission. It wasn't until sometime later that we realized he had smelled our bream in the livewell and wanted us to divide with him. For the second time, we threatened the moccasin with the heavy plastic paddle and he dived again.

We fished in peace for another hour. Lindy once had three bream in the boat at once and I was busy putting his fish in the stern livewell.

"Catch one more and we'll head home," I told him. "It's 11:00 and getting too hot for me."

He acknowledged the remark and immediately pulled in a nice shellcracker, unhooking the fish and tossing it on the deck at my feet so I could reach it. I picked up the panfish, opened the livewell door, dropped the fish in the water and almost unconsciously slammed the lid.

"That cottonmouth is in the livewell with the fish!" I yelled.

"You must be kidding," Lindy retorted.

"You take a look," I said, standing up and holding down the livewell lid. I opened it no more than an inch or two for Lindy to look when that ugly snake popped his head out the opening and looked me right in the eye. I slammed the lid and it pinched the snake three or four inches from the head. It made him fighting mad, and almost instantly he squeezed out of the livewell with his white, wide-open mouth glistening. He struck the padded lid, his curved fangs hanging a second in the plastic. He made a dash for my bare legs. Right then I knew I'd never wear shorts again when I went fishing.

The next instant I was standing with one foot on the Ranger's console and the other on the driver's seat. The mad moccasin was squirming all over the deck where I had been an instant earlier, and he was viciously striking everything he could reach. Fortunately, he couldn't quite reach me on the console, and Evans was high and dry standing on the bow pedestal seat. He had forgotten about fishing. At that moment he probably decided never to fish again. It was apparent that there was no place to run and that four-foot viper had taken over our boat.

I picked up the old plastic paddle in the boat, and armed with that, I looked for an opening so I could bash that snake's head in. But he was adroit at squirming around the gas can, the batteries, the tackle box and even my driver's seat, in openings so small I couldn't get a clean whack at him. Lindy looked for a weapon to defend himself while I stalked the snake from my console vantage point with the paddle ready. I jabbed at him as he squirmed between my seat and the gas tank, holding him momentarily, but it only made the moccasin madder. He used all his strength to wriggle out from my paddle hold and headed for the stern. In a frantic effort to keep him from getting into the bilge well and perhaps under the deck where he would be impossible to dislodge, I rammed the paddle against the snake's neck a few inches below his head. The lick paid off. It paralyzed the moccasin for a moment, and I let him have a blow on the head. He folded up and lay lifeless on the deck.

Lindy and I looked at each other. It could have been a disaster. It would have been easy for the snake to have bitten my hand when I was putting bream after bream in the box. Then when the snake was mad and rampaging wild in the boat and us with no place to go, it's a thousand wonders we were not the object of that snake's dangerous fangs. Certainly that mad monster was trying his best to bite his tormentors.

We made a few pictures of the dead snake draped over the paddle. We were finished with fishing for the day; we headed for home with one thought for boat builders: put a screen across the livewell drains. If that cottonmouth could squeeze through and threaten us, there must be others with the same kind of determination. They will go to any lengths for food, like those tasty bream we had in the box.

HE WAS MORE THAN A DOG

He was probably no more of a thoroughbred border collie than I am entirely Angle-Saxon, but he had all the markings of that species and a heart big enough to endear him to me and the rest of the Carter family for all the 14 years he lived with us.

Dad brought the fluffy bundle of brown home from town, where he worked as a mechanic, and it waddled across the kitchen floor, its short tail wagging and brown eyes blinking, when it was no more than a couple of months old. In a few days we had spoiled the little pup so that it cried when we were not handling him, but oddly, we never kept the lovable little critter in the house. He had to live in the woodshed, and in truth, he objected to coming in the house at all after a few months. He seemed to have sensed that Mama wouldn't approve and even when we forced him inside, he was uncomfortable, tail and ears down and anxious to get out the door and into the yard again.

We gave the pup the unimaginative name of "Rex," a common dog moniker half a century ago. Rex rapidly grew to maturity and took his rightful place as a member of our family. We soon learned that the active outdoor life we lived in that rural community would have been drab without this energetic, many-talented canine that adapted to our hunting styles as no other creature I have ever seen before or since did.

My brother and I helped put meat on the table in those depression years by setting rabbit traps, that we called "gums" because many were made from hollow blackgum logs. With as many as 27 of these to be checked before school each winter morning, we had a daily chore that required time and effort. Rex always made the six-mile round trip with us.

Pulling a rabbit by his hind legs from a trap in the bitter cold can be frustrating. The rabbit comes out kicking and scared and clawing. He will not bite, but his scratching is painful if you don't have a good hold on those strong back legs. Occasionally, one of the rabbits would wriggle loose from our grip and head for the thickets. That's where Rex came in. He would catch those critters within the first 50 yards every time. He wouldn't even kill the rabbits, just hold them down with his front paws until we arrived to retrieve the struggling animal that would adorn the dinner table that night.

We hunted for squirrels almost every afternoon during the season. Again, Rex was the only dog we had that would hunt with us, and if we tried to leave him at home when we proposed to still hunt, we hurt his feelings something awful. He would lie down with sorrowful eyes pleading to go on the hunt and would stay down until we were out of sight. Then he would scamper away at some oblique angle from our path, and a mile or so through the woods, there he was, panting and jumping with joy that he was with his human brothers again. He had outfoxed us, he seemed to think. Usually, we just accepted him and trudged on looking for the hard-to-find squirrels in the hardwood trees. Rex was some help. He would not tree a squirrel in a sense of tracking the critter and then smelling which tree he climbed. But his eyes were like those of an eagle. He would spy squirrels on the ground ahead of us, chase them up a tree and then bark so loud while trying to climb the tree trunk that the squirrel took refuge on the topmost limb and simply shuddered and waited. Usually, when Rex chased one up a tree, the squirrel was easy to find and easy to shoot. They didn't hide like they did when we scared them up a tree ourselves.

But quail hunting was Rex's strong suit and the thing he enjoyed the most. Just as he did when squirrel hunting, he would not smell and track down a covey of partridges. But as he raced along the hedgerows, borders of bean fields, and savannas, he would stop on the proverbial dime when a quail scent hit his sensitive nose. And if we were within eyeballing distance, he would hold that point until we arrived so we could get good covey shots. If he knew we were out of sight, he would pounce on the covey, scattering them in all directions. But that again was one of Rex's talents. Many times he would knock down a late-rising bird, grab him in his mouth and gleefully trot to us with his catch. And when the covey had been shot into by hunters earlier in the day and some cripples left that were unable to fly, he would chase down every one of them and bring them to our stands, usually on the outskirts of a briar patch or new ground brush pile.

Purist quail hunters would not have liked Rex because when he froze on a point, he might just as likely have a rabbit located as a covey of birds. With our hunting, that was immaterial. We were after meat as well as fun and whether it flew above the tree tops or scampered on the ground, we were happy to have Rex spot our prey. Then too, we often missed the creatures and the speedy collie outran many bunnies and saved the hunt and us from being skunked.

I'll never forget the time when we had hunted for hours in a light snow without jumping a single rabbit. By chance we came across one of our rabbit gums that we had missed in the early morning and it had the trap door down. There was a rabbit inside. We hadn't had a shot at anything all day and we were thoroughly disgusted.

"Let's take the rabbit to the middle of that clover field and turn him loose. We'll at least get a shot today," I said.

And thus we walked with the kicking rabbit to the middle of a ten-acre field and let the bunny run. I shot twice with my old double-barrel Ithica and my brother fired once with his single barrel. We didn't cut a single hair from that hare. He ran on into the woods and safety. Rex had been tied to my leg to keep him away from the rabbit we had expected to shoot easily. Rex looked up with an expression that said it all: "You boys can't even kill a trapped rabbit and you had me tied so I couldn't catch him either," seemed to be the unspoken message on old Rex's face.

I went off to college that fall and Rex was heartbroken. The few weekends when I came home he was joyful and wanted to hunt, but my visits and hunting trips became farther and farther apart. Rex seemed to age years between those visits. And then one Friday when I walked into the yard, Mama met me and said, "Rex died last night. He had a broken heart. There was no one here to hunt with him anymore and he watched the road every day hoping for your return. He just couldn't stand the loneliness any longer and old dog that he was, his heart just quit beating. We buried him behind the barn in the pines."

He was more than a dog to me. . . he was my friend and partner. I cried.

CEDAR ISLAND FERRY

The name "Styron" is more popular at Cedar Island on the Pamlico Sound than "Smith" or any other Anglo-Saxon moniker. The Styrons have been there since leaving Ireland three and four generations ago and the talkative family members point out that they settled here at about the same time Edward Teach (the notorious pirate known widely as "Blackbeard") crossed the Atlantic from Ireland in his mother's belly and was born at nearby Bath, North Carolina. The legendary seafaring criminal grew to manhood in the area, was widely described as a womanizer and later a rather famous sea pirate who eventually met his death on the gallows, thus etching a page in history with his lawless exploits.

Captain Tim Styron poses
at the Ferry Dock

The Styrons of Cedar Island today are a sharp contrast to Blackbeard except in their traditional love of the sea. Virtually all of the transplanted Irishmen make a living from the sea, either fishing commercially or aligned with public or private enterprises that ply the salt water of Pamlico and Core sounds off the treacherous Outer Banks of North Carolina and they are solid citizens.

One of the conventional Styrons of this generation is 41-year-old Timothy, one of the ten full-time, licensed captains who ferry load after load of vehicles across the 22-mile choppy stretch of the Pamlico that separates Cedar Island to the south from Ocracoke Island to the north on the Outer Bank barrier islands. It's this treacherous offshore Atlantic where ancient sailing ships, often lured by landlubber pirates, wrecked on the coral reefs, earning the territory the dubious distinction "Graveyard of the Atlantic."

But piracy and lawlessness are not the forte of today's Styrons. Virtually all of them are commercial fishermen. Tim would still be fishing commercially instead of being a ferry

Scott Burleson and Tim Styron talk about the Cedar Island Ferry

captain if he had his druthers and if there was economic security for fishermen. Price fluctuations, bad weather and often a scarcity of fish, make commercial fishing hazardous to the family's health and well-being.

The son of Eugene and Beaulah Styron of Cedar Island, lifelong commercial fishermen along the Outer Banks, Tim served four years in the U.S. Coast Guard after graduating from East Carteret High School in 1962. After graduating on Wednesday night, he was in the Coast Guard at Cape May, New Jersey, on Friday. He liked the service, but preferred to be back home where he could enjoy fishing. He later attended Carteret County Community College for two years.

Captain Styron was officially an able-bodied seaman and he began working on the ferries in 1985, more or less on and off. In 1988 he got his master's license and on January 3, 1993, he reached the pinnacle as a ferry master and he holds that position today with the Department of Transportation.

Ferries out of Cedar Island make the 22-mile Pamlico crossing with up to 55 vehicles eight times a day and a ninth is proposed. There's a $10.00 charge for cars. Pamlico Sound is the largest inland body of water in North Carolina, measuring 65 miles long and 22 miles wide. The ferry captains work 12-hour days from 5:30 a.m. until 5:30 p.m. They have an enviable track record of having never lost a vehicle or man overboard.

Gulls do dive down and take lunch away from some careless tourists who hold sandwiches in their hands while making the two-hour and five-minute crossing. Hundreds of gulls circle the ferry begging for a handout.

Dense fog and rough water cancel some crossings and add to the dilemma of travelers who are stuck at the one-store, one-motel Cedar Island ramp. But camera snapping of picturesque scenery takes up much of their delay time.

"We have sophisticated electronic navigational equipment on the ferries. We could cross in the fog and rough water, but keep in mind this equipment is designed to help you get back to your dock, not take you away from it," Captain Styron notes. "There's too much danger of running over a small boat out there in the fog when you can't see where you are going. That's why we stay in the slip."

The Coast Guard demands that the ferries have quarterly inspections and then a more detailed examination every two years. They ply the waters at 12 knots in good weather and are powered by Caterpillar diesel engines. Jet pump bow thrusters help them to be more maneuverable, easy to turn quicker.

The newest ferry in the fleet is the "Cedar Island" that was built in Moss Point, Mississippi, and delivered in 1995. Others have been built in Mississippi, Florida and in North Carolina.

And is the life of a ferry captain just what the doctor ordered for Captain Tim Styron? Not on your life!

"I would rather be a fisherman than anything else and I did that full time from 1976 until 1985. I like to fish for flounder, mullet and other species and shellfish too, when there's a good market for them.

"We had a 1,500-yard net, five feet deep, that we pulled with two boats in about six feet of water. The larger fish stayed on the bottom, and we caught the best size for market above them. That was fun and you could make a living at it, too," Captain Styron recalls.

He points out that a lot of the flounder off the coasts of the

Captain Styron, Linda Carter and Wren Burleson at the Cedar Island Ferrry

Carolinas are now going to Japan and China. They come to the Carolinas and Florida to catch them. Most of the shrimpers sell their catches locally.

Just what fish would the Styron families prefer on the dinner table? Captain Tim is quick to answer: "I'd choose the fried jumping mullet. I could eat it two times a day and seven days a week."

And what is a jumping mullet? It's that black and gray elongated fish that once was considered a bait fish. It jumps in the shallows, is easy to observe and relatively easy to catch.

"When the jumping mullet has a roll of fat in its belly, it's the best time to catch 'em to eat. October and November is a good time to catch them, and they often sell for as much as $2.50 a pound. Some of the nicer mullet may weigh three and four pounds. The flounder in the fall is a fine fish that is frequently caught in the Pamlico Sound as well as Core Sound to the south," Styron says.

So there have been no vehicles lost overboard off one of the Cedar Island ferries? Captain Styron qualifies that a little.

"No one saw it, but years ago there was a man with a mental problem who walked in here and said he had driven his car off the ramp into the sound. No one paid much attention to him, knowing his retarded condition. Months passed. Someone jabbed a pole down at the entrance to the ramp and got a surprise. There was a car down there. I guess it was the car the mental patient said he had driven into the water," Styron says, a little mystified.

What about close calls? Has Captain Styron had any? He remembers one well back when he was fishing for a living.

A strong line fouled around his arms and body and for several moments he feared for his life. He could have been dragged overboard.

"I knew I had to get untangled fast if I were to survive. I got my hand to my pants pocket to get my knife and was I ever surprised! For the first time in my life, the knife was in the left side pocket rather than the right side. That made it near impossible to reach, but after a lot of grunting and straining, I retrieved the knife, cut the ropes and was free. That was the closest call to death or serious injury that I ever experienced when I was fishing for a living," Captain Styron says. "I always keep my knife in the right hand pocket. Why that particular day it was on the other side, I'll never know."

The Styrons and Captain Tim are legends at Cedar Island. That name will forever be a part of the Coastal Carolina folklore history.

THE USELESS BLACK CROWS

I watched a streaked-head turtle climb up on the canal bank and start digging a hole in the sandy soil along the Black River in Bladen County. Struggling hour after hour until mid-afternoon, that old reptile eventually dug a hole as big as a gallon bucket and only her head peeked out from the deep depression. Now she would do what she came ashore for—lay a couple of dozen eggs that would hopefully help to replenish her species in that swampland. Body fluids poured from her backside. Then she gently scratched the sand over the eggs, packed it down with her rough feet and hurried back to the brackish water in the canal.

Before an hour passed, two squawking crows landed in the yard, looked around to be sure they were not in a no-man's land, and began scratching out the sand that covered the turtle eggs in the hole. Minutes later they dragged out one turtle egg after another until they had eaten and destroyed the eggs so painstakingly deposited by the streaked-head turtle.

This destruction by the crow is typical of the life-style of a bird that mankind and wildlife could well do without. All along the roadways of the Carolinas, the noisy, often pesty, black crow is a regular resident, even though this virtually useless creature was bred for the coldest of winters and his jet blackness is the ideal hue for solar heaters and stoves. Winter does not offend the crow, and his down is just as warm as goose down, giving him a built-in warm, cozy jacket. Yet the deep snows of the northern United States and Canada prod this bird to migrate southward and some say nature even gave the crow a cold morning cough for a call. Certainly it is not a song, and sounds more like an "AWE, AWE, AWE," than a 'CAW, CAW, CAW." That "AWE" might be short for "AWFUL" cold up here.

The crow, while it has a few admirers in the human populace, is generally not considered attractive and man's inhumanity to man has even coined the uncomplimentary phrase "Old Crow" when referring to an unsightly troublesome old lady and what connection it has with the bird remains a mystery.

Like their close relatives the bluejays, ravens, whiskey jacks and magpies, crows do not demand the best accommodations for living. They can survive in the ice or the heat, but they abhor treeless places. They like to perch atop some height to survey their domain. They seldom have warfare among their cousins, but often attack humbler species, killing the young of less aggressive creatures in the bird kingdom. While they detour when larger creatures threaten, they will attack hawks and even eagles during nesting time when they have the advantage of numbers and can dive around the predator while others of the flock are diverting the intruder's attention.

Crows are inclined to pilfer, and people who have raised them from hatching time to adulthood are aware that once this creature is strong enough to fly, he'll steal. It won't be just food, but anything that attracts his attention that he can carry. Often he will sneak jewelry and other bright objects to a cache in a tree hollow or a secret hiding place in an outbuilding. He hoards an armful of trinkets like he was putting money in the bank.

Carolina crows maintain a family group of bachelors, widowed grandmothers, uncles and aunts. All share in gathering food, ranging from a dead snake to the farmers' seed corn in the ground. Some stand sentry duty and others baby-sit. But when there is a real bonanza of seed corn or beans, they all forage at once, descending upon the planted seed like a hive of bees. They are early risers, often sitting on fence posts or nearby trees awaiting first light to swoop down on the corn fields. Once crows are filled, they regroup and fly cross-country for rest or, in the late afternoon, to their roosts.

Crows prefer evergreens for their roosts and they move often for no apparent reason, except perhaps to vary their encampment. They don't sit quietly; rather they play games of tag, hide-and-seek and pom-pom pull-away. Somewhat like the American Indian tribes, they have patrols, scouts and an early warning system around the roost. Crows have one great enemy, the owl, which catches and eats crows. And again we have an expression "eat crow," usually meaning you back up or renege. Crows despise night hunting. They believe in a lot of sleep and don't like the sneaky owl that is like a thief in the night. Flocks of crows, that might better be called a "pack," have a natural hatred for owls and when one is detected in daylight, they swoop down on him with all the vengeance they can muster. Plastic owls set up like scarecrows in their area have been torn to bits by marauding crows. Mockingbirds will also attack crows on occasion.

Again, you have "scarecrow," meaning an object designed to frighten some unwanted species. An untidy person is even sometimes referred to as "looking like a scarecrow."

Despite the crow's unattractiveness, they have pretty babies. The offspring have orange-colored throats and hatch in nests built on high branches with sticks and leaves that dare the weather to dislodge what often seems to be a top-heavy house in the trees.

For almost all people, crows are inedible. The brave who have tried to dine on their bluish-black flesh compare it to pine tar and recapped tires. There's even word circulating that after trying a meal of crow, your fingers curl up like a crow's foot and you have wrinkles like "crow's feet" sprouting from the corners of your eyes, an undesirable appearance again founded on the crow species.

The Carolinas at one time or another have paid a bounty on crow scalps, ranging from a nickel to half a dollar, but the narrow body covered with fluffed feathers makes a poor target for the hunter. Often the difference between cost of skills and revenue is too small for financial gain as the wily crow seldom succumbs to a first shot from his stalker.

A farmer who once raised a crow as a pet, eventually began to wonder whether he owned the crow or the crow owned him. This crow had an accident when he flew into a telephone line, breaking enough bones to ground him for life. Never again regaining flying ability, the crow nevertheless, strutted about the farmyard, intimidating cats and even dogs. For some reason the crippled crow thought all eyes were made to eat, and he always went pecking for those glistening pupils when other creatures were around, even his master's when he set him on his shoulder. After the crow had blinded several cats, he was mercifully executed when the farmer wrung his neck.

Crows might be called man creatures because they have learned it is easier to make a living following behind a plow gulping down the grub worms or eating the planted wheat and corn than scratching for themselves in the prairie or along deer trails. They do still spear a frog at the water's edge along the coastal rivers or pick up a field mouse in the wild when hunting gets tough.

They are one species of wildlife that cares little whether the sun rises or not. They observe sunset like a distant cousin's unconcern at a funeral. Even without exotic plumage, they accept their formal attire with pride and even seem to believe that just living is a wonderment, a great occasion in itself.

In the coastal Carolinas and all over, crows have staked out the shoulders of the roads and highways as their own. They accept them as exclusively theirs for trafficking. It's here where they pull on the shoulder meat of a smashed cottontail rabbit, yank out the intestines of a too-slow 'possum, or sort out the flesh from the bone and shell of an armadillo crunched by speeding wheels. In spite of regular feeding in such a high-risk territory, have you ever seen a dead crow on the highway? You see mockingbirds, larks, sparrows, 'possums, rabbits armadillos, and even squirrels, foxes, deer and bobcats, but never once have I seen a crow killed by a car. Primitive people believed that crows never die. I know that they do die (I have shot several), but there is a lack of evidence that is somewhat troubling.

Crows are not gamblers nor are they afraid, just cautious and take few chances. That's what keeps them alive on the highways. A compelling instinct drives them to get out of the way when something bigger than they are moves toward them.

They live on the ice in Canada and in the heat of the South, some are migrants, and some are permanent residents. They have no native country—they are everywhere. This inedible derelict displays his sovereignty, even when the real thing lights on the outstretched arms of a farmer's scarecrow to scream out his "AWE, AWE, AWE" in open defiance of man's effort to frighten him away from the fruits of human labor. He seems to be stuck on the first syllable of "AWFUL" as he flaunts his disdain for those who would deprive him of another easy meal purloined from his sophisticated neighbors who till the soil.

While crows are generally a nuisance or pest, they are more than that. They are a threat to other wildlife and habitat. They definitely play havoc with other birds. They eat every duck and goose egg that they find. They also scratch out and eat the turtle eggs that are buried in the sand on the shorelines.

If by chance, a few are overlooked and hatch, the crows are offended. They attack the newborn and eat out their eyes and kill them. They then leave the mutilated corpses. They seem to resent other creatures being born that might reduce their food supply in a given territory.

Crows in the Carolinas move in gangs and when they vandalize and murder other creatures, often infuriating wildlife protectors in the park, there's an urge to shoot down some of these culprits. But the crows prove their intelligence. They will circle high enough to be out of shotgun range and will not get close enough to shoot as long as a hunter with a gun is in sight. They are uncanny in their ability to stay out of range.

These culprits actually send out a scout to inspect the premises after a man with a gun has been seen. The scout will look around and sound the "all clear" when he is satisfied there is no longer any danger, then the vandals continue eating the duck, goose and turtle eggs and killing the young near the nests.

SWIMMING FOR HIS LIFE

My bass boat hadn't moved out of the marina for more than a month. It was tied up at a private pier at Sunset Beach while I was traipsing around the country running down fishing feature assignments. The boat had been inactive for so long that dirt dobber nests in the depthfinder had frozen it. A green tree frog hopped around in the dry livewell. Spiders had knitted a sparkling pattern around the spokes of my steering wheel and silky strands extended all the way to the outboard.

I brushed the webs aside, shooed the frog out of the boat, poked the dobber's nest to dust with my knife and putt-putted out into a calm brackish water inlet with hopes of finding a hungry trout around the grass beds on the distant shoreline or a sheepshead under the bridge.

A half mile up the inlet I was surprised to see a big-eyed field mouse emerge from his hiding place beneath the forward deck, and in a state of fright, rush around the bow gunnels in complete panic. There was no safe place to jump from his moving perch. There was water, water everywhere and not a tussock in jumping distance.

Seeing the nylon rope that released my Motor-Guide trolling motor, he grasped what he thought might be an escape route and rushed to the end of the line. Indeed, it was the end of the line and the frightened mouse looked me eyeball to eyeball for an instant and then, in all seriousness, he put his front paws over his eyes and broad-jumped as far as he could. His dive was a belly buster and the little fellow seemed surprised that there was no land there, only water and he had to swim or drown.

With only his nose above the surface, the mouse analyzed his plight, making a complete 360-degree survey of his position. I stopped the boat. This was a predicament few mice ever experienced. I wanted to see what decision he would make. He was not indecisive. The nearest safe haven was a sandy island on the west bank. He began his frantic dog paddling in that direction, his pencil-eraser-size nose all that marked his progress as his tiny wake made a "V" on the waveless surface. He was headed for home. I marveled at the spirit and energy of this gallant swimmer. Even though he was only an unwanted rodent in the world, I had to admire his determination and courage. Perhaps his plight compared to a human halfway to Hawaii in the Pacific.

I felt sure this little rascal would make it to shore. He swam confidently with unbelievable strength and stamina. Minutes passed. His dead reckoning was perfect. Soon he might reach the weedy outskirts of the inlet island. Once he reached that relatively safe footing he would have escaped drowning and the agile, determined little creature could dance on the aquatic growth and perhaps solid ground sometime. It looked like he had beaten the odds.

But it was not to be. It's a world of survival of the fittest. A big old flounder was lurking in the shallows. The fish eyed the tiny wake moving toward her territory. Something alive was kicking on the surface. It would obviously be a nourishing morsel for a hungry flounder, even if it did differ from the usual minnows and other forage on which she usually dined.

The big flounder apparently studied this creature a few seconds. Then bubbles popped up from near the shoreline and a huge swirl indicated a mad dash toward the gallant mouse. There was a noisy splash. The wake came to an abrupt end. Serenity returned. An uprooted weed in the current moved gracefully.

Nature's plan was fulfilled again. One predator had preyed on another. And that is the life and death struggle ever-present in the world.

I cranked the motor and headed for my bridge honey hole. But I couldn't help but feel a tiny tinge of compassion for the little rodent that was so courageous against overwhelming odds.

PRESCRIPTION FOR SUCCESS

Dr. Horace Baker, a retired surgeon with Southeastern General Hospital in Lumberton, North Carolina, grew up in that rural community and hunted and fished like all the other natives of the area. He was no different from his neighbors who tracked cottontail rabbits in the snow, shot squirrels out of hickory trees and fished the black water of the fast-flowing Lumber River.

Then he entered medical school and a traumatic accident to this father, a practicing physician who founded the now-defunct Baker Hospital in Lumberton, changed his lifestyle so radically that he completely stopped fishing. The accident to his father happened in the operating room when he cut the third finger on his left hand—and he was a left-handed surgeon. The wound became infected. For a time it looked like he might lose his hand. He eventually went to Chicago for treatment and survived the ordeal, returning to his practice in Lumberton. But the near-catastrophe to his talented father's operating hand that provided a livelihood for the family, changed Horace Baker's recreation for life. He imagined what might happen to his own career if his eyes or hands should accidentally get impaled on a fish hook. He gave up fishing.

He practiced surgery year after year and bought a summer resort home for his family on the Carolina coast where most neighbors were anglers. Dr. Baker felt ever-increasing pressure from these friends to take up the rod and reel and enjoy the great sport of pulling flounder, mackerel, spots, trout and a variety of other fine fish from the briny deep that ebbed and flooded under his pier.

For years he expressed his gratitude to friends and relatives for their kind invitations to go fishing, always thinking up some logical alibi for not being able to go that particular day.

But the excuses began running out as the invitations continued, and in self defense, Dr. Baker bought a rod and reel. He rigged it up for fishing off his pier. Thereafter, he was a regular fixture sitting in a lounge chair in the sun and watching a bobber dance along the ripples. He seemed to thoroughly enjoy every minute of his fishing. It stopped the day-to-day invitations to accompany others on fishing trips.

No one ever saw him get a bite, much less haul in a fish, but he kept right on sitting there day after day, apparently with inexhaustible patience, awaiting a strike that would challenge his expertise and bring that thrill of a lifetime.

From time to time, someone would drop by and chat. They asked if he had had any bites that day or caught any fish. Always the answer was "no."

The day of discovery came when a neighbor asked the doctor what kind of bait he was using.

"I'm not using any bait," Dr. Baker calmly replied.

"Then how on earth do you expect to catch a fish?" the friend asked.

"Oh, I don't expect to catch one. I not only have no bait on my line, I don't have any hook on it, either. I just come out here every day and flip the line in the water, sit here, hold the rod, and watch the cork float around an hour or two. It stops my good friends from continually asking me to go fishing because they can see I'm already hard at work fishing.

"It has other advantages. I never have to dress any fish that might result in a fin damaging a finger joint, and of course, there's no danger of getting a hook lodged in some part of my body. I get the relaxation of going fishing in the sunshine and fresh air without any of the disadvantages. It's a great way to fish. Then, too, there are rocks on the bottom out here and when you have a hook on the line, it sometimes gets hung. I would have a hard time getting loose. I never get hung with my rig," said the good doctor with a smile that left the neighbor scratching his head.

BELIEVE IT OR NOT

In all the annals of the outdoors, there is probably no more bizarre tale than the true story of a Tabor City, North Carolina, girl's high school ring and a gluttonous 1-pound spot that swallowed a strange meal in the brackish waters along the Tar Heel coast.

Robert Watts, classmate and boyfriend of Debbie Watts, was swimming in the Intracoastal Waterway near Ocean Isle Beach, North Carolina, in June of 1972. He had swapped class rings with Debbie and her ring had accidentally slipped off his finger in the giant waterway.

Chagrined and helpless, Robert told his girlfriend of the lost ring that was obviously gone forever in the brackish tidal water a few miles from the Atlantic.

In the fall of that year, Albert Swartz, of Cheraw, South Carolina, was deep-sea fishing 20 miles off the Carolina coast. He was trolling a Captain's Action Spoon at a depth of 50 feet when he got a vicious strike and eventually reeled in a 50-pound king mackerel.

Later that afternoon when he was dressing the huge kingfish, he noted a knot in the mackerel's belly. He cut the knot open and grinned when he discovered a full-grown spot, still undigested. The spot being whole and unspoiled and a favorite diner table species, Swartz decided to dress the panfish that had succumbed to the big predator.

The decision uncovered a strange believe-it-or-not. It was really even stranger than fiction, but it is documented truth. When he cut open the spot's belly, out rolled a bright, shiny gold class ring. Swartz picked it up with disbelief.

A few weeks later, Swartz wrote a letter to Principal Thomas L. Lewis at Tabor City High School. The letter follows:

"While I was fishing off the coast of North Carolina a few weeks ago, I came across a most outstanding thing, a ring in the stomach of a fish that was eaten by the fish that I caught. We had rigged rather deep, about 50 feet, and had a Captain's Action Spoon doing its usual good job when the rod on our port stern almost exploded. After a few minutes, we landed a large king mackerel.

"That afternoon we cleaned our catch and replayed the day's events. While cutting open our big king, we found another fish that had moments before been devoured by our catch. I cleaned this big spot and when I opened him up, out rolled this class ring from Tabor City High School with the initials "D.W. Class of 1972" engraved inside. I hope that D.W., whomever that may be will keep a tighter grip on the ring the next time as I won't be fishing that area again until next spring.

Very truly yours, Albert Swartz.

Principal Lewis had no trouble determining whose ring had been retrieved from the spot's belly. It was a small school with only one student in the Class of 1972 with the initials D.W. Stranger than fiction? A miracle? Yes, maybe both of those, but it happened just like that.

GOOD SAMARITAN SAVED WILLIE

Thirteen-year-old Willie Green had a toothache. The rest of his family had gone off to church and left the young black boy alone to suffer with his troublesome molar. As he held his jaw in his hand, he remembered his mother had dabbed turpentine on the sore gums when his tooth hurt so badly a few days ago and it brought measure of relief. He would try that again.

Rummaging through the pantry shelves of the unpainted little tenant farmhouse, Willie found the turpentine bottle. He struggled to remove the cork stopper. Then it came out unexpectedly and drenched the youngster's overalls from his straddle to his ankles. Now he was in trouble. His pa wouldn't like it when he returned and found those baggy overalls all smelly with turpentine. Willie stood before the open fire on that cold January morning. He wasn't drying fast enough. He would speed it up by striking a country stick match and holding it close to his wet clothes until he was dry. That was a mistake Willie would never forget. It was almost fatal.

Like gasoline, the turpentine caught fire and Willie found his denim clothing ablaze from his belt to his feet. Engulfed in the flames, he miraculously put the fire out as he rolled in agony on the floor. Screaming in excruciating pain, but beyond earshot of any listeners, Willie cringed on the floor with third-degree burns covering the lower extremities of his shaking body. It seemed like an eternity to Willie before his parents came home.

Hospitals in the Carolinas in the 1930's were not inclined to reserve much space, even segregated as it was, for Negroes. Doctors generally were not anxious to treat them, either. Most doctors had enough practice with the white folks, and Blacks were seldom able to pay for services. But Willie was admitted to the county seat hospital, where he received some medical attention. His condition was critical; he couldn't be turned away. He was virtually knocked out with drugs and his char-broiled legs were wrapped in cotton and gauze from thighs to feet.

A month passed and Willie lay near death in that hospital bed. His temperature hung at 104 degrees. His bandaged legs throbbed and infection wracked him. Liquids saturated the bandages, dried, ate into his burned flesh and he prayed to die day after terrible day. His condition showed no improvement, indeed he was approaching death. His unpaid hospital bill was mounting and the doctor was inclined to mark the patient off the list of the living. He summoned the parents and told them they should carry Willie home. He couldn't save him, but if he did survive a few days, he would need some attention. The doctor suggested that in that case, the parents should look up Randall Burleson, a school teacher and Boy Scout leader who lived in the community. He had practiced first aid at a local industry during the summer months several years and had treated hundreds of youngsters for minor injuries and ailments during they 27 years he had served as scoutmaster of the local rural troop. It was before the day of school nurses and he had been the first aid department in the country school where he had taught for three decades.

Willie's moans jangled the nerves of his parents and brothers in the humble home as he suffered beyond comprehension through several winter days. He prayed harder and harder to die and escape this hell that was slowly killing him. Hopeful that perhaps Burleson could be of some service that might relieve a little of Willie's suffering, the child's father knocked on Burleson's door, half a mile from his pitiful son.

"Mr. Burleson," the giant Negro man murmured, "Would you come to my house and see if you can do anything for Willie? He is hurtin' somethin' awful. We gotta do somethin' for 'im."

"I'll see what I can do," he said, but he didn't relish the thought of trying to treat this suffering boy so near death and so terribly burned.

"When I walked into the house that night, you could smell the sickening odor of his corroding, decaying flesh. The child was doubled up in pain. He was pitiful. How could I do anything for such a suffering bit of humanity so near death? His temperature still was 104 and he was near insane from his weeks of pain.

"I had carried a young man with me that night and he seemed frightened at the sight. But when I spoke to Willie and told him I was going to try to help him if he could stand it, I asked the young fellow I had brought along to help hold Willie. Then I asked the father to help, too, while the rest of the family rushed out of the house, not wanting to see and hear Willie scream, I began removing the cotton and gauze that bandaged one of his rotting legs," Burleson recalled.

"Willie this is going to hurt you so badly you may not be able to stand it. If you ask me to stop, I'll certainly understand, but you must get these bandages off those burned legs if you are ever going to be any better," Burleson told him.

Willie was hurting too badly to talk, but he whispered, "Do something, please," and the good Samaritan picked up the scissors and started at his thigh, trying to dislodge that tight bandage that was literally embedded in the flesh. It had grown into those sores for days, and as he cut, snipped, and tugged as gently as possible and removed piece after piece of the gauze, Willie surged to get away from the pain. Only his strong father and Burleson's unwilling helper kept him on the bed. Slowly, and as tenderly as he knew how, he removed the gauze. Willie was reaching his endurance level when huge drops of blood oozed out from under his exposed knee cap and every turn of gauze laid open raw, swollen muscle. He was skinless where the burn had failed to heal, and the bandage had buried itself into his swollen flesh.

For an hour and a half Burleson worked trying to remove that gauze from one leg. Finally, it was all off and Willie's screams that had shattered the darkness for half a mile quieted down. Burleson covered the wound with some salve the doctor had sent home with the patient and left the gauze and cotton off.

"I'm going to leave that leg open to the air tonight. I'll be back tomorrow to see what we can do for the other leg. The weather is cold and we can't let quilts and soiled sheets press against that raw flesh. Take several of your flat irons, heat them in front of the fireplace, wrap them with some clean rags and lay them beside Willie to keep him warm. Someone will have to keep doing this day and night to keep him from dying with pneumonia," Burleson told the father, and the mother, too, when she and the other children returned to the house.

"Willie," Burleson said, "I'm sorry I hurt you so much, but I couldn't help it. Grit your teeth and try to stand it. I'll be back tomorrow night and we will have a look at that right leg."

Burleson went home, shaky and nervous himself, and vowed to do everything he could for this youngster who was in such great pain.

The next morning the word spread in school and throughout the community that Willie Green was near death and in need. He particularly needed clean sheets and clean rags and the call for help went out. Burleson formulated a plan that just might relieve Willie's pain if it didn't save his life. He knew he could not have those raw legs bandaged again.

After school that day Burleson went to town and talked with the doctor who had treated Willie in the hospital.

"You mean he is still living?" the doctor asked unbelievingly.

"Yes, but he is in mighty bad shape and can't stand much more pain. I'm going to try to remove the bandage from the other leg tonight and I don't want to rewrap it. I'd like to have a prescription for something to treat him with," he told the doctor.

The doctor wrote a prescription for tannic acid and told him he could use that to spray on the burned legs when he peeled off the gauze. Burleson thanked him and hurried home. Neighbors by then had brought in arm loads of the sheets and clean rags that had been requested. He took the materials and went back to Willie's bedside.

The boy was still suffering, but more docile than the day before. He looked scared when Burleson came in and you could see his dread for the ordeal that he faced. But he was willing to have the work done again and his substitute doctor started snipping and pulling the bandage from the flesh of Willie's other leg.

He hollered, he wriggled, he squirmed and he suffered, but an hour later, that leg lay free of bandage but bleeding and hurting. The terrible chore of removing the bandage was over. Near the end of the hour, Willie had mercifully passed out from the pain and that was a blessing for everyone. Burleson looked at those pitiful limbs and wondered if they would ever heal. Could a child who had been so sick for so long and with a temperature of 104 and above survive in this cold, drafty house with nothing for heat except a wood fire? Could anything keep those raw legs from further infection and certain death? He didn't know the answer, but he knew he had to pray for his recovery. He had done all he could with his hands and mind.

"We must build a rack over Willie's legs to hold a kind of tent so we don't have to let anything touch those sore legs," he told Willie's father. He went outside and brought in some old two-by-fours and they fashioned a framework over the bed. On these they draped clean sheets the neighbors had brought just inches above those angry-looking burns on Willie's legs. They folded other sheets and rags around him to absorb the dripping blood and liquids that constantly poured from his wounds. They wondered if Willie would live. Would he continue to suffer? If he lived would he ever walk again?

For two weeks Burleson kept coming back to check on his patient. The drainage from his legs was so great that the rags and sheets had to be changed every two hours for days. But then the boy's temperature started dropping, the tannic acid was sprayed on his dripping flesh morning and night and you could see the drying-up process that meant healing. Willie was getting well!

Willie was burned from the turpentine in January and in July took his first steps. By the time summer ended he was running and playing again.

Burleson happened to run into the doctor in town that fall and told him Willie was back in school.

"You mean he is alive? You can take credit for saving his life. I had no idea anything could save him." the doctor said. It made Burleson feel good all over.

A footnote was written six years later. When Willie was 19 he was involved in a honky-tonk brawl and was shot and killed.

But for Burleson the memory lingered. This little underprivileged boy had been sent home to die. He suffered for a long time, begging to die, but his life was spared for six more years and he lived to play and work again. Often the compassionate Good Samaritan thought about that bundle of misery and the anguish he suffered when those bandages were removed and the blood oozed out of his flesh. He suffered as few ever have before or since, but Burleson gave Willie Green six more years of life. That planted a humility in Burleson that lasted the rest of his life. Maybe Willie Green did more for Burleson than he did for him!

Dr. John Hamlet's Hound Story

Dr. John N. Hamlet died in the rain forest at Bayport on the Gulf of Mexico in 1982, after serving as a naturalist at Homosassa Springs attraction for years. The great naturalist was a remarkable outdoorsman and his experiences are legend.

He headed the Primate Center at Pritchardsville, SC in 1946 where the 5,000 cynomolgus monkeys that he captured in the Philippines were kept for the worldwide research program that eventually led to the perfection of the polio vaccine.

He had a couple of mongrel hounds that were among his best friends in that isolated wilderness. After he had captured these monkeys in the Pacific jungles, the remote South Carolina outpost was sought out and purchased from Lucky Luciano, the deported Mafia godfather, by the National Foundation for Infantile Paralysis. Polio is communicable among all species of primates, including man, and the location of the center had to be miles away from any concentration of people.

So with only his wife and a few local assistants, plus two scholarly researchers in the laboratory for company, Dr. Hamlet cherished the closeness that he had with his canines. They reminded him of his 14 years with the U. S. Fish and Wildlife Service before being loaned to the Foundation for the polio program. He had had a trained wolf for a pet when he was in the West. The dogs also brought back memories of his youth on a ranch outside Rapid City, South Dakota, where he grew up among the Sioux Indians, having left a home that was broken when his father took off for China. He and his Sioux playmates hunted all over the Black Hill country, and by the time he was 14, he had some of the best wolf hounds in the territory.

He had missed having a dog for years as he moved from place to place with the Wildlife Service and later when he was hunting the monkeys in the most remote sections of the Pacific.

But once back at a base that he could call home for awhile, he got an old red bone hound and a little black and tan bitch. The red bone was named "Red" and actually didn't cost him anything. He just took the old dog off one of the local hunters' hands after the dog hung a hind leg in a barbed wire fence, mutilated a joint and the vet had to amputate the limb.

He had given a black man $5.00 for the little black and tan hound. The old cripple and the little bitch became the best pair of hunting dogs that Dr. Hamlet had ever owned. The black and tan could outrun old Red, but her nose wasn't as good. Like his human counterparts, Red seemed to compensate for his amputation by using all of his senses better after losing the leg that had once made him the fastest 'coon dog in the South Carolina low country. His nose was unbelievably sensitive. He had what swamp hunters at Pritchardsville called a "cold nose." That meant he could sniff and animal track from the night before and stay with it until it became a "hot track," eventually flushing his prey.

Red was not just a 'coon hound. He was equally adept at tracking and treeing 'possums or baying foxes and minks in the holes of the river banks. The hunter had to let Red know what he was searching for, and he could do this by letting him smell any old hide of the species he sought. Put a raccoon skin to his nose and he would hunt only for 'coons. Mink, fox and opossum hides would have the same result. It was uncanny the way he could pick one animal scent from another, but he proved this ability repeatedly.

The black and tan usually just followed alongside Red. She could bark and yelp and smell too, but not with the same ability that old Red had. She was more of a follower; Red was a born leader.

One afternoon, William Pickney, a Primate Center neighbor who had farmed and hunted in Beaufort County all his long life, brought a tiny gray fox to Dr. Hamlet's house. It was only a few weeks old and had obviously been orphaned by some disaster. Pickney had found it shivering in a meadow. Naturalist Hamlet always carried a soft spot for every living creature and had nursed literally thousands of wild things back to health at Homosassa and elsewhere. Pickney knew about this compassion and that's why he brought the little fox to Hamlet. He figured correctly that the good doctor would pamper the critter until it was well, strong and ready to roam free in the swamplands.

"I put the baby fox in a cage near the house and kept feeding and watering it every day. It began to grow and soon ate out of my hand. It wasn't long until it was as tame as the dogs and cats around the place. In a few months it looked almost grown and I figured it was time to let it loose so it could join its brothers and sisters in the swamps," Dr. Hamlet related.

"One day I had to go into Beaufort for some groceries, so I put the little fox in a box, set it in my station wagon and headed for town. About five miles down that blacktop country road, I stopped at a particularly dense section of woodland and opened the cage, making the fox jump out. I then got back in the car and headed on to Beaufort.

"I shopped around for an hour or so and drove back to the Primate Center. The first thing I saw when I got out of the car was the gray fox. It was sitting on the front doorsteps, licking its front paws. My wife said the fox was back at the house a half hour before I arrived," Hamlet recalled.

The Hamlets just smiled at each other and decided that if the wild creature didn't want to be wild, it could stay with them in the primate complex. They weren't going to cage it any more, and it could walk out the front gate any time it wanted to leave. They continued to feed it and it became a part of the household.

At first, they tried to feed the fox in a bowl separate from the two hounds, but the fox, not being a believer in "Separate but Equal" would have none of that. It insisted on eating from the same dish as the hounds and they would constantly growl and push each other around, scrapping for the food. While dogs and foxes are normally mortal enemies, these grew to be friends and eventually shared their meals peacefully until all three had a belly full. As months dragged by, they became the best of friends and every stranger was shocked to witness this unnatural alliance of wild and tame animals.

"The building where my wife and I lived at the Primate Center was known as the "Foundation House." It was set on piers well off the ground and the hounds slept beneath the house, directly under our bedroom. When the fox was about grown and had become a member of the canine family, it decided to take up residence and sleep with the dogs at night. They had a kind of communal bed.

"When fall arrived and the moon was full in October that year, I went to bed as usual about 10:30 PM. I had not gone to sleep yet, but was dozing a little when I heard the fox get up under the house, shake itself a time or two and slip out in the yard. It was strange behavior for the fox, and I was curious. I went to the window to take a look. The dogs hadn't moved or made a sound. The fox looked around the yard, then bee-lined for the front gate at a rather fast trot and was soon out of sight in the woods. I went back to bed a little in wonder.

"Thirty minutes or so later, I heard Old Red stand up under the house, shake himself and growl a little. The black and tan arose too. Moments later, I heard them shuffling along toward the yard. Again, I went to the window. They still had not barked or shown any sign of excitement.

"Red looked at the moon, glanced around the premises, then put his nose to the ground where the fox had trotted a half hour earlier and let out a long, ghostly, trailing bark and headed for the gate. The black and tan joined in the music, and they left the compound, barking for all they were worth on the trail of the neighborly gray fox. I listened until they were completely out of earshot, perhaps a mile or more away. Shaking my head in disbelief, I went back to bed confused and my wife and I laughed ourselves to sleep at such unusual events," Hamlet remembered.

"At 1:00 AM, I heard a shuffling under the house in the communal bed. I recognized the noise as that of the gray fox that was panting before he lay down. He quickly bedded down and fell into a restful sleep.

"Twenty minutes later I heard the hounds barking on a trail, getting closer and closer. At exactly 1:30, they came through the compound gates, barking every breath and trailing right on under the house where the fox was asleep. Moments later, they shook off the dew from the long chase, curled up together with the fox and the trio went to sleep for the night. All three were apparently satisfied with their efforts, and were dog tired.

"That cat and mouse game between the two hounds and their own adopted pet fox took place nightly thereafter. It was always the same. They would go to bed together, then the fox would sneak out. Half an hour later, the hounds would get up, find the trail, and off they would go on another three-hour escapade. It always ended back where it began, under our bedroom floor, with the three creature curled up together to rest and sleep," Dr. Hamlet related in all sincerity.

The nightly routine got to be a little irritating to the Hamlets. It interrupted their rest every night, and they decided that the fox would have to go. John had to make a trip to Savannah, a considerable distance from Pritchardsville. They built a little box trap, put the gray in the box and chugged off down the highway toward Savannah.

About 15 miles from the Primate Center, Hamlet stopped the car, set the trap on the shoulder of the road and coaxed the fox out. The fox looked up at Hamlet, who had tears in his eyes when he put the box back in the car, shut the tailgate and started to drive away. For one long moment, Hamlet thought about getting out, picking the little animal up, putting him back in the car and taking him home again. But he remembered those nightly noises that interrupted his peaceful sleep. He drove on toward Savannah, looking back in the rear-view mirror at the fox that was still sitting on his haunches, watching the disappearing vehicle taking his family away.

Hamlet transacted his Savannah business and returned home later in the afternoon. The fox was not waiting for him on the front steps this time. Hamlet was a little crestfallen that at last he had gotten rid of this wild creature who had become so at home in the Hamlet household. It was sad.

A half an hour later, Hamlet heard a scratch at the front door. It was the gray fox, panting and smiling as if to say, "You left me in the swamp, but I'm happy to be back home again."

The nightly cat and mouse game with the hounds continued that night and every night as long as the Hamlets remained at the Primate Center. Months later, the National Foundation sent him back to the Far East on another monkey trapping expedition. He had no room for hounds and foxes on that trip, and he never saw them again.

"I left that strange trio in the compound when I flew to Borneo and I suppose they kept up that little charade until they died of old age," Dr. Hamlet said, a note of nostalgia in his voice. It was a strange kinship.

THE STATE LINE TREE

A grinning Sam Herring, Route 2, Tabor City, spoke with confidence and absolute knowledge of the subject when he talked about the "state line tree" that once marked the boundary between his land in North Carolina and the property of his neighbor in South Carolina 65 years ago. Had it not been felled, it would still mark that border.

Herring, who passed away in 1990, knew about the tree long before he bought the land in 1927: "Way before I got this place here, people would come down the road and see that pine, and see where the state line was. I knew where the state line was, about as long as I can remember," he said.

Herring knew, and his neighbors knew. But the governors of North Carolina and South Carolina did not know. So in 1928 they had the old tree cut down.

Herring, who lived on Route 2, in the Cherry Grove section, remembered when surveying teams from both states reached his property after a march of nearly 40 miles from the Atlantic Ocean that lasted for most of the summer of 1928. When they found the tree, and cut it down upon determining it to be a true state line tree, Herring and his neighbor, the late F. W. Lancaster sawed most of it into lumber for their own use. "Half of it was on his land, and half was on mine," he explained.

The towering state line tree, a long leaf pine, became an important landmark in 1735 when it was blazed as part of the original line dividing the two Carolina colonies. Gabriel Johnston, who became governor of North Carolina in 1735, commissioned a team of surveyors to mark off a compromise line that had been agreed upon by both states in 1730. South Carolina surveyors joined the team.

According to historical accounts, the commissioners planted a cedar stake on the Atlantic shore about 30 miles south of the Cape Fear River. From that point, they proceeded inland on a due northwest bearing. Their line was to continue for about 86 miles until it reached the 35th parallel. From that point, the two Carolinas were to extend westward through unexplored territory all the way to the "south seas" or what is now known as the Pacific Ocean.

The lowland areas through which the original line passed were covered with dense vegetation, and were often swampy. At intervals long the way, the surveyors cut blaze marks in trees which grew on the line. In barren areas, stakes were driven. Nearly 40 miles from the sea, the surveyors blazed a tall pine tree that played a key role in preserving the line nearly 200 years later.

By the early 1900's, the original blazes had grown over, and many of the marked trees had been destroyed or cut down. Landowners marked new trees, but slight variations in the line began to develop. On the coast, the cedar stake could not be found, and disputes arose over fishing rights.

In 1928, Gov. A. W. McClean learned that the 1919 NC General Assembly had acted to re-mark the original line, but that it had not yet been done. He notified South Carolina Gov. John G. Richards, and the two states agreed to undertake an effort to define the boundary.

By March of 1928, North Carolina Boundary Commissioner George F. Syme and South Carolina Boundary Commissioner J. M. Johnson had begun preliminary research on re-establishing the original line.

The task facing the two men and their survey team was not an easy one. Nevertheless, it was not long before the ruins of a Brunswick County "Boundary House" appearing on the original survey map were found. The foundation of the Boundary House, located about two and a half miles from the ocean, provided an indisputable point on the line. Magnetic shifts since 1735 made compass bearings to mark the line impossible, but with the verification of another original boundary landmark, the line could be accurately re-established.

According to a report filed by the two boundary commissioners to the governors of both states on January 4, 1929, "a trial line was next run and a large long leaf pine was located some thirty-one miles Northwest of the boundary house which property owners said had always been observed as a State Line tree, and at which certain properties cornered.

According to the report, "This tree stood in a forest of much younger and smaller growth and towered above the other trees. It was dying of old age and forest fires, and had been freely boxed for turpentine. Only on one side was there a narrow strip of sap wood which sustained its life."

It carried two sets of blazes on the surface of the dead portion of its sides. The age of these blazes could not be determined because they were in dead wood, however, one set was thought to be about 30 years old, and the other possibly 100, but not old enough nor conclusive enough to be considered original marks.

The survey teams cut the tree down and sawed it into blocks, and these were split up until there suddenly appeared an old blaze well inside of the tree and completely healed over without. Feeling sure that this was an original mark, there only remained the counting of the annular rings to conclusively prove it.

A total of 349 rings were counted, and six were added to allow for the time the tree needed to reach the height of the blaze. The age of the tree was estimated thus at 355 years.

Next, 193 rings were counted in from the youngest (outside) ring to the one for the year the blaze was cut. Subtracting 193 from the year 1928 gave 1735 as the year in which the blaze was made, which also was the year of the original survey. The tree was 162 years old when it was blazed.

With two positive points on the original 1735 state line identified, the surveyors were able to connect them and use resulting bearings to extend the line southeast to the ocean and northwest to the Lumber River.

Because of the crucial role the tree played in re-establishing the line, "The block containing this blaze was sawed through the blaze into two parts, one for each state both clearly showing the rings." One portion was sent to Raleigh and the other to Columbia. The North Carolina section is now preserved in the Collection Room of the Archives and History building in Raleigh.

Sam Herring remembered the summer day more than 60 years ago when the old tree was cut down. "I was down there when they cut those blocks up, and split them," he said.

About 200 feet behind Herring's store, within view of RPR 1346, is a four-foot granite marker at the site of the state line tree. On the side facing the road is engraved, "Pine Tree Blazed 1735—Standing Alive 1928."

Herring leaned against the post, which is actually eight feet long with four feet buried in the ground. He pointed across the road. "That marker over there is 37 miles from the ocean," he said. It is perhaps 100 yards from the site of the pine tree. According to the 1928 surveyor's report, the markers were placed along the line every two miles and at major highway and railroad crossings. One was placed on Goat Island as a coastal marker, while additional monuments commemorate the Boundary House and the State Line Tree.

Not many area residents are old enough to remember the State Line Tree and the important role it played in Carolinas history, but Sam Herring did at one time, and so did his wife of 53 years, Nevada, and many of their neighbors.

"Around this country, a lot of people remember the state line tree," he said.

Edward Etheridge - "The Old Man and The Sea"

DARE COUNTY FISHERMAN'S LIFE ON THE WATER

by Chris Street, *N.C. Farm Bureau News*

Comparing Edward Etheridge to the "Old Man and the Sea" brings a smile to the face of the 70-year-old Dare County fisherman. Though he never battled for dominance over a huge fish, he has battled nearly every day for 37 years to make a living from the water.

The reason for his smile could be that the book title reminds him of childhood years spent in Key West, Florida—yes, at the same time famous author Ernest Hemingway lived there.

"Friends of my family lived next door to Hemingway," he recalls, "and they always had interesting stories to tell. Of course, the author was not as well known back then."

The Dare County Farm Bureau Board Member is a second generation seaman. His father spent 33 years in the U.S. Coast Guard, most of them stationed at North and South Carolina ports-o-call. Today he lives in the same Manteo house he was born in along with Joyce, his wife of thirty-plus years. They have two daughters, Amy and Christine.

After graduation from high school in 1943 he followed his father into the Coast Guard, serving until 1946. He says that he would have liked to stay in but tough economic times after World War II led to a reduction in ranks.

He tried his hand at several jobs, including house painting, and traveled as far as Miami Beach and Texas before returning home to the Outer Banks area of North Carolina. In 1958 he seized the opportunity to purchase a used fishing boat and set a course for a career upon the water.

During the spring and summer months he sets out 125 crab pots and also nets shrimp. November starts his oyster-gathering season in the Roanoke and Pamlico sounds.

Today he sports s 26-foot custom-made boat, equipped with a 350-horse Chevy inboard engine. Because his is a one-man operation, he has eliminated the boat's steering wheel and replaced it with a three-foot wooden staff which he can operate with one hand. Watching him pull one crab pot in after another explains the need to keep a free hand.

He moors his boat at Wanchese on the Roanoke Sound because this is where he sells his crabs and other seafood. The equipment he uses for crabbing includes a gigging pole, crab pots (vinyl-coated chicken wire cages) attached to buoy lines—and good bait. His bait of choice is menhaden, a versatile and smelly fish which Edward says, "The blue crabs just love."

Crabbing has been slow this summer. "But," he remarks, "the price is the highest I've seen. They're bringing fifty-five cents a pound—raw weight." He adds that large male crabs, called "jimmies," can be worth over a dollar each, as well as the "peelers" he catches—soft shell crabs. A bushel of jimmies can retail for $85 to $90 while the fish farmer's take per bushel is nearer $45 to $50.

The fisherman takes "slow catch" days in stride, but he is concerned about a continuing decline in the crab harvest. His average catch this summer has been around 300 pounds live weight while he would consider a good day to be nearer 700–800 pounds. A few years back he says there were days when he and a partner used to pull in nearly 2,000 pounds of crab. Things change.

With a note of sadness he gazes across the Pamlico Sound and says, "Blue crabs are on the decline." He adds, "The time may have come to put some controls on crabbing here. One idea is to limit the number of pots you can put out."

"If they don't," he states, "no one will be able to make a living at this."

Edward continues to work as he talks; pulling pots, sorting and emptying crabs into different containers, re-baiting the cages with menhaden and hoisting them back into the water at 75- to 100-yard intervals.

Manteo native lives off the sea

How does a crabber decide where to put his pots? Picking a good spot depends greatly on experience—and a little seafaring luck. "Some spots are definitely better than others," Edward explains. "I usually look for a slough, which is an opening to a shoal in eight to ten feet of water."

Even with 37 years of experience to back him up, the fisherman says crabs can be tricky. "Just like schools of fish, crabs move from one location to another," he says. "One spot may be good for a while and then—nothing."

Keeping track of 125 bobbing buoys in the huge Sound area, and keeping them separated from other crabbers' pots, would seem a difficult task. However, he says there are rules which most professional crabbers follow. "I lay my pots out in straight lines and color code the buoys," he says. "For example, mine are red and white."

There are occasions when Mother Nature makes the task more difficult. The recent uninvited arrival of Hurricane Felix to the Outer Banks helped blow some crab pots off course. "This one's not mine," he says, hoisting in a crab pot attached to a black and white buoy. "I'll take it to the guy it belongs to when we get to shore."

How did a commercial fisherman get involved with Farm Bureau? Considering that the sandy, swampy soil of Dare County does not support a single farmer, Edward Etheridge may be the closest thing.

"To be honest, I started with Farm Bureau because I needed health insurance," he says. "It's mighty hard for an independent businessman to afford this cost and Farm Bureau had the best deal."

However, he became involved with the county organization because of what it stood for. "I've always been a proud supporter of agriculture," he says. "My grandfather was a farmer and if there wasn't brine in my blood, there would surely be dirt under my fingernails."

As a county board member Edward ways he tries to keep up with agricultural issues and lend his backing to matters affecting farmers in other counties. "Some issues affect us equally because farmers and fishermen are both small business owners," he explains.

"Another thing about fishermen and farmers," he adds with a laugh, "We're both pretty independent-minded."

Working in the hot sun on an open boat that absorbs every blistering ray, Edward Etheridge seems to have the stamina of a man 30 years his junior. His hair is still more dark than gray. He smokes unfiltered Camel cigarettes and drinks instant coffee by the jugful as he continues a steady work pace.

How does he keep his strength? "Maybe it's something in the tobacco," he jokes. "Really, I don't know. I think the genes we are born with have more to do with it than anything. For some people there is really nothing they can do to keep from aging."

Judging from his calm appearance aboard a boat, it may also have something to do with the careers people choose. "I find this work relaxing," he says. "There is less stress out here on the water than anywhere I've ever been. But back on shore— well that's another thing."

CAROLINA CLAM BAKE

Many meeting-goers regularly are invited to "clam bakes" that are in reality just gatherings of committees or clubs where clams are neither eaten nor mentioned. It has become a two-word phrase for an informal get-together that is common in the Carolinas.

Then there is the real thing—a feast of fresh clams rooted out of the mud from along the coast. I had such an invitation some years ago when a group of gourmets in Whiteville, North Carolina, asked me to an evening's shindig where clams were featured. Alas! They did have clams but they didn't bake them and the "clam bake" was again a misnomer. But it didn't detract from what turned out to be a meal fit for a king. (Some say steaming is really baking.)

A club of outdoor-oriented gentlemen had hauled in the clams from the marshes, scrubbed them with brushes the night before until they were clean as shark's teeth, then started the gourmet hodgepodge of edibles cooking about 3:00 in the afternoon. The meal was ready around 7:00 p.m.

This unusual feast was cooked in a giant rectangular stainless steel boiler with gas burners underneath and a lid over the top. It must have been about 40 inches long, 18 inches deep and with similar width. In that big kettle, the cooks put a layer of sweet potatoes, a layer of onions, a layer of white potatoes, fresh broiler-size chickens and finally topped it off with a thick layer of the clean clams. They cooked it slowly.

By the time I arrived at the clam bake, the smell was swirling about the back yard of one of the club members who had a kitchen and eating room all fixed up for the occasion in a little building next to his garage. Inside, the smell was even more enticing and the members and guests soon meandered to the cooker. That's when the first inkling of what good eating was in store got through to the first-time guests.

There was a little faucet on one end and at the bottom of the big steamer. Someone handed me a paper cup and directed me to hold it under the faucet. I did. Out poured a dingy liquid and I had little idea of what it was, much less whether it was drinkable. But politely I tried it. It was wonderful. Later, when I learned what a concoction this "juice" was, I wondered how it could have been so tasty. After all, it was the moisture from yams, white potatoes, onions, raw chickens and clams.

At the sound of the dinner bell, heaping plates of all the vegetables, chicken and clams were scooped out of the boiler and it goes without saying again that it was delightful. A wonderful "clam bake" that featured fellowship that really did serve clams.

Catching elusive clams for such a feast requires some labor and expertise. The novices find it easier to just pay $2.90 a dozen at some seafood shack along the coast. But the energetic and pioneering clammers can catch their own and they need not even have a license if they gather only one bushel.

You are most successful with your clam attack at low tide when you can wade smelly mud half-knee-deep and feel the shellfish with your toes all clammed up six inches to a foot deep in the marshes where saltwater has just departed. Clams feed on the nutrients in this salty mud habitat.

Sophisticated clammers have a kind of pitchfork with a grotesque curve in it that you drag through the muck to dislodge the clams from their hiding places. There are even fancier gadgets with more fingers that have a basket above for the clams to tumble into. But by far the most clammers out for a family meal just shuffle through the muck with their feet until they feel something hard and hope it is a clam, not another empty oyster shell or broken bottle. Doing this with bare feet makes finding clams easier, but also leads to plenty of stinging cuts and scratches. Thus, most clammers wear thin tennis shoes if they can keep them on and not lose them in the muck.

Clamming is most productive in sloughs and bays where the water moves rapidly with each tide. And you can go after this delicacy even on Sunday. But you can't hunt oysters on the

Sabbath. You can clam about anywhere that there are no pollution markers.

Those who harvest enough clams for dinner can mix them with the myriad of edibles like the Whiteville Clam Bake affair on a lesser scale atop the stove. Or you can fry clams, make them into at least two kinds of chowder, grill them with a slice of bacon, or any of a dozen other ways. Any cookbook will list pages of clam recipes.

Remember, you may also freeze the cherrystone clams, those three inches or less in diameter, and most seafood enthusiasts think these are sweeter and better.

Then, there's something else you can do if you spend and afternoon searching for these elusive delicacies and fail to harvest enough to eat. You can just clam up.

GOD HELPED HER FISH

I know an old black lady who fishes for bream in the lily pads during most of the summer months along the shoreline of the Intracoastal Waterway near Bucksport. She is scrawny, poorly dressed, sits in an old homemade wooden bateau and fishes with earthworms on a hook and line tied to a cane pole. She has no education and is about as humble a person as you will ever see. But just to fish nearby when she is landing those panfish is a heartwarming experience that makes me appreciate living a little more. It makes me feel a little closer to God.

Each time she pulls a fish flouncing from those murky waters, and it swings like a pendulum right toward her face and boat, she lets it hit the boat bottom just before it would strike her. But she has some words that go with every fish she jerks out of those pads and you can hear her clearly say, "Thank you, Jesus." It's the same expression every time she gets a fish, and she isn't being sacrilegious. She means it! She is indeed grateful that the Almighty has provided these healthy fish for food and fun and prompts them to bite her hook.

Some people will say this is typical religious fanaticism. Some will say God is not interested in such trivial prayers. But is God unconcerned with such trivial things as catching fish?

On the coasts of the Carolinas, you find a people close to God and close to nature. You'll find many who think God is just as interested in helping people catch fish as He is in helping them grow crops. They recall the New Testament books that tell about Jesus Christ asking the disciples to cast the net on the other side of the boat. He was interested in them then and He is interested in the welfare of His people now. That pretty generally sums up Carolinas Christians' faith. After all, the Almighty made this wilderness.

THE KILLER VANISHED

Twice during his tumultuous life as a commercial fisherman in Shallotte, Charles Skipper murdered competitors whom he charged had tampered with his traps and nets. At least, it is assumed he killed them. They disappeared shortly after confrontations with this vicious character who boldly disregarded the law during the tough Depression era. It was widely known that he had once castrated a Negro man and cut off his penis. He was a racist of the first degree.

A violent temper hounded Skipper from early childhood to the end of his life. While he escaped punishment for the two alleged murders of the coastal fishermen, and the brutal crime against the black man, a temper tantrum that led to a third murder was his undoing.

Skipper was walking home from the country store at Bolivia with a bag of groceries under his arm. He had to pass a black family's residence along the way and a barking dog challenged Skipper's right to walk past the house. Mad as the proverbial setting hen at the dog's growling and barking, Skipper picked up a stick and tried vainly to strike the dog a lethal blow. The Negro who lived there, the dog's owner, was upset and he came to the door, called to the dog and asked Skipper to please stop hitting his dog. By that time Skipper was seething. His face was blood red with obvious anger. His uncontrolled temper was evident.

"I'll be back," he shouted, shuffling down the shoulder of the road at a much faster pace than before.

An hour later, Skipper walked into the black man's yard. This time he carried a double-barreled shotgun. The dog again bounced out from under the shanty and challenged Skipper. But not for long! Skipper pulled both triggers at close range and shot two holes as big as your hand through the dog's midsection. He kicked out his life almost instantly.

The black man in the house rushed to the door and groaned in sympathy as he watched his beloved mongrel hound breathe his last gasps.

"What did you have to kill him for?" the Negro asked, with tears in his eyes and agony in his voice.

Without so much as a word of explanation, Skipper turned the gun on the black man. Again he fired both barrels and the Negro grabbed his bleeding chest, collapsed and died instantly.

Skipper turned on his heels and headed back toward home.

Witnesses to the cold-blooded murder called the sheriff's office and reported the bizarre incident. About sunset the sheriff and two deputies arrived at Skipper's riverside cabin and started toward the house to make the arrest. It was not to be that easy! Skipper stepped through the door to the porch with his shotgun cradled in his arms.

"If you officers come one step closer, I'll shoot you down like dogs. I am about ready to eat my supper. I know why you are here, but I am going to eat anyway. Get back in your car and go home. I'll turn myself in tomorrow morning at Shallotte," Skipper demanded.

Knowing that to confront him at that point would have resulted in a blood-letting, the sheriff backed toward the parked car with his deputies alongside. They were angry at this challenge, but knew full well one or more of them would die if they pushed the arrest at that moment.

"Alright, Skipper. We'll leave you alone until morning. But if you are not in the office by 9:00, we'll be back here and we will take you in one way or the other. You are charged with murder and we will not be buffaloed by you or anyone else," the determined sheriff yelled to Skipper on the porch.

Skipper was clean-shaven and in the sheriff's office on time the next day. They handcuffed him, put him in the car, and with the sheriff and the same two deputies aboard, they headed toward the county jail in Southport several miles away.

What happened next? There's no record that he was ever jailed in Southport. As a matter of fact, that's the last time anyone ever saw or heard anything about Skipper. He vanished from the earth without a trace, leaving the world to draw its own conclusions. The sheriff never said anything about that trip to Southport. Many have speculated, but no documentation has ever surfaced. What's your guess?

Sensitive Cat

The James Ward family, among the early residents on the Waccamaw River where they eked out a living off the water and the land, once built a house in the wilderness that had only tree limbs and leaves for siding and sawdust on the floor. It had a good roof, but the rest of the jungle home was pioneering and humble.

Bill, young son of James, had a three-quarter Persian cat named "Tom" that was a pet in the family household. In the cooler months, Tom slept with Bill and actually got under the cover with his head on the pillow.

One night Tom decided it was time to go to the bathroom, which meant simply slipping out through the palm frond siding. Finished with his business, he returned to Bill's bed and jumped right on Bill's bare chest. Startled and not knowing what was on him, Bill slammed Tom across the room and through the limbs and leaves.

Realizing that he had made a mistake, Tom sheepishly returned to the bedside and carefully climbed in beside Bill.

"Thereafter, when Tom wanted to go outside in the middle of the night, he would put a front paw on my chest, extend his sharp claws a little and scratch me enough to be sure I was awake. Then he would go through the wall and soon return quietly and climb back in bed. That was how he learned not to get mauled by scaring me half to death," Bill remembers today.

Tom remained a favorite around the Ward jungle den until one of the married daughters returned home when her husband went in the service during World War II. She brought with her a cocker spaniel and a litter of cuddly pups which were immediately cherished and coddled by the Ward children. Tom was visibly jealous and after a few days of being ignored, he left home, obviously with no intention of ever returning. But like death and taxes, best laid plans of even animals often go awry.

Two years passed. Tom made a living stealing fish out of the boats on the river. The Wards saw him occasionally, but he looked upon them with disdain and ignored their beckoning. He had been rejected in favor of a litter of pups and he could not, would not, forget. He would remain a loner.

Tragically, a fisherman left fish in his boat until daylight and he saw Tom clawing some shiners out of his nylon-mesh net. Angered and afraid that the cat might damage the costly seine, he grabbed a paddle and viciously rapped Tom over the head. Stunned and mortally injured, Tom staggered into the woods. He must have known his day was done.

That afternoon, Tom half-walked, half-dragged himself into the yard of the Wards. Bill saw the pitiful feline with sorrowful eyes as it groaned and moaned in the agonizing throes of death. He picked up the old cat and cuddled him to his chest, remembering how close he and the rest of the family once were to this lovable mixed-breed creature.

Tom died moments later and was buried quietly by the Wards.

HE HELD ON TIGHT . . .

James Samuel O'Hara was a tough old Irishman who grew up and raised a large family along the South Carolina wilderness coast near McClellanville in the 1930's and '40's. It was during the infamous but intriguing era when the desolate coastal rain forests and swampland shanties were home to hundreds of bootleggers and other lawless characters that earned the territory the uncomplimentary name of "Badlands."

O'Hara was not one of those rogues. Generally he was law-abiding, although once or twice he did backslide into bootlegging for a few years when the money he earned catching and selling fish was not adequate to provide for his growing family. He had to struggle for survival during the Great Depression when bootlegging was the number-one industry along the Carolina coasts.

But O'Hara was a good fisherman. By working long hours, often night and day, and with the help of his wife and children, he usually kept food on the table, clothes on their backs and a shelter of sorts over their heads.

He was a tough and determined man who seldom excused inefficiency or carelessness on the part of his family or others he worked with in the inlet and river waters that provided him with a livelihood. Some of his actions could be described as abusive, but his family was quick to rush to his defense and explain that there is a narrow line between abuse and discipline when it comes to your own children. By any measurement, he was rough and tough.

The true story still circulates about O'Hara and his oldest son Sammy, who began fishing with his father when he was still a baby. O'Hara would set him in a washtub, pack pillows around him and carry him out into the brackish water where he sucked his thumb while dad fished hour after hour with a

Calcutta pole for trout and channel bass. He had no money for the sophisticated rods and reels that were just coming on the market and were in the hands of a few doctors and lawyers.

Sammy was the apple of his father's eye, even though other children were being born into the family regularly. By the time he was eight, he was in the boat going fishing with his dad every time he had the opportunity. It was one of these fishing adventures in the Inland Waterway that prompted this scenario.

O'Hara often had Sammy fishing with a light cane pole for pinfish and other forage species that he used on his bigger hooks, heavy line and 22-foot Calcutta poles for trout and other gourmet species that he could sell at the Charleston fish house. Then, when Sammy had a good supply of the live baits in the bucket, he would handle one of the heavy Calcuttas and help his dad land the marketable fish. These poles were heavy for an eight-year-old and they soon tired him out, often leading to his turning to playful behavior and paying little attention to the serious job of catching fish that his dad always insisted upon.

One day when Sammy was fishing with the big Calcutta which cost a hefty $1.50 back then, when fish sold for five and ten cents a pound, he hung a nice trout and was struggling to get the fish to the boat. Prior to the hookup, his dad had told him three or four times to quit playing around on the bow of the boat and be serious about his fishing. He hadn't paid much attention, and when he hung the trout, he let the pole slip out of his hands. It was gone and his dad was furious. He tried to retrieve the pole, but apparently the trout had been big enough to drag it with him into deeper water and beyond recovery.

"If you had paid attention and not played around, you wouldn't have lost my $1.50 fishing pole," O'Hara reprimanded Sammy. Then he cut off a yard or two of the anchor rope and thoroughly thrashed Sammy, who screamed with every lash of the line. "Next time you pay attention!" he demanded, and whether he was disciplining or abusing Sammy is a matter of conjecture. For sure, he loved the boy above all others in his family. The day ended with Sammy still snubbing and hurt.

A week later O'Hara again summoned Sammy to go with him fishing. The boy was reluctant, but dared not disobey. Fishing was an adventure with the foremost objective of making a living for the family. Fun and recreation were secondary, minor fringe benefits seldom considered.

That morning, while holding on to his Calcutta pole and putting trout in the boat for his dad, Sammy suddenly felt a powerful strike on the line. In that day, most fishermen used 65-pound test linen line. They hadn't started using monofilament yet. (Nylon was discovered in 1939, but many anglers did not buy it until many years later). The 65-pound test was as strong as a small rope, and before young Sammy could react, he was jet-propelled over the gunnels of the boat, as a giant channel bass hit his hooked trout and took off for the bright blue yonder at breakneck speed. It could have been a humorous moment had not catastrophe been a real threat.

Sammy was wearing a long-billed fishing hat. The cap bill acted like the lip on a giant crankbait lure as the youngster hung onto the pole desperately with both hands. He skimmed over the surface like he was on a ski board, dipping under the water and then breaking back to the surface as the fish raced away, pulling Sammy at great speed. He was under the water and on the surface about equal time as the big predator dragged him more than 100 yards before his dad got the outboard started and headed for his much-endangered young son. The elder O'Hara feared the worst. And not even a tough disciplinarian wants to lose an offspring.

After several minutes, the monster began to tire as Sammy's weight slowed down the fish. Sammy was still afloat and clinging to the pole. His dad raced to the scene, cut the linen line, and a fish, weighing at least 50-pounds, jumped and was at last free of its cumbersome load. The fish headed out to sea, dragging only the line behind.

O'Hara pulled his coughing and water-logged son into the boat. It had been several scary minutes since the youngster had been jerked over the gunnels by the powerful fish that had been tending to its own business when it gulped down the hooked trout.

"Sammy, why didn't you turn the pole loose?" his dad asked, showing a mixture of anger and relief at the same time.

"You can swim and wouldn't have been dragged all over the Waterway."

Half expecting another whipping, the child said, "Daddy, I didn't want to get another beating for losing your pole." He sobbed as he continued to hold the Calcutta in a firm grasp, fully aware that it was worth $1.50.

That could be the end of the story except that Sammy and his younger brother never forgot the whipping he had received when he lost the pole in the sea that memorable morning.

Years passed. Sammy grew up. He and his brother still worked with their father catching mullet, trout, clams, oysters and other seafood from the ocean. Father O'Hara continued to be a serious fisherman who would not tolerate skylarking even on the part of his grown sons.

One day a big school of mullet was seen near O'Hara's boat. Sammy and his brother were in another skiff a few yards away.

"Cut off that school of mullet! Get your boat in front of them and I'll get this cast net around them!" O'Hara screamed. "Turn 'em! Turn 'em!" he yelled.

The boys tried as hard as they could, but the school of mullet skirted around the end of their boat and disappeared into the deep river. They couldn't stop the pop-eyed mullet that were intent upon escaping.

"You damned sorry boys! You can't do a thing right. I'm going to bring this paddle over to your boat and beat hell out of both of you!" the frustrated father screamed.

Sammy had had enough discipline from his dad. Now he was bigger, stronger and he had the support of a younger brother. He picked up a heavy cypress paddle from the deck. He held it in both hands like it was a baseball bat.

"Come right on over, Dad. We got two paddles in this boat. I don't believe you can handle both of us with a paddle no longer than yours," Sammy yelled back. "I'm not that helpless little boy you beat the tar out of for losing a fishing pole."

O'Hara stayed away from the boat and his boys. He knew his domineering days were over. He never again let his temper get the best of him when his offspring accidentally didn't perform to his expectations. But it was too late to recapture all the love that Sammy once had for him. A short time later, at the age of 16, Sammy left home, never to return.

In a roundabout way, justice was served. O'Hara lost a precious son. His punishment was more severe than Sammy's whipping. Probably deep down the hurt never went away. O'Hara was obviously repentant long before he passed away in the late 1960's. But it was much too late to save Sammy. He received the heart-breaking news just before his death that his son had been killed—allegedly by an estranged wife for his insurance money.

Both O'Hara and his son seemed to have been born to disaster. Justice has a way of surfacing. It was unfortunate that Sammy had to suffer an untimely death. Who knows but what the discipline and punishment he suffered as a child might not have played a part in a life-style that eventually led to his tragic death.

Justice indeed sometimes seems far away.

River Chickens of the Swampland

Traditional chicken dinners were hard to come by in the post World War II era of the 1940's despite its lowly price of 15 cents a pound or less, and many families of the Carolinas turned to turtles for table fare–thus the unique moniker "River Chicken" lingers throughout the coastal Carolina low country.

The ugly duckling critters carry their houses on their backs in the rivers, streams and swamps, providing nourishment (along with semi-hazardous thrills) for the outdoorsmen who stalked them. Rural families learned to like these shelled reptiles for their gourmet meat and "cooters" (as Southern menus call them) remain a delightful seafood for many outdoorsmen today.

Still called "River Chickens" by a few who live off the water and land in the coastal Carolinas, the freshwater turtles remain abundant. The unique, tasty dark meat graces tables as an appetizing soup or a privileged entree for a society of brave "anglers" willing to risk painful bites for a cooter-meat meal. They say the end result justifies the risk.

Methods for catching the streaked head and snapping turtles, two distinct species, vary from one river to another. Several basic techniques are successful, and the expertise matches the free spirits, daring and dangerous challenge practiced by turtle hunters who go after the beasts in the freshwater bayous, rivers and swamplands.

Years ago most of the turtles harvested for food were caught on strong, steel set-hooks tied to overhanging bushes and baited with worms, pork, beef, or chicken gizzards. Baits floated on or near the surface. Turtles gulped the morsel down and were hung; hooks in tough mouths held for hours and even days until the turtleman returned to retrieve his bounty. But set hooks created a problem when more and more fishermen frequented an area. The sharp dangling hooks tied on masonry cord were left hanging from the bushes long after the bait was gone. Set-hook turtle fishing was outlawed in several states after fishermen reported painful injuries from being snared by abandoned hooks as they fished shorelines in search of bass and bream. Cutting hooks out of hands and ears was painful, to say nothing of eyes and lips. Turtle fishermen were rightfully blamed.

Set hooks was the easiest way to catch turtles. You seldom had one clamp down on a finger or hand and hold on "'til it thundered," as experienced snapping turtle stalkers explained how long a turtle locked his jaws. He held on even when his head was cut off.

The era of single set hooks passed, but catfish trotlining emerged. It's a means of catching cats in the swamplands, but the lines with dozens of hooks strung between the trees were often abandoned. Turtles gulped down the helpless fish on the line and were hooked when they made a meal of the catfish. Trotliners often harvested as many turtles as fish on these suspended hooks a few inches below the surface. But, like set hooks, these abandoned trot lines snared fishermen and fouled propellers. They were hazardous to conventional fishermen.

These turtle trot lines in the Neuse and other rivers remained a danger for a long time. But they caught turtles. Tragically, many abandoned trotlines were left unattended even after giant cooters were hooked, and fishermen experienced the gruesome scene of rotting turtles hanging on the hooks for months. Often nothing but the turtle shells remained. They eventually washed off the hooks, and the sad facts lay bleached on the shoreline. It was gross waste, and a testimonial to the insensitivity of some slobs. Such reckless behavior that wasted life and food was abhorred by sportsmen. They believed in using everything that you killed or "harvested."

Other almost unbelievable techniques for catching turtles persist in some river locals. There are devout turtlemen who continue to "grabble" or "doodle" for turtles. It's a unique technique. They poke their arms into holes along the bank and drag turtles out by the feet, tail or even the head. When they can't reach the back of the hole with their arm, they use a leg and foot to coax the turtle out of its haven. Strangely, few admit to ever having been bitten.

Many stories emerge from turtle-grabbling enthusiasts. A turtle stalker was not turtle hunting, but had gone bass fishing in the Black River near Atkinson. He snagged his Rat-L-Trap lure on a submerged log near the dark shoreline. Hoping to save his $3 lure, he paddled the boat to the spot directly above the hang-up and slid his paddle down the line. He expected to push the hook free and move along for some more fishing. Unexpectedly, he felt something alive, a strange action ricocheted up the paddle. He picked up the cedar paddle and was shocked to see a ragged chunk of it as big as his hand missing.

He had planned to stick his arm down in the shallow water to unhang the plug. He was glad he didn't! He put all the pressure on the 20-pound test line that it would stand. Slowly, the hook moved toward the surface. Moments later the flashing eyes of a monstrous turtle stared him in the face. He let go, cut the line and frantically paddled for the landing.

He went to the home of an old black local called "The Turtleman." He told him about the biggest snapping turtle in the world, his eyes twinkling. He obviously relished the news and his boat was anchored on the spot bright and early the next morning. Wading in the shallow eddy, he found the monster with the hook and line still in its mouth. He grabbed its hind legs, and after an amazing wrestling match, put the leviathan in the boat. He turned it over on its mossy back, and it lay there kicking, helpless, unable to right itself. Later he flopped it down on the cotton gin scales at Burgaw. It weighed 129 pounds. The fisherman was lucky. He might have lost his hand, or even his life, had he not poked his paddle in the turtle's mouth.

Along the river shorelines where logs are half-submerged, the trees having been uprooted from swampland muck by passing storms, turtles line up single-file and sun themselves on pretty days. For generations, outdoorsmen have fed their families with income from catching and marketing these creatures. Restaurants have always had a demand for the cooter meat, even during the Great Depression.

Turtles in the lakes where logs provide and easy escape from the water line up head to tail with the largest one in front and the smallest bringing up the rear like elephants in a parade. Often there are half a dozen or more sleeping or sunning on the same log.

UNBELIEVABLE SNAKE BITES

The late Frank Pittman of Kitty Hawk was walking along the waterway near his home when he narrowly missed stepping on a rattlesnake. The frightened viper struck with a vengeance, burying its fangs in the thick rubber boots that Pittman was wearing. The fangs did not get through to the flesh, and thus he suffered no bite. Nearly a year later Pittman noticed one of his boots was leaking. A close inspection uncovered two tiny holes. With his knife blade he picked at the holes and soon removed the two rattlesnake fangs. They had broken off in the boot and worked on through.

His oldest son, Johnny, had an experience with a rattlesnake bite, too. He stepped on one in the dark when he and his father were spreading out a mullet net. The fangs buried in Johnny's barefoot big toe. Amazingly calm about the dangerous bite, Johnny went to the house, found a razor blade and instructed his mother to split the toe open where the fangs had pierced the tough skin. She did, and Johnny put the toe to his mouth and sucked blood and poison out for several minutes. (That was the standard treatment at the time. It is no longer recommended.) With a rag tied around the cut, Johnny went back to work on the fish net. He didn't even get sick. But several months later the toe started swelling and pus gathered under a huge blister. Johnny took his knife and picked at the terrible-looking toe. He hit something solid. Gouging a little deeper, he removed one of the rattlesnake fangs. It had broken off in his calloused toe and had slowly festered there before the swelling and soreness began.

The late Frank Philpott, longtime outdoor writer, and an avid fisherman who fished all along the Carolina coast for many years, drove his pickup along a pig path road for several miles to a freshwater lake. He launched his boat, parked the trailer and fished until noon. When he started to load his boat, he was surprised to see one of the trailer tires was flat. He removed the wheel and carried it to a Nags Head service station to get it fixed. The mechanic removed the tire from the rim and found two tiny holes in the inner tube. He examined the tire. The fangs of a poisonous snake had penetrated the thick rubber tire and then the tube. The air escaped through the hollow fangs. Apparently Frank had come mighty close to running over the viper when he came to the lake and the snake punished him by deflating his trailer tire. Frank and the mechanic were amazed that these small bones were strong enough to go all the way through the tire, but they did.

Trappers Were Surprised

Trappers on the swampland farms are helping eradicate the over-population of beavers that clog ditches and build tree dams that cause flooding of low-lying agricultural fields. It's these energetic little engineers that have impounded many of the swamp ponds where bass and other sunfish thrive in the Carolinas. In a few nights they gnaw down enough trees to block a small stream where the growth is dense. While they conserve some water that would run off and into the Atlantic, a lot of their work is despised by the farmers. It damages crops and floods pasture lands. In an effort to help control these big rodents the North Carolina General Assembly allocated $10,000.00 to subsidize trappers catching the critters. Professionals descended upon the swampland beavers.

Meticulously setting the steel traps just under the surface of the water in one of these swamp lakes near Clarendon, North Carolina, the "experts" were amazed the first morning after placing the traps in the beaver paths to find that two of them had been tripped. But there were no beavers in the traps. Instead, each trap had a 3-pound largemouth bass that had been curious enough to inspect the foreign object in his territory. They nosed around enough to pull the trigger and succumbed to the snapping steel jaws intended for the dam builders. The trappers had a fish dinner, but no beaver pelts. The best laid plans of mice and men often go awry.

Tobacco Good for Something

Robin Durden, the daughter of Mr. and Mrs. Buster Durden, was just 14 years old when she was fishing with her father one April morning in a private pond on their farm. The five-acre lake was adjacent to Grissette Swamp and was long noted for its prolific bluegills and bass.

But it was slow that day. The father-daughter fishing duo put a few bream in the boat, but not enough to really keep them interested.

"Robin, how about going to the house and getting my chewing tobacco. I'll put in a big chaw of that and you can be almost certain the fish will bite when I start chewing and spitting," Buster said.

The young lady dashed off to the house that was but a few hundred yards away and was soon back ready to fish again. But Buster noted that her right jaw was all puffed up like she had a terrible tooth infection or something.

"What's wrong with your jaw?" he asked.

"I have got me a big chew of your tobacco in it. I figured if it would help you catch fish, it would help me," Robin said, with considerable logic.

"But you never chewed tobacco in your life. It will make you sick as a dog in a few minutes," he cautioned.

But Robin kept right on fishing, chewing and spitting. She held a short, stubby pole in her hand that had seen better days before it was broken almost in half and abandoned. Alertly, she watched her cork bob gently on the surface. She could spit the tobacco juice far enough to reach her hook and line and she was enthusiastically chomping on the tobacco.

Then down went the cork and the end of her pole splashed in the water. She had a monster on the hook, she visualized, and began yelling and screaming with delight and excitement. For awhile it was a one-on-one tug of war between Robin and her adversary on the other end of that fishing line. Then a huge largemouth bass broke the surface, shaking his head violently trying to loosen that No. 4 hook from his mouth. But it was all in vain. Robin had hooked that bass securely and minutes later she dragged it to the gunnels of the boat and over the side.

That ended the fishing. Robin and Buster dashed off to the nearest store and weighed the fish in. It tipped the scales at 4-pounds and 4-ounces. Not a record by anyone's yardstick but, nevertheless, a fine fish for a 14-year-old girl.

The amazing story is that Robin continued to chew that tobacco all afternoon and never got the first bit sick. I wonder if chewing the tobacco had anything to do with that fish striking? Or, the other way around, I wonder if catching the bass kept her from getting sick?

COMPASSION SAVED OPOSSUMS

Trapped in a rabbit gum designed to catch cottontails, an old mama opossum died with 13 tiny siblings latched on to her teats and holding on despite her untimely death. A novice rabbit trapper had baited the trap with an apple that had attracted and caught the ugly old scavenger. Then he had waited too long to check the trap and the imprisoned 'possum died with her brood. The mouse-size offspring were near death too when the trapper discovered his unique catch. He was agonized to see the dead body of the old 'possum lying on her side with all that baker's dozen little baby critters hanging on to the 13 spigots on her belly. They were famished, but still sucking away futilely, trying to gain some sustenance from the deceased mother.

He poured them out of the box and pried them loose from the mama. Baby 'possums hang on for dear life, literally, because this species often has more young than they have teats and those who fail to grasp a life-saving milk supply early always perish and are pushed out of the nest. This is one of the examples of the extreme lack of intelligence on the part of opossums, perhaps the dumbest of wild creatures. More of them are killed on the highways than most other wild animals, and even when not accidentally killed, they have a life expectancy of only three years. They have almost no memory. Their greatest defense is playing dead when attacked, thus the expression today of "playing possum."

That hunter, feeling guilty for letting that old mama die in the trap, scooped up the little 'possums and hurried back to the house with his pockets bulging.

"What are you going to do with all those baby 'possums?" his wife inquired. You could feel the compassion she had in her heart for the helpless critters.

"I don't know, but we can't let them starve. We'll have to

try to nurse them until they get big enough to survive," the hunter said.

And so he did.! For several weeks he fed those little big-mouthed, toothy, ugly animals cow's milk with a medicine dropper three times a day. He watched them grow rapidly. Not a one died. All 13 creatures soon were wobbling around in their box and able to walk, rat-like tails dragging behind them.

Eventually they were kitten-size 'possums and the hunter began showing them off at Shallotte. Half of them would hang upside down on his fingers with their curled tails securely wrapped, their heads slowly turning from side to side surveying the surroundings as they do in the wild on their mother's tail when being moved. The others nestled in his pockets. They were pets, but were rapidly getting too big to handle and required too much effort to feed.

Opossums are scavengers that are naturally messy and smelly. Folks who eat them, and there are many in the South who do, usually catch grown 'possums, put them in a cage of some type for two or three weeks and feed them wholesome food like sweet potatoes and sweet milk until they are sure the carrion gulped down in the wild has passed through them. They then kill them for food. They are usually killed by putting a stick across their necks and pulling until the bone snaps. You then scald the 'possum and scrape off the hair like you would a hog. With this done and the insides out, they are usually baked whole with potatoes, onions and carrots stuffed inside. If you have never tried this delicacy, you haven't missed anything. It's about like eating white beef fat or worse.

But the 13 captive orphaned 'possums were not to meet such a fate, at least not by their benefactors. They walked into the dense undergrowth at Town Creek just off Highway 17 and disapppeared. They were reluctant to leave their "mama" and "daddy" and scrambled back to their feet when first set free. But it was time to separate and they were left to forage for their own food. Few people would have worked so hard to save an armful of dumb opossums. But it does go to show that some Carolina residents have compassion for all life, be it ever so humble.

Rx—Fish a Day and a Half a Week

The widely respected Duke Hospital in Durham, NC had a 40 year old patient teetering on the brink of a nervous and general breakdown from long hours of overwork in the fall of 1939. He was Melvin B. Andrews, Sr., a farm boy who, for 16 years, was an educator and then became a super active insurance salesman in Goldsboro, NC. He had tackled his new insurance profession with such dedication, setting himself a quota of 15 interviews a day, that he found himself on the go form daylight until 10:00 PM and beyond, six days in every week. With almost no time left for his wife and five children, he became ill, weak, anemic, virtually disabled, after only a year as a salesman.

A graduate of Trinity College, later changed to Duke University, Andrews called the hospital in Durham and asked to go to the famous clinic for a check-up to determine what was killing him. Given the come-on by the administrator, he reported to the internists and spent five days of intricate physical examination with nine doctors searching for every physical flaw in the patient. They could find nothing.

At the end of the physical exam, the doctors called Andrews to a conference room and revealed their findings:

"Melvin," they began, "You have no disease, no real physical illness. You have seem to have tried to work yourself to death, and may actually succeed soon. You must find something to do as recreation. Can you play golf, tennis, organize a softball league, or anything that will occupy some of your time and take you away from your work?" they asked.

"No, I can't do any of those things," he told them, "but I would like to fish if I had the time."

"Then that's the answer. We are writing a prescription for you today. You cannot fill it at the pharmacy. You are to take no treatment, swallow no medicine. The prescription is simply that you go home and from this day forward, you are to fish one and a half days every week. Do you understand that?" the senior physician asked. "You can continue working, but you must stop to fish."

"Yes, I understand it, but I don't know whether I can make a living and fish a day and a half every week," the sick salesman said.

"Well, it's either that or your family will soon not have a husband and father. The decision is up to you," they said.

M. B. Andrews returned home that September afternoon more than half a century ago and relayed the prescription to his family. Starting that week, he began fishing, often more than just a day and a half a week. He adhered to the advice strictly for 53 years and on September 6, 1980, he celebrated his 91st birthday by going fishing and driving his own car to get his license renewed for another four years.

He fished alone generally, did not use a cane and his doctor told him the week after that memorable birthday that he "was fit as a fiddle and strong as a horse."

Andrews continued to operate his successful insurance business until he was 82, and then returned to be free to fish every day he wanted to. "I have become a terrible crank about fishing. People just want to talk to me about fishing all the time," he said when he turned 91.

Until he was 75, Andrews continued fishing alone in his tiny boat and was adept at catching all the Eastern North Carolina species, especially bass, bluegills and what he called "crappie perch." But when the water skiers became too rambunctious on the Wayne County Wildlife Lake, 11 miles from his home, he began fishing off the piers that are built out back of many of the homes that are on the 100 acre lake.

Fishing from the piers after giving up his boat, he still manages to catch limits of panfish and an occasional bass, all of which he gives to "the widow ladies of the community."

In 1946, NC State College, Raleigh, began sponsoring a fishing school or tournament each year, and at that time it was held in fresh water. It later became a saltwater event. That year the program was scheduled for the beautiful Fontana Lake in the mountains outside Bryson City, NC. The entry fee was $175.00 and included everything—boats, motors, lodging, meals, guides and bait. Andrews landed 16 different species during the three day event and was named "North Carolina's Champion Fisherman," a title he cherished.

"I have fished every hole, pond, lake and stream in Wayne County and at many other places in the eastern Carolinas. I have saltwater fished off every pier on the Atlantic Ocean between Virginia and Murrels Inlet, SC. Of all those piers I believe Barnacle Bill's at Surf City, NC is the most productive," says this veteran of many thousands of days of fishing.

The biggest fish Andrews ever caught in fresh water just might have been close to the world champion crappie. It was landed from a sand hole off the Neuse River and, oddly, he wasn't really there when it was caught, but he considered it his catch. He had set a line with a live minnow on it, tied it to a tree and walked away to eat lunch. The fish hit while he was gone, made a lot of noise with its splashing and another angler pulled it in. The fish weighed 4 1/2 pounds. The world record black crappie of that time was only five pounds.

The biggest saltwater fish he ever caught, he didn't really land either. It was a six foot or longer sailfish and again it was in a tournament being sponsored by NC State University. This time it was in the Atlantic. Andrews hooked a giant sail and fought it a long time. Finally the captain of the charter boat asked to handle the rod awhile. He promptly lost the fish! Although it jumped and dived and was seen and admired by all on board numerous times, it was never landed. In that the captain lost the fish, not Andrews, the Goldsboro fishing champion was given honorable mention in the contest, even though the fish was never brought to the gaff.

"The largest fish I ever actually landed was an 18 1/2 pound black sea bass that I caught in the Gulfstream off Morehead City. I'll never forget it. We set out that morning and there were a hundred or more people on the boat. They got up this pot of money by asking each fisherman to put in $1.00 with the catcher of the biggest fish getting the dough at the end of the day. They asked me to join in but, you see, I am an ordained, licensed Methodist minister, and I preach when asked at churches of this area. I felt this was gambling and was wrong. I would have won the pot had I put in my $1.00 and they really ragged me about it when the boat docked. But I had to live by my convictions, and I wasn't sorry," Andrews said.

Oddly enough, while fishing was so good to him and left him in excellent health at the age of 91, it almost killed him too. In 1970 he was returning home from fishing with a friend driving the car. He was asleep at the time the driver crashed into the back of a truck. It was 45 days later when Andrews revived from a coma in the hospital and had no recollection of the accident.

His wife passed away at the age of 76. She once fished with him regularly until he "scolded" her one day and she never went again. They were fishing off a crowded pier near Morehead City, catching spots and Virginia mullet. Rods and reels were not equipped with anti-backlash apparatus as many are now, and Melvin would cast out for his wife to avoid the bird's nests in the lines and possibly the accidental catching of someone's eye or ear with the hook. He walked away from her a few moments to fish the other side of the pier, and when he returned, she was sitting down trying to untangle a terrible backlash.

"How did you do that?" Melvin asked his wife.

"I decided to cast a little further out and it tangled like this," she explained.

"But I told you not to cast, that I'd do it for you," Melvin reprimanded with perhaps too much hostility in his voice for a wife he dearly loved.

"I'll never do it again," she promised. And she never did. The last 30 years of her life, she never again went fishing with her husband or anyone else.

As Andrews fished more and more in those years when his family of five was growing up and his wife had her hands full taking care of them, she asked him one day if indeed doctors at Duke had really prescribed all that fishing, at least a day and a half a week. He assured her that it was a legal, medical prescription, but try as he might, he could not find it in his records. Nearly two decades had elapsed since he had been told to fish, and now his wife was questioning his putting so much time on the water. He wrote to Duke and explained the circumstances, asking if by some chance they could verify a prescription issued so long ago. A few days later he opened his mail to find a Xerox copy of the exact prescription, taken from his efficiently filed folder in the hospital record room. His wife gave him no more argument on that subject.

Born a hydrocephalic child to a tenant farm family at Suttertown in the Coastal Plains of NC, in 1889, he was abused by his father who whipped and frequently told him he wished he had died when he was a baby. He was subsequently told by the same cruel father that he would beat him enough until he did die. Melvin Andrews survived because of the love of a compassionate mother who cherished and sheltered him the best she could in the face of the inexplicable violence against him.

Believed to be mentally abnormal because of the oddly shaped and disproportionate head, the child was not allowed to even go to school until he was 14 years old. Then, with normal learning ability, he managed to pass ten units of high school by the time he was 18. Melvin wrote to Trinity College asking for admission and was refused because he did not have the 16 required high school credits.

He then penned a letter to the president of Trinity who was to serve even after it was endowed by the Duke family and the name changed. He told him of his abnormal childhood, his abused body and lack of formal schooling, but vowed he could make it if the school would admit him. The school asked him to come for an interview. He did. He was given a job in the library and, in 1913, graduated with a B. S. degree, cum laude. He taught school in Cary, NC one year and returned to get his Master's Degree in 1916. Before entering the insurance business 15 years later, he taught school at summer terms at the University of North Carolina at Greensboro and headed the public school system in Fayettville and in Rockingham, NC.

That baby grew to be a perfectly normal, brilliant, hard working American who resorted to fishing only when his very life depended on it. Later he would take a box of catalpa worms out of the refrigerator, drive to the lake, and catch a mess of panfish for his neighbors almost daily.

"Yesterday I caught 26 bream in an hour and a half off the same pier. Of course, I was there on the major period, and you can just do better during those major solunar periods," Andrews said as he pulled a crumpled booklet from his hip pocket and quickly glanced down the page to see if this is another good hour to catch his limit. Most devout fishermen believe in the solunar times that occur twice daily when the fish allegedly are more active.

"Some of my widowed lady friends really like to eat fish and I'll see if I can't make some of them happy again today," this great senior citizen who had a doctor's mandate to fish, thinks out loud.

In 1983 this unusual outdoorsman died at his home in Goldsboro at the age of 94. He lived by a doctor's prescription to fish a day and a half a week for almost half a century and outlived almost all of his friends and his family.

Coastal Carolinas
Tales and Truths

Fishing, Hunting & Outdoor Stories

As the Day Dawned

Few winter mornings ever promised more "bad weather" than today as I slowly, wakelessly putt-putted my camouflaged old bateau down the winding, narrow Town Creek at Winnabow, just east of US 17. It was a half-hour before sunup and the Spanish moss-draped cypress trees along the swampy shoreline reached toward the sky, their silhouettes providing the only navigational assistance on a dark, moonless morning. But I knew a deep lake was just around another bend and there would be little trouble feeling my way to that favorite spot.

An occasional splash broke the silence as I eased along the shoreline. That would be another leopard frog or maybe an old mossy-backed turtle paddling away and grumbling about being disturbed so early in the morning. That hog-like grunt followed by a much louder thrashing of the water was an old mama alligator crawling off her tussock and scrambling through the grass bed when my boat seemed to challenge her right to that watery territory.

It was raining now. A cold northeast wind whipped the lilies and their pastel undersides began to appear as the first faint rays of dawn pierced through the timberline. I could see a little better now. Cold, rainy, windy, these are the ingredients for good duck hunting the coastal Carolinas, and it wasn't often you were fortunate enough to ferret out such a morning with all three desirables. But this was one. I would soon be in position to shoot the wood ducks that I knew were harbored in the coves and they would be flying low, hunting, looking for a choice place to fill their crops at daybreak.

I had not counted on so many coots that literally covered my favorite duck pond. They had taken refuge there during the night, and when I motored right through their bedrooms, they fussed long and loud, protesting with good reason at being rousted by this human who had so little regard for their peace-fulness that surpasseth all understanding. If I could understand coot language, I'm sure the hundreds of floppy critters strug-gling to fly a few inches above the water so they could quit walk-ing on this liquid stuff, would have been saying, "What fools these mortals be. Here's an old guy out on our lake before day and running his boat right through the whole sleeping flock. He's cold and getting wet and by the time he gets back home he'll be half frozen. Looks to me like he would have just snuggled up in bed and snoozed well into the morning. Then he wouldn't be out here harassing all of us even before we get our eyes open and start looking for breakfast. He is some kind of nut."

Of course, I couldn't read the coot talk, but the squawking sent me the message as they scattered, then sat down a few hun-dred yards away, still jabbering and hostile. But they were out of the way now. I tied my boat to a cypress knee and slumped to the deck to make little or no impression on the sharp eyes of the expected woodies. I shivered and waited.

I heard the air being fanned violently before I saw any-thing. But I knew this meant a duck or ducks were flying close by. Barely visible in the grayish dawn, a half-dozen ducks with the wind at their tails whizzed by. I didn't even get a shot. They were gone. I waited. Again there was that tell-tale fanning of the cold morning air and three low-flying woodies were just yards away and coming directly overhead. I sat up quickly, put the old Browning to my shoulder , and with fingers numb from cold and shaking with anticipation, I pulled the trigger. The lead duck dropped like a toy airplane that had lost its motor. Instantly, I sighted down the barrel at the second duck, now almost over-head, and pulled the trigger again. That old male woody folded his wings and likewise plunged into the water almost within reaching distance.

It was barely dawn now. I had pushed myself out of bed an hour ago, gulped down some black coffee, climbed into this old boat and felt my way down the creek to this memorable spot on the water where I had smiled with success many times before. It was the same today. Yes, I had made myself uncom-fortable for a time. It was cold and I was wet. But there on the water floated two fat ducks. It was my reward. I was the predator. The ducks were the prey. It was man's technology and expertise against the fowls of the water and the air. It was natural. This is what life for the outdoorsman is all about. You brave the elements and the cunning of the creatures. Sometimes you come out a winner. Sometimes you lose. But here in the dawn, surrounded by a beauty untouched by man, I was happy as so many hunters have been since the first loincloth-clothed man shot a rough sculptured arrowhead into the breast of a waterfowl that died to feed his family.

I picked up my success and stuffed them into my old Navy peacoat pocket. It was a good feeling

I cranked the little outboard and chugged off toward the creek mouth. Some people would call this cruel. Some would call the hunt punishment on such a day. I call it fun.

Outer Banks Fall Flounder

Softly, almost as if the flounder rig on the line had tangled with a piece of floating seaweed, the tip of my 7' Garcia rod twitched and then bowed. There was no tap-tap, tell-tale pulsating message on the line. Was something alive really mouthing the three-inch long strip of flounder belly meat on the 2/0 TruTurn hook with the crazy bend?

I looked at the boat's veteran flounder catcher who had fished these Oregon Inlet waters for a quarter of a century. A novice flounder fisherman here needed advice, and on this windy fall day when the tide was rushing across the sandbars, making successful hookups scarce, I didn't want to miss a single strike.

"Mitchell," I yelled to my brother who was captain of this 170 AquaSport, "Is this a flounder strike or am I hung on something?"

An experienced eye searched the bent rod and the flickering tip was instantly revealing. At least it was to the veteran flounder catcher.

"That's a fish! Give him some line for a two or three count, then set the hook with some gusto. Cross his eyes!"

I obeyed the instructions and sure enough, there was a live something on the line. It headed for the boat. I reasoned it must be small because there was virtually no resistance, no surging, no fight. Mitchell idled the motor. We were drifting slowly in the outgoing current within hearing distance of the noisy Atlantic breakers of Oregon Inlet on the North Carolina side of the Outer Banks, the "Graveyard of the Atlantic." Historically, the shallow, rocky reefs along this Tar Heel coast played havoc with early American ships that floundered and sunk. Today, the floundering off these Outer Banks is confined to catching the gourmet species of one-sided fish that abound in the sounds, surf and sea.

Reeling almost frantically now, I saw the two foot leader break the surface, and then there was the dark, flat image of the strange shaped flounder with both its eyes on the same side of its head. The fish came toward the boat, docile and humble, until it saw me. Suddenly, it was no longer the gentle creature I had reeled up from 60 feet behind the boat. The strength of a flounder is enhanced by its flat shape and huge tail and dorsal fins. My fish dived for the bottom and away from the dip net above that spelled his capture. For an instant, I held on to a vicious, steady tug. Then it was over. The flounder came unbuttoned. He quickly disappeared in the briny, tidal water of Oregon Inlet.

"What did I do wrong?" I asked in all sincerity. I had tried hard to hang and land this elusive, challenging species that provides more native Carolinians and tourist seafood lovers with dinner than any other fish other than the hand-sized panfish known as "spots," too small a variety to interest most sportsmen.

"You didn't let the flounder have time to wallow the bait around and get it in his mouth. He was just gumming it when you set the hook. He held on until you got him close to the boat. Then he saw he was being caught. He turned everything loose and swam away. He wasn't hooked. Next time, give the fish more line so he can gulp the cut bait down. Then when you get him near the boat, have the net already underwater. With it under the surface, drag the flounder's head into the net. A flounder will always struggle and surge that last moment to stay out of the net when they see it in the hands of a fisherman. He is the predator and the flounder instinctively spots danger, thus the last minute struggle to escape."

We were slowly drifting across a shallow sandbar near the Oregon Inlet three-mile-long bridge that connects Hatteras with the northern section of these barrier islands. It's a famous floundering area of these productive sounds that are real fish havens all the way north to Kitty Hawk, scene of the Wright brothers' famous first airplane flight. A nor'easter was kicking up a roaring, rough surf just a stone's throw away across the narrow spit of land that separates the North Carolina mainland from the historic Outer Banks. These wind-swept sand dunes are federally managed as part of the National Seashore Parks. There is still great surf fishing on nearly 100 miles of the Outer Banks strand, but most of the floundering is done on the Oregon Inlet side of the land spit. Charter boats and private fishing vessels ply the calmer water from spring until early winter with fantastic success.

Excellent public access launching ramps are available from Kitty Hawk in the north to Ocracoke at the extreme southern tip of the Banks.

Numerous RV parking areas are available, and moderately priced motels are scattered all along the scenic miles of coastal highways (158 and 12) from Corolla in the north of Ocracoke on the Pamlico Sound, across the bay from Cedar Island. Fishermen who do not take the northern route (Highway 264 and 64) to the Outer Banks can enjoy a 2 1/2-hour ferry boat ride from Cedar Island to Ocracoke. Boaters can reach this flounder-catching honey hole from the Intracoastal Waterway by cruising across 6.1 nautical miles of Albemarle Sound using NOAA Charts 12204 and 12205. You set a course from flashing day-beacon #AS to #MG that puts you on Croatan and Roanoke sounds. Dredging and a new high-span bridge across the Roanoke has opened new avenues for boaters traveling the waterway to this fishing ground.

Excellent country-style food is served at a myriad of restaurants in the islands. Prices remain comfortable here for fishermen.

On the mainland at Manteo, the west side of Oregon Inlet, there are motels, tackle shops, restaurants, guide services and charter boats, making whole and half-day trips from spring to fall. In addition to exposing clients to some spectacular coastal scenery, flounder and other estuary species are commonly caught in good numbers by even the novice fisherman.

Flounder found here in the warm months are generally known as "summer flounder." They are not all alike. Some are light tan in color. Others are covered with spots that look like eyes on their top side. Deeper in the marshes where the flounder go to ambush forage food, they are almost black on top.

They miraculously camouflage their bodies to the habitat in which they live, an adaptation which offers a lot of protection from the harpooning fishermen who harvest the flatfish with lights and a gig at night. Fish eyes are easy to see, like a firelighted deer. Gigging is legal as long as the flounder are at least 13 inches long. Natives have gigged flounder for the dinner table since the days when the Native Americans occupied the coastal lands and made spears from bone and wood. Today, anglers fill freezers and preserve many fine wintertime seafood meals.

You can carry home coolers full of flounder without gigging, a less sportsman-like technique than fishing with a rod, reel, hook and line. It's a matter of perfecting the technique, the revealing feel of a flounder bite.

Most avid flounder fishermen use a 12-pound test line with a special leader rigging that includes a mud minnow or cut strip of belly meat impaled on a 2/0 hook above a one-ounce slip sinker. The novel part of the rigging is a two inch oblong red or yellow cork a foot in front of the bait that keeps the hook off the bottom. The idea is to drag the sinker across the fish waiting in ambush in the mud. The bump of the sinker wakes the fish up, he eyeballs the moving bait and pounces on it. You have to remember a flounder is slow in getting the bait beyond his sharp teeth and it takes a few seconds of patience to be sure of a successful hookup.

The sounds of Oregon Inlet today are among the very best floundering waters in the country. A little expertise, proper trolling rig, boat-handling acumen in the tidal current and slow dragging of a bait on the bottom from spring to fall will often fill freezers. There's the thrill of victory in catching these one-side oddballs. There's great satisfaction when the tasty filets are browned over an outdoor fire in an iron skillet and enjoyed at day's end. As the TV commercial says, "It just doesn't get any better than this."

FISHING TIME IN DIXIE

Tired after a long flight from the frigid North, purple martins chirp and flit from gourd-draped double crossbars on a 20-foot pole that rises from a garden along the marshy shoreline at Louisiana's Bayou Barbary. Selfish red-winged blackbirds battle each other for mosquitoes swarming over lily pads along the river banks. A haggard bald eagle, the emblem bird, refurbishes her 500-pound nest that's anchored in the tallest pine tree on a Sandy bluff overlooking the Intracoastal Waterway. A half-dozen water snakes entwine in a single mass on a drooping myrtle bush in the shallows of Sparkleberry Swamp in South Carolina's Santee-Cooper country. Red is beginning to show on the maples that hover over the water along the shore where the dingy Big Pee Dee River meanders.

The natives and visitors who wait out the cold months expectantly, hopeful, confidently are suddenly aware that it's that fishing bonanza time again in Dixie. And for those who know their geography and closely observe water levels and temperatures they are almost guaranteed thrills and gourmet meals. These are the signs that spring has sprung and there is no better time to catch the gamefish that are prolific in the South.

Every freshwater fisherman has his favorite stream and semiprivate cove where he landed limits of bass, bluegill, crappie, chain pickerel or other gamefish in years past. He expects them to be there again when the water temperature reaches the seventies. Or maybe he is getting his directions secondhand from a friend, relative or professional guide. Many have experienced the fierce appetites of these Southern fish when the sun eases northward to scatter welcomed warmth that is absorbed by the fresh water of the lakes, rivers and impoundments in the cypress, palm, magnolia and live oak tree country where the Spanish moss decorates the shoreline with nature's own artistry.

Pre-spring fishing success is noted first in January and February in the far South where the lakes attract hundreds of thousands of anglers who have witnessed the feeding habits of spawning crappie and bass. From the tropical region, the warmth spreads north and west bringing good fishing to state after expectant state from February through June when much of the nesting has been completed and anglers have had a season of field days fishing in the not-too-cold and not-too-hot weather that is generally enjoyed those months of the year in the Carolinas.

Here are some best bet locations for spring fishing in the Southern states:

South Carolina—Among the best fishing spots in America for more than 40 years from February until the hot months of summer is the 171,00-acre Santee-Cooper watery complex. The two lakes of Marion and Moultrie, along with the creek tributaries of Potato, Wyboo, Mill and others, and the flatland shallows of Sparkleberry Swamp and Rimini, offer crappie and largemouth bass fishing equal to any in the country. Crappie are caught stump jumping in the deep water with live minnows or jigs as well as in the shallow portions of the lakes where they spawn and will hit almost anything that drops in their faces. The two big lakes of this impoundment above the Wilson and Pinopolis dams, offer the novice and the astute veteran some striped bass fishing that you can write home about. Using cut herring or live shad, the domesticated rockfish that abound here, bite so consistently that they leave a lasting mark in the Isaak Walton clan annals throughout this impoundment. Many of the purists still prefer trolling big fish look-alike lures or casting Sassy or Shimmy Shad for the stripers. In either case, live baits or artificials, the spring fishing at Santee-Cooper generally pays off with creel limits normal rather than the exception.

Wildlife officials have considerable confidence in the Wateree River early in the spring. This small river, near Columbia, has been noted for an abundance of medium-size crappie and the last several years has become a big producer of yearling-size largemouths, too.

A little further southwest in the Palmetto State are Lake Hartwell and the Clark Hill reservoir on the Savannah River. These lakes have not been outstanding for bass or crappie, but hybrid stripers have been taken by the boatful in many of the deep water areas where the water is backed up over standing, dead trees. Many devout fishermen here prefer the night hours and talk of "catching hybrids in the treetops." They mean that literally. Using live shad, they drop these morsels about 30 feet in 100-foot water to the tops of the submerged trees after spotting schools of hybrids on depth finders and sophisticated charters. The action is furious when you locate these suspended schooling fish early in the spring. You'll catch some catfish with the same baits and in the same places too.

North Carolina—When warm spring days begin to heat up the giant estuary of Currituck Sound along the North Carolina-Virginia border near Manteo, the bass, crappie and bluegills are pulled over the gunnels in such numbers as to be almost unbelievable. There is no more productive water in the world, if you do not get caught in a northeastern wind that blows the water out. Veteran bass casters, who release virtually all the largemouths they catch, do not have to stretch the truth to tell about 100 and more fish landed in a single day. Some float or wade fish. Most use boats. These fish are generally caught along the Eurasian water milfoil line with floating lures or weedless plastic worms. There are others who have reported fantastic success using live runt eels and shiners. These bass are not generally lunkers, mostly weighing one- to three-pounds, but the numbers are phenomenal. An eight-pounder is uncommon, but some are caught here.

These same waters, especially around Knotts Island, are just as remarkable for the panfish. "Find the wood and you find the bedding fish" is the rule of thumb as fishermen drop minnows for crappie or crickets for bream around duck blind pilings, abandoned piers, boats, and navigational markers to bring home coolers filled with gripper-size flatfish. It is unbelievable success in April and May.

Further south in North Carolina is the oft-ignored Waccamaw River. Ignored, that is, except for the local anglers who have been feeding families from it since barges hauled out giant ton timber to Georgetown, South Carolina, nearly 100 years ago. This swamp-colored water moves through 40 miles of scenic wilderness from Lake Waccamaw in Columbus County on Highway 74, until it joins the Pee Dee and the Atlantic at Georgetown. The redbreast, bluegill and bass fishing here for those who can handle a small boat, slingshot a popping bug a few inches from the bank under an overhanging brier patch, is as good as it is anywhere.

Other fine coastal fishing spots for spring in the Tar Heel state include the Northeast Cape Fear River, near Wilmington, the Black River at Burgaw, and Atkinson, and the Lumber River between Whiteville and Lumberton on Highway 74.

With alertness, expertise and perhaps a little professional assistance from local guides on your first trips to the waters mentioned here, you'll be pleased with the results. And it gets you off on the right fishing foot a few weeks early before you dare take your boat out of mothballs where it has rested most of the winter while you switched to deer hunting.

There's No Substitute

Two veteran saltwater anglers were tirelessly casting a variety of grubs, jigs, spoons, spinners and crankbaits close to the oyster bars as the tide slowly receded, uncovering the crustaceans where redfish, trout and other species feed at the mouth of the Cape Fear River. Nothing seemed to be interested in any lure they cast. They hadn't had a strike in an hour.

A stone's throw away, a young man in a homemade boat was fishing alone. Regularly he was reeling in another nice trout or redfish, catfish and even a flounder or two.

Observing the two quiet fishermen who were skunked, the youngster had a little compassion. He though maybe he might be of some help.

"What kind of bait you fellows using?" he politely inquired.

"We been throwing about every lure in the tacklebox, but nothing works," one of the discouraged anglers replied.

"I'm catching fish on live shrimp. I can sure tell you something. There ain't nothing as much like a shrimp as a shrimp," the successful young native philosophized.

He was so right!

Spot Time in Carolina

While mackerel, marlin, sailfish, wahoo, white sharks and other giant species get most of the headlines, the real fish attractor to the coasts of North Carolina in the fall and early winter is the humble spot, or Norfolk spot as it is called by some oldtimers. It draws more people to coastal fishing than any other species and has since the time the Indians inhabited the Tar Heel State. It's popular in South Carolina too.

As the water temperature starts to drop, spots migrate southward and most of the myriad of piers along the coast are filled with shoulder-to-shoulder anglers casting double and triple hook rigs baited with bloodworms or bits of shrimp into the shallow water where the waves break and the suds boil. These yellow-belly fish seldom reach weights of more than one and a quarter pounds but they are easy to catch, tasty and perhaps most importantly, they are so plentiful that they can be landed by the thousands and frozen for gourmet winter meals when it is too cold to catch anything along the coastal water.

Every beach resort in the Carolinas has half a dozen of more long piers that jut out into the Atlantic, and for minimal costs, you can buy bait, fish all day, and carry home a cooler full of hand-sized spots. If you are a night angler, often these panfish descend on the piers in even greater numbers than in the daylight. Many coastal working people put in their hours, drive to the coast and catch a big stringer of spots before bedtime.

When spot fishing, it is important to have a small hook, No. 4 preferred, with a light line in the six- to eight-pound class. The rod should be limber and when you feel the slightest nudge or see the rod tip dip, just start reeling in. Spots have tender mouths and generally little or no hook setting is required.

If you have a boat and want to escape the crowds that pier fish for spots, the Intracoastal Waterway, estuaries and inlets along the coast are filled with spots when the water begins to cool and into winter. Just anchor where the tide creates a current around a bend or near some deep holes, put the bait on the bottom, keep the line tight, and reel in a cooler full of spots.

SMOKERS SAVOR CIGARS

Plowing through some medium-height swells on an early fall morning in an 18-foot Grady White boat, pushed along by a 140-horsepower outboard, we were suddenly captivated by a milling school of mackerel that were in a frenzy chasing small forage fish all over the surface. The scene was unbelievable only in its scope. Feeding fish off the mouth of Masonboro Inlet that leads to Wrightsville Beach and the Intracoastal Waterway in this southern tip of North Carolina are common from spring until winter year after year, and anglers normally make good catches of these charging mackerel when they are found on the surface. But this wasn't just a fish or two. There were thousands of them, covering many acres. It was a sight to remember.

We quickly tossed out some of our favorite lures for these snake-size kings and lunker-size Spanish that seemed to be intermingled in the school. Strangely, the fish ignored all the spoons, crankbaits and colorful jigs that we cast or trolled through the melee on the surface. Nothing seemed to interest the feeders except the live, three-inch shad that were humpbacking in fright all over the place.

"Why don't we try the drinking straw gimmick that is the talk at every tackle and bait shop on the beach?" my companion suggested.

"Good idea," I said, with hope that this humble lure, a plain old soda straw with a line through it and a hook on the end with an ounce or two of weight in front, would turn these snakes on. Early American fishermen used to use waterfowl leg bones, bleached white in the sun, hollowed out and strung on a line with hooks in the stern. They were apparently replicas authentic enough to fool the fish into thinking they were striking the American eels that have always been an important part of predator diets along the coastal Atlantic. The soda straw was a good imitation of that bird-bone lure.

I pulled a 20-pound monofilament line through an 8-inch white straw, snapped on a hook, and tied the line to a stout rubber band looped around a cleat on the gunwale. It was a hand line that would run close to the surface, and often was more productive than rod and reel lines in holders. The rubber band on the cleat maintained a tight line on any strikers that hooked up, and few escaped this kind of rigging.

Bingo! The hand line with the soda straw tightened and jerked. Something had struck the straw. I grabbed the line and hand-over-hand wrestled a fish to the gunnels. I lifted a snake-size Spanish over the side. It flopped on the deck and we had unlocked the secret bait that this size mackerel liked, Spanish or king.

Moments later, another big Spanish was yanked in and then a 24-inch kingfish that was obviously cavorting with the Spanish in this giant melee.

We had made a discovery for ourselves, these big Spanish and snake kings are suckers for the soda straw lures. Indeed, snakes *do* strike straws.

With enough snakes in the boat for a family seafood dinner, we left the milling mackerel in search of larger fish, the *smokers* as veterans at Masonboro call lunker kingfish.

Three miles off Masonboro Inlet and a few degrees south, a sunken liberty ship is covered with 25 to 30 feet of water. It's a prized location for many mackerel fishermen of the Carolinas. We quickly reached the buoy that marked this manmade fish haven, and on a hunch I impaled a six-inch cigar minnow on a No. 8 Kahle hook with two sets of trebles trailing a few inches apart. Hooked through the lips, the frozen cigar minnow almost obscured the unbaited treble hooks.

We dropped the bait 30 to 40 feet behind the boat and trolled across the wrecked ship.

"Grab the rod!" I yelled. "Something's on the lines."

My fishing partner yanked up the stiff eight-foot rod with the reel strong enough to draw water on a bucket from a well, and held on as nearly 100 yards of line zipped off the reel. He tightened the drag and the fish headed back to the boat. He pumped and reeled, taking in the slack and maintaining enough force to make the fish work. His hands began to tire, and he wondered if he would have a blue belly the next day from the abuse his stomach was taking from the rod butt.

The mackerel made a second dash when he saw us and the boat, but this time he didn't run as far or as fast. My companion patiently held on and reeled. The mackerel turned on the surface. It was a smoker all right. The kingfish that liked the cigar was more than a yard long and well into the 20-pound range. We gaffed the fish as he bellied up after running underneath the boat and trying his best to foul around the outboard foot.

We looked over our catch. The nice kingfish had hit the cigar within seconds from the time the bait was in the water. Obviously smoker mackerel savor cigars, cigar minnows, that is.

Subsequently we caught several others and proved our point. Smokers like cigars and snakes like straws. At least that's a certainty off Masonboro Inlet at Wrightsville Beach in the fall.

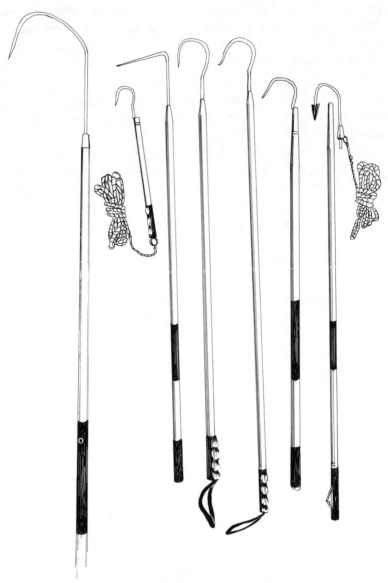

Gaffs come in all designs

GAFFS—FISH HOOKS ON HANDLES

Sport fishing could survive without the gaff. By any measurement it is not an instrument designed to preserve the fish populations of the seas and streams. But this fish hook on a handle is the coup de grace that has put many big fighting monsters over the gunnels which would otherwise have escaped just an arm's length from the boat. Many of those escapees would have died and rotted on the bottom after a gallant battle that wrestled their hearts into failure and death. This sharp hook is most often popped into the belly cavity of a fish too big to haul over the boat side with a monofilament line and too cumbersome to drag into a landing net.

Most sports species are netted, beached, or yanked over the gunwales with a strained, bent rod. But sheer weight or size is not the only reason for gaffing instead of the more conventional-type landings. Speckled trout (weakfish) in the estuaries are often easier gaffed than netted, and the toothy bluefish, and even striped bass can be kept at arm's length on a hook with a handle. The gaff often saves a fisherman from chewed-up fingers and bloody legs when cavorting fish cut through skin and flesh with sharp dorsal fins. Then, of course, there is the light tackle sportsman who must get his fish in the boat by some means other than the strength of his line, and gaffing is often appropriate when netting is impossible.

Many an old-timer has mourned the loss of what he considered a record of a species because he couldn't get the fish headed into the net. Perhaps he could have saved his trophy with the proper gaff. Gaffs are fish hooks greatly modified from those carried in the tacklebox. They come with short handles, long handles, with barbed hooks and plain. Some have detachable hooks with stout lines attached that give the angler assurance of saving his fish once he has set the gaff, even if his monofilament breaks. In this case the fish surges free to release the line from the pole, either by his pressure, or by the angler simply tripping a trigger that frees the hook and line from the pole.

While gaffs are made commercially in a variety of styles for various purposes, many are still homemade affairs in which fishermen use their own inventive genius to design a hook on a handle to exactly suit their individual purposes. One can custom-make his landing gear, "roll his own," if you will. Some homemade gaffs are called "hammers" and are nothing short of a club loaded with lead on a curved rod. Some gaffs are carried in belts with plastic point covers to protect the angler from gaffing himself. But most gaffs used by wading anglers are left lying on nearby shoreline where they can be easily reached when a giant of a species is struggling on the end of a line and you must have an implement to save him. A few fishermen throw caution to the wind and hang a gaff over their shoulder—expectantly and confidently.

Some gaffs are made for one-hand operation and can be efficiently used at long distances with a single hand. But longer handled gaffs usually require both hands and are pulled into the fish by a companion other than the angler struggling with the reel in his hands. These are most efficient when pulled straight into the fish and not used in a passing swipe like you might with a shorter, one-handed gaffing technique.

Bridge and pier fishermen have a totally different kind of "gaff" often used to hoist up larger fish 20 feet and more when line strength is questionable. They simply lower giant treble hooks on stout rope beyond the fish's gills, yank sharply, setting one or more of the hooks and then, hand over hand, they bring their prey to the railing and the cooler.

Gaffs used on boats are always a mixed bag of various styles. Some captains often carry a spare or two in case of a mishap, broken shaft or loss overboard when a big fish challenges the fisherman's prowess and wins. It's important to remember that a boat gaff's length is determined by the distance between the gunwale and the water, the freeboard.

A unique gaff with a sharp point at right angles to the shaft is known as a "pick gaff," It is somewhat like the lead hammer that surf casters use, but the pick has no head and is simply jammed into the fish when it heads for the boat. In that it has no hook, it will slip loose unless you are adroit at handling a squirming creature on a piece of sharp steel similar to an icepick on a broomstick. But most gaffs have U-shaped hooks with tapered points, some with barbs and some without.

The "gape," or hook size, of a gaff and diameter of the rod or shaft, is determined by the size of the quarry the angler seeks. The gape should be only wide enough to allow easiest penetration of the fish flesh and it is better to have a smaller gaff head than one too large.

The intriguing detachable-head gaff known as a "flying gaff" is what the big species are brought home with. The head is attached to the shaft and a rope releases from the shaft when a huge fish is harpooned with it. With the line secured, the fisherman has won this battle unless the gaff head comes loose. That's not always the case with fixed head and shafts where the fish often masters the man.

While gaffing of various species of fish has its place in the sun, sportsmen must keep in mind that generally it is a technique that should be abandoned when you have all the fish you need to eat, the large trophy you want to preserve, and putting another creature in the boat serves no purpose. Gaffing anywhere other than in the lips (as some fishermen drag up tarpon), is a fatal maneuver. There is no release to fight again once a gaff head has been jerked into the body of your catch. It is finished! It will thrill no other fisherman. Your grandchildren won't be able to feel minnows flouncing in their veins when that fish's ambition to be free tugs on their lines. There are times when you should use your net or simply cut your line and let your sportsmanship show.

Ancient stone age people carved crude gaffs out of tree limbs and bones of fish and mammals. Later as civilization advanced, gaffs were forged or beaten into sharp hooks for snaring fish from the streams of Africa, Asia and Europe. In every facet of life, sophisticated changes have evolved since those ancient men walked this earth. Gaffs changed with the times too, and today they are designed to make it easier, faster, and safer to put a big fish in the boat or on the beach.

Gaff history marches on along the scenic and prolific Carolinas coast.

Unique Triggerfish

The often despised triggerfish that swallows almost any bait that drops near him in the deep waters off the coasts of the Carolinas, is a delicious dinner meal if you know how to handle the ugly creature. Triggerfish hide is almost as tough and rough as that of the garfish that the American Indians used to cover their shields when they went to war. To get to the white, fine-grain meat that is like tenderloin on each side of the backbone, you need a sharp knife to puncture the skin and then start cutting until the blade stops on the rib cage. There is only about 30 percent of the triggerfish's gross weight that is usable for food and that is the two tenderloins along the back. The belly and rib meat is too difficult to separate from the bones to be practical as food.

Once you have cut the meat away from the backbone, jerk the tough skin off with a pair of pliers or some such instrument. You'll have two fillets that vary in size from four to six inches long and an inch deep and wide. It's a gourmet protein that you can cook a variety of ways.

If you like fried fish, these tenderloins can be dropped in deep fat and fried a golden brown after salting, peppering and rolling in cornmeal. In a few minutes they'll look like fried chicken nuggets and taste much better.

If you don't go for fried fish, then broil these white pieces of meat over charcoal or a gas flame after salting, peppering, and dripping lemon juice or butter on them as they slowly cook. They are delicious broiled.

You may also take these white fillets, cut them into nugget sizes, boil for two or three minutes, then take out and dip in butter or lemon juice and have a protein that tastes very much like lobster or scallops.

Triggerfish chowder cooked with the same ingredients you use in clam chowder is great for soup eaters. The fish has great flavor and cooks to pieces quickly.

Try triggerfish any of these ways and you'll be convinced this is not a worthless fish as some contend.

WACCAMAW BREAM AND BASS

Cradled in the low country swampland of Southeastern North Carolina, a mile off U.S. Highway 74 near Whiteville, is the largest natural lake between the Great Lakes and Florida. It bears the Indian name "Waccamaw" from a tribe that once lived off this land and water and is believed by many to have absorbed the settlers of the Lost Colony established by Sir Walter Raleigh four centuries ago. Today pristine water covers snow-white bottom sand and weaves its way around grassy shorelines decorated with ancient cypress trees, and it has some of the finest springtime bass and bream fishing you can find anywhere in the country.

This five-by-seven mile lake that averages only eight feet in depth, was created instantly in the distant past when a giant meteor crashed to earth wrapped in searing flames. It smashed this depression in the wetland woods in what is now Columbus County, North Carolina. The fire burned out and water filled the hole. It became the headwaters of the Waccamaw River that laces its meandering path into South Carolina and empties into the Intracoastal Waterway just south of Conway and Myrtle Beach. The 40-mile-long scenic river has a shoreline virtually untouched by man's development. For miles willows drape the banks and grasses wave in the currents and sloughs where bass and bream abound.

The water of the lake, but not the river, is not as pure now as it was when the Indians lived here, as homes now dot much of the lake periphery. But the fine gamefish have not been seriously disturbed. They thrive in the great aquatic plant habitat, much of which grows 100 yards and more out into the lake from the cypress line along the bank.

Spring of the year draws the bream to the grass where forage fish school and feed off the insect life. Largemouth bass are not far behind and both species can be caught with live bait or artificials. Fishing pressure has not hurt the bream and bass populations.

The best time of day is early morning or after sunset. Often you can be skunked throughout an afternoon and then suddenly have so much action that you don't realize that darkness has settled over the lake. It's not unusual to put a half-cooler full of panfish in the boat from a single house-size grass patch while landing a dozen bass from the same spot with the same tackle. Most fishermen release the bass, but the bream are saved for the dinner table.

A few years ago most of this grass patch fishing was by locals with cane poles, a single shot on a monofilament line, a small bobber on the surface and a No. 4 hook a few inches from the bottom with a wriggling native earthworm dangling from its midsection. Sometimes they let the worms squirm right on the bottom. Bluegills, shellcrackers (redear) and grass perch (punkinseed) sucked up the baits. Bass were just as hungry and a lot of fun was found here when some real lunkers struggled on the line, doubling the limber poles and thrashing through the thick sawgrass.

Sophistication of the grass bed fish has taken over in the last decade. Plastic worms flutter to the bottom in holes in the grass as flypin with 7 1/2 foot rods, heavy test monofilament line, and strong rods are used by locals and tourists to haul the bass over the gunnels. There is still some cane pole fishing with real live worms. Some bass are still caught that way, but live baits with modern tackle are now more productive.

There is also some good fishing with crankbaits and spinners on the fringe of the grass. This works in the middle of the day when worm flippin' isn't very good. If the angler is ready to adjust and diversify, he can catch bass here all day long. He may land lunkers weighing five or six pounds or more but the bulk of the bass catch in Waccamaw is in the two- to three-pound range. They are fine eating size bass for those who like these fillets in the skillet and on the table. While most bassers here release their catch, as conservation is a much practiced habit at Waccamaw, the yearling bass from the gin-clear water provide a tasty protein. And there's nothing wrong with eating a few bass.

Bream, as all the flat panfish here are called by Southerners, today are caught on crickets, earthworms, maggots, wasp nest larvae, sapheads and catalpa worms by pole fishermen. The purists catch them on small Mepps Spinners, Tiny Traps, Mini-Jigs and Hal-Flies retrieved or vertically jigged around and in the covers. Spinning tackle is the usual equipment, light or ultralight.

There's one season when every fisherman goes topwater. Late in May or early June, millions of mayflies fall from the trees and flutter on the surface. Every hungry bass or bream in the territory rushes to the tree line. The water often boils over myriad acres as many species gorge themselves with mayflies. These insects stick to the leaves until the dew begins to dry and the wind picks up. Then they lose their grip on the leaves and tumble into the water. It's dinner-on-the-ground time as a unique feeding frenzy sweeps across the lake.

Boat fishermen catch bream and bass with long lines on poles with small popping minnow bugs or with similar topwater lures or fly lines or ultralight spinning tackle. Few are fly rodders from boats.

Some fishermen don waders. The water is shallow for several hundred yards and fly rodders have a heyday casting and moving along through cascading mayflies that are singing their swan songs. The bonanza of mayflies may last only a few days, but occasionally continues for about two weeks. The great fishing lasts as long as the mayflies do.

While it is a great moment for topwater fishing, bassers often surprise themselves by hauling in nice catches on crankbaits and plastic worms, even crawfish and dummy frogs. The Burke Snakebait and Swimmer Worm retrieved near the surface around the mayflies have been deadly by those who have tried it in these Waccamaw waters.

A swamp tributary on the north side of Lake Waccamaw is Big Creek. It winds into a desolate swamp. Bass love to linger in the mouth of this clear creek. Almost any popular crankbait or worms will catch fish in the creek mouth where numerous grass patches polka-dot the surface. Live bait bassers do well when anchored in this six- or seven-foot water with big shiners flitting under corks on the fringes of the grass. Some hooked bass make a dive for the grass after attacking a shiner, but with gusto hook-setting and experience, most bass, even big hawgs, can be hauled out of aquatic growth and to the boat. A tight line, raised rod tip, proper drag set and patience help the fisherman outlast the largemouths.

There's a low four-foot-high dome in the south end of the lake that keeps the water level fairly constant in this natural resource. On high water, bass often are attracted to the swift current that sweeps forage food past a myriad of grass patches. Topwater bass plugs cast into the current and retrieved sometimes bring fantastic action. This is not an every day pattern, but it can be great just after a spring or summer freshet that dumps more water into the lake than it can handle.

For anglers interested in other species, yellow perch are caught here the year 'round, many in the 1 1/4-pound class. Black crappie are plentiful in the open water. The aggressive white perch that come a-runnin' to any water splashing noise strike minnows and lures in every warm month. There are also some carp and pickerel.

There are good, hard-surfaced launching ramps on both the north and south sides of the lake. Tackle and bait are available at the ramps as are rental boats and motors. Good restaurants are located on the highway a mile from the north shore of the lake. Lodging can be found there and in Whiteville, ten miles to the west on Highway 74.

Lake Waccamaw is a place of great beauty and if it is true that bass like pretty places, then surely they will continue to thrive in this giant hole in the ground made by a stone that fell from the heavens and buried itself in the swamp.

CAROLINA SWAMP PONDS

Slow dark water flows quietly through much of the sandy swampland of the eastern Carolinas on its way to rivers, estuaries and bays along the Atlantic coast. It passes through private lands in the dense rain forests, some areas stripped for lumber in the years past, others still covered with standing cypress, gum, ash and other low country trees that can live with water around their feet without succumbing to the wetness. It's these runs through the swamps of creeks, branches, canals and natural ditches that have created a relatively new bass bonanza all along the coastal Carolina lowlands. Farmers and beavers have dammed the flows to impound acres of fresh water literally covered with logs, stumps, brush and standing timber. While they are called "ponds" by many, they are not farm ponds in the usual concept of the word. They are not pushed-up cattle watering holes or irrigation impoundments. These are fish ponds, made for recreational fishing and for providing food, and the largemouth bass population in these manmade (aided by beavers in many places) lakes have exploded in numbers in the last decade.

Some of these impounded swamp waters cover hundreds of woodland acres, but many are only 20-50 acres. The habitat is so ideal with shade and food that the bass thrive and fishermen thrill to the challenge of landing trophy size lunkers from cover so dense that some anglers fear to tread it. Bream, crappie and warmouth perch abound in the ponds, too. Often the bushes harbor giant wasps anxious to protect their paper houses and snakes thrive in the jungle-like habitat. It most certainly is not the type of water where you want to risk an antique lure. The lures are often planted on the bottom, anchored forever on stumps, irretrievable in the deeper water of the swampland lakes, where snakes and 'gators make it uninviting to dive for a lure even if it did cost five dollars.

Where the contour of the land has not been attacked by man, most of these impoundments are no more than four or five feet deep and logs and brush literally cover the bottom when builders economized by not clearing the land, just backing up the water. There are a few deeper holes. This gives shade to bass and enhances the cover where forage fish hang out. Deep water up to 15-20 feet is often found a few yards away and always near the dams that give the bass easy access from ideal bedding bottom around logs in the shallows nearby to more comfort in the cooler, deep holes where they can suspend and wait for early and late meals to come within striking distance. Most of the natural baits, bluegills, warmouths, shiners, gambusia and crawfish, are found in the shallows and the supply is unlimited as the same ideal habitat for bass reproduction applies to the food fish populations. It's always the survival of the fittest in the shallows of these swamp lakes where bass love to meander along gulping down morsels of live critters.

Some of these swampland ponds are so private that only the owners, families and friends fish them. Others are open to the public for an annual fee, usually a modest $100.00 or so. Still others have daily charges of $2.00 or thereabouts, and some are leased to individuals and small clubs that pay a yearly sum that entitles members and guests to use the facilities at their own discretion.

Near the Columbus-Brunswick county line two such swamp lakes owned by Hugh Williamson, a gentleman farmer of the rural section known as "Mollie," were built a couple of decades ago. With connecting short canals, three of the lakes total 66 acres and there's a stickup of some kind in every five square feet of water. Small one- and two-man plywood bateaux are about the only kind of boats that can make it through these lakes and not stay hung up on snags that lurk just beneath the surface. It's tough to rock a big, flat-bottomed boat off one of these springy obstacles.

The late A. E. (Ed) Prince, of Tabor City, a long-time hunting companion and friend of Williamson, leased these two lakes for several years. He sub-let the rights to fish in the ponds to about a dozen friends. His record of bassing success in these

swampy waters is astounding and is reason enough for other land owners along low country streams to consider building such recreational facilities that give the angler an opportunity to escape the crowded public waters where you almost have to buy a ticket to find a space to anchor your boat during some seasons. Prince not only caught yearlings, he landed some real trophies, too, as do others who share the lakes with fishing privileges.

His son, Bernon, not a devout bass angler by any means, landed a 9-pound, 8-ounce largemouth in the lake on one of his few afternoons there. A local resident fishing from the bank of the dam with a live shiner on a line tied to a14-foot cane pole and a snap-on cork as big as your fist, dragged a 12-pound, 4-ounce bass ashore. Prince and his companions regularly put big fish from 5-pounds to 8-pounds in the boat.

Prince was particularly proud of a five-fish catch he made one spring. Fishing a few hours before dark each afternoon of a week in June, he landed and documented on the scales five bass that weighed 36-pounds, 6-ounces. That's a size that would win almost any bass tournament—an average of over 7-pounds.

Most fish in these swamp lakes are caught on weedless artificials, like the plastic worm, Sputterfuss or spinner bait with the hook protected. Topwater chuggers are great too. Even with these hooks you lose a lot of strikes, but some fish are worked around the logs to open water and hauled over the gunnels of the tiny boats that are used in these lakes. Topwater Devlhorse lures plopped into open holes and twitched a few times produce strikes and fish from spring to fall.

Most of the boat fishing in these tree-studded ponds is from unique little crafts that some people call "floating coffins." Usually no more than eight or nine feet long with one or two inches of freeboard, you fish with caution, care and without too much fidgeting about. It doesn't take much movement to rock the boat enough to dip water and put the fisherman in the drink. Most of these are one-man boats, but some carry two people. You feel like you are fishing in a rocking chair when casting from these tiny crafts. Fortunately, not much of the water where the heavy cover lies is deep enough to be over the head of a boater. Those who take an unscheduled swim in these ponds (few reports have been heard of drownings), usually just stand up on the bottom, turn the boat over enough to pour the water out, then pull it by hand a few steps to the hill where they board again and go on with their casting. The wet clothes just cool you off on a hot summer day in the swamps. A big bass on the line presents a challenge to land her without capsizing the boat.

Most of these lakes are too small for outboard motors. Fishermen usually use a small trolling motor custom-fitted on the stern with some handmade foot pedals and ropes secured in the bow where the angler controls the speed and direction with his feet, leaving the hands free to cast and lift bass over the gunnels. Outboards would be digging into logs so regularly that they would be of little service. The distance from ramp to fishing hole isn't enough to require any power boating. Many old timers showing disdain even for trolling motors, still move their tiny boats along with "one-handed paddles." These are hewn out of cedar or cypress and usually are about two-and-a-half feet long and light. The astute paddler can put his boat where he wants it and hold it there with one hand while fishing with the other. These ponds seldom have any current and tall trees and dense growth along shorelines protect the fishermen from most winds that would make movement difficult in open water. There are many accurate casters in this society of swampland bassers who can hit a pork and bean can with a lure regularly at 40 to 50 feet.

If you are a true outdoorsman who doesn't have to bring home a stringer full to enjoy an outing, you will be impressed with the swamp ponds of the Carolinas. Beavers are plentiful and they are the architects of their own dams and burrows in many of the impoundments. You often can see them at work early and late as you quietly move along through their domains. It makes you feel like Daniel Boone. Muskrats are likewise at home in these waters and flip their flat tails like rudders as they speed to holes in the dams when boats approach, leaving a quiet wake behind. There are even a few bobcats that stalk their prey at nightfall and flit in and out of the bush. Early in the mornings and at dusk the call of the bobwhite quail is crisp and distinct. Osprey nest nearby and shriek a warning as intruders appear.

Wood ducks and mallards swoop past with wing beats thrilling the observer so that he feels like minnows are flouncing in his veins. Whitetail deer are numerous in the surrounding woodlands and one often slips out of the bushes to drink when the quietness makes him think he has this territory to himself. The swampland lakes are close to nature and indeed with just a little help from man, they are God's artistry, nature's masterpieces. You cannot help but feel close to the land when you ease out on one of these desolate swamp ponds.

They provide fun and food. Prince and his friends looked forward to almost weekly cookouts when they got together in a 100-year-old refurbished home on the banks of a swamp lake. The walls are filled with mounted fish, ducks, deer heads, and even a raccoon and a bobcat. These outdoorsmen cook their fish and feast on them along with the farm-fresh tomatoes, potatoes, cucumbers, slaw and corn dodgers.

EELS BEGIN AS TINY ELVERS

All American eels are spawned in the 1,500-foot-deep Sargasso Sea in the Bermuda Triangle. They surface and float along the U.S. shoreline and into the Carolinas coastal waters on the wind and tide. Many drift up coastal rivers and creek inlets and live for years in these waters where they may grow to as large as 13 pounds. One of this size was unearthed by a dredge operator in Eastern North Carolina near Harker's Island.

Known as elvers when they are infant eels, it takes from 3,500 to 5,000 to make a pound. Elvers have been sold to China and Japan for $464 per pound. The elvers are grown out to eating size and are considered delicacies in the Orient.

Life expectancy of an eel is unknown, but one that had been in captivity in Sweden for more than 30 years died during the German occupation of World War II. The Germans let the eel starve.

CATFISHING THE CAROLINA LOWLANDS

The cork above a gob of worms squirming on a hook on the muddy bottom of the Cape Fear River sank slowly. Six inches below the surface it stopped. There was no movement and I wondered if a blue crab had decided to partake of my enticing bait. It was a warm spring morning when a rush of muddy water was pouring in from the swampland canals following a near cloudburst the night before. I flicked the end of the rod, only half expecting any resistance, but the tip bent, the line tightened and in that instant I knew there was no ghost taking my bait. I had a fish and he was running like the devil was chasing him.

It didn't last long. The fish stayed down, but he soon tired and I reeled in a 30-pound flathead catfish. A tasty meal went into the cooler.

All over the Carolinas, many species of catfish await the sport and commercial fishermen who use everything from traps, rods and reels to cane poles and bows and arrows. These omnivorous feeders will eat anything, spoiled or unspoiled, dead or alive, and that gives sportsmen and meat hunters plenty of leeway when it comes to putting a mess of these whiskered critters on the dinner table. They do not have to be giants of the species like the blue catfish and flatheads to be a thrill to catch and gourmet fare on the table. Even the kittens, as some natives call the smaller catfish, make real gourmet eating. Indeed, those tiny critters the size of jumbo shrimp, are a dining delight when fried in deep fat. Really something special! You only have to know how to eat the meat right off the flexible backbone and ribs to know you have a protein that is truly finger-licking good. The small ones are best cooked whole, not filleted.

Virtually unprotected by law at any level, catfish have been netted, trapped, gigged, trotlined and seined by commercial and recreational fishermen for decades. They are shipped to seafood markets everywhere. Public waters have teemed with catfish of various kinds for generations and no particular water has had any monopoly with lakes, creeks, rivers and even man-made ponds readily acceptable habitat for Carolina catfish. While some lakes have had enough commercial pressure to curtail the harvest for brief periods, the catfish always bounce back and become plentiful again, as a single big mama cat may produce as many as 50,000 fry in a single season. They are so prolific that they often infest lakes where they are not welcome and haven't been stocked by any agency. They just seem to miraculously appear and thrive.

Always caught on purpose by some sports fishermen, catfish often are pulled from the water on hook and line by accident. Often an unwanted variety, they must be loosed from the hook carefully to avoid the painful sting of the needle-sharp spines on either side of their slick heads. They are equally disliked by many sports fishermen who frown on having to skin rather than scale the critters before putting them in the skillet, even if the meat is tasty.

But there is a growing fraternity of catfish fishermen who are discovering the simplicity of catching these cats in a myriad of manners, none that is costly or sophisticated, relative to other freshwater angling. It's a way of providing protein that is tasty without damaging an already over-spent family food budget. They can often be caught closer to home, saving that high-priced gasoline, and the bait that attracts them is free—often the scraps you would ordinarily toss in the garbage. It is fast becoming the practical fish to catch, even though unfashionable in the minds of many bass and other game fish anglers, who show only disdain for followers of the lowly catfish. It once was considered a trash fish, but no more.

Whether you are fishing a low country farm pond, lake or river, you'll catch more cats immediately following a freshet when the water is rising rapidly. It even seems to help if the water is muddy from the onrushing runoff that brings in worms and insects from the surrounding soil and vegetation. The food wash-in stimulates the catfish to feed and it behooves the fisherman to get there as soon as the water starts rising or the foraging feeders will get their fill quickly and not be interested in your hooked bait. But as long as the water is rising and the channel cats haven't satisfied their appetites, you can keep right on catching them.

The most ideal place to cast bait in this freshet situation is about where the onrushing fresh water slows down in the existing stream. It's there that the drowning insects are deposited, sinking to the bottom, and the whiskered fish lie in wait. This type of catfish angling is particularly successful after a long drought when the insects have been scarce on the water.

Often when the water is rising, you can detect the movement of catfish in the grass and weeds along the shoreline. This is like shooting ducks in a barrel and the cats will eat anything you drop in front of them.

In fishing for these catfish in this situation, there is no better bait than grasshoppers, but if you have a really hot spot, you probably can't get enough of those insects to keep fishing long. Earthworms are the classic bait for these fish any time. But you will probably do better with some kind of blood bait. Skinned beef melt or spleen is a good blood bait as is any type of animal meat or organs.

If you are fishing for channel catfish at a time other than the freshet, you'll do better with the liver, heart or kidneys of a wild rabbit or squirrel. Entrails from quail, doves, pheasants, and ducks are also good blood baits for catfishing. The wildlife organs are better than domesticated species generally, because the tame ones are bled out thoroughly and quickly, leaving almost no blood. Wild animals are almost always left longer with the blood in them and it settles in the internal organs.

You can freeze these wild animal parts in bait-sized pieces. Then when you are ready to fish for cats, you thaw them out and dangle them in the honey hole where you believe the critters hang out. As the blood dissolves in the water, the catfish pick up the scent and they will rush to strike. These blood baits are great for fast-running water, particularly just above obstructions. Catfish often congregate in brushpiles near a rapid flow of a stream and you may catch a sack full with blood baits allowed to drift toward them.

When you are fishing a blood bait, don't be too anxious to move it. Often it takes a little time for the scent to flow some distance to attract the fish. But they'll come a-runnin' when they get a whiff of it. Also, don't move on when you have caught one. There will always be more than one that has smelled and moved toward the scent.

One fish biologist has refined this scent fishing bait to a point that, for some, the end result can't be justified, even when the catch is successful. He mixes equal parts of limburger cheese and beef brains and lets the concoction season in the sun for several days. He then dips a piece of sponge in this gooey mess and puts small pieces of the sponge on his hook. It naturally sends out a strong scent to the catfish, and he says they bite it.

If you are fishing fairly swift moving water, you can catch cats by drifting dead and smelly minnows with little or no lead over logs and obstructions on the bottom. If there are pools or eddies, the floating bait will often be gulped down every time it slows down in the stream and sinks in the deeper places. If there is an eddy that is covered with trash, you often can work a hole in it, drop the bait in the hole and sit right there and catch cats constantly.

If you are using live bait, catfish will eat those too. The best technique with minnows is to use a bobber and hold the swimmer just above the submerged grass or moss. The cats will rise from the cover to take the struggling bait.

Catfish are nocturnal and do much of their foraging at night, but they won't turn down a morsel of food if it confronts them in the daylight. You can put them in the boat easier at night, if you prefer that kind of fishing. They prowl more looking for food after dark. From 9:00 P.M. until midnight is the best time.

There are some wading catfishermen who have good success, particularly in creeks and rivers where there is a ring of grass or lily pads near the shoreline. You can wade out near enough to the open water to cast a minnow, crayfish, a gob of worms, or other good catfish bait in the edge of the aquatic growth. You can use a bobber if you like with a little weight, or no bobber at all. You need some slack line regardless of which way you fish the grass. When the fish strikes, let him take some line. He will usually strike and run. If the line is tight, he may turn it loose.

A number 2/0 gold hook, like many people use for crappie while stump-jumping, is an ideal catfish hook. They are sharp, light and hang in the rough catfish mouths easily. Few channel cats will straighten out a hook, although it is weak in comparison to others. Many cats even in the 12- to 15-pound class, have been boated with these hooks, but most native species aren't going to challenge the hook's strength. You'll catch most of your catfish in the 1- to 3-pound size. In the Cape Fear and at Santee-Cooper they grow to giant size.

Once your fish has had time to take up the slack, set the hook hard. You are not likely to jerk it out of his mouth. After setting the hook, if you are in a lot of grass, weeds, or brush, it is wise to actually give the catfish a little slack. He will head for the open water and untangle your line from the rough habitat where you hooked. him.

Some catfishermen go after this species only when they have been run off their favorite lakes by water skiers and crowds of other sports anglers who are out after bass, bluegills, crappies or perch. Catfishing is a change of pace that often is a welcome reprieve. The best natural catfishing holes aren't generally crowded in the Carolinas, not even on holidays and weekends.

The more you learn about this fish, the better your catch success, true of any species. When you learn their habits and life-style, along with a little biology, you'll find the action is fast. They don't commit suicide to get in the boat, but landing them is easier, simpler and usually more certain than with many other kinds of fish.

It surprises many veteran fishermen to know that the catfish has better sound perception than other freshwater fish. They are "cypriniformes," that is having their air bladders attached to the inner ear through the Weberian apparatus, a unique set of bones. The bones transfer noise to the inner ear from the bladder, and amplify the sound. Their sound discrimination is far ahead of most fish species, even the largemouth bass and other cautious fish.

The catfish has several strange behavior patterns not thoroughly understood, even by the most astute biologists. For instance, while they inhabit much of the same water as the carp, they do not feed actively at the same time the carp forage. Biologists call this situation one of timing and territory. While several species may live side by side, using the same habitat to feed and live, they are active in the area at different times. This keeps the species from bothering each other in the process of feeding. For the catfisherman, it might be a tip-off that he can't expect much action if the carp are tearing up the water. There is an exception to this in the spring, when both are scouting for spawning space, but after that, each species has its moment and the other knows to stay out of the way.

These two species often share habitat and carp fishermen, if they stay at their post over several hours, will almost always catch some of both. They fish right into each species' time for action. In that case you most often are fishing with a bait that is delectable to both, as long as it isn't alive. Carp almost never eat anything that swims. The catfish eats both dead and live baits.

A hooked catfish, whether six inches long or a 50-pound blue or flathead, has strength. They never jump, but hang to the bottom like an American eel and you must use brute strength to make them surface. They make no line-singing runs like bluegills and largemouths, but there is pure thrill in landing cats of respectable size. It's a change of pace and a tasty meal. It's also a chance to go home with something in the cooler and anything is better than being skunked.

BULLHEAD CATFISH COUNTRY

A virtual wilderness maze of swampy rivers lace through the cypress, willows and gums a few miles off the Atlantic Coast in the South Carolina Low Country and the labyrinth eventually converges just above Georgetown and pours into Winyah Bay. The black waters of the smaller rivers merge with the clay-colored Great Pee Dee and there are miles of creeks, branches and runs where the once-despised bullhead catfish thrive and today provide real gourmet dining for those fishermen with the expertise to ferret them out of deep holes and the energy and determination to skin and clean them for the skillet.

Bill O'Quinn, of Loris, South Carolina is one of the frequent anglers in these wilderness rivers who brings home good catches of catfish when it is more difficult to fill a stringer with bluegills, crappies, redbreasts and largemouth bass that also abound in these little-fished waters. Still not considered a gamefish by wildlife departments, and little protected in the Carolinas, these prolific breeders continue to dominate many of the deep holes in the Waccamaw, Little Pee Dee, Lumber, Sampit, Black and the Great Pee Dee rivers as well as in other tidal waters of the Intracoastal Waterway that parallels the Palmetto State shoreline from Little River on the northern border until it reaches the estuary at Georgetown.

These rivers have a tide as regular as the ocean, but it is delayed as much as seven and eight hours many miles upstream from the inlets at Little River and Georgetown and the usual tide tables available at marinas and tackle shops are of little value. You must keep the time yourself to establish high and low tides that are extremely important to catfish catch success in these dark brackish waters, some completely fresh, but often with a touch of brine a dozen miles upstream.

"Generally, you cannot expect to catch many catfish or anything else when the tide is high and the swamps flooded. The best time to fish is when the tide is ebbing and at least one-third out. But you can also catch fish as it starts rising and before it floods," O'Quinn says.

"I fish the deep holes in these rivers and time of year seems to have little effect. One of the advantages of fishing for cats, in addition to the fact that they are good eating, is that you do not have to wait for spring or summer or spawning season. They school up in the deep holes, especially where there are some logs or brush that stays put on the bottom and you can catch them with just about any kind of bait, dead or alive.

"I really prefer a wad of earthworms fished right on the bottom, but sometimes when I'm fishing for crappies in the same deep holes in the cold weather, I'll catch nothing but bullhead catfish with my live minnows. Catfish are not usually large in these waters I fish. Most of the time they are just good eating size and that means from about a half pound to a pound and a quarter. I think these little fellows are better for the frying pan than bigger ones, but I do hang on to some big 'uns. Even the little cats give you a pretty good pull when you hang them in 15 feet of water in the heavy cover. You have to handle them just right to keep them from snagging and coming unbuttoned.

"I especially like to fish the dark water downstream from Conway on the Waccamaw River. I put my boat in at the landing on 501 By-pass and go downstream about five miles. There's a log across a hole in a deep cove and there's a really giant catfish in the hole. Three times I have hung this monster, only to lose him when he broke my 12-pound test monofilament line. I just let my worms or some kind of stink baits flutter to the bottom, fishing across the log. This big cat sucks it in and takes off. I haven't seen him yet, but I'm sure it is a big catfish.

"These streams do not have the exotic giant flatheads and Arkansas blue cats that have been stocked in the Santee-Cooper. The catfish I catch are natives, but that big 'un that keeps getting away is sure no little fish. I know it is a giant," O'Quinn says about the one that got away.

While Bill usually fishes with earthworms or minnows for the catfish, he knows that there are many other good baits, including beef liver, stale chicken parts, grasshoppers, crickets, chunks of almost any kind of smelly fish, white soap, dough bait, cut shrimp from the ocean, or the tiny grass shrimp from the fresh waters that can be strung on a hook to make a tasty morsel. Even stinky cheese makes a good catfish bait. In a pinch you can cut your live shiners used for bass fishing into small portions and entice catfish to bite.

"The Big Pee Dee is murky, but you can catch fish in that colored water. I do most of my fishing on that largest of these streams up some creeks. You only have to go a few hundred yards from the main flow to get in dark water like the rest of the rivers here. That murky water in the Pee Dee comes from the erosion way up in the Piedmont section of the Carolinas. The river gets a lot of mud in it up there and some stays in the water right on into Georgetown. When I go up these creeks, I try to find a deep spot where the water is circling a little and where there is bottom cover. Insects and other types of catfish food float into these holes and the fish congregate here to feed. Sometimes if there is much movement, you have to put several good-size shot on the line to keep the bait on the bottom. That doesn't stop the catfish from biting like it does bream and crappies. They pick it up and gulp it down regardless of how much weight you have on the line. To stay in these honey holes, it's better to tie your boat to an overhanging limb, but you can anchor in most places and hold.

"I like to use a steel No. 4 Eagle Claw hook on catfish. It seems to hold better than some other sizes and it isn't as hard to get out of their mouths while you try to avoid the painful sting from the spines on both sides of their heads. I carry a pair of pliers to snap off those spines as soon as I get the fish in the boat and take the hook out with the pliers. Catfish have no teeth and if you get those horns off, there isn't anything left to hurt you.

"When I fish the big Pee Dee, I launch my boat at the Yauhanah Bridge on Highway 701, just north of Georgetown. I run downstream usually from there a few miles to find the deep catfish holes. I look for those creeks that have the dark water. If there has been a lot of rain recently and water is pouring in from ditches or little branches, the mouth of those places is great for catfish. They seem to lie in the swirls and eat everything that floats by," O'Quinn says.

There are some fine cat fishing holes in the other rivers of the area, some with intriguing names, and O'Quinn fishes all of them at one time or another. He likes the water around Parker's Landing on the Little Pee Dee. When he fishes there he takes Highway 378 out of Conway toward Lake City and crosses the water on the Teddy Bear Ferry. He then has to ease down an old dirt road to get to Parker's where he catches a lot of fish.

"There are some really big catfish down the Waccamaw around Peachtree Landing near Socastee just off Highway 544. Then on down the river near the Waterway there is an area called 'Enterprise' that has some good cat fishing and some deep holes. In the waterway around the section is Bucksport, just off Highway 701 South from Conway where you can get gas, tackle and food. It has some really deep water. Yachts and barges pass through here and catfish hole up in deep spots. You have to be careful of the barge wakes if you are in a small boat, but find a quite deep hole and you can pull in some catfish.

"I guess because there is an old chimney still standing on the shoreline, dating back to slave days, there's a Waccamaw River section known as 'Old Chimney.' It's fished more than some of the other more desolate areas, but it still produces and has good catfish holes. It's between Yauhanah Bridge and Conway and there are some good places on the Waccamaw at Bull Island and Sandy Island. There is not much development along these scenic wilderness shorelines and fishing is as good here as anywhere in South Carolina," says O'Quinn. "It's not as publicized, but those of us who grew up here know it still offers great fishing.

"There are some grown 'uns in the Waccamaw, Little Pee Dee and the Big Pee Dee. While these catfish are not giants like those at Santee or in the Mississippi River, they are sure bragging size for this part of the country," says this veteran cat fishing native who spends just about every vacation, Saturday and holiday fishing these swampland rivers.

POOR MAN'S FLY FISHING

A wide-brimmed, weather-beaten old straw hat shaded the eyes of a swarthy preoccupied fisherman riding alone in the bow of a homemade plywood bateau that quietly drifted with the current around a bend in the desolate, scenic Waccamaw River that winds its way through the Green Swamp in Southeastern North Carolina and on into South Carolina. It crosses the border into the sister state and on to its destination in Winyah Bay at Georgetown, South Carolina. The serious angler hardly noticed us as we slowed the outboard, and eased upstream past his wake in our sophisticated bass boat. We were scouting these black water, low country swampland flats for largemouths that often live to ripe old ages without having had the opportunity to reject the best laid lures of modern man. It truly is a picturesque Southern river with cypress-clad shorelines and dangling Spanish moss that make every turn in the narrow stream another picture postcard that you could write home about. We were aware of this uniqueness, but the presence of this old native stoically situated in his boat with a limber cane pole and unusually long line got our attention quickly when we saw wild splashing on the surface beneath a willow bush, heard athe envied noise of a fish in distress, and then the finale when the angler lipped a 2- or 3-pound bass. He quickly lifted it over the side and into his livebox built into the center of his tiny boat right behind where he sat on a six-inch pine board that was his bow seat.

This drama transpired in a matter of moments as we had simply intended to ease past this old-timer on our way to alleged greener pastures a few miles north where some of the natives who live off the water at the village of Crusoe Island find bream and crappie the year around. Perhaps there was a lesson to learn here, and from a distance we watched, holding on to an overhanging myrtle bush as the native angler's boat floated on toward the next oxbow in the Waccamaw.

With expertise obviously gained from years of experience on these river flats with overhead, surface and underwater obstacles arrayed as far as you could see, this veteran knew what he was doing, and his humble innovation from the normal fly fishing technique was the way to put fish in the boat. This was apparent as he put another crappie and two fine copperhead bream in the boat before he floated out of sight 200 yards downstream. We just observed with mouths agape. We knew we must learn more about this fisherman's method that was obviously successful, yet without outboard, trolling motor, rod, reel, net or anything electronic. He was really back to the basics with a two-foot, one-handed paddle keeping him 30 feet from the bank and straight in the slow-moving water.

I turned loose of the limb that was holding us in place, cranked the motor and with more than the normal courtesy, we pulled near the old fisherman, passed along a friendly "Hello" and attracted his attention.

"Sir, can we talk with you a minute?" I asked politely.

He glanced up, pulled the paddle a couple of times through the water, put his pole down in the boat, and grasped a limb from a sweet gum tree top that was half-submerged on the west bank.

"Whatcha want to talk about?" he asked in an almost hostile tone, or at least it seemed so.

I introduced myself and my companion. "We have been impressed with how you are catching fish, and just wanted to see if you would share your experience and know-how with us."

"Oh, I don't know all that much about fishing. I just live up the swamp apiece. Born there. Fished and hunted this old Waccamaw all my life. I farm a little patch or two, but I makes a living fishing and hunting. Mind you, I don't do nothing against the law. I do sell some catfish, but these other fish I eat just about every day of the year. I do some whittling of dough trays, and once in a while I chop out another boat from a big cypress log. They's always a market for those log boats. My name's Dodo

Clewis. Everybody knows me around here," he said, and there was an unspoken hint that perhaps sometime in the past he had had run-ins with game wardens.

"We know something about fly fishing, and we catch our share of bass with that system and with rods and reels, but you seem to have unlocked a secret here with your cane pole. You are using it like a fly rig but without a reel. Can we take a look?" I asked.

"Ain't nothin' to it. I just got some of this old plastic line and tied it onto a 14-foot pole. I use a white bug for bait. You can see that this river is narrow here, no more than 40 or 50 feet in places, and if you tried to use one of them fly rods like I see on TV, you'd stay hung up half the time. With this little old boat, I kind of slip up on the fish, and I can flip that bug under the bushes where the fish are laying out. On cloudy days and early in the morning, you can catch a mess of crappie and bream just about every time," he revealed.

That was it. With an 8-pound test monofilament line about four feet longer than the pole, this veteran could hit a pork and bean can at 30 feet under the overhanging shoreline bushes. He was amazingly accurate, and convinced that unless you can "put the bug in about six inches of the bank" you won't catch any fish. He emphasized that just about every fish he caught struck the bug just a hand's width from the swampland shore in the darkest shade he could find.

He had a preference for colors. White was number one, but he liked that "light green" (chartreuse) bug too. He was using a medium size popping bug with red eyes, and black hair sprouting out from the No. 4 Eagle Claw hook in that cork body. Four white rubber legs about an inch long protruded from around the bug's eyes. His technique was much like that we had experienced many times with more conventional fly gear. He put the bug in his honey hole, let it float motionless for half a minute or more. Then he flicked it a time or two with a twitch of the cane pole tip. If nothing happened, he snatched it out of the cover, let it buggy whip out in the open and back it went within seconds to another likely-looking fish hideout under the bushes. His speed and accuracy were uncanny, made possible by years of trial and error, and no doubt many cusswords vibrated through this swamp from snarled lines on both sides of the river before he became the expert that he is today.

"Sometimes there's a spot under the bushes that's hard to get to with flipping the bug across the bow like I usually do. But it may be just the place where a big old copperhead or slab crappie might be looking for something to eat. I take the bug in my fingers, make a bow out of the pole, aim it right for the spot and let it go. Most times I get it where I want's it, and I get some big 'uns out," Clewis said, demonstrating his technique of sling-shotting the morsel into tiny openings along the bank where no normal fly fishing expert would dare to tread.

"Do you ever use any other kind of bait for these fish with that fly-fishing system?" I asked Dodo.

"Yeah, sometimes I use a spinner, a gold 'un. If the fish just ain't going after my bug on top, I knows they are there somewhere. I put on a shiner and maybe a cricket or worm, but sometimes nothing but the spinner. I flip it in the same holes as I do the bug, and I catch some good bream and goggle-eye (black crappie). I have some baits that look like a caterpillar worm on a gold hook, and it floats a spell, and then sinks kind of slow. It'll catch some bass and bream too on this old river," he said, and it was apparent that his old river rat was getting more talkative and sharing all his secrets.

"Is there any time of the year that this kind of fishing is better for you?" I asked.

"Yep, it's better in the summer and fall. You can catch some when the frosts quit in the spring, and a few crappie will strike even in the coldest days in the winter, but most of the fish hide under the bushes when the sun's bearing down. Then in the fall when the insects are plentiful and topple off the bushes, the bream bite real good. I think the fish know they can get something to eat when these insects get cold and fall off the leaves. They just hang around in the morning 'til the sun comes up and the skeeters and bugs start losing their grip on the bushes. Then I flip my little old bait right where the skeeters fall, and the fish are ready to swallow it," Dodo said.

"Until a few years ago I never saw one of these bugs that I

bought at the hardware store in Tabor City. I just dug me a can of worms or caught some grasshoppers and crickets. Bream will still bite them too, but it's easier to get these bugs. They don't cost but about a dollar, and I can use them a day or two if some old mudfish or jack don't come along and take everything with him," Clewis acknowledged.

"Did you ever fish this way at any other place?" I questioned this expert again.

Yeah, I fish Lake Waccamaw sometimes. That's the headwaters of this river. The river is hard to get to up the swamp because of the trees that are all over the place and block the water. But you can put in at the lake apiece off the highway that goes from Whiteville to Wilmington (Highway 74). They's some good ramps up there, and fishing is good around the cypress knees all around the lake and the grass patches in the water at the river mouth are full of crappie and grass perch (punkinseed). I use this same old pole and same baits. I just pop it along the grass line or around the cypress stumps and stuff where it's not so light. The water's clear in Waccamaw, and you got to be quiet, and put the bait on the other side of the tree or somewhere that the fish don't spook. It's good to have a little boat like this. It's hard to get in some of the close spots with a big boat like you fellows have, but you can fish the grass lines, and you can use those fly rods and reels there without getting hung up much like you would in the river," Dodo shares some of his know-how.

He was right on just about every count from the good months of the year, to the dark spots in the cover, to the fishing in Lake Waccamaw. We learned that on subsequent adventures when part of the time we adapted to Dodo's unsophisticated gear, and caught limits of bream and crappie in the river after we learned to manipulate that bug into dishpan-sized openings along the shoreline. But we were even more successful when we went to the lake that Dodo talked about. Lake Waccamaw is the largest freshwater lake created by nature in the South, except for Okeechobee in Florida. It was formed centuries ago by a meteor that blasted a five-by-seven-mile hole in the Columbus County low country. Averaging about eight feet in depth with a pure white sand bottom, it has long been fine freshwater fishing haven for many species.

We went there with fly rods and reels, tapered lines, wet and dry flies and all the sophisticated equipment in a new bass boat. The fish cooperated, and we had a thrilling adventure. We shifted to casting and spinning rods and reels and likewise put middle-size largemouths in the boat in quantities of bragging proportions. They loved spinners, crankbaits, topwater and plastic worms. We had a ball more than once in that North Carolina fishing hot spot.

Reflecting on the experience, we owe Dodo Clewis some gratitude. He helped us find a good fishing hole, and showed us the way to use humble fishing gear and still taste success. As a matter of fact, we find ourselves back up that narrow, desolate river frequently. It's a near-undisturbed Paradise where neither the fish nor the fisherman are so refined that yesteryear's methods are frowned upon. And how can you imagine a more thrilling moment for a fisherman than that instant when he slingshots a man-made bug into a dark hole din the cover, and then feels like minnows are flouncing in his veins when he has both sight and sound tickle his senses as a fish explodes on the surface after the offering? It's a moment you'll remember up the Waccamaw.

THE WHITES RUN THE YADKIN CHAIN

Brisk winds made my thick quilted jacket feel good that early March morning as I stepped out of the boat to the bank and then slowly waded over the rocks in the shallow, cold and clear water that seemed to chatter as it flowed rapidly from the little mountain creek that entered the beautiful Uwharrie River, a small tributary of the Great Pee Dee River between Stanly and Montgomery counties in Piedmont North Carolina. It was white bass running time here and I knew they would be holed up in these headwaters as they sought spawning space in this season that borders either side of winter and spring.

It took only moments to verify that history was repeating itself and these fighting, but relatively small fish had indeed fought their way out of the Yadkin chain of impounded waters into this unpolluted stream where spawning was possible and eggs would hatch as they floated unmolested for miles over rocks and gravel toward the calm and deep reservoirs of the river's bowels.

I flipped a tiny red-headed jig with a hairy white skirt into the rapids where the fish were teeming and in eyeball distance of me and several other anglers who had braved this chilly morning to challenge the whites on their spawning maneuvers. It jerked back as soon as it touched the water and I reeled in a flopping, flouncing, struggling 12-ounce fish that fought like she was much heavier. I flipped the same bait in the honey hole again and there was instant replay, a Xerox if you will, and a similar white bass joined its mate on the stringer I had tied to my belt. During the course of that morning, I put two dozen of these first cousins to the striped bass on the stringer and there were few moments without action, thrills and satisfaction that March morning.

White bass swarm all over the Yadkin chain of lakes that includes Tuckertown, Badin, and Tillery, north to south, on the

Big Pee Dee River that once was called "Yadkin" in the Tar Heel state and changes its name at the South Carolina line. These three lakes are impounded by separate dams and all provide excellent white bass, and other species of freshwater fishing in the piedmont area of North Carolina.

Spring or late winter is the ideal time to catch these small fighting whites in the shallow tributaries that rush out of the Uwharrie mountain range, these hills are tall enough to be called "mountains" and are some 50 miles east of Charlotte and nearly 100 miles from the real mountains of western North Carolina. Not only are these desolate creeks and tiny rivers great for fishing, the area is among the most productive deer hunting ranges in the South.

Some of the avid white bass anglers in the Albemarle area who fish these streams regularly use this red-headed jig with a tiny cork about a foot up the line. It suspends the jig just off the bottom in many of these moving waters and the whites often will gulp it down better than one that flits on the rocky bottom.

P. E. Miller, Jr., a Richfield, North Carolina resident, is a devout believer in this jig with a cork and has caught limits season after successful season with this kind of rig. He not only catches them in the fast-moving water in March, but also in deeper water later as the warm weather approaches when the white bass school on top and tear the surface apart.

Like the Uwharrie stream where whites spawn in March, Mountain Creek is another tributary of the Pee Dee that often is flooded with schools of these itinerant fish looking for areas to spew out their eggs. The creek eases into the river impoundment with little or no current, but it is a rapidly flowing stream near the headwaters where the creek forms from the mountain runoff. It's in this headwater area where most whites are caught by fishermen in the cold of March.

They are not only caught on jigs, but all kinds of small lures like Mepps spinners, Rebel Deep Wee R plugs, tiny buzz baits, floating popping bugs and even wet flies on flycasting equipment.

While these March runs are great times for catching limits, those less astute anglers who do not care to brave the cold of frosty mornings can catch their share of white bass a few weeks later when they begin to school in calm waters of the impoundments. They literally are in a frenzy when they surface to attack forage fish and they will bite just about any artificial lure that isn't larger than they are. It is not unusual to land a fish on every cast for several minutes before they spook and head for the bottom.

Even that sounding to the bottom doesn't necessarily stop the angler from catching a good mess of white bass. Like Roland Blalock, a Stanly County fisherman, says, "You can catch white bass right on the top or right on the bottom." Whey they stop feeding and go down, they are still ready to hit just about any kind of small jig that you dangle in their faces.

In addition to catching them in the calm waters when they are schooling, there are times when they literally infest the turbulent waters just behind the Tuckertown dam. This is a maze of rocky little channels where the water streaks from the dam outlets after turning the dynamos and heads downhill in a mad rush. The white bass like this churning, foaming water and many anglers take stands on huge boulders that are high and dry and drag the whites from their refuge.

Most Pee Dee or Yadkin chain white bass are not the size that you write home about. Some are caught that are as small as five ounces and a good one is usually in the one-pound range. Of course, there are always a few giants of the species that weigh more. But if you fish this chain with the realization that you are probably going to come away with a good stringer of white bass that you can fry three or four or more at one time in a 12-inch skillet, you can have an exciting, wonderful fishing adventure. The whites are plentiful and you can load the boat livewell or your stringer if you are wading. And while there are other species that are not as strong to the taste as the whites are, it is still a good meal for most anglers, especially those who take to the creeks on a cold March run and then come out, dress the catch on the river bank and fry them over a wood fire at high noon.

Waccamaw's Redfin Pickerel

Twitching his Rebel floating minnow patiently toward the boat after casting the treble-hook lure near a fallen tree top that was half submerged on the shoreline of the Waccamaw River in Horry County, South Carolina, Albert Mayberry Johnson, known as "Al" to family and friends, felt a vicious jerk on his line and for an instant he hesitated before reeling a fish over the gunnels that was soon certified a state and world record.

Al was three weeks away from his twelfth birthday that Saturday afternoon when that redfin pickerel (*Esox americanus*) struck and he thought he had just hooked another chain pickerel or jackfish like those of that species he had caught here previously in Bluff Lake off Worthman's Landing near the North Carolina border.

"But when I got it in the boat I knew it was not a jack and my dad quickly recognized this redfin for what it was. He knew this fish that most people around here call a 'pike' was something special," Al tells about his experience.

The pike that Al refers to is the redfin pickerel that abounds in the swamp lakes of the Carolina Low Country, among other waters. This fish is most often caught on a spinner and a cane pole or with some form of red or white attractor fastened to a hook and pulled rapidly near the surface. They love to strike a strip of red balloon, red velvet, white pork rind or a strip of belly meat and fins cut from one of their cousins. Most fish of this species weigh only six or eight ounces, but they are tasty and make many gourmet meals for natives of the area who go after them in the fall. An intriguing factor about this species of small fish is that many people scale them by dumping several in a tin tub, throwing in pine bark chips and stirring rapidly. The bark quickly scales the pickerel and they are ready for gutting.

The redfin that this young Florence, South Carolina, angler caught that afternoon weighed in at 1-pound, 8 3/4-ounces. It was 16 1/2 inches long and had a girth of 8 3/4 inches. It broke the South Carolina state record by 2 3/4-ounces that had been previously set by Charles L. McCord, of Manning, South Carolina, June 3, 1983. Prior to McCord's record the largest redfin was a 14-ounce fish weighed in by Reese J. Taylor, also of Manning, in 1980.

While Al's big redfin was an all-tackle world record when biologist David W. Croshet of the South Carolina Wildlife and Marine Resources Department certified it August 19, 1983, the all-tackle mark has since been broken by Gene Brantley in Georgia. But young Johnson's fish remains the 10-pound test line world record and the all-tackle South Carolina record. Brantley's monster of the species weighed 2-pounds, 10-ounces.

Hal Beard, fisheries biologist for the S.C. Wildlife and Marine Resources Department says the redfin pickerel is basically a low country black water species usually found in slow-flowing water and mill ponds. It is often called a grass pickerel or redfin pike, but its true name is redfin pickerel. It is easily identified by the reddish-orange margins on its pelvic, caudal and anal fins. It was this distinctive marking of Al's fish that caused his father to sit up and take notice when the fish was flouncing on the deck. He knew it was an unusual size for this species. Beard said the fish is sought by avid anglers looking for fish with savory sweet flavor, but it is not generally considered a popular game fish.

Al caught his record fish on the Rebel plug, a Rapala-type, elongated minnow with silver, red and black colors that is his favorite artificial lure, using a Zebco Omega model 181 reel and Zebco Sundowner rod. He had Trilene XL 10-pound test line that was later certified to be a true test of the monofilament. While young Johnson likes to cast and is usually throwing his artificials around, his fishing father is more inclined to go after bluegill, crappie, redbreast and other species with crickets or minnows. Al says he still likes to fish with crickets and a cane pole too.

Al has fished with his father, an entomologist on the faculty of Clemson University and an avid angler since his childhood. He grew up in the Floyds Community a few miles from the Waccamaw and Little Pee Dee rivers, since he was six years old. He has used a rod and reel astutely since he was eight and considers himself fortunate to have a dad who gives him so many opportunities to enjoy the out of doors. He has been catching bream and other panfish species virtually all of his life and once landed a 6 1/2-pound catfish in the Santee Cooper complex of lakes.

The father of this young record holder says Al really likes to fish the artificials more than he does. While his son is casting along the shorelines, big Al puts a lot of panfish in the boat and says he has the "little boy instinct." He likes to see the cork go down when he is holding a cane pole or a fiberglass Breambuster.

"I think I can catch bigger fish with a rod and reel and lures than I can with most live baits," Al says, and he is probably right. He likes the action even when they are not striking rather than holding a pole and waiting patiently.

Believing in water safety always, Al's dad insists on wearing life jackets when they are moving from one place to another in his two-man river boat and they are careful all the time. Al is a good swimmer and during his half-dozen years fishing regularly with his dad, neither has had to use his swimming ability. Al did get a hook in his hand once when a sister inadvertently walked into his line while he was tying on a lure. They removed the hook almost painlessly without a doctor's help.

While Al and his father were knowledgeable enough to meet all the requirements necessary for recording the champion fish, not all of the big ones get a fair chance at this recognition. A lot of records are eaten before the fisherman discovers his fish is worthy of attention.

Some basic guidelines for young anglers interested in seeking a state or world record include:

A prerequisite is that your fish be caught according to the laws and rules. It must be caught by sporting means using tackle or pole and line. No fish caught in a trap or net is eligible.

The legally caught fish must be weighed on a set of state certified scales—such as those in most grocery stores—and two persons of legal age must witness the weighing. (This varies by state but is generally true.) Witnesses must sign an affidavit form and it is a good idea to get their addresses and telephone numbers if you don't know them.

Immediate steps should be taken to preserve the fish until it can be verified by a wildlife department fisheries biologist. It can be preserved by putting it on ice, but it should be frozen as quickly as possible. The fish should be wet and placed in a dark plastic bag if possible before freezing. If freezing facilities and ice are not going to be available for several days and the fish is dead, it can be partially preserved by salting heavily and wrapping in wet newspapers of thick mats of grass. A photograph of your fish helps in further documentation.

South Carolina is among the leaders in world record fish, with four other marks a matter of record in the Palmetto State. The other four world records set in South Carolina are a 2-pound redbreast caught by D. R. Turner of Nichols with a Mepps Comet in the Lumber River; a 2-pound, 3-ounce warmouth caught on an earthworm by W. L. Singletary of Manning in Douglas Swamp in Clarendon County; a 58-pound channel catfish caught on a bucktail jig by W. H. Whaley of Pineville in Lake Moultrie and a 21-pound, 8-ounce mudfish (bowfin) landed by Florence's Robert Harmon in 1980. (These records are broken regularly.)

The 12-year-old Al Johnson is proud to be among the record setters in freshwater fishing and except for his devotion to Little League baseball, he would rather be fishing than anything else. And he has a dad who is justly proud of his offspring and happy to have a chance to fish together in the prolific streams of the South Carolina Low Country.

Max Clarke, a Tarheel native, lands a sheepshead

Sheepshead Challenge

With the close of the school year, families schedule a breakaway weekend, and many head for the coast and a day or two of saltwater fishing after being landlocked for months with the cold of winter. In the Carolinas, where there are a variety of quality saltwater species available in the summer, there is a fraternity of anglers who go after sheepshead, that crafty species known as "convict fish" because of its white and black stripes, as well as its ability to take fiddler crab baits off your hook time after time without so much as a nudge or a bump reaching the sensitive fingers of the fisherman holding the line.

Some of the finest sheepshead fishing along the Atlantic coast is found at Southport, Wrightsville Beach, Sunset and Holden Beaches, Surfside, Garden City, Murrell's Inlet, Myrtle Beach and Charleston. There are good launching ramps at all these places, but generally you will need to take your own boat. There are few boats for rent along the Inland Waterway where the 'heads congregate around bridge abutments, pier pilings and any other stickups in the tidal waters not more than a couple of miles from the sea.

Sheepshead are generally bottom feeders that suck the bait from the hook. They feed on barnacles, oysters, shrimp, minnows and small crabs that hide around shell-covered stickups. They are also caught off oyster and clam beds in the open water, but that is not where most Carolinians find and hook them.

You need a tough monofilament line in the 30 to 40 pound test class to catch a lunker sheepshead. The fish will dash around the pilings and cut most lines unless they are manhandled with a stiff rod and strong reel the minute the fish is hooked. He cannot be played. The object in sheepshead fishing is to put the fish in the boat as quickly as possible.

Sheepshead will bite live shrimp, raw oysters, barnacles, sand fleas and other creatures, but most Carolina anglers use the Chinese fiddler crabs, the one-armed, dangerous-looking little critters that run backward and forward with equal speed in the marshes along the waterway during every warm weather low tide. They can be scooped up by the hundreds and trapped in a bucket where they will live for days. It's a cheap bait that you must catch yourself. They are not for sale at tackle and bait shops.

Sheepshead bite best when tides are half out and half way back in again. They are difficult to entice to the bait at high tide or ebb tide.

When you lower a baited hook to the bottom around a piling and feel the slightest movement on your line, set the hook with all the force you can muster. If you don't hook the 'head, rebait and try again. Many times, a sheepshead will stay right there and feed on a dozen or more of your offerings before you finally sink a hook in his bony mouth that is filled with protruding sharp teeth that give the species its name.

The meat of the sheepshead is white, flaky and tasty. Along the Carolinas coast, you may catch them as small as a bluegill or as large as 12 pounds or more. Big or little, they are powerful fighting fish that will thrill any angler when he finally gets a hook set in a fish which the makes a dive for the pilings that may often mean freedom.

HATTERAS ISLAND—MACKEREL MECCA

Hatteras Island, on the historic North Carolina Outer Banks, was a beehive of activity on the crisp fall afternoon as dusk began to creep over the dunes. Many of the 30 charter boats that dock in the snug little harbor at Hatteras Village had just chugged through the narrow rock-jettied inlet from the tumultuous Atlantic.

Mates sweated on the fantails of a dozen boats as they unloaded what, to the novices, appeared to be a fabulous eight-hour catch of giant king mackerel. Kibitzers stared open-mouthed with disbelief as one huge barrel after another was filled with fish and pushed onto the narrow pier. The barrels overflowed with now stiff, giant-size kingfish that stood on their heads with their sleek, once powerful tail fins protruding above the top of the drums, attesting to the success of the day's remarkable offshore mackerel harvest.

This is a scene often repeated at Hatteras Village from early April until the middle of November, sometimes beyond, when sportsmen from a myriad of eastern states flock to this remote barrier island chain to catch big fish with rods and reels. It is an angler's Paradise.

Captain Jerry Shepherd, of the charter boat Tuna Duck, was one of the professional guides with a catch worth writing home about that memorable October afternoon. His first mate, a four year veteran helper from West Virginia, Steve Coulter, was shoving one container after another onto the dock, each filled with the individual catch of an angler aboard the Tuna Duck. They had left the harbor at safe light. Understandably, the tired quartet of anglers were all smiles as they looked over their barrel of mackerel. They were anxious to tell in detail of their fine day, how they pulled these giants over the gunnels after experiencing gallant fights. Bystanders were plentiful and eager to lend an ear.

Captain Shepherd and his party dragged in 20 big mackerel that day, ranging in weight from 20 to 46 pounds, totaling more than 700 pounds. On a fluctuating fall seafood market, their catch was worth at least $1,400, to say nothing of the glorious excitement they enjoyed. With that included, who can say what the experience was worth?

A half a dozen apron-clad teenagers stood before homemade sinks and splash boards at the end of the dock. With sharp knives and a lot of expertise, they were rapidly preparing mackerel steaks and filets for the coolers while the quartet of Tuna Duck anglers looked on. Angling success was even felt by the fish-dressing shack workmen who would collect 20 cents a pound—a good day. Literally tons of fish were backed up in the drums on the dock, waiting for their turn in the dressing shack assembly line. They would pay for a lot of grits and gravy.

"I'm glad I don't have another charter trip tomorrow," Captain Shepherd commented, "Steve and I can go fishing for the market, and if the kings keep on hitting like they did today, we will make more money than we can by taking sports fishermen out for $350 or $500 apiece." You could easily understand the economics behind his reasoning.

An old salt who was smoking a traditional pipe in silence while the boats unloaded looked into the face of the crowd who were still stunned with what they saw.

"They got a pretty good catch, but I've seen much better. On a good day, a single boat often comes in here with as much at 1,900 pounds. Sometimes the kingfish are so thick out there off the beach that you give out pulling them over the rail. You kind of hope you don't hang another big 'un," the veteran native mused.

Charter boats like the Tuna Duck, a well-maintained, 30-foot diesel, are safe in almost any of the wind and weather that harasses the Cape Hatteras coast, the legendary "Graveyard of the Atlantic," where hundreds of vessels have floundered on the shallow reefs since the New World was discovered. Astute captains like Shepherd, with experience and modern electronic gadgetry, seldom worry about such dangers.

It's a great place to catch the mighty King Mackerel.

A Minnow Is Real

Harold (Spud) Picklesimer, of Gastonia, North Carolina, and his partner Buddy Wright of Chapin, South Carolina, burned up $300 worth of gasoline and together spent a thousand dollars scouting out Clark Hill reservoir the week prior to the World Championship of Striped Bass fishing at Thomson, Georgia. They believed they had really nailed down the location of the hybrid congregation and had a good shot at the $12,000 Ranger first prize. It was not to be!

Picklesimer, whose unusual name leads some to suspect he is a newcomer to the South, is very much a native. He and generations of his family have been mountain men in the Murphy section of the Tar Heel State. He guides at Santee-Cooper and Lake Murray when he isn't busy at his vocation as an electrician.

Wright is a manufacturer's representative and lives on Lake Murray, where he is one of the most successful striper and hybrid anglers in the land.

Picklesimer's astuteness as a striper catcher earned him the leadership in eight competitive tournaments one year and he once won the $1,000.00 "Angler of the Year" award from DuPont Stren, a big promoter of the striper world championship event.

But despite these credentials and five days of intense observation and study at the Clark Hill site, these veterans found that either a sudden change of weather or the shift from live bait to artificials makes all the difference in the world. The morning the championship opened, there was a severe drop in temperature and an equally disturbing cold wind. In addition to that, this tournament had set rules that hybrids must be caught on artificial lures, not the live shad that Picklesimer had used so successfully in the eight events leading up to that world series of striper fishing.

During those practice rounds from Monday through Friday, Spud and his partner had traversed all of the Clark Hill impoundment, even making the 53-mile run to the foot of the Russell Dam. But after all the scouting, they came to the conclusion that the place to win the championship was in the deep water under the Little River bridge, just a hop and skip from the Raysville Marina.

"We are not going to run far. We'll be at our fishing spot in a matter of minutes after the starting gun and we will fish that one place all day," Spud said when I crawled into the boat prior to commencing the competition. "You see, we know the fish are under that bridge. We saw 63 caught there Tuesday and another 23 yesterday."

That seemed like reason enough to cast your lot under the Little River bridge that has giant boulders at both ends and a bottom covered with similar feeding ground for these fast-growing hybrids that have reached weights above 20 pounds in this backwater of the Savannah River.

But Picklesimer noted that those big catches under the bridge were made by amateur anglers from the area using live bait. He and Wright had not done as well on their artificials, but they had put some nice stripers over the gunnels with Sassy Shad, Shimmy Shad, Mister Twister and some Rapala-type lures worked deep in this cider-colored water. They had even caught some nice fish with white jigs fluttered just above the rocky bottom covered with 30 feet of water. Spoons had also produced when weighted and worked with an up-and-down motion where the hybrids had schooled and were stalking their prey. The very fact that it was a certainty the fish were there is what brought the glint into the eyes of Spud and Buddy. They were confident they could entice those critters to bite on Saturday and Sunday and need not burn up any great amount of high-priced gasoline traveling half a day to and from the distant dam.

We tied up the Glassmaster boat to the bridge and began eight hours of offering those persnickety stripers with the broken lines along their sides a vast variety of the best artificial baits that money can buy. Alas! The fish would have none of them.

As the hour approached for the check-in at Raysville, Picklesimer didn't have a fish. Neither did I. Buddy had managed to catch one on a Mister Twister, a pretty, white, lead-headed bait with a flat tail that looked like it was good enough for any fish to eat.

That's only half the story. The real trauma in this adventure was triggered less than 40 feet away under the same bridge. There in a bass boat sat Gerald Partridge, a young construction worker from nearby Appling, Georgia. All during that frustrating day this native was pulling in fish. He had an assortment, too. Some were nice crappie. He had a largemouth bass. But most interesting were the hybrids that he boated. That was the species we wanted so badly, but only his lines ever tightened and jerked with a fighting fish on the hook. Why? Well, Partridge was using plain old Missouri minnows about two-and-a-half inches long for bait. He was impaling them on a 2/0 hook with a wraparound lead a foot above the hook and he was fishing about ten feet deep, where the fish were obviously suspended. We had fished that same depth many times that day without success. Obviously, the minnows were the difference. And while hybrids would have preferred some four or five-inch-long shad, they still chose those little minnows over everything we had to offer. Some 50 feet away at the adjoining bridge abutment, two young fellows in a streamlined canoe were busy catching fish too. Frustrating? Yes, it most certainly was.

Partridge injected the finishing touch. Indeed it was a bit of wisdom that even Solomon could not have improved upon: "They ain't nothin' that's as much like a minnow as a minnow," he said. He was right! And while many of our artificials looked like good imitations, obviously those fish at Clark Hill were not stupid. They were not making mistakes. When they bit, they were after the real thing, something with protein and not plastic or balsa.

No doubt there are times and places when you can catch hybrids, bass, crappie and most other species just as well or better on artificials than you can with the real thing, but at that particular time and place, they were choosy, looking for something alive.

Some of the diehard purists won't believe this. Some will say that any time you can catch fish on live baits, you can catch them on lures too. Yet Picklesimer and Wright were experts and they couldn't entice the strikes that day despite a day-long effort. Both were sure they would have enjoyed success with some native threadfin shad. And I believe it too.

But then those purists have a rebuttal for that too. As one told me recently, "I wouldn't even eat a fish that I had to catch on a live bait." So be it! Pass them along. I'll enjoy the fish and the fishing, whether they are caught on my Deep Wee R Rebel or on a soft shad that I trapped with a cast net in the shallows. There's a challenge, at least to me, in catching fish on naturals or artificials.

WHY FISHERMEN ARE CALLED ANGLERS

Did you ever wonder why fishermen are called anglers? Well, it all dates back to 1350 A.D., when Dame Juliana Herners wrote the book entitled "The Treatyse of Fysshinge with an Angle."

Netting, trapping and other means have been used to catch fish from the beginning of mankind in the world and they were called "fishermen." Then, as man focused upon catching fish, he began fashioning a kind of hook from a piece of steel that he bent at an angle. The angled steel led to the term "angler" for all people who fish with a hook and line, and solves a lot problems for writers today who can use "angler" for both men and women rather than have the gender problem created with "fisherman." Netters and trappers are still fishermen, not anglers.

WARMOUTHS—A WELCOMED SPECIES

My tiny bream cork disappeared like it was alive and the strike was obviously vicious. But then the line stopped. The bobber stayed down and I wondered if a real lunker hadn't carried the bait under the cover, disgorged it and left my line hung but good on the bottom, where decaying brush made sheltered nesting havens for a variety of Carolina panfish.

I yanked on the cane pole, expecting resistance of one kind or another. But the line came up straightway out of the water with only the tiniest trickle of life and motion. Unbelievable! I had a two-finger sized warmouth perch not nearly as long as any of the gob of night crawlers used for bait and yet that little critter had jumped on my hook and carried my cork to China almost like he had hands. Honestly, when I eased the little fellow off the hook he seemed to be grinning at me with an expression like, "Fooled you that time, didn't I?"

Such experiences with the warmouth perch, that range over the Southern sates are legendary. There isn't a freshwater game fishing enthusiast in the country who hasn't had a myriad of momentary thrills from this gallant little species that will bite anything from a crayfish as big as he is, to a broken-back Rebel lure with three sets of treble hooks trolled along the bottom in search of stripers or largemouth bass.

These stumpknockers, as they are known by many anglers, are not afraid to attack anything dead or alive that is flaunted in their faces and if it gets by without feeling the hook the first time, it will come right back and strike again and again, much like the chain pickerel. Even if you do land the critter, it may come back to bite again within moments if it hasn't been hurt substantially, and you keep on fishing where you caught and released it.

And most warmouths are released. They are generally caught by mistake because few anglers go out to catch a creel limit of warmouth except in some remote rural areas where the native fishermen have caught them for food for generations. Those select few know that whether this species is large or small, it is a fine gourmet meal if you catch it early before the water gets too warm and they get that strong, muddy taste. They are not appetizing then, but neither is a bluegill under the same circumstances.

Warmouth inhabit dense weed beds, soft muddy bottoms, around stumps and brush, rocks or logs, anything that offers cover and protection from the larger predators and any territory where minnows and other panfish fry are likely to provide an abundance of nutritious meals for a species with a healthy appetite. They are generally morning feeders and will gulp down any kind of larvae from the aquatic growth and any fish that swims that isn't too big to go down. All insects and crayfish too are among the favorite foods of this hungry species. They generally do not feed much in the afternoon and the really devout stumpknocker anglers go after them at safe light and either have their cooler filled or have struck out before noon.

Those warmouth fishermen who actively seek the species have perfected the system. Mostly they "lead line" for the warmouth with several big shot on a strong monofilament line, a stubby cane pole, No. 4 Eagle Claw hook, load it with a wad of worms and jiggle it on or near the bottom in the thickest brush piles and log jams in the still waters of lakes and streams. These fish are not fond of fast-moving water, preferring instead the calm areas from a few inches deep to four or five feet. They have an amazing ability to live in muddy water, much like the bowfin and catfish, where most more actively hunted panfish wouldn't want to be found. They will hit a wad of worms being moved around and you have a good momentary tussle with one of average size. That means one in the seven- to ten-ounce class.

But they are not all just average. Those that live to be senior citizens in the fish family, seven years old or more, reach lengths of 8 1/2 inches or thereabouts and many have been caught in the 1-pound class. The largest one on record was landed by Carlton Robbins of Sylvania, Georgia, on May 4, 1974.

It was officially weighed in and recorded at two pounds even.

There may be no best time of year to catch a warmouth. But those who study their lifestyles and fish for them with intensity, believe that they are bedding and therefore the easiest to catch in the Southland when the dogwood trees begin to bloom. By the time the petals fall, they have about ended the spawn, but are still caught frequently right in the bluegill, shellcracker, bass and crappie beds. They recognize a good dining table when they see it and will make their home there as long as the eggs and fry are plentiful. It is during these months that anglers for other species often put warmouths over the gunwales whether casting an artificial minnow into the grass; jigging a fly for bream; dropping crickets, shrimp or worms in the lilies; or even trolling live minnows in the open water nearby. Warmouths are not that persnickety about what they eat. If it moves, they'll come after it.

There are warmouth fishermen in Carolina honey holes who use the old throw gear system and still catch good messes of this species. This is a light monofilament line on a limber cane pole, tiny cork, little hook with a cricket, worm, live grass shrimp, grasshopper or crayfish for bait. They flip this bait in the thick cover, under overhanging bushes and around the maiden cane and cattails to roust the warmouth out of the cover.

Many today use a small piece of Uncle Josh's white pork rind on the shank of the hook, above a live bait. It is an attractor that often brings the warmouth a-runnin'. Before the time of the more sophisticated attractor now commercially available, these avid fishermen cut tiny pieces of white fatback and threaded it on the hook above the bait. Either addition seems to make the bait a little more enticing for the warmouth than the plain bait, but brave little fellows that they are, they will attack just about any offering.

The largest warmouth I ever put in the boat was caught on a lead line with a gob of live wiggly worms on the hook. It weighed 14 ounces and the next time I dropped the bait to the bottom, I pulled in another one exactly the same size. It was an instant replay situation. Both looked huge for warmouths, and I have never again caught one that big. Those two were caught in the Waccamaw River in North Carolina where they are called "Morgans" by many, for some unknown reason. Other names by which they are known in other parts of the country include "goggle-eye" and "goggle-eye perch." They are also often mistaken for rock bass. The thick-bodied sunfish does resemble the rock bass, but it can be distinguished by the three spines on the anal fin, teeth on the tongue and small spots on the anal and dorsal fins. It has a large mouth extending beyond its reddish eyes and it is never longer than 11 inches. It is olive or gray in color, with mottled markings on its sides and back.

One of the great attributes of the warmouth perch is its lack of fear that makes it readily catchable for even the rankest amateur or first-time-out child. Regardless of the noise you make, splashing that ruffles the water, and ineptness in putting on the bait and presenting it to the fish, almost any angler can bring a warmouth out of the water. Fishing from the humblest bateau, jon boat or even from the bank, warmouth are usually catchable.

Never was this more dramatically exhibited than a few years ago when a Cub Scout pack was out fishing in Lake Tabor in Tabor City, North Carolina. One of the youngsters had never had the pleasure of doing any kind of fishing in his life, and when I handed him a cane pole with a worm bait on it and gently let it sink a couple of feet in the water near a cypress trunk, I casually remarked that he would have to watch it for a bite in that good-looking place.

"How will I know when I get a bite?" he asked, and I was astounded that an eight-year-old didn't know how to tell when a fish bit.

"Well, you'll know you have a bite when that cork on the surface goes under," I told him patiently.

Several minutes later, when I had the other dozen youngsters anxiously expecting a bite and a big fish on the line, I came back to the little scout who didn't know how to recognize a bite. Amazingly, he was using the end of his pole to push the cork under.

"What are you doing that for?"

Just as sincere as a deacon in church, the little fellow said,

"Well you told me I would have a bite and could catch a fish when the cork went under."

At that same instant, the cork stayed down and the line was almost tight. Sensing something on the line, the Cub Scout jerked with all his might. A little warmouth went flying through the treetop like he was shot from a cannon and came to a bouncing stop in the palmettos 40 feet from the river bank. Moments later a happy eight-year-old was clutching his catch in both hands and beaming a smile worthy of the most professional basser with a wall mount in his net. It was an incident that truly dramatized that the warmouth, minor species that he is, still has a place in America's water and that he will bite regardless of the lack of expertise or knowledge of the angler.

And there should always be plenty of these little critters for the young and old to enjoy. A single female will lay up to 126,000 eggs in a season. They become sexually mature when the are three inches in length and will grow half that long the first year of life. In the scheme of nature, there is no such thing as an insignificant species. For a lot of anglers who take up a hook and line only once or twice a year, the little old warmouth is important.

Catching Mullet That Don't Bite

It was one of those freakish early winter days when the temperature along the Carolina coast dropped to low in the 20's. It was far too cold for most anglers to brave the wind that swept across the salty estuary at Murrell's Inlet, just off Highway 17 south of Myrtle Beach, SC, but some tourists from a couple of hundred miles upstate had made the trip with the idea of catching speckled trout (called winter trout locally) that often bite when the weather is the most inclement. Despite a hearty effort and hands nearly frozen from the ordeal, no trout rose to the live shrimp offered on hook and line.

Resourcefulness paid off when the alert fishermen, despite the freezing temperature, observed literally thousands of popeyed mullet virtually powerless in the two foot water that separated the Future Farmers of America pier from the marshy mainland. An idea was born.

The anglers had no treble snare hooks, but they used some monofilament line to lash three big hooks together, tied on a one ounce sinker and began casting and yanking those hooks through the water where the mullet were schooled. Action was immediate. The hooks began taking hold of the two pound fish in the sides, bellies and backs, and in an hour or so there were 17 of these fat creatures lying on the pier. The anglers had the mess of fish they came for. They were cold, but happy and as anyone who has ever fried a plump mullet just an hour or so after it was taken from the freezing salt water is aware, there is no better tasting fish to be found. It was a fishing morning with lasting memories as determined fishing tourists didn't let the weather or the fact that the fish had lockjaw stop them from bringing home the protein.

FISHING FOR FROGS

Some people are squeamish, reluctant to eat fried frog legs, while others declare they're the finest of seafoods. In the Carolinas this deep-throated amphibian is sought by a unique society of night-stalkers with four-pronged gigs from boats and they have never lacked for a market for their harvest. Other frog fishermen hunt these gourmet jumpers for family meals. But make no mistake, the species is definitely depleted and the size today does not compare with that of even a decade ago.

Ray Morrison was alone one warm spring night. His wife elected to sleep at a coastal motel while he skirted the wetlands and the lily-covered shoreline searching for those beady eyes that meant another frog was on the surface looking for his nocturnal meal of insects. More often than not, she was riding with him on his old boat that had slid over millions of acres of marshlands during the many years that this outdoor-oriented couple had made a living harvesting frogs.

Never staying at one place more than a day or two during the spring and summer froggin' harvest, the young hunters thinned out the tasty creatures quickly in any area and moved on to greener frog pastures. They were professionals and not interested in just a few legs for Sunday dinner.

An expert at frog gigging in the dark of night from his moving, elevated swivel seat, Ray could pick up a pair of flashing eyes 40 feet away when the beam of his miner's cap reflected and echoed the presence of another jumper quietly floating on the surface or resting in a grassy hassock.

With a deftness seldom equaled by even the most avid sportsman, Ray gigged frogs while his boat idled along, almost never stopping, and the kicking, squirming critter was quickly stripped from the barbed gig and jammed into the two lengths of stovepipe behind his seat that angled down into a tow bag on the deck.

269

At three o'clock in the morning, Ray was dead tired and ready to call it a night. He had roused innumerable alligators that slithered away with threatening grunts and suspicious glances at this creature with a light on its head. Snakes by the dozens crawled on and off the airboat, some poisonous, some harmless, but all ignored by this frog hunter who lived nightly with them without a semblance of fear. When they got too friendly, he just brushed them off the boat with his foot and made sure they didn't get a mouth inside his tow bag, once used for fertilizer and referred to by some as a "croaker sack." Frogs make up a good portion of 'gator diet and they are also plentiful where frogs abound.

Ray revved up the old boat engine and skidded across the water to camp. At the landing he tied the mouths shut on two bags full of frogs and went inside for a few hours of sleep and rest. Froggin' is a nighttime task, but it doesn't mean you can loaf around all day.

The Morrisons were up and working shortly after the sun rose above the cypress tree tops at the fishing camp motel. With cloth gloves they began the task of skinning what they estimated to be at least 400 pairs of frog legs from rather small creatures. Ray did the chopping of the hind ends from the body just behind the front legs and his wife yanked the skin off the remaining edible meat.

"How long will it take you to dress those two sacks of frogs?" I asked.

"Not more than two hours," he said, to my amazement. These experts had this skinning process about as pat as possible. Dressed frog legs went into a huge pan of water and the carcass into a waste bucket about as fast as Georgians can shell peanuts at a country store.

"How much will these frog legs weigh?" I asked.

"These frogs are small and it will probably take 12 to 14 pairs to weigh a pound. We must have 30 or 40 pounds here."

"How do you sell the fog legs?" I questioned.

"We have restaurants that take what we catch at $3.75 a pound. The price is down right now. Sometime later in the year when they get scarce, we get as much as $4 a pound or more, especially when we get in to some of the big frogs in the swamplands where three or four pairs of legs weigh a pound. Everybody would like to have the big frog legs, but we catch whatever size is available in the lake we are fishing," he said.

In less than two hours, this froggin' couple had finished the task, loaded the boat on a trailer and were off to market their catch, find another lake to gig, and repeat the scene the next day. They had grossed about $90 for their night and morning's work, but from that came motel rent, meals, gas for the boat and for the pickup that pulled them to the location. It was obvious they weren't going to get rich quick in this business, but working together and traveling throughout the state was obviously fun as well as a livelihood, and as long as there were no children to tie them down, they might continue this making a living off the land, or rather the water, for life. It was an interesting, different kind of life that was appealing to the Morrisons. They were professionals.

But most froggin' is a nocturnal "hunting and fishing" adventure designed just for individual family tables. In a good year, there may be a few pounds surplus that can be sold to help pay the gasoline bill.

Don Braddock is one of those frog hunters who gets a thrill just seeing the moon rise over the wetlands when he speeds his boat toward the frog flats, and a few hours of gigging.

"Once I could get ten pounds of dressed legs in two hours. Now I barely get enough to pay the gas bill. What I get now are no larger than the rain frogs in my kitchen sink. We have green or leopard frogs and bullfrogs here. The bullfrogs are called 'pig frogs' because of the grunting noise they make. A leopard frog is the smaller type that barks just as he leaps from his perch into the water.

"I have fished for frogs in the deep South for years without getting any big ones. The Seminole Indians in the 'Glades of Florida are expert frog hunters and they work much of the area where the best froggin' is down there. There are thousands of acres of sawgrass in those Everglades and plenty of frogs are living there. But you have to really be brave and nervy to take off across those marshes in an airboat. Everything looks alike and if you aren't careful and a good navigator, you just might never find your way out," says Braddock.

Braddock says the best time to go froggin' is the first night in spring when the temperature reaches 50 degrees. The frogs come out of hiding at that temperature. He also thinks a good time is right after the first frost in the fall when some of the vegetation along the shoreline is bitten and droops. But if that frost doesn't come mighty early, Braddock doesn't take advantage of the fall froggin'. When the deer and dove hunting seasons open, he is through froggin' and his recreation is confined to hunting until the season closes in January.

Braddock has a homemade froggin' light made from a motorcycle headlight reflector and a bulb mounted on his hard hat. His gig is a product of his own hands, too. It is four giant-sized fish hooks straightened out and mounted on a seven-foot bamboo pole. Some froggers use conduit instead of bamboo. The four hooks are not aligned in one continuous row an inch apart as in yesteryear. Froggers now mount these hooks at four corners of a one-inch square. You have to be accurate with your spearing, but few frogs escape these experts who sometimes gig the leapers when they are moving 10 or 15 miles per hour.

This old outdoorsman has a keen eye to go with his expertise with the gig. While his light doesn't really put a frog in a trance, as some people believe, it does blind him and stop him from jumping. There are frogs that are easily spooked and escape, often when a quick stop sends a wave ahead of the boat. But most of Braddock's quarry float motionless on the surface or on the bank and seem to dare the frogger to use his barbed spear.

Tom Cassels is another of the family of froggers, although there are times when he has a little excess meat that he can sell to neighbors and friends. He makes a living building and repairing airboats.

Cassels thinks the fast-rising population of alligators is destroying some of the frogs. He notes that every time he finds a heavy saturation of frogs, there will be several alligators taking up permanent residence alongside them. Cassels thinks an alligator's diet is made up of the easy-to-catch frogs, and that this is reducing the froggin' harvest. He also notes that frogs make up a good portion of the food supply for numerous water birds. Eagles and osprey abound in coastal areas, as do herons and hawks. All take their toll of frogs, as do largemouth bass.

Cassels says he once gigged a giant frog in a private pond that had two monster-sized legs that tipped the scales at one pound even. He is aware that few bullfrogs ever reach such proportions, but points out that there seem to be more big frogs in private lakes than in the public ones, perhaps indicating less pressure on the privately owned property.

"The legs off a small frog are better to eat than the large legs. They taste better. The older a frog gets, the poorer quality meat. But the public wants big legs. The front legs are just as good as the back ones, but they are so small you can't get much meat off them," Cassels says.

There has been amazingly little research or study made of frogs anywhere in this country by agencies of the state or the federal government. The last study was early in 1950.

The froggers have observed the species long enough to know some of its characteristics. Loose in the wild, a bullfrog ceases to be a tadpole or polliwog, and develops four legs at the age of two. One year later he will reach eating size, but two years are needed to reach real maturity. There are few facts documented about the frog's life span, but biologists speculate the normal length of life at seven or eight years.

There are almost no regulations governing the harvesting of frogs. The frogger must have a regular, fishing license, but he can hunt any time, any place and make whatever disposition of his catch that he chooses.

"I believe we could have an increased yield by protecting the reproducing frogs at critical times during the season," a biologist says.

The late Dr. John N. Hamlet, a naturalist with the U.S. Fish and Wildlife Service for 14 years, was in charge of animal health with several wildlife attractions for years. He said the U.S. has been slow in studying the protein potential and economic possibilities of frogs. Other countries have beaten the U.S. in frog production studies.

273

"I presented a proposal to congress at several sessions years ago asking for an appropriation of $50,000 for frog research. The request was headed 'Sex Life of a Frog.' The congressmen laughed at the request and turned the grant down year after year like it was a joke or something. They never took it seriously," Dr. Hamlet said.

He noted that as a result of the congressional inaction, other countries have far surpassed the U.S. in frog production and we are now importing large quantities of legs from Denmark, Israel, France, India and Japan where they are being successfully grown for commerce. Cuba also is producing frog legs for export, but they are not allowed to enter the U.S.

While there are still some giant bullfrogs in the Green Swamp of the eastern Carolinas, they have their beginnings in many other deep swamp areas. The tasty frog is not as bountiful where man has intruded. His habitat is shrinking and unless more time, effort and money are used to protect and produce them, there will be a few domestic frog legs adorning the tables of Americans in the next generation.

BACK LEGS ONLY

When rabbits were thick in the thickets of the eastern Carolinas as well as in the jungles along the river banks, hunters with dogs often went after the bunnies with no weapons other than an axe handle or four-foot stick of some kind. The swamp rabbits and cottontails were bopped over the head when dogs chased them near the hunters. It was popular, especially when there was snow on the ground.

Wild rabbit meat was a delicacy to rural Americans for generations all over the South and elsewhere. In the era when they were hunted so eagerly in the Carolinas, most natives ate only the back legs of the rabbits. They are the biggest and best part of the rabbit, but front legs and the back have plenty of meat also.

Perhaps the hunters compared them with frogs. You eat only the back legs of frogs.

ROANOKE RIVER STRIPER FISHING

From its mouth to the Roanoke Rapids Dam, a distance of 140 miles, every inch of the Roanoke River offers excellent striped bass fishing. The striper, a wild, anadromous species, dearly loves to spawn in the Roanoke River that empties into Albemarle Sound in Eastern North Carolina. Furthermore, if you prefer to catch the land-locked stripers, nearby Kerr Reservoir has part of the same Roanoke River-Albemarle Sound striper population. These rockfish are isolated in the giant impoundment. As in the Santee-Cooper, they have adapted to the times, and now make spawning runs up the Dan River in North Carolina and Virginia.

While there is a huge commercial striped bass business conducted along the Roanoke, it remains among the best sport fishing waterways anywhere, with studies carried on since 1955 verifying the fun rockfish anglers have when these big bruisers leave the sea to hunt free-flowing inland tributaries.

Skipping the study until 1970, you find that sports fishermen landed 28,257 stripers in the Roanoke-Albemarle that season. It then improved with 65,399 in 1971. In 1974, the sports catch was 38,257 fish, but declined to 22,219 in 1975. Apparently tied to some kind of cycle, the catch in 1976 was 40,799 fish, a figure that dropped by a mere 8,000 to 32,983 in 1977. By 1980, the catch slumped to 15,239, and it is now time for an up-cycle again in these normally productive waters.

The catch per effort (C.U.E.), a measure of the number of fish caught per person, per fishing trip, hit a high of 7.82 in 1971, and was 3.64 in 1980. It must be noted that a lack of fish in the Roanoke in 1980 instigated a considerable decline in fishing effort. Often a decline in the number of fish in a given body of water does not seriously discourage the more expert and die-hard fishermen, but it does turn off the novices. The less skillful and intermittent striper seekers will curtail their efforts in such circumstances.

The Weldon area of the Roanoke River is located in the center of the striped bass spawning grounds, and is fished more intensely than any other part of the river system in the eastern NC complex. While no study of sport fishing catch can be entirely accurate, the most complete striper data come from this productive section.

While sports fishermen were catching fish by the thousands from this river during the studies, it is interesting to note how many striped bass were hauled in by commercial anglers with nets, traps, seines and trotlines during the same period.

The annual average of stripers caught by commercial fishermen in these waters is approximately 595,000 pounds per year. The commercial harvest peaked in the Roanoke-Albemarle Sound waters from 1967 to 1969, when catches averaged more than 900,000 pounds per year. While sportsmen were having good success, they were actually harvesting a tiny fraction of the fish available in those waters during the spawning runs. The smallest commercial catch in the Roanoke was in 1979 when 243,744 pounds of striper were hauled in. That is the lowest figure during the study for the area. This decline of commercial fish that occurred after 1976 brought considerable criticism of management policies and the discussions which followed resulted in restrictions on gill nets and bow nets in the Roanoke in 1981.

Striped bass are abundant in other areas along the NC coast and the average mean total commercially landed for all the years on record is 790,000 pounds per year. That harvest hit a peak in 1971 with 2,318,000 pounds. The heaviest catches ever recorded by the commercial harvesters were during 1968-1976. These records were due largely to a great population of striped bass in the Atlantic along the Outer Banks.

The record catches of rockfish during those years precipitated bitter controversies between resident and non-resident commercial fishing crews. There was also some controversy between sports fishermen and commercial fishermen operating within the Cape Hatteras National Seashore. The National Park Service adjucated some of these disputes, and federal regulations cleared up confusion between the activities of sport and commercial fishermen for the stripers. There has been a minimum of controversy and hostility since that time.

With stripers in abundance each spring in the Roanoke, the devout anglers for this species, who now enjoy catching them in 36 states where they have been transplanted, are anxious to try their expertise with jigs, spoons, plugs and live baits where the fish is still truly wild. Most experienced rockfish enthusiasts believe that a fish right out of the saltwater is even more of a battler than his freshwater cousins.

Accessibility to the Roanoke River by boat is readily available. There are numerous sites along the 140 miles of river bank. Public boating access areas are maintained by the North Carolina Wildlife Resources Commission near the mouth of the River at Hamilton (river mile 62), Weldon (river mile 130) and at Roanoke Rapids (river mile 134). Other public ramps are located in the lower section of the river at Plymouth (Weyerhaeuser Plant, river mile 7), Jamesville (river mile 18) and at Williamston (river mile 30). The section between Hamilton and Weldon has no maintained access areas open to the public, even for a fee. Consequently, this is one of the least fished areas of the Roanoke, and a great area for sports fishermen to try their hand at landing the giants that come in from the sea.

A growing fraternity of striped bass anglers is evidenced all over America as the exotic has become commonplace almost everywhere. But there is still something special about enticing one of these natives of the Atlantic to strike a man made lure and then pulling the big lunker over the gunnels. At Albemarle Sound and the Roanoke River, in spawning time, you can still do well with unusual regularity.

TAR HEEL TARPON MAKING A MARK

Rays of morning sunshine peeked through fast-moving clouds in the narrow creek that sprouted off the Cape Fear River in Brunswick County in mid-August. John McLean, George Bear and Lawrence Cook patiently rocked in their 15-foot jonboat as the tidal waters of the Atlantic swelled and subsided in the waters of the dingy creek, its banks lined with empty shells that had once housed a myriad of crustaceans in this Bald Head Island fishing paradise. The trio of avid anglers had selected this creek behind Bald Head for their morning quest for these big silver sides.

Isolated from the mainland by two miles of water, Bald Head is a narrow spit of land in the mouth of the Cape Fear that was barren until about three decades ago. Now many affluent have built homes on the isolated sand dunes and suddenly it has become a fishing mecca with a skyrocketing reputation for tarpon schools with the arrival of each fall season.

The three seemingly useless fishing lines swayed in the breeze from McLean's humble flat-bottomed boat. Nothing had bothered the heads of half-pound spots that baited each No. 4/0 hook as they quivered on the bottom of the eight-foot-deep creek where the tidal current pushed them around and made the heads look almost alive. Then McLean's rod tip fluttered, stopped and then went down to stay. The limber rod was tested in the succeeding seconds as it seemed the very devil had gulped down the panfish head and was fleeing.

Bear and Cook hurriedly reeled in their lines and quickly hauled up the anchors as McLean set the hook with gusto. It was obvious this critter on the hook wasn't coming to the gunnels without a tussle. He didn't!

It was 9:20 a.m. when McLean hooked the fish and the monster had the weight, energy and stamina to fight the tight drag and 20-pound test line for three tiring hours. McLean held on as the fish on the line dragged the boat and the three Lumberton, North Carolina, anglers up the river to the Pfizer Terminal, almost three miles from where the strike and hookup occurred. Then the fish tired and slowly came alongside the fishing bateau. The gaff hooked the huge tarpon in the gills and moments later he was gasping for air on the deck. He was long enough to cramp the quarters of the three anglers who looked at each other and smiled. Surely, this was the day that tarpon fishermen would use to document a fact—tarpon are back in the waters off the Carolinas.

Outdoorsmen no longer have to drive hundreds of miles southward to fish for these giants of the sea. The tarpon renaissance in Tar Heelia is here. McLean's monster weight 80 pounds and was long enough to practically fill the boat.

Dr. Ernest Brown, also of Lumberton, has some tarpon stories of his own to tell about his experiences at Bald Head.

One August he went by the fish market at Wrightsville and bought a dozen hand-size spots for bait. He cut off the heads and had the rest of the fish dressed for the dinner table. With his fish heads on ice, he motored to a calm spot near the island and found a gentle east wind blowing. With the moon waxing, he considered the conditions ideal, as do many tarpon hunters. The east wind and growing moon on a falling tide are ideal for the movement of tarpon in the Cape Fear tidal waters. They seem to feed more under those conditions.

Brown, with his wife Sue and daughter Rachel Hall, a practicing attorney, anchored the 20-foot boat and settled down to watch the rod tips. Bingo! Both Sue and Rachel's rods dipped and stayed down at the same time. They yelled and set the hooks. Both succeed in hooking their quarry and the wrestling match began.

Miraculously, the ladies fought those tarpon around and around the boat, passing the tackle under each other's lines time after tedious time. They out-muscled the fish and eventually got both of them to boatside. Sue released her fish, but Rachel insisted on keeping hers for mounting. It weighed 65 pounds and still adorns her mantel.

"I use a fish finder rig and fish the bottom with about two

ounces of lead and a big steel hook. I usually use spot heads for bait, but some people prefer heads of blues, menhaden, pinfish, whiting and other species. When the tarpon are in the shallows no more than 150 yards off the Bald Head beaches, you can catch 'em," Brown says. They go up the creeks, too.

L. B. Bennett, of Long Beach, is one of the knowledgeable natives who fishes a productive hole in the Bald Head area that is widely known as the tarpon hole. They hang out and stalk food here.

Northward up the Carolina coast in the Beaufort area, tarpon are attracting attention more than they have in years. Thousands are in the Pamlico Sound off Cedar Island across from Ocracoke and tarpon are often seen greyhounding in the hot months of summer. Most anglers in that area use dead whole panfish for baits and fish the holes in the estuaries. Some tarpon have migrated from Florida since the '20's and veterans like Ralph Forrest of Oriental have caught many of them in the Pamlico River and sound.

Fishermen for years have believed that tarpon seldom roam further north than the Pamlico River, but for the past five years they have been caught by devout tarpon stalkers in the Chesapeake Bay off the Eastern Shore of Virginia. One man acknowledges catching 23 and another 18 in that huge bay. They prefer to remain nameless, but tarpon are in the Chesapeake Bay.

Virginia fishermen are not particularly anxious to encourage tarpon anglers. The natives are kind of closed-mouth about where and how they fish. They do not believe they are plentiful enough for great tourist pressure on the species, but some admit to fishing with whole dead panfish.

There is some reluctance to divulge the secrets of tarpon fishing at Bald Head in Carolina. Most veterans say the fishing is simple. There are no guides, but if you have your own boat, maneuver it close to the island or some of the nearby creeks in the month of August when there's a little wind from the east and the moon is filling, the silver kings will be there and with patience and practice, you can put them in the boat. But you are on your own. You won't get much help from the locals. That makes tarpon fishing in Tar Heelia challenging.

PANDEMONIUM WHITE PERCH

Few species of fish are so rabbit-like in reproduction that their population is never threatened by angling pressure, but biologists agree the racket-loving white perch can fill livewells in the Carolinas and never suffer depletion. This gourmet panfish is unique in many other ways, among them its ability to thrive in fresh water, brackish estuaries and even in the sea itself.

Perhaps its most remarkable characteristic is its attraction to surface noises that is a big assist for anglers stalking this species. Because it is found more often in freshwater lakes than elsewhere, many sportsmen consider the white perch the most fun to find and catch of any of the panfish.

Though it runs in wolfpack schools in estuary waters all the way north to Maine, it does not often make the headlines like it does in eastern North Carolina from Elizabeth City to South Carolina. The Waccamaw is a clear water lake named for a small Indian tribe that once thrived along its white sandy shores in the Green Swamp. Tar Heel anglers have dragged in this testy and tasty fighter for more than half a century from this seven-by-five-mile natural lake in Columbus County.

Generally weighing less than one pound, but with an occasional 2-pounder to brag about, white perch gulp down almost any small bait, dead or alive, when it is trolled, drifted or retrieved near the surface. They feed in giant schools in open water, almost always considerable distances from the shoreline. And when you can locate these schooling wolfpacks, they can be caught by the bucketful the year around. While they are reported to be the most active from April through October in Lake Waccamaw, hearty sportsmen who wrap up and motor out into the lake often find and catch 50 and 60 a day, even on the coldest days of winter. They are a gluttonous species, always hungry and always cooperative for anglers stalking a mess of fish for the dinner table.

White perch is among the easiest fish to find. Taking a paddle and splashing water around the boat apparently makes the white perch think there's a school of forage fish nearby. You can see them coming to that kind of noise several hundred feet before they reach your boat and bait. Often you know about where to stop your boat and start the racket by the telltale ripples on the surface. Schools of white perch will attack small minnows, mayflies, mosquitoes, worms and anything else that floats on the surface. They make no effort to conceal their presence from anglers. In a boat on a near-windless day, you see them working a football field away. The excitement begins when you motor close to the feeding frenzy and cast, troll or drift a spinner, tiny plug, jig, fly or a live minnow, cricket or wriggling earthworm near their mad attack on the food supply.

Some anglers prefer to anchor and drop their artificials or live baits near the bottom where the species will return as soon as they have gulped down the surface protein. A bait fished just off a muddy bottom will get strikes from available white perch but most of the devout sportsmen who go after the species, catch them near the surface on lures or minnows dragged on or inches beneath the surface.

Half a century ago, when there were few outboards or good boats, a troop of Boy Scouts from Albemarle, North Carolina, camped out for a week on the shores of Lake Waccamaw. In that era camping was really roughing it. The scouts carried live chickens that they dressed and cooked as they needed them. Other uncanned staples were kept on ice in a tin tub. There were no frozen foods. Several meals were confidently planned around fish from the lake. The scoutmaster knew white perch could be caught even by young novices.

One July morning he scheduled a fishing trip for the dinner meal. Guides were scarce, as was money, but he found Charlie Pate who lived in the village of Lake Waccamaw. He would carry a group of scouts fishing for half a day for $10.00. With the price established, the scoutmaster paid $2.00 and eight scouts paid $1.00 each. That secured the guide fee and the boat putt-putted off from the north shoreline the following morning at safe light.

Guide Pate first crossed the clear and beautiful lake to the south shore, got out of the boat with a 12-foot drag seine, and asked an older scout to help. They made two fast dips in the clear water around the cypress trees and had hundreds of two-inch minnows trapped within five minutes. He dumped them in a minnow bucket, pushed the boat off from the shoreline, and slowly motored a few hundred yards off shore.

With a soft south wind blowing, he cut the motor and told the boatload of young anglers to stick a hook through a minnow just below the dorsal fin and drop the lines on the windward side of the boat. Each scout had a 12-foot cane pole, braided cotton line, a piece of wraparound lead from a junked car battery and a big round cork the size of a golf ball four or five feet above the hook. Admittedly, it was humble tackle, but that memorable morning those enthusiastic and crowded scouts dragged in 91 nice white perch. They fed the whole troop at dinner time.

Perhaps the most unorthodox lesson learned that morning was how these fish loved to come to a noise. That old native guide spotted the ripples on the water where the white perch were active when he had crossed the lake to get the bait. He put his boatload of enthusiastic fishermen right on the school quickly and the excitement reigned until the last minnow was eaten. The shock to the scouts was how he made a noise to attract the fish. They had been taught from childhood to be quiet while they fished even from the shore. Charlie Pate debunked an old wives tale.

White perch fishing by today's experts still defies the teaching of most authorities who declare it is O.K. to talk but don't bang around in the boat and cause vibrations. Today's best white perch fishermen often stomp their feet in the boat, even take a paddle and bang on the gunnels. Obviously, there is a difference between bass fishing and going after white perch. Noise isn't a perch danger signal.

Among the two best white perch anglers in North Carolina are Pete Strickland and George Fipps of Chadbourn. They have caught livewells full of white perch from the brackish waters of the Chesapeake Bay to the inland ponds around

Greenville, North Carolina, and in their home county where Lake Waccamaw is located.

"We prefer our white perch fishing on days when there is a little wind that helps us drift slowly and when there is some cloud cover. Perch seem to rise to the surface frequently when it is cloudy and we like to drift better than troll. We have no trouble locating the schools. If it is not too rough, you can see the circles the feeding fish make on the surface. We get close to the commotion and start casting a tiny minnow-like lure near the breaking fish. Meantime, we put out cane poles with plain minnows on the hooks. We fish some with corks and some without corks and each line has a lead shot or two five or six inches above the bait. It's not unusual to have two or three white perch on our lines at the same time. We catch many in the 2-pound class although white perch generally weigh a pound or less," Strickland said.

"I know it doesn't make sense considering all we have ever learned about fishing and making a racket, but we not only catch a lot of white perch after splashing and beating on the boat, we catch several 4- and 5-pound largemouths on the same hooks and lines right in with the perch. They apparently are feeding with the perch and the noise sure doesn't run them away," Strickland says. "They are busy eating.

"I can tell you something else. These white perch are fine on the dinner table. They have firm, almost hard, white meat that is delicious. The last time we went after these perch was in June and we caught 141. They will bite early and late in the day, every month of the year and the moon doesn't mean a thing to white perch," this veteran Tar Heel fisherman said.

Like most panfish, the white perch lack the stamina to struggle for a long time on a hook. They make a gallant first run and thrill the light and ultralight tackle fisherman. A large perch sometimes gets the line across his shoulder and does a lot of bucking and running that is challenging for a short period. The slab-size fish may struggle in circles and then dive for the bottom. Most anglers feel that the search for the schools, the vicious strike and the cavorting antics of the bigger fish make white perch fishing a memorable sporting experience.

Some white perch fishing is done with flyrod tackle. The perch will hit small bugs and poppers from size 8 to 10. But nymphs and dry flies that are similar to their natural diet are the most effective. In Lake Waccamaw, lures that mimic mayflies that fall in the spring are the ideal fly bait. Floating patterns like the Cahill, Black Gnat and Black Ant are also good fly fishing lures.

While it doesn't seem to be appropriate for Lake Waccamaw, in the ponds of Elizabeth City and the Chesapeake Bay estuary, some white perch fishermen say the fish rise from deep water at sundown and remain active until dark. There are even reports of white perch after dark going near shallow shorelines to feed. But generally it is an open water fish like the striped bass that it closely resembles.

Perch populations cycle, but where they are found, they are in abundance, and no amount of angling pressure has ever reduced the population. State fishery experts have netted tons of perch from small lakes year after year without affecting the standing crop. The annual production of a single pair of 1-pound perch will more than replace all of the species that fishermen catch. A careless spawner, the female may hatch as many as 150,000 eggs when she is only two years old or less. The eggs will adhere to anything they touch and will hatch within five days after being fertilized by marauding males. The hatching ratio in relation to other species is enormous. Trout eggs take 50 days. Perch have a long lifespan, commonly reaching ages of 12 years, with some documented at 17 years.

Almost everything works in favor of the white perch except that unique trait of being attracted to noise. That puts the fish within catching distance of the angler who might never find these panfish in the deep water where they normally live, if they did not fall to the ancient ploy of noisy splashing on the surface that relays a phony message of something to eat in the offering.

White perch is a pandemonium species. They all have ravenous appetites comparable to wolves. Hundreds forage in packs stalking anything dead or alive that promises to satisfy their healthy appetites. Fishermen cause many to make mistakes. They can't tell the difference between a splashing paddle and a school of shad on the surface. Nor can they distinguish a mayfly from a hairy hook on a line or a plastic minnow from the real thing. As long as they continue to rush toward the rackets man makes and strike whatever contrivance anglers flaunt in their faces, white perch will be a favorite for a special society of sportsmen who fish for both fun and food in the Carolinas. More anglers than ever go after these noise-loving panfish that simplify the search.

MENHADEN GIVE THEMSELVES AWAY

The perch-shaped menhaden trolled for mackerel and other species of big fish around and over the Masonboro manmade reef off Wrightsville Beach, pour into the Waterway and inlet throughout the summer and fall months. While some other species are betrayed by diving birds and predators, the menhaden give themselves away.

They move about in huge schools and flip and frolic on the surface in eddy areas near sandbars and off marshland sloughs. Sometimes they move right in around structures, piers, docks, bridge abutments and buoys. Cast netters eyeball the surface at dawn when the fish are the most active and sneak close enough to the flipping bait fish to encircle them with a 12-foot bloom. Often you can catch a morning's supply at a single cast.

Menhaden will spook when a boat moves near them and they will dive. But a little patience and an alert vigil will pay off. They will surface again in a matter of minutes and usually not far from their original playground. The species is widely known as a "fertilizer" fish and they are caught by the billions in the open Atlantic and used in agriculture. But enough of them swim into the Wrightsville Beach estuary to provide sports fishermen with a good supply for trolling over shipwrecks just offshore from the sunbathers on the strand.

SLASH CREEK'S MIRACLE OYSTERS

Did you ever hear of a one-year-old oyster reaching a super-select length of over five inches? Normally it takes oysters along the Carolinas coasts two years to be of harvesting size, and that's generally conceived as much less than five inches. But a creek with the crazy name of "Slash" at Cape Hatteras, North Carolina, is turning out the oyster giants every 12 months and biologists have launched a study to discover why Slash Creek oysters grow so much faster and bigger than in other estuaries with similar capabilities.

Old fishermen around Cape Hatteras have known for years that the Slash Creek oysters were bigger than any others and told some tall tales about their growth. The stories got back to Hughes Tillett, a Sea Grant marine advisory agent in Manteo. He decided to check out some of those old salt stories. Sure enough, the oysters there were giants as compared with those of most surrounding oyster-producing waters.

Tillett launched some experiments designed to determine just what the Slash Creek oysters had that others lacked. He wanted to unlock the secret and he gathered some spats (baby oysters) the size of air rifle shot, and planted them in trays in the Slash Creek oyster fields. Bingo! There was something unusual going on in the life of Slash Creek shellfish.

Those tiny spats grew out of the trays so fast that Tillett had to scatter them to keep them from smothering each other. In half the time it normally takes to grow oysters to harvestable size, Tillett's planted spats were ready for market.

Amazed at this growth explosion, Tillett gathered some samples of his crop and carried them to Glenn Patterson, a biologist at the University of Maryland. Patterson's study discovered that these unusual oyster freaks had twice as much sterol of several kinds as normal oysters. And sterols are what influences growth and other body activities in oysters and all animal life. This dramatic difference led Patterson to believe that these compounds were responsible for the robust Slash Creek giants.

Apparently the Slash Creek water is filled with a food supply that the oysters glut on that quickly produces these sterols and perhaps is responsible for the rapid growth.

Patterson thinks it is possible that environmental changes have destroyed the preferred food of oysters in most waters while it still exists in abundance in Slash Creek. There the shellfish can still get a square meal and grow to proportions of yesteryear before man polluted the earth, and made it harder for the water to support fast growth of sea creatures. Maybe the Slash Creek species is what once was normal everywhere. Now others are stunted while that small area has the purity to grow real lunkers. That's at least a possibility.

Future research may unlock the secret so scientists can learn how to give the typical oysters in other growing areas the same robust health that Tillett found so evident in the creatures of Slash Creek.

BIG FISH MIXED BAG

Submerged in about 50 feet of water four miles off the mouth of Masonboro Inlet at Wrightsville Beach, North Carolina, are an old sea-going tug and a larger freighter that were planted on the bottom a number of years ago to encourage gamefish to congregate and thus enhance the outside sports fishing off this Tar Heel coast. It has been amazingly successful from spring to fall and great catches of a variety of challenging gamefish are caught by thousands of anglers who crisscross over these abandoned boats trolling artificial lures and live menhaden. Big fish are pulled over the gunnels of humble jonboats and sophisticated 30-foot fishing machines. While much of the attention of fishermen here is focused on king mackerel, still the primary species sought by both tourists and locals, memorable experiences of fighting big cobia, sharks, dolphin and even a few sailfish, are recounted almost daily at the launching ramps at day's end. Obviously, the manmade reef that is so conveniently located only minutes from the strand, has proven its worth and continues to bring smiles to fishermen after the catch of their dreams.

There are still those bottom-fishing enthusiasts who simply anchor their skiffs alongside the wrecks and dangle cut bait on the bottom for black bass, grouper, snapper, flounder, spots and many other edible species. But the society of bottom fishermen is small on the Masonboro reef as compared with the armada of trolling boats, often numbering near one hundred, that putt-putt over and around the reef trying to entice giant species to strike.

The Masonboro reef is near enough to the shore that even river boats often dot the horizon on calm mornings heading for the wrecks. Northeast gales discourage ventures by small boat fishermen but often in the summer months there are more little craft trolling over the reef than larger, safer vessels. Small boat anglers catch their share of big fish, too, and it is a moment to remember when a four-foot green cobia is pulled over the side only half tired. Chaos reigns until the powerful fish is tranquilized with a rap over the head with a fungo bat or similar club. Some broken bones, smashed tackle boxes, crushed coolers and ruined rods and reels are credited to hooked cobia antics.

Permanent markers are anchored at each end of the sunken ship reef. It's near these two buoys that cobia often loll around from daybreak until an hour or so after sunrise in most warm months. While some cobia are caught by trolling fishermen, many are hooked by casters who flip live eels, pinfish or other natural baits into the shadows of the markers. The ugly cobia go after live dwarf eels ten or twelve inches long more often than any other bait, real or artificial, and when the hook is set, cobia fight with the stamina and determination of the devil himself. Big cobia often pull a small boat around like it was a cork on a line until the fish tires and succumbs to the gaff or the net. The Masonboro reef is one of the best cobia fishing locations on the Carolina coast. They are not there every day, but when they are, you can often see them just below the surface and put a bait in their faces. Often you will see the cobia dash out for the hook before he strikes.

But cobia is just one of the several big fish species that inhabit the Masonboro reef. The most sought-after fish is the king mackerel, and they are more abundant than cobia. Strangely, the kings almost always strike best in the early morning, and preferably when there are some ripples on the water. Their sharp eyesight helps them spot the angler before he spots them on calm days, especially when there is no overcast. Often the fishing day is done by nine or ten o'clock when the kings simply turn off and stay turned off. Occasionally, they will come out of hiding and hit again near dusk, but most of the Masonboro reef fishing is done in the early morning. The wind often becomes a factor for the small boaters as the day wears on.

All sizes of fishing boats carry anglers to this prolific deep-water hideout. In calm weather, most of them are skiffs in the 16- to 18-foot range and virtually everyone trolls for mackerel. Some veterans prefer big topwater lures or shallow diving crankbaits with a few successful with big bright-colored, bucktail jigs, like the Christmas Tree artificial. There are always a number of bigger, more sophisticated fishing boats that intermingle with the smaller craft. But whether they are large or small, fully equipped or just a single fisherman with a rod and reel in his hand, the bulk of the mackerel anglers troll live menhaden about 100 feet behind the boat and near the surface. Some tie on heavy weights and let one rig tempt the suspended fish atop the buried tug with its menhaden moving along. A few use downriggers. But mackerel apparently know that the fertilizer fish is a surface species normally and most of the strikes are on top.

Veterans learned years ago that the best homemade hook arrangement for big mackerel is a three-pronged device. It has a big steel hook in front with the menhaden hooked through the lips or nose. Then No. 4 treble hooks are four inches and eight inches behind the one with the live bait. The first treble hook is pushed through the bait's dorsal fin and the last one dangles behind the trolled bait. Mackerel almost always strike the whole hook and bait conglomeration, but are hung on the trailing trebles.

When a king strikes the menhaden, most old salts do no hook setting. Certainly there is no gusto yank on the rod. The fish hits when he is charging at full speed and with the reel free-spooling the mackerel takes out yards of line as the clicker screams. Most big fish have the hooks well in their mouths by the time the fisherman gets his hands on the reel and they are hooked. With 17- to 25-pound test line that is used by most mackerel chasers, you generally save your fish if the drag is properly set. A few will come unbuttoned. Some will break the line if you have been careless and not cut off a few feet after your last catch, where nicks have weakened your monofilament. Even the piano wire leaders occasionally break if a kink has been left in the wire. When it straightens out, it often snaps and the fish is gone.

Mackerel over the wreck usually make two long, fast runs and they are through. You have a pretty good idea of what species you have before it is in sight if you have fished here for big fish and remember their traits. Their fight pattern gives this species away.

Sharks abound over the reef. With myriad species of panfish sheltering in the sunken vessels, sharks prowl the area for food. When a menhaden trolls past these big critters, they may strike it with the same gusto as a mackerel. But you'll usually know quickly that it's a shark on the line. They tend to stay down and to shake their heads from side to side as they attempt to dislodge the hooks. They may make a run or two, but not with the same characteristics as the big kings. Sharks are notorious line cutters. Their sharp teeth and violent side-to-side head shaking cut many lines that would have held a king fish. No longer considered a trash species, most black tip sharks and some other types are filleted for the dinner table when they are landed at Masonboro. They are challenging giants on the line that are growing in popularity. Some fishermen are exclusively shark hunters.

Some dolphin are hooked at Masonboro on trolled menhaden and even a few sailfish make mistakes and thrill anglers with their acrobatics. Few fishermen are here just for dolphin or sailfish, but almost weekly there are some good stories at the Wrightsville Beach marinas about the billfish that got away or the one that didn't.

Bottom fishing along this reef is still the choice of a few tourists and natives. Mostly they reel in spots, flounder, pinfish, triggerfish, snappers and sea bass. But that isn't always the case. In the fall, there are times when big groupers visit the wrecks, and they will go after shrimp, squid, crabs or almost any kind of cut bait that reaches the bottom.

Then there is the convict fish: sheepshead. Growing almost to hand-towel-size, these powerful flat fish suck sand fiddlers and other baits on the bottom. They are one of the most difficult species to hook. They give no discernible tap-tap bite that most fish relay up the line. The are bait thieves and you may feed a sheepshead a dozen fiddlers before you hook him. But when a ten- or twelve-pound 'head gets on the line, you have a struggle to remember. Sheepsheads like to feed on the barnacles and other crustaceans that grow on the rusty, sunken ships, and bottom anglers with patience often drag up real giants of the species. It's a fine meal on the dinner table, too.

Whether you are fishing on the surface, on the bottom or somewhere in between where the sharks glide along, you have a good chance of hanging a real saltwater giant over the Masonboro reef that will test your skill and endurance. You have only to listen to some of the veterans who know where and how to catch menhaden that is by far the most productive bait. You learn how to keep them alive in an aerated plastic tank, but that they won't live overnight. Catching menhaden for bait is a daylight chore that can be fun when you learn how to properly throw a big cast net. Some people say it is as much fun catching the bait as it is the fish. When you have unlocked a few of the Masonboro reef secrets, you'll start catching big fish close to shore and easy to reach even with lake and river boats. It requires a little caution. The Atlantic, even close in, can get rough quickly. Unless the morning is calm, it is foolhardy to challenge the waves to run to the reef. Discretion is the better part of valor and small boat anglers will do well to be patient for another day. There is one factor that enhances safety on the reef—every day from spring to fall the area is covered with an armada of boats. Many have good ship-to-shore radios and the Coast Guard is only five miles away. If you are in trouble, help is usually not far away. It's a great mixed bag spot for big fish that doesn't take but a few minutes to reach. It's on the horizon and there may be a big king there now waiting for your menhaden bait to pass by.

CARP—HERO OR VILLAIN

My three-inch oblong bobber lay dead in the water. The single shot on the line and the four kernels of sweet roasting ear corn impaled on the No. 4 steel hook rested atop the mud in the 171,000-acre Santee Cooper reservoir in the South Carolina Low Country. I was bank fishing with a cane pole in the diversion canal that joins Lake Moultrie with Lake Marion. This cider-colored water was 12 feet deep and warm this calm May morning. There just had to be some giant German carp here. We had been baiting this hole with chunks of corn bread in a loose mesh onion sack for more than a week and it always brought these old buglenoses a-runnin' as their appetites are notorious and seldom satisfied. The bobber dipped ever so slightly and small rivulets danced in ever-bigger circles from its disturbance. It moved an inch or two and stopped. There was not another indication of activity. I waited. Nothing but stillness. Something must have sucked my bait off the hook, I surmised. I'll bring it in and rebait. I turned the reel handle a couple of times and started the retrieve. Oh yeah! The devil was hooked. And so it seemed for the next quarter hour as I tussled with one of the strongest fresh-water fish in America—the much-maligned German carp that thrives in 40 states as well as in most other countries around the world. That big mama weighed over 18 pounds and if you hadn't been told that she was not good to eat, you could feed the family some quality protein for several days. Unfortunately, the word has spread in the last half century that these fish are not the very tastiest to eat and the carp is no longer a delicacy at the dinner table in America. But in millions of homes around the world where that message hasn't been heard, people continue to eat and enjoy this ultra-prolific species that grows to giant size in almost any kind of polluted or unpolluted water.

"Whether carp are good to eat or not is a matter of education on eating," says Ed Chateau, of the U.S. Fish and Wildlife

Service. His office has conducted extensive studies of carp and discovered there is an abundant population of the species.

The late Dr. John N. Hamlet, noted naturalist who captured the monkeys used to perfect the polio vaccine, and a native of Rapid City, South Dakota, says, "In the West, where nobody told us that carp were not good to eat, we ate them regularly and liked them. But just as soon as the word got spread around that they were not good to eat, people started disliking them."

In truth this cyrinid from Asia, brought to Europe in 1227, was relished as food for half a century after it was introduced as a source of food in this country in 1872. But it became little appreciated as an abundance of tastier meats became available for the dinner table. Yet, worldwide, it is still the most avidly sought freshwater protein, and in China and Russia it is a leading food species, usually cooked whole in the oven and served head, eyes and all.

The carp story began in America in 1872, when J. A. Poppe of Sonoma, California, shipped 83 carp from Holstein, Germany. Only five sick fish survived the trip, but they were nursed back to health in a private pond. They eventually spawned and Poppe had a thriving business raising and selling these fish not only in the United States, but in Central America and the Hawaiian Islands. Those five six-inch carp grew to 16 inches from August until May and produced 3,000 healthy offspring. Poppe was on the way to great wealth.

"Every fish I can possible send to market sells readily for one dollar per pound (much higher priced than they are today, even with inflation). Farmers who have natural facilities on their places for making ponds and who have access to canals or rivers communicating with large cities, can greatly increase their income with small trouble and expense," Poppe wrote.

"There ought to be one person in every county who would raise choice carp as stock fish to sell to others to fatten for their own tables. It would be a cheap but sumptuous food and at the same time very convenient, as they are ready to be eaten at all times of the year," Poppe expounded over one hundred years ago.

The U.S. Bureau of Fisheries took an active part in the distribution of carp and in 1883 at the peak of the importation, 260,000 were obtained from Germany and distributed to 298 of the 301 congressional districts.

By 1899, there were 3.6 million pounds of carp harvested by commercial fishermen in Lake Erie. In the Illinois River the population had exploded so that by 1896, 22 million pounds were netted and sold.

Wisconsin in recent years has determined that carp will produce up to 439 pounds per acre and that they thrive on domestic sewage, as they do in China today. In 1972 Minnesota's Lake Minnetonka yielded 225,000 pounds of carp in a single netting operation by a state fisheries crew, an unprecedented record seine haul.

While in the beginning sportsmen were enthusiastic over the introduction and expansion of carp in this country, by the turn of the century some anglers and fishery agencies were beginning to reevaluate and some condemned this prolific mud rooter that was turning shallow bays and lakes into mudholes.

Edward Prince, a Canadian, warned, "German carp are nomadic in their habits and wander apparently aimlessly into all accessible water, hence if introduced into any streams, will spread rapidly over the whole system. . . . Like undesirable weeds, they have spread everywhere and it is practically impossible to limit their progress or to effect their extirpation."

Carp soon became destructive of the habitat as they dominated lakes and rivers and destroyed much of the wild celery and wild rice that once covered many inland marshes. It soon led to wholesale poisoning of many carp-infested waters as sportsmen and governmental agencies analyzed the species as a threat to all others as well as to waterfowl, especially the canvasback duck.

But the old freshwater fighter still thrives in much of America, except for the coniferous region of the North where the waters are not as fertile as in the South and West. The largest concentration of carp is now in the Mississippi River system and the eastern Great Lakes. Carp are still commercially harvested there, but their value has plummeted. The average price for the 28 million pounds harvested annually from 1955 to 1969 was 3.8 cents a pound.

Easily understood today, that price is way out of kilter as inflation has skyrocketed and carp are being sold in many areas of the country now for 50 to 80 cents and more a pound as other protein foods have inflated prices out of reach of many American families and that economic factor is bringing carp sports fishing with hook and line back to some semblance of respectability in many parts of the country.

While the quality of the carp as food faces many challenges, and it is put down for its muddying of the water and destructive habits, there has never been any skepticism about its prowess as a fighter on the line when sportsmen decide to hunt for this big game of fresh water.

As John Wilson wrote in 1978 in the Kentucky Department of Fish and Wildlife Resources magazine when he was fighting a carp on the line and was asked what on earth he had hooked, replied, "I don't know, but if it is a bass, I don't think I want it in the same boat with me!"

That fish that Wilson was struggling with bulldogged near the bottom and he reasoned that if it were a bass, it had to be a world record. Ten minutes later he began gaining some line and his wife Sally netted the fish and heaved it over the side. The carp was not even particularly large, just over 7-pounds, but Wilson declared, "It gave me more fight than any bass I'd ever caught, including my largest—a 10 3/4-pounder. Although there were no spectacular tail-walking leaps and long runs, I've never caught a fish that evidenced such power or put up a more determined battle. The carp, I decided right then, is a worthy adversary."

Despite its power and challenge on the end of the line, there are many in the angling fraternity who begrudge space in the water for any species other than the one they fish and they label everything else "rough fish" or "trash fish." That moniker includes catfish, shad, white perch and several varieties of suckers. Many are unaware that in some parts of the country the popular largemouth bass and its cousins, the smallmouths have at some time been considered trash species. Even today the bluegill is legally a rough fish, since only black bass, white bass, rock bass, crappies, walleye, sauger, rockfish, yellow perch, muskellunge, northern pike, chain pickerel and trout are officially game fish. Without trash fish, the forage species, there would be no gamefish. These are the food supply of the species people prefer today.

Some so-called rough fish have become excellent tablefare. Almost everyone now respects the catfish as a delightful dinner meat. And worldwide the carp is equally respected as it has been raised for food for a thousand years. But the old saying about one man's trash is another man's treasure prevails in the United States.

All freshwater fish are edible. Some have more bones than persnickety diners are willing to remove. There are some oily species that concentrate impurities from the water into their flesh, giving them a strong or muddy taste, an off-flavor. Some cooks can circumvent objectionable qualities with techniques and commercial processes convert any species into fish sticks and patties that are acceptable.

Catching carp is an art and more carp are not caught because many fishermen do not have the skill, finesse and patience necessary to induce them to bite. Carp are caught all over the country and in almost all seasons except where the water temperature drops below 50 degrees. They hibernate at that temperature. Lakes, rivers, impoundments, swamps and even dugout mudholes are homes for this hardy species that requires a minimum of oxygen and can survive in a mixture of mud and water that is so dirty there is no depth perception.

Carp will eat almost anything dead or alive, and the best baits for them vary widely. While there are commercially marketed baits in the tackle shops, most carp anglers make their own from flour, cornmeal and seedless cotton kneaded together and rolled into marble-size balls that the small, sucker-type mouth of the carp can swallow along with the embedded hook. But either fresh or canned whole-kernel roasting ear corn is a great bait and will stay on the hook a little better than the conventional dough bait. Cheese is a good carp attractor, too, as is white soap and Irish potatoes.

Carp are most often caught in warm water and they feed infrequently when water temperature is below 50 degrees Fahrenheit. Frost often marks the end of carp fishing season. Their appetites increase with oxygen content and this accounts for some biting frenzy at times when it is windy or rainy. In shallow lakes, carp in midafternoon are likely to be near the surface if there is little wind, the sun is shining and water temperature is over 70 degrees. They often glide around with their dorsal fins above the surface. Others will hang motionless in the weeds. They will show no inclination to bite anything.

As dusk arrives, the temperature drops, they become more active and feed both on the surface and the bottom. They begin jumping and will move toward the east side of the lake as the last rays of sunlight focus there. On cloudy afternoons with the temperature falling rapidly, they move into deeper holes or in the shade to prevent radiation loss. Carp often feed all night and this becomes a choice time to fish for them with hook and line. They seek out the warmer places in the lake and will school there, anxious to bite if the water is about 60 degrees.

Carp begin to leap in the Carolinas as temperatures rise and for reasons no one really understands. It may be an action preliminary to feeding, but that is conjecture. If there has been a lot of boating activity in the lake, carp may have been so alarmed as to stop biting completely until after dark when the chaos has subsided.

When carp have full stomachs, they are often impossible to catch as they will rest, digest their meal and await another feeding period. Anglers will then have their best success if they get in on the beginning of a favorable temperature period and other desirable conditions.

Carp anglers do not go out for this species with a sewing thread line, flimsy rod and toy-store reel. These giants that easily reach weights up to 40-pounds and above, will destroy skimpy outfits and leave you holding only a handle. You must have heavy spinning or casting equipment or a bamboo pole as big as your wrist to fight these muscular, tackle-busting brutes. Monofilament lines should be at least 20-pound test or more.

Baits are usually lowered to the bottom, but if there is so

much mud you fear the morsel will be hidden from the nosy bottom-eaters, you can put a tiny cork a few inches above the bait with a small lead on the bottom. This will keep the bait visible and easily available for the marauding, feeding fish. You can use a cork on the surface that lies flat with no weight pressure and it will indicate when you are getting a bite, but only after the carp has picked up the morsel, sucked it down and started moving off. Often you have the fish on the line several minutes before he moves and before you are aware he has eaten your offering. You'll know it once the line is tightened and the fish knows he is hooked. He'll fight you every second until you put him in the boat or drag him out on the hill as many natives do in carp country like Santee Cooper.

Some carp anglers fish for these hefty critters with a tight line against their rod tips. The line is tight from the slight pull against the sinker, not the bait itself that must float free. But when the cautious carp nibbles on the bait, the rod tip dips ever so gently a time or two. You withstand the urge to set the hook for several moments while the nibbling goes on and when the tip stays down, you know you have the fish with the hook in his mouth and you set it with some gusto. The fireworks will then begin.

Carp will often accumulate in the same areas that catfish gather. If there is a fish dressing spot where guts, eggs and other residue are put into the lake every day or at least on a regular basis, both the catfish and carp will prowl this territory for food. Chummed, so to speak in the area, carp will take bits of fish, roe or other meat parts impaled on a hook. Often you can catch fish here during the middle of the day periods when most gamefishing devout are experiencing an "off" period for their favorite species.

These mud-nosing carp will eat small worms and larvae that they root out from the bottom and, of course, these same bits of fish food are productive as baits.

Chumming an area is a common way of attracting carp as you get the mountain to come to Mohammed rather than trying to locate the fish yourself. You can chum a hole with bread, corn-meal, cow or chicken feed, fish parts or grains of corn, and in time it will attract carp to the feeding ground where you then lower some of the same stuff or similar morsels impaled on a No. 6 or No. 4 hook and wait for the fish to gulp it down.

Carp seem to have a preference for different baits in different sections of the country. Dan Gapen, an expert at carp fishing, notes that there are portions of the St. Joe River in Michigan where you can get bites only on night crawlers. In Illinois he says there is a lake where the carp prefer a paste containing alfalfa and whiskey. In Oklahoma the preference is sweet corn and Gapen vows the fish have been educated to theses local choices.

But by far the most popular bait remains the doughball baits about the size of a marble that will hang on the hook awhile or a few grains of sweet, fresh or canned corn.

When a great carp is hooked and heads for the other side of the lake, like a locomotive out of control, you'll suddenly forget about all those thrills you had the last time you hung a 5-pound bass after 10,000 casts. You'll get interested in catching some more of these giants with the bulldozer power. And catch them you can as both young and old, day and night can succeed in landing carp once you unlock the secret of their feeding habits and have the expertise to properly rig a strong carp rig for the tussle of your life.

Izaak Walton, the legendary daddy rabbit of hook and line fishing, wrote, "The carp is queen of the rivers." Indeed, in this day of pollution and game fishing pressure, it may be that the carp will reach that lofty pedestal again and you may have a carp in your future.

From Santee Cooper and many other Carolina lakes and rivers, carp are again being enjoyed on the dinner tables of many families. It's still a fine, healthy food.

Spadefish Off Fripp Island

Jim Wescott's 17-foot SportCraft tossed in the swells off Fripp Island in St. Helena's Bay and the 39-year-old skipper suddenly turned into the waves and pointed seaward. He had spotted what he was looking for. Just inches under the surface hundreds of purple jellyfish, known along the South Carolina coast as "blue balls," drifted and propelled themselves along with their array of tentacles on their undersides.

"That's what we are looking for. That's the best bait you can find for spadefish. Grab the landing net and start dipping them up," Wescott yelled. "We need a lot of them for the hooks and for chumming."

My ex-wife Brenda is a real saltwater enthusiast and she quickly leaned over the side and began scooping up the transparent jellyfish that ranged in size from golf- to baseballs. They were a cinch to catch, moving much too slowly to escape the adroit netting of Brenda and the astute maneuvering of the small boat by Wescott. In a matter of minutes, more than 100 of the soft, harmless balls of clear jelly were trapped in the plastic bucket on the deck and very much alive, albeit crowded in the few gallons of salt water.

"That's all we need. Now we will run out to 6HI and see if we can catch some of the fine spadefish that make a home around this mile-long manmade reef. Spadefish live on structure and when reefs are built along the shore, they flock to the cover. This reef we are going to fish is just a few miles off Hunting Island and it is No. 6 buoy that marks it. All the locals call it 6HI and I've had some great experiences fishing for this little-known species. It's a 14-mile run from the Edisto Island inlet to the reef, but both Fripp and Hunting islands are much closer," Wescott revealed as the boat rushed through the gentle swells toward a distant marker.

The Atlantic spadefish has common names in various parts of its range that runs from New England to Brazil, including the

Gulf of Mexico. It is called angelfish, moonfish, porgy and paguala, among other monikers. A member of the *Ephippidae* family, it is easily recognized by its deep, compressed, silvery body with four to six broad, black vertical bars that give it the appearance of a giant freshwater angelfish. These bars are found in specimens as small as three centimeters although they fade somewhat in larger fish. But off the South Carolina coast the bars remain distinct even on the largest spadefish. However, they soon disappear when the fish dies.

Spadefish mouths are small and have rows of brush-like teeth. The outer series of teeth are slightly enlarged. The two dorsal fins are joined, and the third spine of the first dorsal is long, unique and pronounced, as are the anterior rays of the second dorsal and anal fins. These tall spines often prove the undoing of the spadefish.

"Jim, there's some kind of fish swimming around on the surface, I can see its fin," I hollered to the captain just as the boat neared one of the three buoys that mark the reef with the words "South Carolina Artificial Reef."

"That's a spadefish. He's after one of the jelly balls. We'll rig up some chum and see if we can get some strikes," Wescott said, as he idled the motor and began rigging up lines and tackle in a manner totally different from anything I had ever observed before.

First, he fished up four of the jellyfish from the bucket and threaded them on a a 25-foot piece of braided fishing line by sticking a needle-like wire through their bodies several times. The four tied-out jelly balls were grouped on the end of the line and Wescott dropped it over the stern, tying the line to the cleat. They fluttered and squirmed on the surface as the boat drifted slowly.

Second, he rigged another similar four-jellyfish-in-a-wad line and made sure it was long enough to reach the bottom in this 40-foot deep water. He tied it to the gunnels and dropped it over the side, gingerly fingering the line to make sure it was near the reef structure and the impaled blue balls were on the bottom.

Finally, he handed each of us an open-faced spinning reel

on a seven-foot rod. Tied on the 25-pound test monofilament was a strong, steel No. 2 hook and five feet up the line from the hook he clamped two buckshot-size lead sinkers.

"Now you are ready except for the bait," Wescott said, and he dipped up two more of the jellyfish, dropped them on the top of the cooler and cut them into four pieces, each about the size of two short fingers. "Thread these on the hook and when I give you the word, drop them out beside the boat and let them kind of filter down toward the bottom."

Wescott turned the boat around and eased it back toward the buoy where I had first spotted the dorsal fin of a spadefish. He dropped the anchor and it held.

"I can see a lot of fish on the flasher. They must be spade-fish," Wescott said, and he began slowly lifting the line with the impaled jellyfish up and down off the bottom. "Yeah, I can feel them nibbling at it."

The words had no more than left his lips when Brenda hollered and I was not far behind. Both of us suddenly had a horse on the line and it was man against fish. Meantime, a whole school of giant spadefish surfaced all around the boat. In seconds they had riddled the four tied-out jellyfish on the surface and by the time Wescott got his weighted bottom chum to the boat, he had only the lead sinker left. We were reeling and grunting as our fish took out line and the star drags squeaked. It took about eight or ten minutes and the hooked fish surfaced. They were beautiful flat, striped fish that Wescott dipped up and grinned as they glistened on the deck. Almost round, but two inches thick, these fighting beauties looked like twins and weighed over 8-pounds.

For the first time we realized what a great gamefish we were after. Spadefish have tremendous strength and ounce for ounce compare with the fight and stamina of a freshwater shellcracker. Consider you are hooking these monsters 30 or 50 feet deep and you can imagine the challenge the angler experiences before he puts the fish in the net.

There is no trick to hooking the spadefish, even though they have small mouths. They see the chum in their faces and the cut jelly balls dangling nearby. They gulp it down and run. There is no need nor time for hook setting. The spadefish is on and the thrill of a doubled-up rod and screeching reel brings excitement to everyone aboard.

Wescott threaded on some more chum on the surface and the bottom line and dropped them out again. It was like instant replay. Brenda again hooked a fish, fought it to the boat and was smiling when my rod bent and another struggle ensued. We had four spadefish in the boat and the day was young.

The tales we had heard were true. Spadefish congregate over structure in loose schools by the thousands. They love shipwrecks, reefs, buoys, rock jetties and oil drilling platforms. They are often found down-current from major pieces of bottom structure if not directly over it. The spadefish swim in circular patterns around the water column surrounding the structure material. Spadefish are often visible on the surface, as was the one I spotted that prompted our anchoring. they surface after floating food. Schooling behavior for the species is so strong that sometimes an entire school will follow a hooked fish right to the boat when he is being played. It is a fish frenzy that delights spadefish enthusiasts.

Spadefish taken by hook and line along the South Carolina coast usually weigh between three and nine pounds, averaging about 6-pounds. But there was something special about this particular spadefish adventure and we sensed it at the time.

With the action subdued, Wescott suggested we pull anchor and try some other spots on the reef. he moved slowly across the structure and stopped. "There's a whole school of big fish right here. Let's hope they are spadefish," he said, as he slid the big anchor down again in the 40-foot water. He had learned how to use his flasher and was almost certain of the species.

Again he threaded on the chum for the surface line and the bottom attractor. This time he also chopped up half a dozen jellyfish and tossed them over the side. The pieces of cut blue balls had hardly disappeared when both rods bent and the struggle began again. I put my 10-pounder in the boat and was admiring it before Brenda finally got her fish to the net. It was a real beauty. We didn't realize it at the time, but her fish beat the South Carolina all-time record for a spadefish by 3-pounds, 15-ounces. She had boated a 13-pound giant that was a magnificent specimen. We learned later that even in the southernmost range of the spadefish, 12-pounders are rare, although some literature on the species tells about 20-pounders off the continental shelf in 30 fathoms of water.

Only when we returned to Bay Creek Marina and the scales at Salty Mike's were we sure that this was an exceptional day of spadefish angling. We had nine fish that weighed more than 100 pounds, including the unofficial new state record of 13. The old record was caught by Mrs. J. Brooks, at Murrells Inlet, near Myrtle Beach, in July of 1965. It weighed 9-pounds, 1-ounce.

Moreover, we could have caught many more spadefish if we had wanted to. They were plentiful and easy to hook. We caught no small fish, just giants as big as a wash pan. At 2:00 in the afternoon we gave away our supply of jellyfish to some envious observers on the reef and headed back to the ramp. It was fish dressing time.

Spadefish have tough hides and it takes a sharp knife to cut the fillets from the bone, But huge chunks of fine white meat come from the spadefish and gourmet diners swear there is no better species in the world to broil, bake, fry or even prepare like the Cajun blackened redfish delicacy.

The species is not one that is hunted frequently by conventional anglers. its feeding habits and behavior have not been discovered by many fishermen but its challenging fight on the line and food value most certainly will soon make it more popular. Recent studies of the species have found that it will strike shrimp, squid, small crabs and even pieces of cellophane that resemble the cut jellyfish portions. But nothing beats the two- to three-inch strips of real jellyfish. Its firmness makes it an excellent bait that stays on the hook and it is not venomous like the man-o-war that stings and hurts when touched. The jelly ball bait is found easily along the Carolinas and Georgia coast and sometimes is found near the shore in New England, the Gulf of Mexico and all the way to Venezuela.

Atlantic spadefish are plentiful in the oceanic waters of South Carolina throughout the summer, from May through November and in Florida waters it is a year-round resident.

On the hook or on the table, spadefish are a delightful species that will soon have a society of enthusiasts stalking them on the reefs made by man and the natural offshore structures.

SANTEE'S DROSES THREE

Frank Drose drifted his big boat within 40 feet of an overhanging willow bush in Santee Cooper's Wyboo Creek. Quietly he told his middle-aged bass client to cast his purple worm right into the shadow of the growth, and then to let it sink in the four feet of water. "There ought to be a nice bass around that bush," he muttered with optimism.

The vacationing angler cast in the direction of the willow, his plastic lure falling four feet short of the shadows. He tried again and missed the spot by even more as the boat slowly moved along.

Frank picked up his casting rod and reel and deftly flipped the plastic lure within three inches of the willow limbs and let it settle in the darkness of the upstream shadow. Bump! Then bump-bump and this knowledgeable guide had the message. He set the hook with gusto. A fighting 5-pound largemouth leaped clear of the water, splashing and struggling to dislodge the No. 2 hook that pierced her upper jaw. It was no use. Drose had placed the lure in front of her nose, she had gulped it down and soon was in the dip net and flouncing on the deck.

"The secret to catching largemouth bass here is to be accurate with your casts. We have so much cover, logs, limbs, trees, bushes and grasses, that the largemouths hide around and under that you have to really tempt them with a lure up close to make them leave their lairs," Frank says.

This likable 53-year-old native of the Santee Cooper complex in the South Carolina Low Country, is the middle brother in a trio of guides who are second generation professionals on these 171,000 acres of watery wilderness. Joe, at 55, is the oldest and Don, 45, is the youngest. They moved to the Manning, South Carolina, area on Lake Marion when Don was only two years old and their father before them led many a visiting party of lunker hunters to full stringers.

All three Drose boys served four years in the Navy, but virtually all the rest of their lives have been entwined with guiding and fishing with tourists for bass and stripers in these prolific waters.

Frank still guides for both largemouths and stripers. Joe and Don stick with white bass and the stripers exclusively.

"I used to guide customers for bass until my spider monkey died," Joe jokes. "I had that monkey to run down the lines and unhang the lures that my parties kept tangled in the trees and the bushes. When the monkey died, it just wasn't worth it any more."

And Joe gets back to his primary point that to catch largemouths in this jungle of forests and aquatic growth, you need to be talented with a rod and reel. Just any amateur can't bring home the lunkers when he can't cast within a few inches of a honey hole.

Joe insists that only about one fisherman in ten that he guided for bass knew how to cast and really fish. And those who didn't know how were so much trouble that he just shifted exclusively to the striper family that does not require much accuracy in bait casting.

"In our kind of business, you must enjoy people. We can help even the novices catch stripers, but it's harder to help them catch a nice-sized bass. Those fishermen who come to Santee, especially for the first time, who want to fish for bass should hire a good guide on their first day here, not the last day. Often they can learn enough in a few hours to get by pretty well the rest of their vacation time," says Joe.

"You get some bass fishermen here who assume that if you will just cast often enough that you will get a strike and put a fish in the boat. They pay little attention to where they are throwing their lure, just as long as they have the reel spinning and the lure being retrieved. They are almost always fishing in vain because they do not cast close enough to the stumps and the logs. Frank will watch this futility awhile, then just reach down and pick up his rod and put the lure where the bass are. "Bingo!" He gets a strike immediately and the customer stands there wondering why he didn't catch that fish," says Joe. "It's the ability to hit the spot within two or three inches that makes the difference. And Frank knows where those spots are."

Frank chips in, "The real art in being a good guide is helping other people catch fish. As guides, we can almost always catch fish, but our job is to help our customers catch them. I hear people talking when they come in off the lake and saying 'We caught 18 fish today, but the guide got 17 of them.' That's not what we are getting paid for. We are taking the money from our clients to help them catch fish, not catch fish ourselves, although all three of us like to fish for fun. But sometimes you have customers who just haven't done their homework and are not experienced sufficiently in the mechanics of rod and reel fishing to be successful.

"I get a real kick out of seeing my customers catch fish," Don notes. "Some months ago I carried three senior citizens, 74, 73 and 70 years old, out stump jumping for crappies. They just wouldn't have been good bass fishermen. But I knew we could catch some crappies around the logs and stumps. All four of use were in my 19-foot boat, but it was a calm day and safe. They all caught fish, some crappies weighing up to 2-pounds and those old fellows had the time of their lives. Each of them decided to have his biggest fish mounted. That's my real reward for such a guiding trip—to see people really enjoy themselves."

The Droses guide parties the year around at Santee, but are quick to point out that the hot months of July and August find most species inactive and harder to catch than during other months. Most fish lose weight, especially stripers, during these hot months when they feed very little. The best bass months are in the spring and ten-fish limits are not uncommon for Frank Drose.

Conversely, the best time for big stripers is from December 1 to January 15, particularly in the lower part of Lake Moultrie. Then from April 15 through June, older people can have a lot of fun catching smaller stripers on live herring. You do not have to be as alert to catch the stripers then and the weather is better for old fishermen," Don points out.

All the Droses emphasize the need for heavy tackle in these waters regardless of the species you are fishing for. "You never know when you are going to hang onto a big monster, and I don't like to see my customers have weak and inadequate tackle. I believe, like the Boy Scouts, in being prepared with heavy tackle regardless of the place or the season," Joe advises.

Don uses strong seven-foot popping rods and Ambassadeur reels and prefers Trilene line by Berkley. Joe has a preference for the pink tournament grade Ande line.

He likes the Shakespeare Ugly Stik for his striper fishing, but says they cost too much to put in the hands of some of his amateur customers. The client must pay for any rods he loses or breaks.

"I pay for any tackle that is broken on a fish. It's the equipment that is stepped on or dropped overboard that is the customer's responsibility," Joe says. "I had a customer who left a bait dangling a few inches out of the water last year when we were moving. I told the guy he better put it in the boat, but he ignored me. A fish struck the bait and jerked the rod and reel in. He hollered for me to stop. I asked him if he thought the tackle would float, and I didn't even slow up. In this big water, you can't even find a sunken boat, much less a rod and reel.

"We hang some stripers on the outskirts of the dead forest that just parade right on through the woods and don't ever stop. They take your line and go on their merry way. Those are the ones that are too big to handle almost regardless of the kind of tackle you have," Joe says.

"Anybody who hasn't chased a school of big rockfish through the standing dead forest at Santee just hasn't lived. Why sometimes my boat just sits and pants to get going after those stripers in the woods when they are nesting," Don says.

Among the best artificial striper lures are the purple and yellow, 4 1/2-inch, deep-running Rebels. The Droses contend that stripers will not bite the natural colored baits and that the purple color is now difficult to find. They say that a tiny difference in the shade of green turns some stripers off, while another green brings every rockfish around running to swallow it. Some years ago, they say they sold more deep-running Rebels than any outlet in the country. The water was low then and the lure ran about 14 feet deep. It was attracting the stripers all right, but the low water made it hang up on stumps and logs and a lot of lures were lost. They contend that if the water is muddy, the best lure is yellow. You'll never convince the Drose brothers that stripers are color blind at any depth. On the contrary , they believe even the tiniest variation of color is detectable by the fish.

One year Joe carried out parties on 44 consecutive days in the spring. He was about exhausted from his daylight-to-dark, seven-day-a-week chore when he finally got a day off. "No sooner had I announced that I didn't have a party for that day when my wife quickly outlined some chores she wanted done around the house. 'Darling, I'm tired,' I told her. But she couldn't believe it. 'Well, I don't know why. You don't do a thing but fish,' she said. Wives just don't consider fishing work," Joe shakes his head.

The Droses always have a sense of humor, like when Don says, "Women are always wanting to waste money buying clothes or furniture and stuff when you could take that same money and buy fine fishing tackle."

Joe and Frank used to have some fishing poles hid out along the river bank where the blacktop road laces along Lake Marion's shoreline. They waited for the school bus there each morning. Frequently they caught their limits before the school bus arrived, tied them out under a bush and lugged them home to mama in the afternoon.

"The best way to catch a lot of stripers is to keep one hung and in the water flouncing and fighting as much as possible. The fish will draw others from all around when he is hooked. He will regurgitate and others will rush in to eat the vomit and the commotion itself will attract his cousins. The more people you have fishing an area, the better the fishing will be. You don't catch many stripers when you are out there alone. You need some fish on the hook all the time for the most fun," Don says.

"A lot of people come down here in the wintertime and because this is in the South, they don't think they need to have any warm clothes. Let me tell you, it can get mighty cold on this water from December through March, and you need some good, warm clothing. When the temperature drops to about 20 degrees, you can't live in this water but about 30 minutes, and you never know when you might hit a submerged log and tear a hole in your boat. I hit a log last winter and cut a three-inch hole 15 feet long in my boat. I managed to keep the motor running wide open and got to the landing without sinking.

"My customers caught about 20,000 pounds of stripers one year, and that's a pretty good record. We had 2,500 pounds from the first week of July until the first week of August, just rockfish. We also had 15 catfish in the 15- to 30-pound class and had to outrun three tornadoes.

"The next world record striper is still in Santee. I have seen several that were records. They just broke off everything we had and got away. But Santee still holds a 60-pound striper and we will get her one of these days," Joe Drose predicts, and he may be right.

But with all the striper talk, Frank, the devout basser turns the conversation back to the largemouths. Frank often fishes with Roland Martin, the most renowned professional bass angler in America, who started his fishing career at Santee,

A guide since he was old enough to paddle a homemade bateau with a tiny kicker to push him out in the lake, he later fished from what looked to avid bassmen like a Noah's Ark. It was a 20-foot Sea Ox with 30-inch sides and enough room to play ping pong on the deck, and a tall windshield in front of the driver. On the bow he mounted a trolling motor with a five-foot shaft. It was custom-made so it would be long enough to reach the water from such a big boat. Other than tackle boxes, there was nothing else on the deck to get in the way of the customers he guides 250 days a year.

"I try to keep the deck neat so my clients can walk around and be comfortable, but one year I had a couple who insisted upon drinking more and more beer all day until one of them finally fell face down in his own open tackle box. He got up with lures hanging from everywhere and we had to bring him in to get the hooks out," Frank remembers.

On a recent morning when Frank was about ready to shove off with two novice bass anglers, a sleek, trim, fully-equipped, low profile, high performance boat pulled alongside at the dock and cut the motor. Frank had never seen the fishermen before.

"What you fellows going to fish for today?" the driver in the pretty bass boat asked Frank. "You must be going to chase stripers with that battleship."

"Oh, I thought we would go see if maybe we could find a few largemouths this morning," Frank quietly and calmly replied.

Before noon that morning Frank returned to the landing with his two paying customers. By chance, he tied up alongside the very bass boat that was there earlier in the day and the two occupants of the sleek craft were stepping out on the dock with two small yearling bass on a string.

"They sure weren't biting out there today," the talkative hotshot bassman said, shaking his head and glancing at Frank, who sat quietly under the wheel while his passenger disembarked.

"I see you got two little fellows," Frank said, and he then opened his cooler slowly and began tossing bass out on the pier. One, two, three, four, five and on up to 20 he put the largemouths on the dock, some weighing up to 8-pounds and his companions for the morning were jubilant.

"We didn't get but 20 this morning of whatever kind of fish these things are. I guess it was because our boat was just too big. If we had had a nice bass boat like you fellows, we might really have caught some of those largemouths you fellows wanted," Frank said with nary a smile, as he tied up the stern of the boat, put the cooler full of fish on a stringer and posed while the marina proprietor took some pictures.

His critics of a few hours ago just kept their mouths wide open with surprise. For the first time they were speechless.

After the loudmouths had left, Frank elaborated.

"I know this is a big boat, but these 171,000 acres with 450 miles of shoreline is big water. Winds and thunderstorms come up fast and often do. You need a long boat with the 30-inch sides and a wide beam to make it across the lake safely and try to stay dry. The smaller and faster bass boats can't cope with some of the rough water that slips up on you here.

"Then, too, I take a lot of ladies fishing. Ladies don't mind getting wet if they decide to get wet by themselves, but they just won't stand for you getting them wet. They have to want to get wet to like it. With this 20-foot Sea Ox, I normally can keep them dry and comfortable," Frank philosophizes.

"But even with this big boat, there were three times one year when the lake got so rough that I couldn't safely cross it with my customers. I had to tie up on the opposite side and call my wife to come after us in the car," he says.

The Droses three, real fishermen who are always at home on the water and with expertise seldom monopolized in one family.

AMERICAN EELS—A UNIQUE CRITTER

There is no better cobia bait than a dwarf-size American eel. But this critter is repulsive to some people and admired for various reasons by others. It's safe to say the eel is truly a unique creature.

In medieval times, eels were said to be horse hairs that came alive in the water. In early America, these snake-like creatures were believed to be male catfish. Because they squirmed when cut into pieces and fried in hot grease, many people refused to consider them for the dinner table. In the Orient, they are a favorite food, smoked, jellied or broiled. They are also a delicacy in parts of Europe and many are trapped in this country and sold overseas for prices ranging from 85 cents to more than $2.50 a pound.

Edible eels must weigh at least three-quarters of a pound, be about 16 inches long, and those caught smaller than that by commercial fishermen are the best cobia baits.

All American eels are hatched in 1,500 feet of water in the Sargasso Sea. As tiny elvers they float along the Carolina coast, many wriggling up tributaries where they may stay for a lifetime. Some return to the Sargasso to spawn. Others float on to the northeast and across the Atlantic past Africa and eventually back to their breeding grounds.

Impaled on a hook to attract cobia, they will live all day if not attacked by a big predator.

INTRACOASTAL WATERWAY FISHING

When engineers charted a barge route from the metropolitan northeast across Maryland, Virginia, the Carolinas, Georgia and on southward to the Florida Keys, there had to be a considerable distance along this 1,246-mile journey cut by man and machines through swamplands, marshes, rivers, lakes, estuaries and bays. These smaller bodies of water were connected by canals dredged out to depths of 20 feet and more to guarantee inland commerce by water routes. These manmade streams today link the natural water to form the busy Intracoastal Waterway, that generally parallels the Atlantic shoreline, and much of this 100-yard-wide canal is so far from the saltwater of the ocean that no brackishness exists despite the regular rise and fall of water level from the ocean tide pressure as much as 25 miles away. It's in some of these blackish waters of the coastal South and the tributaries that sprout out from it that some of the best largemouth bass fishing in the nation can be found today.

Among the very best of these bass havens is a long stretch in South Carolina, beginning just below Little River on the Carolina border and ending at Georgetown, some 60 miles downstream. It's where the Waccamaw, Little Pee Dee, Black, Edisto, Sampit and the Great Pee Dee call it quits and the water that they have carried all the way from the Piedmont in the center of North Carolina slips into the sea.

This waterway in the South Carolina Low Country, and in North Carolina to the north, is laced with shoreline strips of lily pads, weeds and grass, intermingled with stumps, logs, overhanging willows and uprooted tree trunks that provide fantastic cover for freshwater game fish, notably largemouth bass, redbreast and bluegills.

Generally these areas are underfished, as most of the devout bassers are not aware that where this water rises and falls like the ocean, it is really not salty and accommodates good populations of largemouths. The bass like the heavy cover of the shoreline and feed from the abundant supply of freshwater shrimp, tiny shad, fingerling mullet and giant schools of small bream of several kinds, including warmouth perch, crappies, bluegills, shellcrackers and redbreasts.

It is not the kind of habitat that makes for much success with diving crankbaits. There is so much bottom cover and aquatic growth where the bass are that most casts end in fouled plugs and few strikes. Plastic worms are effective when you succeed in dropping the lure in a hole clean enough for the bass to find it and gulp it down. Good catches are reported by worm fishermen, primarily using black and dark blue colors. The seven-inch size is most commonly successful.

The best of baits in this constantly-running water is a topwater that is at least somewhat weedless. Flipped in the jagged little indentations along the bank where water eddies and then swirls around tree trunks and roots of cypress trees and myrtle bushes it gets attention. The bass stalk the minnows in these shallows and from March through November in the Carolinas bass can be caught in good numbers in the Intracoastal Waterway itself. If you are an accurate caster with experience, you can catch bass on Rapala-type topwaters that are not weedless, but you will likely lose some plugs to hang-ups.

One of the prerequisites to success in the Waterway is to watch the tide. Study it for several days and don't waste your time fishing when it is either on the extreme flood or the extreme low. Bass leave the cover for the deeper water as the tide falls and it is unusual to have much success fishing for them when they retreat to the dredged portion of the waterway. They seem to suspend for awhile and stop feeding. They won't even bite when marked with a fish finder graph or blip. But as the tide comes halfway in and the water begins covering the grasses and licking at the roots of the trees on the shore, in come the largemouths again as the gambusia gather and fishing becomes exciting once more. Reeling even a yearling in after he reaches some fast water is thrilling.

It is not a daily occurrence to catch real lunkers in the Waterway itself. Most of the bass caught in this tidal water are in the two- to three-pound range, but they are always healthy and robust. They fight much longer and more enthusiastically than most lake bass, and when using light or ultralight tackle, they afford thrills a-plenty for the sports fisherman. Occasionally, a monster in the eight- or nine-pound class comes over the gunnels for the Waterway bassers, but that is not an everyday expectation. You need to be content with the 14-inchers to fish the Waterway.

If you are after trophy-size bass, the tributaries that wind their way through the abandoned rice fields of the last century or desolate but scenic swamps still unspoiled by man's intrusion along the banks, are bouncing with wall mounts. Rivers like the Waccamaw and Little Pee Dee are honey holes for veterans with expertise who catch bragging-size bass almost the year around.

In the narrow sloughs that separate the old rice fields, many native bassers still sneak along in one-man boats less than nine feet long and run a jigger on the surface with a shaking hand holding a 16-foot bamboo pole. They put bass on the bank in creel limits using this unsophisticated system that was really designed more for the meat fisherman than the sportsman. Often they hang the bass on an eight-inch line and simply flip her into the bushes on the shore. Minutes later they retrieve the fish. It's easier than putting up with a flouncing monster in a boat that's as unsteady as a rocking chair teetering on a waterfall crest.

But up the rivers from the waterway, you can catch some write-home-about lunkers with conventional lures and rods and reels. This habitat is pioneering too, with overhanging tree limbs, stumps, log jams and aquatic growth. But fishing the current and drifting along the shoreline, you can find productive havens in the coves and lakes that mosey out into the wooded flats. Worms continue to be the best single artificial lure, but Rebel and Bagley, among other crank and buzz baits, attract bass too.

You have to be prepared for the unexpected when fishing the Waterway along the Atlantic and its tributaries. Giant rockfish and striped bass pour into these waters in the spring and are sometimes present in the late fall. They go after much of the same forage fish as the bass and they often strike the bass fishermen's lures with gusto, often taking hook, line and sinker as they challenge the equipment most often used here. These stripers are real hogs, sometimes in the 30- to 40-pound class. There are also numerous instances where other saltwater species strike bass lures, with marauding flounder commonly caught. It's almost scary to pull in a flat slab with a lure. In the deep water there is even an occasional sturgeon hooked and lost, as well as some bluefish and trout when the water nears the salty estuaries and ocean varieties prowl the shoreline for live foods.

Spawning season is always a good time to catch the bigger bass in almost any body of water. And this is particularly true in the waterway. The big mamas settle on sandy spots along the shoreline of the tributaries and up the sloughs that drain farms and pastures. Waterway spawning bass in Florida usually seek out bedding areas in February and March. Slowly the species moves to the beds in March and April in Georgia and the Carolinas. The spawners may even carry on their nesting into May and June in coastal Carolina and Virginia, and further north it is often even later.

All spawning is keyed to the weather in any particular spring, and in recent years winter has lingered later than some decades ago, pushing spawning times later , sometimes even into the summer.

Bassers who do not consider it a sin to fish for some freshwater species other than largemouths, often shift to Beetle Spins and jigs in the Waterway and coastal rivers when lockjaw sets in on their favorite fish. With these small lures adroitly flipped into the cover wheich the bass have abandoned, many a gourmet meal of hand-sized redbreasts goes into the cooler. These panfish are plentiful all over the freshwater shorelines of the waterway, and unlike those in the tributary rivers, they will bite spinners, jigs and other small artificials better than they will hit the usual natural baits of earthworms, crickets and shrimp. They strike with a vengeance and you have to fight even a 12-ouncer every inch of the way to the boat. It often saves the day for the basser who fears skunking and in desperation goes after fish for the table rather than a bass to brag about.

The Intracoastal Waterway is a unique fishing experience. It differs greatly from most river or lake fishing. Few novices who have not studied the species in tidal waters and do not do their homework will have much success. But if you once learn the habits of the bass as the tides rise and fall, watch for the action in the shallows where the forage fish are in a frenzy from being chased by predators. Take some precautions to keep from hanging on the ever-present stickups, and you can have some fabulous bassing adventures from Virginia to the Florida Keys in fresh water just a few stone throws from the Atlantic.

There must be one other word of caution here: Beware of the commercial boat traffic. Giant barges and yachts ply these canals constantly. Sometimes there are half a dozen or more together as they congregate to pass under revolving bridges or those that rise to allow vessels to pass under them. Many have dangerous wakes that disturb your fishing holes along the shoreline and bring out a few cuss words from the bassers. But more importantly, some of these wakes are big enough to break right over the bow of many low-profile bass boats. It behooves the angler to be careful in these waters. When possible, pull into a creek or cove until the traffic and wakes pass. If you cannot do that, at least stop fishing long enough to put your boat's bow into the wave and hang on a few seconds. Once the wake subsides, go right back to your casting. These bass apparently have learned this water disturbance is not a hazard and they will often strike a lure tossed at them before the rivulets from the wake have disappeared from the shoreline.

It's a unique bass fishing experience and if once you master the technique for locating and enticing the largemouths, you'll be back for more.

Yet there is still one more warning: There are many areas along uninhabited waterway shorelines where rivers converge. Pay attention or you can easily get lost. All the tree line looks much the same. If you are observant, you'll take note of buoy numbers, colors and locations. They mark the commercial channels and you can get back to the launching ramps by simply paying attention. It's embarrassing to have to stop a passerby to ask how to get back to your car and trailer. Don't let it happen to you.

Yellow Perch
—At Home in the Carolinas

Yellow perch, known by a lot of other names in North and South Carolina, is a coldwater fish that flourishes from Maine to the Georgia border and then westward as far as Kansas. It is a fine gourmet fish for those who have the patience to scale them and it is eaten by many in the Carolinas. (But in Northern Ireland where the species is so bountiful that it roots the trout and salmon out of the lakes, it's called a "coarse" fish and those who land them throw them out in the woods with a few choice Irish cuss words.)

In Eastern Carolina rivers like the Black, Cape Fear, Northeast, Lumber, Pee Dee, Waccamaw and the Edisto, the elongated, striped trout-shaped fish comes up from the tidal water of the Inland Waterway and the swamplands to search for spawning space in the coldest weather of winter. January is usually the month when most of them are caught in the headwaters of these rivers.

They are not persnickety about what they hit when they are nosing around river headwaters for a place to nest. While most Carolinians go after them with minnows, worms and crickets, these robust perch will hit spinners, small crankbaits, jigs and even plastic worms that are not too long.

Perhaps because of their long, striped bodies, native Tar Heel fishermen have referred to this species for generations as "redfin trout" or just simply "redfins." In truth it is not a member of the trout family at all and is in the perch clan even though it is not a flatfish as are most people's concept of a perch. This fish is also called a "raccoon" perch in many areas of North and South Carolina, among other monikers.

They cut all the words away from the species in Ireland and just simply refer to it as a "perch." But make no mistake, it's the same fish that you pull out of the Cape Fear River in January or the Lumber and Pee Dee in South Carolina when the weather is so cold that most fishermen hover by the fireside and hope for spring. Ireland's waters are always colder than most streams in the Carolinas, and thus this species bites the year around and hits just about anything. The most used perch bait in Northern Ireland is maggots, raised in moist wheat flour and sold in tackle shops. They are not wet or messy. They are in wood shavings and totally clean and dry. You impale two or three of these little white worms on the tiniest hook you can find and flip it around grass beds, pilings, bridge abutments or near rocky shoreline structure. The perch that tops 1 1/2-pounds is rare in the U.S., but in Lough Erne (Lake Erne) in Ireland, near the village of Kesh, you can catch a boat load that are that size and the Irish record is over 5-pounds.

An indication of how this "coarse" fish abounds resulted in a "match" held in Ireland. They do not call their competitive fishing "tournaments." They are "matches." In a five-hour match, one man hauled in on a hook and line 258-pounds, 9-ounces of coarse fish, mostly perch. Normally, every contender in such matches will catch no less than 72-pounds in a five-hour period.

If you have never dressed a yellow perch, you are not aware of the chore that it is if you do not fillet them. We do not fillet any fish. We scale, dehead and gut our fish, wash them good and fry them whole. That's the way I like fish best. Brenda and I, on a trip to Ireland, once caught and scaled 11 nice perch. It was difficult. The scales seemed to be cemented to the skin and it took an hour or more. But we completed the job and they looked appetizing. Then we ran into another problem. They do not have cornmeal for sale in Ireland, and that's what we roll our salted and peppered fish in before frying. We substituted brown whole wheat flour. The lady at our guest house cooked the fish after getting some advice from us. She had never fried fish like that before. We ate them and they were finger-licking food.

Humorously, an old Irishman came by when we were dressing the perch. He looked at us and then at some other observers and came up with what must have been an astute observation. "That's the first time I have ever seen any poor Americans." He surmised that anyone who would dress and eat yellow perch had to be hungry and thus poor. We didn't mind being called poor. The Irish wait for brown trout and salmon on the dinner table.

But we have eaten this species in eastern North and South Carolina as long as I can remember. Its only liability is the difficulty of the scale removal. Yes, it has bones, but when it is cooked crisp and you know how to use your fingers, the meat can be "filleted" from the bones easily and separated so that you have little chance of getting a bone in your throat. It, and few other panfish, should not be eaten with silverware unless you do cut away the meat from the bone and waste about 30 percent of the resource. For me, it tastes better cooked with the bone in and the skin on, and I like to eat with my fingers anyway.

In Ireland the few people who go after the perch buy a tiny hook that is smaller than anything I have ever seen in America. Its metal diameter is smaller than most human hairs. From the eye to the bend in the little hook is less than 3/8 of an inch. The bend itself is about 1/8 inch. You have to be rather dexterous with big fingers even to hold this little hook, get a line through the eye and bait it. Irishmen use this hook that easily earns the name "hair hook" because the maggot baits are tiny. This little hook allows several to be impaled at once and obviously the yellow perch have no difficulty swallowing them. They can gulp down a crawfish three inches long, and this little morsel on a hook can be used for catching even the smallest perch.

When Carolinians go after the perch species, they pull on all the heavy coats they can find, wear some insulated boots, a cap with ear flaps, maybe even some warm gloves, and motor through the cold of winter to a spot where there is fast water in a creek or river mouth. Then with light or ultralight tackle, or even a long limber cane pole, we flip a minnow hooked through the eyes into the current with a little cork up the line and a shot or two a few inches above a No. 4 hook. Or, when they are biting like mad, we may just cast Beetle Spins or small jigs into the current and bring in some nice fish.

In the Carolinas we generally have to face the cold on a boat to get to a fishing place in the winter where the yellow perch are congregated. In Northern Ireland, wildlife agents make fishing more comfortable for their populace. They use the abundance of rocks to build masonry structures out into the lakes all along miles of shoreline. The rock walkways have a circular area at the end about six feet in diameter where the fisherman can stand or place his lawn chair. He is far enough away from the shoreline to easily permit casting into holes that are ten feet deep and more. He can bundle up and stay comfortable even when the weather plunges below freezing. He doesn't need a boat and his catches from these lakes are astounding. One of the days that we were fishing in Lake Erne, an old-timer sitting on one of these short walks caught so many fish he couldn't carry them back to his car in one trip. Mostly he had nice perch, but he had a few brown trout and even a couple of Atlantic salmon.

It wasn't a bream day. I couldn't get a bream bite, but after a half hour my cork ran off. I pulled and up came a little six-inch yellow perch. I dropped the fish in the bottom of the boat, rebaited and tossed out the line again. It had hardly straightened out before the cork plunged under and I came up with another small yellow perch. Both lay flouncing on the deck as I put the hook back in the water again. Nothing happened! I looked at the yellow perch and picked up my rod and reel that I had brought along just in case I saw a bass jump in the grass beds. What the heck! I'm not doing any good. I'll try something new. I tied on a big hook, threaded a cork up the line a couple of feet, picked up one of the yellow perch and stuck the hook under its dorsal fin. I flipped it a dozen yards near the swaying sawgrass patch.

I snuggled my coat up around my neck to fight off the stinging north wind. The cork trembled and shook as the yellow perch was lively and full of action. Pop! I heard the round cork go under. The line played out! I set the hook and soon struggled with a 3 1/2-pound largemouth. I finally lipped the fish and lifted it over the side and into the livewell.

I reached down and picked up the other yellow perch that was still breathing. I impaled it on the hook the same way and flipped it back to the same place I found the other bass. The cork wasn't still a minute until it went down and I came in with an even bigger largemouth. I put the rod in the boat and hurriedly started fishing for some more yellow perch live baits. In a little more than an hour, I caught four nice bass and lost two other yellow perch baits to the predators. I couldn't get another perch to bite. So out of bait, I cranked up and went home. But it surely proved one thing—in the winter time when the shad, shiners and minnows are scarce and these perch come up from the river, the bass are hungry and ready to strike. I wouldn't be surprised if the game fish of Ireland wouldn't like to strike a tied-out perch on a line, too.

Some wag has said that "One man's trash is another man's treasure" and surely that is true in the case of the yellow perch. While it is a "coarse" fish and unappreciated in Northern Ireland, it is a thrilling fish to catch and tasty on the table in the Carolinas. The smallest ones are good bass baits too. I wish they were as plentiful here as they are there.

MARSHLAND TROUT

Veteran speckled trout fishermen along the marshland trenches of the North Carolina coast near Cedar Island prefer to stalk the tasty saltwater fighters in October and November, but you can catch them any month of the year. Sometimes they never leave regardless of the season and at other times they disappear in what are predicted to be the real bonanza periods.

"They often surprise us locals and show up in early spring ready to strike our grub lures and other artificial and natural baits much like they had gone all winter with nothing to eat," says David Hamilton, a veteran senior citizen angler from Stacey, North Carolina, who has fished the narrow ditches and creeks of the coastal waters along the roads and highway near his home for a lifetime.

While the brisk wind from the northeast puts a crimp in fishing these ditches during the coldest months of winter, November through January, the venerable Mr. Hamilton contends that the trout are often still present in these many miles of tangled trenches dug to find base dirt for the roadways. They come here to feed and to spawn.

"Often the trout are still here when it is bitter cold and I have put many a mess on the dinner table in the winter. You have to know how to cast a light grub fairly accurately and learn the touch of a slow retrieve. It takes some experience to catch these trout, and at times I get a good stringer of fish while some of the tourists alongside strike out. There is a definite feel that you have to learn to catch these trench trout," says Hamilton.

A labyrinth of trenches are on both sides of state route 12 just south of Cedar Island, right on Pamlico Sound, across the inlet from Ocracoke, where there is a spit of islands known as the "Surf Fishing Capital of the World." But Hamilton prefers to fish comfortably in these roadside ditches rather than on the famous Outer Banks where you face a throng of people and a lot of wind and cold in the fall and early winter. He doesn't like to waste two and a half hours riding the big ferry to Ocracoke across the Pamlico from the jumping-off berth at Cedar Island even though there are 175 miles of unique beaches that make the spit of sandy barrier islands attractive to anglers. On those Outer Banks from Kitty Hawk on the north end to Cape Lookout to the south, anglers land channel bass, giant blues, sharks, mullet, flounder, spots, trout and other species, especially on Hatteras Island. Most of these fishermen are surfers, wading in the sudsy Atlantic where they make great catches from April into winter when the cold gets too bitter for most saltwater fishing enthusiasts. It never gets too cold for a devout few who thrive on surf privacy and the thrill of combat with a big fish in the waves of the Atlantic.

Old salts who live at Cedar Island, Stacey and other tiny towns along highways 70 and 12, bring in fine stringers of gourmet speckled trout without facing the wind, sand, currents and waves of the Outer Banks where the shifting reefs shallow the ocean and create the centuries-old shipping hazard that earned these waters the dubious distinction of "graveyard of the Atlantic."

These deep manmade trenches stretch along both sides of state route 12 and in places the water is eight to twelve feet deep. Dark, brackish tidal waters fill these ditches from John D's creek and the canals perpendicular to the trenches that reach into Core and Pamlico sounds and the Neuse River that converge here. Sawgrass and saltgrass line the banks of these trenches and creeks and fish foods flood from this cover as the tide changes. It brings in the gamefish and knowledgeable anglers catch full stringers from the comfort of lawn chairs by casting lures or floaty live shrimp and minnows into these productive streams. At times, it is equally fruitful to cast cut bait into these ditches and wait for trout and flounder to snatch it off the bottom. Some boaters anchor in these narrow water passages and fish, But there is more activity from the banks and bridge abutments.

Best places to catch the tasty trout that feed here are where the perpendicular creeks and manmade canals cut through the wetlands and junction with the trenches alongside the blacktop road. There's a always a current where these water merge and insects, minnows and other forage foods collect in the small eddy swirls where the shallow flows meet.

"I fish only artificial lures, preferably a Stingray green grub with red bead eyes. It's a Tom Mann bait that I cast into the junctions of these ditches and creeks and then retrieve slowly with spinning tackle. Sometimes I have to retrieve faster than at other times, but when the trout are here they'll hit these green grubs retrieved in their faces," the old corncob pipe-smoking veteran fisherman says.

"Some seasons are unusual in these creeks and trenches. Normally I catch trout here in the fall when the weather begins to cool. But the trout one year came in April and hit all summer. Sometimes they go back into the sounds and the ocean in summer and return to the creeks for food in October and November, but they may stay here the whole year. They keep right on biting into winter if you can stand the cold," Hamilton reveals. He doesn't fish from a boat. He brings his light-weight folding lawn chair, sits it on a level spit of land, and starts casting a grub along the grassy shorelines of the streams where the tide always creates some current.

Ralph Palmer, of nearby Cedar Island village, was often a fishing companion of Hamilton. They fished about the same way and had similar expertise. Palmer moved about more, often fishing under and around the bridges where trout are prone to hang out and stalk forage food. Palmer moved to this unique village in 1982 from the North and was not a native like Hamilton, but he loved this desolate coastal county and the great fishing so close to his front door. In 1987 a thief broke into his coastal cottage while he and Hamilton were trout fishing. He surprised the robbers when he returned and a real tragedy resulted. The robber shot and killed Palmer.

"Our trout caught here in these ditches and creeks along the road range from 1-pound or so up to 4- and 5-pounds. You can take a boat and go up in the bay and catch them even larger. But what we catch here are fine eating, pretty fish and we don't have to go boating to catch them," Hamilton says. "They put up a pretty good fight, too."

Flounders are caught off the highway 12 roadway and in the merged creek mouths, but Hamilton and Palmer concentrated on the speckled trout. It is more challenging to catch trout than flounder, but both are fine eating.

Tide ebbs and floods influence saltwater species' feeding habits along most coastal water, even when it is barely brackish and often many miles from the Atlantic. But Hamilton takes exception to that generalization.

"These trout here bite on any tide, rising, falling, low or high. The only factor that counts is whether they are here or not. If they are, they'll hit these green grubs," Hamilton says with assurance. He differs from most veterans about the tidal influence.

Hamilton has some bits of advice for the novices who go fishing for these coastal trout in the trenches. These fish have weak mouths, some areas of tissue almost as weak as a Kleenex, and you cannot use much gusto in setting the hooks. It will tear out the hooks. Also, these fish should be netted. They may come unbuttoned if they are in the 4- and 5-pound range if you attempt to land them by lifting them out of the water and dragging ashore.

The trenches of Cedar Island's marshland are convenient, easy-to-fish waters and require no sophisticated tackle, boats or vehicles. You don't even have to buy a fishing license to fish North Carolina salt water. It's a great place for the novice or the veteran to carry home a stringer of gourmet fish.

Further information about trout fishing the trenches or the Outer Banks is available from the Travel & Tourism Division of the N.C. Dept. of Commerce, 430 N. Salisbury St., Raleigh, NC 27611. Phone: 919-733-4171.

PIER AND INLET ANGLERS HIT THE SPOT

A brisk north wind rattled my unbuttoned raincoat as it flapped against the railing on the Garden City, South Carolina, pier that jutted out into the Atlantic that November morning. Shoulder to shoulder I stood with fishermen from all over the Carolinas who were almost frantically jerking, reeling, baiting and landing the migrating spots—a small but delectable salt-water panfish that heads south each fall. It is the most sought-after species in the Carolinas, as nearly half of all coastal anglers are spot fishermen in these states.

Amateur as well as veteran anglers had a heyday that morning, our party of three landing 256 of the hand-sized, half-pound cousins of the croaker that seems to have constant hunger pangs when traveling. These spots had abandoned all caution and were swallowing every edible object their small mouths could scoop from the sandy bottom. Called "roe spots" when they reach Florida, they are simply "spots" from the New Jersey coast through Georgia waters and are a favorite food for literally millions of hook and line and net fishermen.

This silvery-colored fish is punctuated with a blackish spot just behind the gills from whence cometh its name, and the species has provided fun, thrills, success stories, and entertainment, as well as food for families for generations. Indeed, thousands of anglers who will not chase flounder, trout and redfish or even the more glamorous sails, kingfish, swordfish and marlin, delight in spot fishing from piers and in boats of inlets along the Atlantic's Carolina coasts.

From early spring until Christmas and beyond, spots flock along the coast, ranging from deep water to the surf no more than a couple of feet deep, constantly searching for nutrition and the competition with each other for available tidbits makes them easy prey for even the novices. Moving in huge schools all the way from the New Jersey coast, these faintly yellow-striped cousins of the croakers with flashes of blue and silver make them a pretty sight as they are reeled across the surface and hauled 30 feet to the pier railing, flouncing and squirming, often two or three on the line at the same time.

A primary reason for the popularity of spot fishing is its simplicity. Anglers for spots need not be experts, they do not even have to change tackle from that they customarily use in farm ponds, lakes and streams back home. Any light spinning tackle used in fresh water is adaptable to spot fishing easily and inexpensively. And so are bait-casting outfits regularly used in bass, crappie, bluegill and catfish adventures. There are even many successful spot anglers who never use anything more sophisticated than a handline dropped straight down in the rolling waves a few feet from the pier pilings or virtually underneath their parked boat in the sounds and inlets.

Most spot veterans use two or three small hooks on the line, size 4, 6 or 8, and tie these directly to a light monofilament on short loops four or five inches long and ten inches or so above a pyramid, one-ounce sinker. Leaders are not required, in that spots are no challenge even to six- and ten-pound lines. Those that are lost usually escape by pulling the small hooks from paper-thin mouths, not from destroying even light and ultra-light tackle.

Another thing that makes spot fishing attractive to so many is the ease in procuring acceptable bait. Most spots are caught on cut shrimp, usually available at beachfront piers or tackle shops at marinas. And it is a choice diet of traveling and hungry spots. Equally as good, even better in the minds of many, are bloodworms, also for sale at many piers. These worms are tough and you may land half a dozen or more spots without losing your bloodworm bait.

Other successful spot baits are the lowly earthworm used in fresh water, bits of clams and oyster muscle, and even tiny pieces of filleted fish or belly meat from members of the same family you have already lifted from the school. They strike almost anything to keep a neighboring spot from getting there first.

Spot fishing from piers and small skiffs is often a family

affair, with wives, husbands, and children of almost all ages participating. They take turns fishing and making fast trips back to snack bars for coffee or cold drinks, as the weather dictates, or to buy more bait as cup after cup quickly disappears when spots are attacking.

Several times over the decades that I have spot fished, I have seen these vicious little critters brought aboard with two and three hooks firmly hung in their lips as they showed their gluttony by gulping down all available baits quickly, before the angler felt the tap-tap bump that signaled a bite and hook-setting time. The ability and carelessness of the spots also creates some confusion when two or more elbow-to-elbow fishermen frequently reel in the same fish, as it swallowed two baits along the sandy bottom before becoming aware of the impaling barb embedded in those tasty shrimp tidbits.

Also making spot fishing attractive for families, including the inexperienced, is the ability to catch these fish without casting. Normally, you need only to let the line run free straight down until the lead strikes the bottom. Failure to use this simple system has led to many an argument where hooks being cast in a crowd resulted in caps being snared, even noses, eyes and ears.

My most noteworthy memory of casting for spots getting someone in trouble happened to a 91-year-old angling friend of mine, the late Melvin Andrews of Goldsboro, North Carolina. He and his wife were spot fishing and doing fairly well, but not sensational. He had told the less experienced wife to just lower the bait in the water and not to cast while he walked further toward the end of the pier, looking for greener pastures. When he returned a short time later, the wife was sitting on the pier deck struggling to untangle the worst bird's nest backlash you ever saw.

"How did you do that?" he asked, somewhat harshly.

"I tried to cast out a little from the pier and this happened," she said.

"Well, I told you not to cast out," he reproached her.

"I'll never do it again," she said. And she didn't. That happened when my friend was 40. His wife died at the age of 87. She never again went fishing with him.

"It just goes to show that if you want your wife as a fishing partner, don't scold her," he said philosophically a few years later.

Not only are piers often crowded with anglers when the word goes out that the "spots are running," small boats converge where schools are numerous. Frequently the rush brings fouled anchors as well as tangled monofilaments when everyone is concentrating on putting the bait in the one honey hole where most of the spots seem to have gathered.

For those who both abhor the crowded piers and have distaste for boats anchored close enough to fish each other's livewells, there are some small inlets and tidal creeks with drop-offs from palmetto trees and myrtle bushes where even bank anglers can carry home a few skillets of tasty spots. Bugs and biting insects are more of a nuisance on the hill than they are on piers and boats, but spots can be landed even in such habitats.

In the long ago, families trudged to ocean beaches in the fall to seine or hook-catch spots that were salted down for winter food. With the coming of easy travel, deep freezers and convenient seafood markets, few preserve their catch in that manner any more. But millions still seek this easy, economical fish that can be harvested six to eight months each year on almost any kind of tackle, any kind of natural bait. Indians in particular still cherish the spots and many make annual treks during the big fall runs to fill larders for the winter.

When the spots are scampering along the coast, and if you can get your pier or boat position set before the throng arrives, you have only to flip out a baited hook, thumb the tightened line, and wait for that tell-tale tap that signals another bottom feeder has found your offering. Reel him in and enjoy a tasty morsel at the dinner table.

Spots have one idiosyncrasy more peculiar to them than other surf fish. They almost never will swim under a pier. Skin and scuba diving observers have watched them for hours. Million in a school will be traveling along at four or five miles an hour. A pier juts out into the sea in front of them and they make a 180-degree detour around the pilings. That's why you often see hundreds of spots cranked up from the water on one side of the pier while a few steps away there is nary a strike for even the best spot fishermen with identical bait and tackle. Other species have similar habits, but the spot seems to respect these manmade objects more than just somewhat.

Thus, for those anxious to get down to serious spotting, find your place on the side of the pier that the spots are approaching and don't get squeezed out. Cast sparingly and cautiously with tiny shrimp tidbits on little hooks and light lines with enough lead to get your tempting food on the bottom. That's about all you have to do except be sure you have a cooler partially filled with ice. If you don't, you just may get so enthralled in reeling in the spots that you'll let them spoil in the sun.

Most spots weigh only half a pound or so. But they are fun to catch and are sought by every segment of society—particularly those who lack patience to challenge more cautious species.

BEST BAITS FOR CAROLINAS SALTWATER

Saltwater fishing along the coasts of the two Carolinas attracts throngs from early spring until Christmas and a survey of veteran ocean anglers comes up with these proven baits for the most sought-after species:

SPOT: This hand-size panfish is the number-one sought-after species in Carolinas salt water. They bite best from April through November, but sometimes are plentiful on into the colder months. Bloodworms, redworms and shrimp are leading baits and the fish are caught from piers, waterways and inlets.

FLOUNDER: These are plentiful in inlets, rivers and off some ocean piers during the hotter months and favorite baits are live shrimp and live minnows.

WHITING: Often called "Virginia mullet," this is a cold weather fish caught on cut shrimp from March through December.

TROUT: Cool water in the fall and early winter brings these gourmet fish to rivers, inlets, waterways and close offshore reefs. Trout are suckers for fish-like lures trolled or retrieved, but will also attack live minnows and shrimp, In very cold weather, cut mullet fished in deep holes on the bottom will often prove productive. It has been a favorite in Lockwood Folly River for years.

RED SNAPPER: A year-round fish offshore in the Carolinas in water 100 feet deep or more all the way to the Gulf Stream. Cut mullet and squid are best baits.

SILVER AND GRAY SNAPPER: Often found at the same time and strike the same baits as the red snapper.

KING MACKEREL: Now a species with competitive anglers going after tournament prizes worth many thousands of dollars from May through September, this plentiful giant ranges from the shoreline to 50 miles offshore. Devout mackerel anglers swear by spots and menhaden live baits for best results but others prefer large Rebel lures and the Cisco Kid, usually trolled. Sometimes they are trolled near the surface and on other occasions used with planers to take bait deep.

SPANISH MACKEREL: This is a warm weather fish usually caught trolling Johnson or Clark spoons rather fast on or near the surface from June through September. Sometimes in the surf or just beyond and up to 25 miles offshore.

BLUEFISH: A vicious, toothy species that will strike almost anything dead or alive either in the surf or just a few yards offshore from the breakers. Any spoon, spinner, minnow-lookalike attracts the blues from midsummer into late fall or winter.

BONITO: November is a good month for fast trolling for these big fish offshore with spoons, feathers or cut strip baits.

BLACK SEA BASS: From April through December these abound in water from 40 feet to over 100 feet whether close offshore or well out to sea. They are bottom feeders, preferring shrimp, squid, pork, octopus and cut mullet.

BLUE MARLIN: A Gulf Stream species that is caught fast trolling in fall months with whole mullet, bonito, Spanish mackerel or squid and skirted strips.

WHITE MARLIN: Another species usually in the Gulf Stream where they are caught by trollers with rigged mullet, flying fish, ballyhoo and skirted strips.

SAILFISH: A warm weather species caught top trolling near the Gulf Stream with hte same rigged baits that catch marlin.

SALTY MIKE'S PLACE

Mike Altine is marina manager at Edisto Marina, Inc., at Edisto Island on the southeast corner of the South Carolina coast. But this fifth-generation Greek from Charleston is more than that. He runs Salty Mike's restaurant and thus follows in the footsteps of his father who operates a restaurant in Charleston. He also has a ship's store and fishing supplies for visiting anglers from around the nation. Still, he is more than that. If you are looking for a place to sleep, need a fishing guide, or just advice about where and what fish are biting, Mike has a lot of the answers.

"The Spanish mackerel are right off the beach a short distance. Amberjack and barracuda hang out around A-can, a buoy marking the Edisto Island inlet. An hour off from A-can you can catch sailfish, dolphin and king mackerel. But while the amberjack and other species are good eating, most tourists are interested in the mackerel. They bite all summer and right on into fall.

"I have a tournament for the mackerel fishermen and we give away no money to the winners. We just furnish a lot of good free food for the contestants and have a lot of fun," Mike says.

"We have some tarpon off Edisto but not many of them are caught because not many people fish for them. Fishing for tarpon is kind of like bass fishing. You have to study the species and know its lifestyle and behavior to be successful," Mike says.

"The nice thing about Edisto is its laid-back atmosphere. It's quiet and friendly and a great place to live. A lot of people have moved in since Oristo Corporation sold out and Fairfield Ocean Ridge developed the island with fine homes. The last several years have seen this island really growing. The Bay Creek Villas owned by Terry Collier is a fine addition to progress here, too," Mike says. His operation is located at the Bay Creek complex.

Captain Jim Herlong's charter boat "Precious III" is available for offshore trips ten months of the year and Mike handles some of the bookings. A full day's fishing for four people costs $450 and a half day is $250.

"We have some good inshore fishing here too for speckled trout and other fish, or you can go up the creeks and rivers far enough and find some good largemouth bass in the brackish and fresh water. We catch our live bait up the creeks in the fall and that's a fine trout bait. When the live bait leave, you can still catch trout with grubs and Mirr-O-Lures. Some spottail bass are caught inshore here too," says Mike.

"The spadefish off the reefs are a challenge to catch. They have small mouths, but are great fighters when you get one on the line," the 31-year-old businessman reveals.

"I like to fish and hunt. I hunt ducks, doves and deer and fish for anything I can catch. My dad is a good fisherman and he knows these waters, having lived in Charleston all his life. He taught me the restaurant business and I love it. I would choose my lifestyle here above all others. I just like what I am doing," says this genial young man with conviction. If you are looking for a charter boat trip, a fishing guide, lodging, food or fishing supplies, call Mike Alpine at 803-869-3504, or write to him at 3702 Dock Site Road, Edisto Beach, SC 29438.

If you are interested in renting a luxury condo for a few days, call Fairfield Ocean Ridge at 800-845-8500 if out of state and 800-922-3330 in South Carolina, or write to them at P.O. Box 27, King Cotton Road, Edisto Beach, SC 29438.

Chain Pickerel Is a Fighter

While some sections of the country have a society of fishermen who hate chain pickerel, call them snakes, throw them in the brush for the weasels and raccoons with a few cuss words when they land one, they are rapidly enhancing their reputation in many parts of the Carolinas and throughout the South as challenging fighters on light tackle with taste-bud attraction for the diner's palate when properly prepared by a cook with some expertise.

Pickerel, known more frequently as "jacks" or "jackfish," strike artificial or natural baits with the power of a coiled spring, and they are not normally persnickety about what they strike, be it dead or alive. Furthermore, if he misses with the first lunge, he'll come back an instant later to strike viciously again and again until he is hauled over the gunnels or left flouncing on the bank.

Usually lurking in the shallows with good cover of fallen trees, lilies, grass patches, or rocky ledges, the fish is an alert and swift stalker of forage fish and in his own way competes with the largemouth bass, stripers and other predators for food. His preference of artificials is for small, shiny spinners or lures tied directly to a fairly light monofilament line without swivels, metal leaders or other hardware. You need a strong steel hook and the sharp teeth will fray even the best mono line so it will need to be cut off a foot or two after each jack landing.

While some jacks have the personality that defies explanation and will gulp down bait, leader, swivel and all, there are some a bit more cautious that shy away from too much hardware around the lure. But as a rule of thumb, a pickerel will strike anything dead or alive that passes in front of his face that is not bigger than he is.

The smallest of the pike family, a first cousin to the Northern Pike, which he closely resembles except for his pointed nose, jacks of the Carolinas usually are no more than 20 inches long, but there is an occasional 30-incher. They average about two to three pounds, but once in a great while, a six-pounder will come aboard.

They are particularly hungry in the fall and winter when wild natural forage fish are not as plentiful and it is then that they are easiest to find and catch. They will snatch a red-winged blackbird off a lily pad, swallow a swimming squirrel if it will go down the jack's throat, consume several baby alligators in the swamp waters, and gorge itself on frogs, insects and crayfish. They have a preference for cold rainy weather and when you can catch nothing else, pickerel in Tar Heelia are ready to strike. Even the novice lure caster can hang them as accuracy has no significance in pickerel fishing success.

Most pickerel are caught accidentally as bass, crappie or bluegill fishermen suddenly feel something unusual on the line. But there are some devout Carolinians who go after the jacks, usually with cane poles and live shiners around willows and cover in ponds, lakes or quiet tributaries of dark water rivers. Not blessed with fins that give him the lateral movement of a bass, the chain pickerel is still a fine physical specimen with athletic ability that gives him great straight forward propulsion and he will run fast, pull hard and die slowly.

Pickerel often will cut the angler's line after it has been dropped on the deck of the boat. It will shake its head back and forth violently with an evil eye fixed on the human predator and its hacksaw teeth will cut the taut monofilament if the fisherman still has pressure on it.

You can get a lot of advice about how pickerel should be caught, but it is not always consistent. Most successful pickerel catchers who go after them on purpose use strong cane poles and live shiners impaled through or under the dorsal fin. They drop these tasty pickerel meals around aquatic growth with a cork a couple of feet above the hook and sinker. The jack will hit the shiner with the speed of a jet and zip through the water. Let him have it awhile! Don't be too quick to set the hook. He has the shiner in his teeth at first like a cat and he'll juggle it a moment before swallowing. You need to let the cork go down and stay down a few seconds. Then yank hard and you'll have a tussle when the hook sinks in the hard, bony mouth.

Many fishermen frown on eating pickerel because of the small, limber Y-bones that are difficult to fillet out. But those who have experimented with this species for years know it is among the best flavored, white, fine-grain meat you can find. The best way to handle the cleaning, cooking and eating of a pickerel is to scrape off the scales, remove the head and guts, then slice in 1/4 inch steaks through the backbone. The thinner the better. The pieces will resemble a pair of frog legs. Drop these thin slices in deep, very hot fat after rolling in corn meal and salt. The Y-bones become brittle and edible. Only the round back bone is left and it is easily removed. It makes a fine fish dinner.

Where in the Carolinas can you find chain pickerel and be able to catch them? The answer is almost anywhere that you have aquatic growth and some still water. But specifically here are some fine pickerel honey hole locations:

Lake Waccamaw, Columbus County, North Carolina, just a mile off Highway 74-76 east of Whiteville. It's a five-by-seven-mile natural lake, clear and with ample launching ramps. There are nearby cottages and motels with good food.

Lake Tabor, a 388-acre, 100-year-old, man-made lake just off Highway 701 east of Tabor City, North Carolina. There is a good concrete ramp and a motel within sight of the water.

The Cape Fear River and its tributary, the Northeast River, run through Wilmington, North Carolina. North of the city is a community known as Castle Hayne where ramps are accessible and motels and cafes are close by.

In Piedmont North Carolina, the central section of the state, the Great Pee Dee River flows with hydroelectric dams impounding water every few miles. These impoundments are known as Lake Tillery, Badin Lake, High Rock and Tuckertown, among others. All have jackfish. There is little pressure on them. But those with know-how catch them up the creeks and in inlet mouths. In Stanly, Montgomery and other counties along this big waterway, there are Wildlife Commission launching areas and bait and tackle shops are not far away.

In eastern North Carolina in Pender County is Black River

with ramps near Atkinson and Kelly and motels and restaurants in these small towns. This is a remote section with an abundance of pickerel in the sloughs.

In Brunswick County, traversed from north to south via Highway 17, there is the small village of Winnabow. Town Creek flows through the Green Swamp here and into the lower Cape Fear River. It has some good fishing holes. Bait, food and rooms are available on the highway.

South Carolina has a numer of good pickerel lakes. The Low Country rivers of Sampit, Little Pee Dee, Waccamaw, Edisto and Santee-Cooper all have eddy water where jacks abound. These locations are just short hops off Highway 17 South. They have some desolate sections, but launching is easy and accessible near good roads. Food, bait and rooms are never far away from the landings.

Other states along the Atlantic coast have great pickerel fishing too, and more people than ever are going after them. Try the pickerel holes then try them in the skillet. You'll come back for more.

REDBREAST
IN SOUTH CAROLINA'S BIG DITCH

My astute fishing companion guided the bass boat around the stumps, logs, sandbars and jagged points of grass and lilies that protruded out from the swampy shoreline, parts of which were so dense and desolate that you wondered if anyone had walked through this jungle since the Indians lived here a few hundred years ago. He was a bass fanatic and cared little for catching anything else. But I am not so dedicated. I like to catch fish when I'm on the water with a rod in my hand. I'm not so persnickety about what species comes over the gunnels and later into the frying pan. He wasn't setting the woods on fire, although he had disturbed a couple of yearlings that swirled, splashed, hit his topwater plugs and scooted away into the cover, leaving him with a frown on his face and an unprintable word or two on his lips.

It was time for a change. I laid down my casting rod and reel and picked up a close-faced

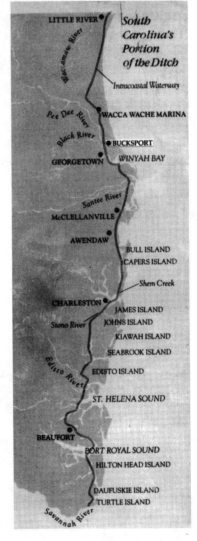

ultralight rig that I had brought along just in case—just in case it was mid-morning and we didn't have enough fish in the boat to stink up a skillet at noon. It was mid-morning and the tide was right. No sense in losing the opportunity.

I tied on a yellow Beetlespin and flipped it 40 feet into the shade of a myrtle bush that precariously leaned out over the water, its roots nearly all exposed to the air as the slashing waves and constant change of tide had eroded away the black muck in which the plant was trying desperately to stay grounded and nourished. The water underneath was no more than a couple of feet deep, but it was dark from the tannic acid and was cider colored near the bank from the rivulets that forever ate away at the dark sandy dirt. It was a likely place for a panfish and any veteran freshwater angler in the coastal Carolinas could spot it.

The Beetlespin moved toward me only a few inches from where the slow retrieve started before there was a throbbing bump-bump on the line and the monofilament tightened like a banjo string. It sang like a scared honey bee as it split the surface and the lure headed for the open water. There was no need to set the hook. I had a fish and it was just a case of patiently reeling, guiding the line away from obstacles and eventually proving the 4-pound test line was a match for a fish if the drag was properly set, and I didn't get in a hurry. Moments later I lifted the fish over the side. It was a 1-pound red bream, known all over the coastal Carolinas as a "redbreast" because of its fiery red color on the chest from the gills to the anal fin. Ounce for ounce, there is no fish that I have ever seen with the strength, determination and speed of a Carolina redbreast in the Inland Waterway and its tributaries. It is also second to none when it comes to gourmet eating, if you are the seafood eater who can enjoy a fish cooked whole with only the scales, insides and head removed. Most redbreast are too small for filleting, but are absolutely delicious when salted, rolled in corn meal and cooked to a golden brown in a skilled filled with peanut oil.

This morning's fishing adventure was in the 2,000-mile-long Intracoastal Waterway, known more intimately as the "Inland Waterway," that glides through South Carolina from Little River on the North Carolina border to near Savannah to the south and on down through the east coast of Florida. It traverses the nation from Massachusetts to Key West.

As it passes through South Carolina, it winds along sandy bluffs near Ocean Drive, Myrtle Beach and the Grand Strand, past Socastee, Sandy Island, Hobcaw Barony, Bucksport, Murrells Inlet, Pawleys Island, Cat Island, once a a part of the Tom Yawkey estate, saltwater bays and estuaries providing a water route for barges, yachts and other vessels preferring the protection of nearby land to the open sea. There are other places along the way with intriguing names like Daufuskie Island, Seabrook, Fripp, Edisto, Kiawah and Hilton Head.

This picturesque waterway that locals refer to as "the big ditch" in the Palmetto State, ebbs and floods past abandoned rice fields, relics of once-proud and regal Magnolia-South mansions, wilderness swamps and pine and cypress forests as it cuts a 100-yard-wide swathe filled with darkish tidal water. The South Carolina portion of the waterway in the Socastee area where we were fishing that morning is calm as compared with other areas where winds and waves keep it disturbed. It's generally a peaceful liquid highway where you can get the smell of mud flats, marshes, sawgrass and the friendly odors of fresh fish from numerous seafood packing houses. Further south you admire the unique village of McClellanville where visitors stop yachts to see the ancient oaks, narrow streets and museum-like homes of Civil War days.

Completed in 1936 after it was started nearly 150 years earlier, this waterway through the Carolinas is polka-dotted with things to see, sounds to hear, smells to adore and wildlife to photograph. Managed by the U.S. Corps of Engineers, it remains a stream through the scenic wilderness of the Carolinas. Long strands of Spanish moss dangle from trees and bushes along much of its 200 South Carolina miles, and cabbage palmetto and wax myrtles mixed with turkey and blackjack oaks make many views typical color posts cards. Bald eagles and American alligators are at home along the shoreline, whitetail deer drink in the freshwater areas, and masked raccoons snatch gambusia minnows from shallows where creeks and tiny streams trickle into the ditch.

While it's worth any fisherman's time to just simply put his gear in the boat and admire the scenery of the big ditch from Socastee to Bucksport where the fascinating Waccamaw River empties into the waterway, the serious angler gets a bonus if he moves his boat along the shoreline and flips a lure in search of that thrill you get when something alive strikes and runs.

The Socastee area, just a couple of miles below metropolitan Myrtle Beach, has a public ramp as do most other communities with names along the waterway. It's here that I usually slip my bass boat into the water in search of largemouth bass and redbreast bream. While the tide rises and falls four feet or more in the waterway, usually about five to six hours later than it is on the beach a mile or so away across Highway 17, a spit of land and some beach houses, there is no discernible salt in the water. It's too far from the ocean at Georgetown to be even brackish.

This water had long been known by natives as among the very best for redbreast. And, strangely, these fine gourmet fish seem to prefer small spinners like the Beetlespin or Hal Flies to the natural cricket and worm baits that have been used here for generations.

While many of the locals still catch redbreast for the dinner table with a limber cane pole and a cricket on a No. 4 hook below a tiny shot and thimble-size cork, my success in this waterway area has always been greater with ultralight tackle and a spinner cast around the stumps and logs that are half-submerged on high tide and bare and ominous during the ebb.

One thing is for certain the year around, you'll catch most of your fish when the tide is going out and before it gets low. Half-out to half-in is the prime time for either the largemouth bass or the redbreast and bluegills that apparently gorge themselves on insects and creatures that float out of the swamps when the water recedes. Once it stops, the strikes are few, but there are some good hours from low to half-in.

A word of caution: carry along a good supply of spinners and other small lures. The underwater obstacles are plentiful and you'll get hung time after time if you cast under the bushes where the redbreast hide and start your retrieve. Just break off the spinner and start over. You can seldom unhook a lure set solidly in a cypress knee four or five feet under the water. The other even more important caution is to be always on the look-out for long chains of loaded barges that ply these waters where commerce is the main objective. Heavy barges frequently suck out a foot or two of water and may leave your boat high and dry along the shoreline or even splash a barrelful of water in your boat. The stream is narrow and you'll do well to head your boat directly into the barge wake or scoot up a slough or creek until these craft pass.

The current is not usually a severe problem in the water-way. I find it is an asset when I move along the shoreline with my bass boat, using the trolling motor only to keep straight or detour around protruding logs or treetops that just may have a hat-size wasp nest hanging over the water. With a strong troll-ing motor you can buck the current, but most regulars on the waterway move with the current as they cast.

You have the added advantage of being able to fish the Waccamaw River when you launch your boat at Socastee or Bucksport. (There's gas and food at both places.) The river pours into the waterway between the two points, only a few minutes on a fast bass boat from either ramp. This river has long been noted for its bream and bass fishing, as well as catfish for those who prefer the bewhiskered species. Few yachts pass up the Waccamaw and you escape all of the big barge traffic. It does have more fishing pressure than the waterway itself, perhaps because of the harassment of the commercial vessels, but fine stringers of fish still come out of the Waccamaw River between the waterway and Conway and on into North Carolina where the headwaters are in Columbus County at Lake Waccamaw. You can motor up the river almost to Lake Waccamaw, a stretch of about 20 crow-fly miles, but more than that via the winding river.

While you may come in with a live-box full of redbreast from the waterway, you are not likely to have any of wallmount size. These fish are normally about four fingers wide and eight or nine ounces in weight, but tasty and ideal for frying either along the river bank or in the back yard when you get back home. Often you can catch some much larger redbreast up the

Waccamaw a mile or two, but the numbers are reduced. You kind of take your pick whether you want to pull in some bragging size or just eating size.

And where do you find a honey hole for redbreast? It's a fish that demands moving water. Almost every time that you catch them in numbers, you must find an obstacle over or around which the water pours rapidly. On the eddy side of these stickups, redbreast hover and stalk food as it rushes past. An accurate caster who can put a tiny spinner into the eddies, often no larger than a ten-gallon hat, will catch redbreast. And if you are a cane pole angler, you need to drop that natural bait in the same little whirlpools and watch the cork spin around and around a few seconds. If the redbreast are there, they will gulp it down.

Another productive redbreast spot is around sandbars that drop off into deep water, particularly when there is a bend in the stream or a point. Where the drop occurs there often is aquatic growth in the shallow portion and redbreast congregate there. A Beetlespin twitched in their faces is irresistible. They'll strike and you'll vouche for the fighting strength of these little fellows that object to being reeled in from their cozy habitat. They will fight all the way to the gunnels.

Because the waterway weaves in and out of the Atlantic at a number of places and is salt water or brackish, some anglers do not think they have to buy South Carolina freshwater fishing licenses. But you must have a license in the waterway when you get inland enough that freshwater species are abundant. Most such areas are marked with signs at highway bridges advising where you must have a freshwater license.

The big ditch through South Carolina has much to offer the outdoorsman. You can catch bass, bluegills, pickerel, catfish and more redbreast than in most other water. Fish the tide. Watch for the commercial vessels. Cast in the eddies and admire the flora and fauna. It will combine to make you a day to remember and you will be back to try it again and again.

TIME FOR GOOD WILL

Winter sunshine peeked through the cypress trees on the shoreline as the first faint rays of dawn glistened on the peaceful surface of Lake Sutton, near Wilmington. Mark Whitley glanced up at the horizon from his pedestal-seat perch on the bow of his sleek fishing boat, and then settled back to carefully watch his half-dozen bobbers floating in the stillness. Any moment Mark expected a bobber to disappear. It was speck-biting time.

Nothing happened. But so what! Everything was beautiful, and he surely would catch the mess of crappies that Martha expected before the morning passed. She wanted enough fillets for the small grandchildren who would be arriving late in the afternoon. He fished on and other boats settled down around him, propping out enough poles on the gunnels to make the crafts look like giant spiders. Maybe they were sprouting. But then his boat looked like those of his neighbors.

Mark flipped the switch on his Motor-Guide trolling motor, adjusted the speed so his hooks would pass a foot or two off the bottom, and set a course toward the south end of the lake. If a breeze sprang up, it would probably be from the northwest. That would put it on his stern where he wanted it.

Lady Luck was smiling. Corks disappeared on both sides of the boat. Mark carefully, steadily lifted one pole after the other from the holders, and three 1-pound slabs soon flopped on the deck. He was off to a good start. In the hour that followed, he put ten more fine specks in the livewell. He was pleased.

"Hey, mister, what you doing in that boat? I been watching you catch a stringer full of specks, and I ain't had a bite. You must know something I don't," a bearded stranger from a nearby boat hailed Mark. A tiny quiet figure in the back seat held a pole in each hand, intensely watching two corks. He stole a quick look at Mark, glanced at his dad, and the six-year-old's eyes returned to his lazy, luckless bobbers.

"I'm fishing like I always do in the open water. I got several colors of Super Jigs and Crappie Rattlers on my lines with a small minnow hooked through the eyes. You see how I troll them slowly through the water with the oblong corks making tiny wakes on the surface," Mark relayed a bit of his technique.

"I just got minnows on my hooks. I ain't got no jigs," the unsuccessful fisherman muttered with a little chagrin.

Corks continued to pop under, and the tips of several of Mark's B 'n' M fiberglass poles splashed in the water as big specks struggled to get unbuttoned. He admired the big pop-gutted female crappies that were ready to spawn when they gulped down another meal before heading for the shallows. They splashed in the livewell.

The neighboring fisherman wore a tragic, disappointed countenance. He hadn't had a bite despite trying so patiently. Mark suddenly was obsessed with a feeling of guilt. Little voices seemed to be telling him something. He sat upright in his seat and looked around. He was letting his imagination play tricks on him. Or was he? The compelling urge to do something engulfed him. He got the message.

That neighboring angler could use some help. Why not live a little of the golden rule? Mark turned his trolling motor toward the other boat, put his port-side poles on the deck, and moved a few yards to boatside of the fishing stranger with the wisp of a child huddled in the stern.

"Fellow, would it irritate you if I shared a few things? I know you haven't been catching any fish. I think I can help," Mark cautiously approached the unknown fisherman almost apologetically.

"I would appreciate any help. This youngster I have with me is fishing for the very first time. We will have a mighty disappointed child if we go home skunked."

Mark held on to the side of the boat, and for the first time looked at the quiet child. Bright steel braces were fastened to the shoes on both feet. The face bore the semblance of a smile and long, blonde hair tucked under an old fishing cap testified that this was a little lady. Polio or meningitis had made her a cripple. Yet, she wanted to fish with her daddy and was trying ever so hard.

"I have plenty of these small Super Jigs that help me catch fish. Here, take this handful! Put one on every line you have. Make sure you have pink jigs on some of your hooks. The specks seem to go for pink this morning. Use your smallest minnows. Those four-inch minnows with a jig make the morsel entirely too big for most crappies to strike. Also, slow your trolling motor down a little. Put a couple of more lead shot on your line a foot above the jigs and let's see if your luck changes," Mark shared his jigs and advice. He started to push away from the boat.

"That monofilament line looks mighty heavy. What test is it?" Mark asked as he saw the little girl's line flitting in the air.

"I think it's 25-pound. It's been lying around the house for a long time," the fisherman said. "I don't get much chance to fish."

"It's far too heavy," Mark said, and he pushed his boat back alongside. "Little lady, hand me your poles. I'll change your lines." Ten minutes later, Mark had put new 10-pound test line on the little girl's poles and helped her dad re-rig his with the new, lighter line.

"You're all set now. Let's get back to fishing," Mark said as he trolled away and watched his new acquaintances drop the jig-minnow baits in the water.

Almost like a miracle, the child's yell signalled success. She struggled with a big speck that slammed against the boat, took a ride across to the other side, and finally, like a pendulum, fluttered in the air above the deck. Smiling, her dad turned around, unhooked the fish and said, "Get the hook back in the water. That's a real beauty."

Instant replay kept the rest of the morning thrilling. The little cripple had the time of her life as she put eight or ten nice specks in the boat. Her dad concentrated on helping her, often ignoring his own strikes. And Mark didn't even bother to fish. His reward was the yells and smiles of the little lady.

It was time to head for home.

"Well, maybe I'll see you around again. And be sure to bring that youngster back fishing often. She's going to be a real pro," Mark chided as he cranked his outboard and roared toward the dock.

There was a unique warmth in Mark's chest he had seldom felt. It lingered even as he began dressing his fine catch. He had more fish than his grandkids would eat. The old widowed lady at the end of his street might like a few fillets. He put four in a plastic bag and dropped them off at her house on his way home. She was so grateful. His warm heart was lighter than ever. What a great world he lived in.

He wiped the dirt off his wet shoes at his back doorsteps and went in. Martha was putting lunch on the table. She smiled at his bucket of fillets.

"What are you so happy about?" she asked, observing the glow on Mark's face and the glint in his big brown eyes.

"Oh, it's nothing. Nothing at all. I guess I am caught up in the season," Mark smiled, and the subject was dropped.

It was Christmas Eve.

THREE BUCKS IN ONE DAY

Bragging rights for harvesting a trophy deer have escaped young Dean Ulmer of Elloree, South Carolina, in the Low Country of the Palmetto State. But he accomplished a feat that certainly sets him apart. He killed three fine bucks in a single afternoon while still hunting near his home. That's legal in South Carolina, where the season runs from August 15 until January 1 in most areas. That's the longest deer hunting season in the nation.

Sportsmen: The Endangered Species

Bumper stickers flash a message that teeters on advocacy of violence, boldly declaring: I'LL GIVE UP MY GUN ONLY WHEN THEY PRY MY COLD, DEAD FINGERS FROM AROUND THE BARREL. It is meant in definite terms to indicate the determination of hunters to keep their rifles, shotguns and other weapons despite wowser pressure to push laws through congress that would control gun ownership in America.

The anti-hunting and anti-fishing organizations and individual proponents, a growing aggressive force that threatens the very existence of sportsmen in the decade ahead, has concentrated its lobbying and propaganda effort against the hunters and their guns primarily, while openly admitting that they fiercely oppose fishing for fun too. They don't propose to confiscate our rods and reels, but hope to kill sports fishing by eliminating wildlife and game species sought by sportsmen. The avowed objective of the so-called Friends of Animals, Inc., and the misnamed Committee for Humane Legislation, Inc., is to destroy the Pittman-Robertson and Dingell-Johnson Acts that preserve and restore fish and wildlife.

The anti's "back to nature" movement would leave the reproduction and expansion of wildlife to the survival of the fittest without regard to the usefulness of the species as a natural resource. No species would have the assistance of human agencies that would promulgate fish and wildlife desirable for harvesting by sportsmen. Indeed, the wowsers make it clear that they would like to see fewer deer, turkeys, bass and stripers for outdoorsmen to "kill." They object to the use of the word "harvest" in connection with hunting or fishing. And scientists "collect" instead of "kill."

These radical groups are acutely aware that man's constant infringement upon the habitat of the game species in the forests and in the streams threatens the very existence of edible, challenging animals. They know that these creatures could not exist many years without sophisticated, planned programs of conservation and restoration. But they could not care less whether there is anything to hunt or fish or not. If there are no game fish or animals, the wowsers will have accomplished their purpose—hunting and fishing will cease while the land fills up with cockroaches and the lakes with garfish.

What they propose is equal attention to the useless non-game species. Unfortunately, the rats and weasels can survive in the midst of man's garroting pressure on their habitat better than the sought-after food species that pit man's ability and equipment against the cunning, acute self-preservation instincts and senses of the wild creatures.

When the ugly head of the wildlife wowsers first appeared in the 1950's, it seemed destined to an humble place with little chance of a following sufficiently muscled to challenge American outdoorsmen's self-evident privilege to hunt and fish. But with the rebelliousness of the '60's in many spheres of life, thousands of people broke from tradition and searched for a cause that they could espouse. Opposition to hunting was a natural for some who challenged the establishment.

In the beginning, the anti movement was little more than printing and handing out circulars and tracts, eventually made available to schools and clubs. Then came appearances by the antis at forums, television talk shows, radio programs and some celebrities got in the act when exaggerated brutality was shown on TV of mutilation of baby seals in the frozen north and the infamous "Guns of Autumn" pictured hunters as slobs intent upon cruelty to animals.

The formation of organized groups with phony names that seemed designed to protect wildlife increased contributions from all over the country. Few original promoters visualized a movement that would soon advocate total abolition of hunting and fishing. Even fewer suspected that extensive litigation would be in the federal courts with the admitted objective of designating the use of hunters' and fishermen's excise taxes to expand the game populations of the land. Almost no one suspected that a bill would be introduced in the House of Representatives that would abolish the highly successful wildlife and fish conservation programs in the United States. But both were realities by 1978-79.

Considering the youth of this country and the near hero-worship children of a few generations ago had for history's notable outdoorsmen like Daniel Boone, Davy Crockett, Buffalo Bill Cody, among many others, it's little short of miraculous that the antis could have made such inroads against sportsmen in a few decades. Several of the anti groups quickly established budgets of almost a million bucks a year and when there was virtually no organized opposition by sportsmen in the early years of this campaign, the antis got a head start in propagandizing a large segment of young people. They enrolled many converts who still are determined to undermine wildlife sports.

In a nutshell, the difference between the objectives of the antis and those of the sportsmen hinges on whether you are a consumptive or non-consumptive user of wildlife. If you hunt, trap or fish you are a consumer. If you watch, photograph, paint and study, you are a non-consumer. But will such distinction stand scrutiny or is it ecological nonsense?

Articles, films and literature distributed by the antis portray a smugness, paternalism andvituperation against sportsmen, a holier-than-thou attitude, as if their hands were lily-white, while the hunters and fishermen were covered with blood. Not true!

Ano Nuevo Point, California, has a colony of elephant seals. When they come ashore in the spring, the "nonconsumers" spray graffiti all over their backs with paint. Some youngsters slide down sandy banks to bronco straddle and ride the blubbery backs of the big seals. Harassment? Nonconsumers?

Scientists who "collect" species are presumably clean and without blood on their hands. But consider a project in Alaska in 1975 when they "collected" 80 species of birds, 20 species of fish and 20 species of mammals. There were 79 black-footed kittiwakes, 110 tufted puffins, 224 redpolls, 23 savanna sparrows and 32 black-capped chickadees. Of the fish "collected," 179,697 were three-spined sticklebacks and 2,988 Arctic char. In the mammal group were 1,046 tundra red-backed voles, 5 wolverines, 34 Arctic ground squirrels and 6 Arctic foxes, among others. I am not here trying to condemn that "collection." It was probably justified and within the sustaining limits. But the point that does need to be made is that these scientists were consumers, just as surely as are the hunters and fishermen. Furthermore, the scientists kill more species and take more in breeding season than sportsmen.

What about the puritanical image of photographers and beachcombers? On Cape Cod, Massachusetts, a flock of Arctic terns that numbered more than 40,000 was reduced to just 24 survivors in one decade when picture taking and beachgoers caused such intensive disturbance that they would not reproduce. British beach tourists eliminated the Kentish plover as a breeding species. The little tern was destroyed in Sweden from the stresses of having man in its habitat. High school classes in beach areas have stripped the strand of tide pool and beach animals while studying nature. Nonconsumers?

Thousands of acres of green wildlife habitat is trampled, eroded and burned in national parks and forests every year as throngs of "nonconsumptive" users enjoy and overrun the homeland of the wildlife.

Consider the consumption of a moose that a hunter stalked and killed and compare that with an equal amount of beef. Nature produced the moose without plowing up the land, spreading fertilizer or spraying pesticides. The energy used in getting a moose home was less than shipping a beef from Texas to Chicago to Alaska.

Then you analyze the meeting of "conservationists" at the 1977 Earthcare Conference. They destroyed more quail habitat than if every one in attendance had gone out and shot a pair of the birds. And if hunters had shot the pair of quail, there would have been some funds made available for restoration. But the money the Earthcare proponents spent for prime beef rib only helped to destroy wildlife habitat.

The point here is not to point an accusing finger at the scientists, beach lovers, the school classes, the bird watchers, the park hikers or the Earthcare conservationists, but to note that there is no one group that can be singled out as "consumers" while everyone else has clean hands. We are all consumers of wildlife, one way or the other. When you drive your car, wear wool or cotton clothing, heat your home or burn your lights, you are a wildlife consumer. It takes strip-mind land, oil fields, pipelines, plowed land that replaces oak and pine woodlands—all these one way or the other "consumes" wildlife.

There is not such thing as a nonconsumptive user of wildlife. There are just those who care and those who don't and the tragedy is that the hunters and fishermen are getting most of the accusing fingers while the mass of people share no shame because the wowsers are loudly condemning sportsmen. These false distinctions play into the hands of that mass of people who simply don't give a damn.

So where do we go from here?

While there are dozens of good, energetic, aggressive organizations with huge memberships in this country that represent the interests of hunters and fishermen, the impact of their voices is subdued by virtue of its diversity and scatter-gun action. There is a definite need for a consolidated spokesman who can produce TV shows, send competent lecturers to school chapel programs, defend the rights of sportsmen on network talk shows, distribute truthful, informative literature to both high and low places. Sportsmen need a strong lobbying arm to compete with that of Friends of Animals, Inc., and others. One that will let the lawmakers of the land respect the rights of sixty million Americans who have the determination to hunt and fish as long as they live.

That bumper sticker with the message of the cold, dead fingers being pried from a gun barrel can be enlarged to encompass, not just refusal to give up firearms, but to preserve and promote fish and wildlife conservation and restoration forever.

We have the numbers. What we need is consolidation and leadership. Will the real voice of American sportsmen please take the stand!

CRUSOE ISLAND HUNTER

Born on an island in the remotest section of the Green Swamp in Columbus County, North Carolina, shortly after teh turn of the century, Dodo Clewis grew up in that scenic wilderness without an opportunity to go to school. Thus, he never learned to read and write and he lived and made a living off the woods and waters, never having been outside the Crusoe Island area. While Clewis had no book learning, he was Phi Beta Kappa in the outdoors. Whether he was armed with a rifle, shotgun or an humble bow and arrow, this old recluse of the swampland was an expert at hunting deer, bear, boar and even the wily wild turkey. He spent most of his 70 years stalking these game animals for food. Listening to his experiences over the many years, you are acutely awawre taht this old hunter was after both fun and food in those scenic jungles in decades past.

some of his adventures were so unique that they were almost unbelievable, but if you ever knew Dodo Clewis, you relied on his integrity.

Some would say Clewis was poor, pitiful and in need of help. They would look at his tiny, rundown home that he made himself on the river bank and lament his poverty. But if you asked this swamper, he would be quick to say he was fine, lacked nothing and perhaps enjoyed life far beyond that of the wealthiest city dweller in the country.

Life in the swamps had a few complications. You worked generally only for food, clothing and shelter and Dodo's requirements were humble. His homemade house kept him dry when it rained and reasonably warm in winter. The shade from the giant cypress in his yard was the nearest thing he had to air conditioning. Cucumbers, cabbage, sweet potatoes, roasting ear corn and butterbeans came from his hand-tilled garden alongside his house. For luxury, he raised a few watermelons and cantaloupes. For meat, he headed into the dense jungle with his bow or gun or climbed in his cypress dugout canoe and went fishing. Proficient as a hunter and a fisherman, this old bachelor never went hungry.

Clewis was a deer stalker, not a tree climber or a ground-level hunter who blended into the forest waiting for othe buck to come by. He knew their trails and with the caution and cunning of a cat, he crept through the maze of vines, bushes and trees and sat within shooting distance of his whitetail prey. He was an expert marksman with a rifle and seldom missed, even in the thickets where the deer lived along the river. He was just average with a bow and arrow.

Some deer are just too tough to stalk successfully and Clewis reminisced about one old eight-pointer that he trailed time after difficult time. Finally, he conlcuded that he was never going to be able to slip up on this buck in the swamp. He would have to devise some other plan. He surmised that the buck would come to drink along the river bank late every after noon and perhaps about dawn in the morining. That habit was the buck's undoing.

"I have a 10-foot canoe that I chopped out of a big log. It's what I use to fish in on the Waccamaw where I catch a lot of bream and some catfish, too. I can handle this canoe fine wiht my one-handed paddle. I looked my boat over and decided it would help me get that buck that was alwllays giving me the slip. I picked my time and one afternoon, just before sundown, I pushed the boat in the river and climbed in. When I got to the open water, I flattened out on my back in the boat and drifted along. I knew the buck I wanted lived about a mile downriver. I kept peeking over the side as I moved along, my rifle ready beside me. Sure 'nough that old buck was standing on the river bank. He looked up and down the river and all he saw was a log flating along. If I had been in a fancy boat, the deer might have spooked, but he wasn't scared at all of a cypress log.

"When I got within about 50 yards of the buck, I sat up quickly and brought my gun up. That buck didn't seem to believe it, and he just stood there. I shot him right in his throat and he fell in his tracks. I pulled the deer in the boat and paddled home with my meat. That was a long time ago, but I'll never forget how I outfoxed that old buck," Dodo told the story with obvious pleasure at having used his basic equipment and expertise to put meat on his table.

"One other time I was bow huhnting along the river and

had something happen that you won't believe. I killed a deer without actually putting an arrow in him. The buck saw me about the time I saw him and headed for the water. I's narrow up-river near Lake Waccamaw, and by the time I got to the bank that buck was coming out on the other side about 50 yards away. I threw my bow up and fired. That buck went down like I had shot him right through the brain. I waded across the river. It was only about straddle deep then. When I got to the buck, he was rolling his eyes and trying to get up. I cut his throat and he kicked a few times and died. I saw no arrow in him. There was not a speck of blook. I scratched my head. Why had the deer dropped if I hadn't hit him? I looked and looked and found what had happened. My arrow had struck the buck right at the base of his horns. I had actually chipped off a chunk. The blow had stunned that deer without hitting anythign except the antler. It gave me a chance to get across the river and kill the deer with my knife. I have the horsn on the wall now," Clewis says, and he strips the antlers from a peg and shows you how he got a buck wwithout hitting anything but the horns.

"I guess the time I killed a buck with an axe is the oddes thing that ever happened to me. It was one cold fall morning and I was out of firewood. I picked up my little axe and walked down the edge of the field to an old hickory tree that the wind had blown down. I was going to chop up some limbs for the fire. Before I hit the first lick, I hears a deer snort. I looked up the hedgerow beside the soybean field, and there was this big buck walking toward me and looking around with his head way up in the air. I know he had smelled a doe and was looking for her. Like some men, he didn['t have a thing on his mind but sex, and he headed right for me. I slumped down in the grass at the edge of the field and waited.

"That bucvk came within 15 feet of me and he didn't see a thing. I raised up and threw the axe. It hit that buck right between the shoulder blades and it buried. The deer fell kicking. I had hit him just right to break his backbone. It was all luck, but it put some meat on the table for me and my neightbors," Dodo revealed this almost unbelievable experience years later.

But it is not beyond belief when you get to know this old outdoorsman who was adept with a gun, knifem, axe and the ancient fishing equipment he used, a can pole cut from the river bank, line, wrap-apround lead, cork from a bottle and some store-bought No. 4 hooks. He put most of his protein on the table with this fishing trackle. Panfish were hiding under every bush along the river bank and Dodo could slingshot a cricket, saphead, wasp larvae, wriggling earthworm or catalpa worm right into a hole no bigger than a pork 'n' bean can at 20 feet or more. Bream can't leave a natural bait alone when it is flipped so accurately.

While another deer story unfolded in these swamps, it didn't actually happen to Clewis, he just eard about it. It seems one of his hunting buddies had shot a deer and dragged it back home to dress. When they pulled the hid off the buck's head, there was a knife, completely enveloped by the hide. YOu could see only a bulge where the knife was embedded. Apparently, someone had tried to kill the buck with a knife, lost his weapon and the deer. It stayed under the hide and hext to the skull of the deer long enough to heal.

"I got myself a deer one time way over in the swamp when I didn't even shoot and I didn't kill it with my axe, either, " Clewis volunteered another story.

"I was hunting by myself like I usually do when I heard some deer hounds hot on the trail of a deer or womething. I think they must have been wild dogs, because I never saw or heard any hunters with them. I knew they were headed for me and I stood still, hopoing the deer might get close enough to shoot. But that dder stayed in the cover so I couldn't get a look at him until those dogs were right on his heels. Then he charged out of the gallberry bushes wide open and came right at me. I didn't have time to shoot. I just dived out of the way. The deer flew by me, treid to go between two sweetgum trees and his rack was so wide he couldn't make it. He broke his neck on the charge. I went over and slit his throat, ran the pack of dogs away and had my deer without firing a shot," the wily old woodsman recounte diwth pride his accomplishment.

Law and order came to the swamplands about the middle of the 20th century, but in the distant past, few of the swampers bought hunting and fishing licenses and they generally disregarded the game laws. They had lived here for generations, and many considered game and fish their property and not subject to state and federal regulations.

A serious wildlife officer years ago heard that Joseph was hunting deer without a license and he was determined to catch him. One morning from a distance he watched Dodo leav his house and head into the swamp, obviously going after deer. He had his rifle and surely was hunting. The game warden followed the deer stalker for miles staying a safe distance behind, but close enough to catch Dodo if he shot antyhing. Then the swamp silence was shattered by the blast from teh swamper's gun. Ghe game warden quickened the pace and soon walked right up on Clewis, who was bending down over his dead buck.

"Well, I got you this time," the officer said. "I knew if I stayed after you long enough I'd catch you shooting deer without a license. so ou pick up the deer and come along with me. I'll need the deer in court for evidence."

Now Clewis was uneducated and couldn't read, but he was no fool. If that offercer wanted the deer for evidence, he would have to haul the deer o ut of the woods himself. It was a hot day and it was miles to the nearest road. He wassn't going to work himself to death getting that deer out for the officer.

"I'm not taking that deer anywher. If I xcan't have the deer, then you get it out the best way you can," dodo told the officer.

The officer had little choice. He grunted disapproval, but picked up the heavy buck, lifted it across his shoulders and headed out of the swamp with Addison trudging quietly along behind. Three times the officer had to put the heavy load down, wipe sweat form his forehead and rest a bit. Finally, he reached the road where he had left his pickup truck and he plopped the big buck on the tailgat.

"Well, I got it back even if you didn't' cooperate and I'll write you a citation for deer hunting without a license," the officer said, obviously irritated that Clewis was no help. He pulled his book out from the sun visor and started to write.

Clewis fumbled through his walleet and sheepishly walked over to the officer.

"Is this any good?" Clewis asked as he showed a card to the warden. "I went with my sister to the courthouse last week and paid seven dollars for it."

The officer was without words for a moment as he stared at a valid hunting license.

"Damn, you've go t a license," he then stammered.

Dodo picked up his deer and headed for home.

BOWHUNTING IS BACK

The late noted naturalist, Dr. John N. Hamlet, handed me a deerskin pouch bowtied with a leather thong, his conception of a gift wrapped package, and wished me a Merry Christmas. Cautiously, I unwrapped the unique bundle, half expecting a snake or something equally unusual to pounce out like a Jack-in-the-Box. But there was no animate object here. Instead, I spread out four antiques of nature and the distant past that brought a huge lump in my throat as he explained each object.

"This is a whale's tooth from Hawaii. This egg-shaped rock that is split in the middle with a leaf etched between the halves came from a mountain in South Dakota. This other flat piece of stone with a fish fossil clearly pictured on its surface was dug from a Wyoming mountain," he said.

"They are wonderful," I interrupted, "And you don't have to tell me what the other one is. That's an Indian arrowhead. I have seen plenty of those around the Indian Mound near Ellerbe, NC."

"Wrong," said this expert on all things out-of-doors, "No Indian ever saw that arrowhead. It was used in France about 30,000 years ago. Bows and arrows were not inventions of American Indians. They were in use by stone age people and were really the first forms of mechanization in hunting and warring following clubs and sharp rock axes."

I stood corrected by this retired author, scientist, wildlife film producer, world traveler and renowned naturalist who captured the 5000 cynomulgus monkeys and built the primate center at Pritchardsville, SC where the animals were kept for research that perfected the polio vaccine. Raised with the Sioux Indians in South Dakota, this 70 year old retired outdoorsman later served as naturalist at several tourist attractions after receiving his honorary Ph.D. from the University of South Carolina. He admits the sophistication of today's bows and arrows is a revolutionary departure from the weapons of those ancient ancestors, and he was aware that most Americans think of arrow heads in the same manner I did—a primitive weapon of the Indians.

In truth, the bow and arrow has determined the destiny of mankind a myriad of times since the beginning of civilization. Man's fortunes have been determined by archery in conflicts of man against man, time and again when the superior weapon and expertise won battles.

It is even more historically significant as a hunting weapon that has sustained man throughout the ages and there are still primitive tribes today that would go hungry and unclothed if denied their bows and arrows.

There is no exact date recorded that establishes the invention of archery as a hunting tool, but stone age paintings depict bowmen standing with hairy mammoths lying at their feet, arrows protruding from the beast. Others picture dead elk with bow hunters, and most historians believe archery may have evolved 30,000 years ago or more. Archery ranks along with speech communication and the discovery of fire as one of the three most important cultural advances in the history of man.

Successful bowhunting demands stamina, courage, perseverance, skill, patience and a woodsman's knowledge of wildlife. It ranks among the greatest of modern conservation developments, is self-perpetuating and a sport that promotes itself. State after state recognizes bowhunting as a conservation method and designates exclusive bowhunting areas and seasons. Crack shot rifle hunters of both large and small game have been converted to bowhunting with its special challenge that tests prowess and knowledge of animal behavior. Even the most adroit, experienced hunters are flocking to the archery community. Bowhunting, for many, provides added opportunity to stay in the woods longer since the patience required for success enhances the enjoyment of nature by giving the hunter more time to admire his surroundings.

Giant technological advances in today's bows and arrows are greatly responsible for influencing the mushrooming interest in bowhunting. While there are some purists who condemn advances in design and mechanization of archery weapons, and look to the original longbow as the only true challenge, it is the modern innovations that have made the sport attractive to the masses. In hunting circles, the advances to recurves, double-wheeled compounds, plastic fletching, sighting devices, rangefinders and aluminum arrows have not cheapened the sport. While less sophisticated but talented and successful longbow archers are lauded by all sportsmen, the modern advances have done as much toward effective promotion of bowhunting as Henry Ford's T-Model car did for private transportation.

Even with today's "Cadillac" standard of archery weaponry, a bowhunter often goes days, weeks, even years before releasing the first arrow at a legal deer—and then he may miss. But the veteran bowman accepts this as part of the challenge. He knows this sport is for the patient and experienced, and gets his kicks from the effort—much as a bass angler would from a thousand casts in the right places that left him skunked at the end of the day.

Avid archers know that months of preparation must be invested just to get a chance to shoot a deer, and then success or failure—hit or miss—may be had or gone in an instant. But those hours of mental and physical training will not have been experienced in vain.

Neither enthusiasm and desire nor even coaching and listening to other bowhunters relate stories of buck fever, loss of poise and other problems will give the novice bowman self-control when he sees the first big buck down the shaft of his arrow and in easy range. That confrontation, whether it puts antlers on the mantelpiece or simply puts a deer into a mad rush through the palmettos to freedom, makes every bowhunter feel like minnows are flouncing in his veins. It's that thrill that keeps a bowhunter in the woods season after season. It's a precious moment never to be forgotten, the nourishment that sustains them until the next hunting season. Next time he'll do better, but even if he doesn't, there's that memory of the moment, the thrill, the challenge, the simple enjoyment of the hunt, whether or not it puts meat on the table. Marveling at the sights and sounds of the out-of-doors, the bowhunter will patiently return to his favorite deer haunts and stick with the sport. His time to win will come again.

The odds are stacked against the first-year bowman in favor of the deer. He has a less than ten percent chance of success in his initial season. A veteran in an area with good deer population, possessed of skill, nerve and some of that intangible something called luck may have a 70 percent chance of downing a deer, season after successful season, but even the novice who is dedicated to his sport will be so determined that luck, skill and patience will combine to bring that harvested buck to his table.

Advice for the would be bowhunter? First, seek out a reputable bowhunter, archery club or specializing sporting goods store. Talk about your hopes and plans and what you want to hunt. Buy archery equipment fitted to your physical ability and personal preferences. Then you'll have to raise $200-400 for a middle-priced bow, some arrows with field points, hunting broadheads, quivers, an extra bowstring or two and some finger and arm guards. For another $50-100, you can get some camouflage clothing, string noise dampeners, brush buttons, etc. With the purchase of equipment completed, learn the best shooting techniques from a seasoned bowhunter and become a wildlife expert on the game you expect to hunt. Diligent practice, making you a more accurate marksman, will tone muscles and instill confidence—all important to your success in the woods. On top of those tidbits of advice, learn about animal scents, wind and weather, safety measures, and even how to field dress your expected trophy. You are now a bowhunter, be it ever so humble.

Bowhunting has been a part of man's way of life from the stone age onward, and Maurice Thompson, who some say fathered today's bowhunting explosion, believes it is here to stay. As he puts it, "So long as the new moon returns in the heavens, a beautiful bent bow, so long will archery hold the hearts of men."

BASS BITE TINY TURTLES

Henry Spivey and his partner had cast about every lure in their tackle boxes from early morning until near noon in the murky, cypress-laced waters of the Neuse River. No matter how accurate their cast or how promising a likely-looking honey hole they put those lures into, there had not been a rise, not even a swirl. Yet, these avid anglers with years of experience searching for largemouths and despite having seen numerous lunkers active in the grass and lily cover and around some of the fallen trees that jutted above the surface all along the wooded shoreline, were skunked.

"There are plenty of big bass in here, but for some reason they just don't want what we are offering them," Henry moaned, as he cast again into a shadowy hole under an old log and watched six turtles scramble into the water from their sun-basking, lolling lazily above the surface on the dead tree trunk.

Turtles line up on logs all along the swampland rivers. The largest heads up the group and the youngest of the brood trail off on the tail end of the column. What seems to be a family is actually just a group that has come together for security. Twenty turtles can see danger better than one or two. They are long-lived and large ones may be 50 years old or more. They never see their own young after they bury their eggs and leave them.

When anglers approach these reptiles lolling on a log or the bank, they fall all over each other scrambling for the water. They drop to the bottom and hide, but they must surface periodically to breathe. They can only stay submerged as long as they can hold their breath. Once the danger or suspected danger passes, they pull themselves back onto the log and relax.

"I wonder if fish eat those turtles?" Henry thought out loud. "Let's see if we can get one of them, put a hook through his tail and turn the critter loose in some of the brush tops where we have seen the bass striking." Agreed. They couldn't do any worse than they were already doing and the innovation was worth trying.

Catching some of the little fellows was no easy task, but the long-handled minnow net in the boat pushed along the bottom in some of the mud and muck around the tussocks paid off. Finally, they had several about an inch and a half across the back.

Henry put a No. 2 steel hook through the short, tough tail of the smallest captive turtle, took the cork off the line of a cane pole lying in the boat, and flipped the little creature into a dark hole under a willow that spread its branches out over the water.

Only moments passed before Henry felt his walking bait speed up, stop a moment, and then head for open water. He set the hook and was all smiles when he saw a fine 3-pound largemouth break the surface. He quickly put the bass in the boat.

In the course of the next hour, he and his companion put bass in the boat with every turtle they could catch and rushed home to show off a nice stringer that fell prey to the most novel bait either of them had ever tried.

Since that memorable day, other bassers have come up with similar success using these tiny turtles that are now a proven bass catcher for those who like to flip a live bait in front of a largemouth.

But what happens to the turtle once it gets into the stomach of the bass? That's the first question being posed by scholars of the bass species. And there is no real documented answer.

A veteran fisherman dressed a 5-pounder that had four turtles inside its stomach, each measuring about two inches in diameter. Some appeared to have been swallowed many days previously. They had changed color, but the shells were still hard and the bass did not appear to be anemic or in poor health.

Some biologists believe that over a period of weeks, maybe months, the bass will have enough acid in its stomach to actually dissolve the shells and pass them out as normal residue. But not all believe this will happen. Some think a continued diet of such baits will end in death for the predator as his stomach clogs and his bowels lock.

Douglas Hannon, the astute bass scholar, author and TV personality of Odessa, Florida, has caught bass with turtles in their stomachs. He is sure that once the nutrients in the turtle have been fully absorbed, most lunkers regurgitate the shells and are no worse off for the unusual meal. However, he says, it does not always work out well, because he once found a giant 12-pound bass floundering on the surface in Alligator Creek with a four-inch cooter wedged in its throat.

"I have seen the bass in my 7,000-gallon test tank swallow, or partially swallow, other fish that were too large for them to get down. Sometimes the head of this mouthful is far enough down to be digested by the bass and it will carry the meal around for days, eventually getting the rest of it down, or spitting the remains back out.

"While there is no documentation of what happens to bass with turtles in their stomachs, I am quite sure that the fish does at least have the ability to vomit these shells up. Not many species of wildlife will gorge itself on something that is lethal. While bass are easily fooled by many poor imitations, Nature's "great plan" is precise and purposeful. I feel sure they would not become gluttons on turtle shells or any other naturally-occurring food, that would eventually end their lives. I'm certain they can get these shells out and go their merry way," says Hannon, the man who watches this species the year 'round in his backyard research tank, and speaks with authority based on years of experience.

Hannon knows that fish can digest some tough stuff and he backs that up by citing research that shows it takes a great white shark only 11 days to digest the thigh bones of a man.

How or if the bass rids himself of the shells remains unsubstantiated. But make no mistake—these little turtles are great bass baits, as Henry Spivey and others have proven. Apparently, the old largemouths have been stalking these walking, swimming creatures for years without any fear that there might be a hook impaled in their tails. But with some fishermen inclined to try anything when the fish have lockjaw, those bass in turtle-infested lakes in the future better watch out. The meal may not be as easy to swallow as it first appears.

Rabbit Hunting Revived

With hunting at a near standstill during World War II when thousands of the hunting-age young men were in the service and shells were difficult to buy if you stayed home, it was reasonable to assume the cottontail rabbit population would explode. These hyper-sexually-active bundles of fur often raise two or more litters in the same summer, each litter numbering from three or four to as many as a dozen. I once had a tame rabbit that gave birth to 13 tiny bunnies at once.

But the rabbits began to swiftly decline after the war rather than increase.

It was a disappointing revelation to many of the devout cottontail hunters who grew up jumping and shooting these wily critters and then ending the day with fried, baked or stewed rabbit on the dinner table.

Modern chemistry, modern at that time, was the villain. The widely-used insecticide DDT had come into its own and farmers and fruit growers were spraying field after field with this deadly poison. That kept the insects under control without resorting to a lot of tiresome, time-consuming, tedious work of picking the destructive invaders by hand as tobacco and vegetable growers had done for years. Insecticides were a time-saver, a money-maker.

This deadly poison even when directed to tobacco, also saturated the crab grasses and other edible vegetation nearby. The rabbits ate a bellyful and soon died from the fatal DDT. The bunny population plummeted and a few years into the mid-fifties there were hardly enough cottontails to interest the hunters.

Other factors added to the demise of the rabbits. Ditch banks and hedgerows were cleaned up, and many acres of new ground residue were burned to make room for more and bigger produce crops. It greatly reduced the hiding places for the rabbits as well as nesting habitat. The once plentiful cottontails were scarce, hard to find and hunters were turned off for about 30 years.

A new day dawned slowly in the 1980's. Many agricultural poisons were outlawed. More and more land was allowed to lie fallow, untended year after year as surpluses led to farm subsidies for *not* growing crops. This launched a revival for cottontails in the eastern Carolinas and both the cottontail and the swamp rabbit have enjoyed a renaissance. They are relatively plentiful again and more and more rural residents have beagle hounds in backyard pens that yelp, jump and celebrate when a hunter with shotgun in hand approaches. They know it is time for play day.

Rabbit-hunting beagles jump and trail rabbits around a circle and often back within shotgun range of the waiting hunter near the rabbit's original hiding spot, usually a hole in the ground where leaves and straw camouflage the brown rabbits perfectly. Many rabbits would never be shot at if they remained in their lairs and backed up so that only a sunlight spark reflected from their eyes is their only giveaway. But beagles sniff them out and make them jump and run many times when otherwise they would have remained hidden from man and other predators.

There are rabbit hunters who are gifted to the extent that they can find and spot setting rabbits even in the best of cover and camouflage. In the days when most rural hunters were after rabbits for meat for the dinner table, these specialists, who found the bunnies huddled in their nests, shot them between the eyes with a .22 rifle. Some even harvested many a mess of rabbit for the family with a homemade slingshot and a marble-size rock that they could shoot accurately at distances of 15–20 feet.

But it takes a real eagle-eye hunter to spot the setting rabbits. As my daddy once said, "I never saw but one rabbit setting and he jumped up just before I saw him."

Most rabbit hunters today are sportsmen more interested in the beagle chase than in harvesting the cottontails. But few outdoorsmen frown on bringing home a sack of rabbits that make a gourmet meal when cooked a variety of ways, even broiled over a spit above red live coals of a campfire when day is done.

The rabbit's comeback is a blessing to many Carolina outdoorsmen who prefer hunting the small game to deer, bear and hogs. Hopefully the bunny crop will continue to expand and thus provide food and fun for the generations of hunters as yet unborn.

Rabbit hunting is great fun when it's too cold to go fishing.

Discarded Flounder

Sheepishly, Sam Heinz of Cleveland, Ohio, recalls an embarrassing fishing experience that happened to him shortly after he moved to the Carolina Outer Banks.

"I was fishing off the strand. A number of other anglers were also fishing for anything that would bite. I knew nothing of saltwater species, but I kept that a secret from my fishing companions. I didn't want to look stupid.

"I landed a few whitings and other nearby fishermen fought and finally reeled in some huge skates. They tossed them back into the ocean with a few cuss words. The skates were the first ones I had ever seen. They looked like the ace of spades and each angler who caught one hurled the critter back with the words 'Damn skate,' " Heinz recalls.

"Finally, something struck my line, gulped down my cut shrimp bait and headed slowly out toward Europe. I hung on for several minutes and prayed not to lose this biggest fish I had hung in my life.

"I was finally rewarded for my tussle with something almost too strong for my 10-pound test line. When I saw a big dark fish break the surface 20 feet from the shore, I gave the fish time to lose a little stamina splashing in the water. Slowly I reeled it in. During all this battle, an old lady fishing nearby was absorbed in my fight with the whatever-it-was fish on the line.

"I hoped for a big sea trout that I could put on the dinner table, but when that thing came over the breakers, I knew it was not a trout. It was a big, flat, fanlike rascal. I was disappointed! Certainly it was a no-good species, but my big fish of the night must have weighed at least 5-pounds and was shaped like a pancake. Not wishing to be outdone by the other fishermen, I picked up the big fish and flung it back in the ocean with the normal oath 'Damn skate' that I had heard several times that night," Heinz recalls with chagrin.

"The old lady who had been kibitzing during the fight to save the big fish walked over to me with anguish written all over her face. She almost shuddered when she saw my fish hit the water and disappear.

"Why did you throw away your fish? That was a fine summer flounder that would have made you some great eating,' the old native fishing lady said."

Heinz's doleful eyes told the story. He had to learn the difference between a skate and flounder.

HARKERS ISLAND FLOUNDER

Some tourists have been spending vacations at Harkers Island, North Carolina, for generations and carrying home enough summer flounder to fill a freezer, ensuring a supply of gourmet protein throughout the year. While this flatfish is unsightly, with both eyes on the same side of its head, it is definitely not a flat-tasting morsel on the dinner table. It's delectable and among the very best seafood caught off the Carolinas Atlantic coast.

These bottom feeders are always plentiful off Harkers Island, near Beaufort, and they begin striking trolled minnows, cut baits, shrimp, grubs, crankbaits and the ancient Seahawk lure from the first warming trend in the spring until it gets too cold to face the ocean gales in late November. They are harvested by the thousands with hook and line off Core Banks in the sound off both sides of the Beaufort shipping channel for eight months or more every year. It's a beautiful coastal area with a minimum of disturbed inlet marshlands where wild horses still wade feeding on the saltgrass, and gulls, pelicans and osprey entertain flounder fishermen trolling the tidal shallows in search of the flounder on the bottom.

This is a tiny community with homes scattered along both sides for half a dozen miles when you turn east off Highway 70 north of Beaufort. The blacktop road deadends in Core sound and along the narrow spit are a few service stations, small grocery stores, fish houses, restaurants, a church, campgrounds, motel facilities, boat launching ramps and marinas.

Just south of Ocracoke and the famous islands that earned this section of the ocean the dubious distinction of "Graveyard of the Atlantic" when sailing ships wrecked here for centuries, Harkers Island is a peaceful refuge for fishermen. While the area was once a graveyard for U.S. ships torpedoed during World War II, it is a single fisherman's paradise today. But it is treacherous water to fish, with numerous sandbars and shoals hidden by the barest layer of waves and water. It takes some experience to navigate and the astute study of a chart of the area before rushing out into the inlet in search of the popular flounder is using good judgment. The careless often waste much of their time pushing off the sandbars, although they are not normally in any mortal danger.

Perhaps these thousands of acres of relatively shallow waters, with aquatic growth along the island shorelines, and a bottom often covered with oyster shells is what attracts the feeding and spawning flounder to converge there. The tidal current raises the water level three feet twice a day, washing in food for the predators. The water is alive with forage food from sand fiddlers with their uplifted single claw to popcorn shrimp that thrive in the marshland sloughs and an array of minnows from the anchovy species, called "silversides," to schools of what the natives have named "fatbacks" and "ring necks." All are good flounder baits when rigged so that they will tempt the fish that wriggles its body under the sand with only the eyes protruding and attacks everything that isn't too big to swallow that crosses its path. The bait doesn't have to be alive, it just must look alive as the bulk of the regular fishermen here use dangling cuts of shark belly, cobia stomachs or even a three-inch strip of the white side of a flounder to entice the stalking predators to bite. Live shrimp and minnows are hard to beat. Seahawks, grubs, spinners and crankbaits catch some fish here when cast or trolled on or near the bottom, but the biggest catches are generally made on the natural baits.

Harkers Island flounder anglers troll for their fish. They use a flounder rig tied to a 17- or 20-pound test monofilament line on a relatively small reel and a stiff rod. A flounder rig is a two-foot leader with a swivel at one end that attaches to the line. Halfway down the leader is a red or yellow oblong two-and-a-half-inch cork threaded on the line that runs a foot above the hook and gets the bait off the bottom. A one-and-a-quarter-ounce slip sinker stops on the line above the cork when it strikes the swivel. Just above the hook is a single leaf silver spinner blade and two colored beads that attract the attention of the observant fish. The hook behind the spinner is a 2/0, with a unique special bend that most anglers of Harkers Island call a "flounder hook." Minnows, shrimp, cut bait and even blood-worms are impaled on this hook. Fishermen run out of the good marinas at Calico Jack's or Fishermen's Inn, among others, to the channel, then ease off the waterway a few hundred yards away, and get the wind on the stern of the boat, toss out the baited flounder rig, let it hit bottom 30 or 40 feet behind the boat and hang on as the boat drifts.

The bouncing sinker on the bottom gives the novice a tap-tap feeling that makes him think he is constantly getting strikes. But he is misled. The real hit is not a tap-tap or bump-bump like the bass fisherman feels. It's a sudden stop of the vibration as if the hook has hung a shell or a root. Veterans know when a floun-der is hanging on to the bait, sometimes just the tail of the min-now. They relax the line a bit, give it a three count, then set the hook, but not with all the gusto they have. If the hook-set is timed right, there will still be the heavier than usual pull on the line, even if there is no throbbing, quivering sensation normally associated with a live hooked fish. Flounder, even big ones are content to swim with the retrieve for several yards. They make a dash for freedom and you get the thrill of the catch only when they see the boat or you and your landing net. Then they dive and give most anglers enough fight to make the catch memo-rable. It's always a good idea to net a flounder. Most flounder that come unbuttoned escape when they evade the net and dash off when they are near the boat. It's never a good idea to try to lift a big flounder over the gunnels. They have a habit of falling off at the last minute. They come unbuttoned when you horse them too much or leave slack in the line.

This flounder catching rig is most conventional along the Carolina coast. But it is not the one that A. J. McMillan of White Oak, North Carolina, and his family use at Harkers Island where they have floundered for the past thirty or more years. This se-nior citizen farmer, cattleman and fisherman catches flounder when almost everyone else fails. Others may yell at the wind and the inclement weather that reduces their catch to a few or none, while the McMillans catch hundreds of flounders every day. They fish from several boats that are big enough to with-stand the wind and waves, and are stoic about all weather.

"We do not pay much attention to the tide nor the wind. We have found that we can catch fish on the ebb tide as well as the flood tide. We can catch them on a nor'easter or when we have no wind at all as long as there is enough current to move us along," the personable veteran angler says. The McMillans flounder differently from other fishermen who are not always as successful.

"We pull our minnow seine through the surf and catch a bunch of fatback and ringneck minnows to begin with. I don't know what the real names of these little fish are, but that's what we call 'em. We prefer these live baits to cut meat that most folks use. In that we catch our own, it isn't expensive like it is if you buy your minnows or live shrimp. We fish as a family with my son, David, Ralph Godfrey, my son-in-law, and others. We come here for a week or so every year and we carry back all the flounder we need to eat during the winter," McMillan says.

McMillan shares the secret, although a little reluctantly. Aware that many fine flounder are lost when the fish chops off the dangling tail of a bait and misses the hook, the McMillan clan has customized a system that fools the wily species. They seldom miss a strike anymore since their innovative expertise was perfected several years ago and they use it exclusively.

These flounder fishing experts wanted a hook with a super long shank. None could be found in the tackle shops. They turned to a manufacturer and negotiated a deal with Mustad for 10,000 white steel 1/0 hooks with a four-and-a-half-inch shank. They had to be made in Norway. It's an awkward looking hook like none you will find on tackle shop shelves but it was designed with a purpose. They tested it at Harkers Island and their successful strategy is legendary. It catches fish while other hooks are reeled in with only a minnow head.

These veteran flounderers fasten a one-and-a-quarter-ounce weight two feet up the line to pull their minnows to the bottom and they also use the bright colored, oblong cork above the bait and the same single blade spinner and snap on this long shank hook rather than the odd bend flounder 2/0 used widely for this species. They thread on their recently-caught live baits and the ohs and ahs from spectators at day's end are proof of their success.

They push the eye of the hook through the fish from the anus in the belly to the mouth of the minnow. When the eye emerges, they snap it on the rig and toss it behind the boat where it is trolled just like others by fishermen in an armada of boats all over the sound. The hook is hidden from the predators inside the minnow except for the hook point and it is only an inch or so from the tail of the bait. This rig has stopped the flounder from biting off baits and swimming away without getting hooked. The McMillans hook and land almost all the summer flounder that strike. That's why they catch fish when others fail. They say they land about 85 percent of their strikes.

Once when they fished three June days while camping with McRoy and Hilda Suggs of Winston-Salem at Harkers Island, there was a strong northeast wind that blew constantly. Many fishermen left the campgrounds and motels and headed for home. But not the McMillans! During those three days they landed 350 flounder, some in the four-pound class. On the worst of those days, with a 25-mile-per-hour gale forcing most anglers off the inlet, they caught 107 flounder while drifting across the sandbars of the inlet. It was normal success for this fishing family that almost never fails. A couple of nice bluefish and several blowfish hit their minnows threaded on their custom-made Mustads.

"We eat everything that we catch and keep. The blowfish tails are good and the blues are too. We also catch some sharks and they are fine eating. We do not believe in wasting any of the resource," the elder McMillan reveals his conservationist habits.

Summer flounder at Harkers Island are not giants of the species. They are edible size from one pound to about four pounds. You'll even catch a few too small to keep. They must be 11 inches to be legal. But generally you are catching panfish just right for the skillet when cooked whole with the head removed. It's no trouble to remove the bones from a cooked flounder even if you do not fillet the fish.

Colors of summer flounder vary at Harkers Island. Some have spots. Others have a light brownish hue. Around the marshes some are almost black as they tend to adapt to the bottom color. It's these dark colored fish around the sloughs of the marshes that are the largest. Flounder gigging fishermen go after these lunkers from spring to winter and some real slabs are brought to market that succumb to the three- and four-prong spears.

Flounder start life just like any other fish, swimming upright, possessed of a float bladder, their skeletal structure a model for anatomists. Then something happens. They really aren't stepped on; the change comes about naturally.

When the fish is a couple of inches long, one of its eyes begins to wander over onto the other side. The float bladder atrophies, and finally disappears. The fish begins to lean to one side as it swims. The dorsal fin lengthens until it is continuous, head to tail. Finally, the bodily changes complete, it takes up a sedentary life on the bottom, flat as a flounder, always looking upward.

Flounders are all sinistral, meaning they have their eyes on the left side. If, like the Pacific halibut, they had them on the right, they would be dextral.

Don't assume the flounder is a mild-mannered scavenger just because it lives on the bottom and is shaped like a throw rug. Flatfish are audacious predators, with long, sharp teeth. When caught, they chew a lure savagely, and refuse to open their mouths when it's time to be unhooked. Their jaws either grip firmly or snap convulsively, and can cause painful damage to unwary fingers.

As related in "Fish Stories," published by the American Littoral Society, skindivers have spent hours on the bottom, watching these bizarre fish. Sometimes the flounders weary of lying half buried in mud or sand, and turn over to scratch their backs/sides/flanks or whatever you call their upper halves. In playful moments they scull to the surface, then glide for long distances, using the water like a turkey buzzard soars on atmospheric thermals.

Hungry flounders prowl along the bottom on their median fins in a walking motion. Their eyes work independently, searching for prey. Spotting a victim, they bunch their fins, seem to coil up, then burst forward in a flash of speed, much like striking snakes. One writer says they are "as fast as any fish we have observed."

Flounders find most of their food by sight, rather than by smell, devouring mainly small fish. They also sleep at night, and can sometimes be picked up and handled without giving any sign of being disturbed.

"Turkey" is the moniker used by most sportsmen to refer to the former proprieter of Calico Jack's. Turkey recalls weighing in a 14-pound flounder that a gigger brought to his marina. "It was a real monster," says the personable shopkeeper.

Calico Jack's is at the "end of the road" at Harkers Island. Turkey ran a full service operation including restaurant, motel, tackle shop, grocery, double launching ramp, boat storage docks, scales and campground. Turkey is a registered pharmacist who got tired of rolling pills after 17 years and bought this sportsman's corner. The intriguing name of "Calico Jack's" was tagged to the business by a previous proprietor, Jack McCann. He named the operation after the infamous Jack Rackham, a notorious pirate who harassed these waters, wore calico clothing and became known as Calico Jack. The nickname stuck.

Charter boats go out from this dock for bluefish, mackerel, marlin, sailfish, grouper and snapper off the bottom. Business flourishes during all the warm months. Fisherman Inn is another fishing facility of note at Harkers Island. Located on the water three miles before you reach the end of the road, four miles off Highway 70, there are a good launching ramp, boat storage facilities, campground, small motel, tackle shop and grocery. Prices are not inflated here and rooms for two are economically priced.

Harkers Island natives believe that the abundance of grass beds that lace the island shoreline as well as the offshore spits attract an abundance of forage fish and thus the summer flounder population comes in from the Atlantic to feast. It gives them a bountiful supply of easy food. The smaller flounder are caught from early April until mid-July. Thereafter, they are larger but you do not normally catch them by the hundreds like you do in the spring. Many of the real lunkers come several miles inland and feed around the marshland grasses. They lie in the mud and stalk their food.

Sea Grant College at North Carolina State University has researched flounder lifestyles and behavior. They know the fish congregate at Harkers in numbers and they have searched for the reason. Long-time observers believe that the species migrates southward when the first warm days of spring appear and they are attracted to the sandy beaches of the island because of the food and their spawning instinct. They hang around feeding and then spawn all the way to Frying Pan Shoals further south. But they are caught more frequently at Harkers than in most other inlets.

Les and Sally Moore used to live offshore from Harkers Island on Core Banks where all houses have now been removed by the National Park Service. They really know and love this desolate area.

"When the Moores lived on the banks, they would often see flounder in the surf so thick that they would butt up against your legs if you waded. They would send me word that the flounder were coming and we could catch them by the tubfuls. I remember once when they saw them in the middle of February on an unusually warm day. They passed the word along, and we caught them as fast as we could reel them in. They could be caught everywhere that we fished," Turkey recalls, and you envy such an experience.

Throngs of anglers from all over the country do not pour into Harkers Island like they do the more publicized Outer Banks fishing spots to the north. Most of the fishermen here come from North Carolina and Virginia and they tend to return year after successful year. Those who have unlocked the secret of catching these tasty summer flounder, like the McMillans from White Oak, need no other fishing spot. Harkers Island is the end of the rainbow, a real angler's bonanza and they are not scouting for anything else. This is their Shangri-La.

MACKEREL OFF MASONBORO

Rowell Burleson and Rusty Carter had left their Wrightsville Beach, North Carolina, cottage at dawn, intent upon getting past the jetties of Masonboro Inlet and outside the breakers where the king mackerel were known to have schooled the previous day. But first there was the matter of catching the menhaden, a popular live bait along the Carolinas coasts and called "fertilizer fish" by every native.

They stopped their Boston Whaler in the calm inlet where a few flips of fish tails announced the presence of the forage fish and began casting ultra-light tackle, with treble snare hooks into the school. But it was not a day when Providence smiled brightly on them. Try as they might, they were having only bad luck in putting the menhaden in the minnow bucket. A nearby fisherman with a giant throw net wasn't doing much better, even though he cast time after time above the school, only to come in with an empty basket.

Finally, four menhaden were snared, each about seven inches long, and they put the slightly injured bait in the live well. But by now the sun was high in the sky and they knew at least half their fishing time this morning was gone. Even worse, now two of their baits were dead from the snaring.

"Let's go with these four baits. Maybe we will just get lucky," Rusty said.

They cranked up the 85hp Johnson outboard and rushed out a few hundred yards past the end of the jetty. It was fall and the weather crisp but beautiful with just a breath of breeze. They quickly had their two live menhaden impaled on a conventional mackerel fishing rig for this Carolina fishing hot-spot. It was a 40-pound Stren monofilament line with a five-foot steel leader, a No. 9 Penn reel and a strong six-foot fiberglass rod. On the end of the leader was a 2/0 hook that was fastened through the eye socket of the menhaden. Then attached to the swivel on the leader was an eight-inch additional leader with treble hooks on the end. This rig was designed so that the treble hooks would be gulped in by any predator swallowing the menhaden and usually these dangling trebles caught the fish, not the hook holding the live bait.

Carter idled the motor down to almost a stall and the boat moved at a snail's pace, the manhadens on the two lines without any bobbers were fluttering and swimming on the surface a few yards behind the boat. Bam! The water exploded, a starboard rod bent and line played out fast like the devil himself was chasing the menhaden. Burleson grabbed the rod, let the line run for a five count, and viciously set the hook. He made contact. A fish was hung. Thirty minutes later the two fishermen gaffed a 38-pound king mackerel that was to feet longer than their 96-quart cooler. It was a proud moment and indicative of the success thousands of anglers enjoy off the North and South Carolina coasts each fall fighting the king mackerel, one of many species of large fish that are caught by thousands of saltwater enthusiasts. This species has become so important that more than a dozen tournaments are held annually, climaxed with the Arthur Smith King Mackerel Tournament each October. This tournament draws more than 2500 fishermen.

There are many other species of sport fish caught from Kitty Hawk, hard pressed against the Virginia line, to Hilton Head Island, near the Georgia border. These species include marlin, bonito, wahoo, sailfish, sharks, swordfish, dolphin, among others. Then there are the giant blues that strike almost any and everything of both surf anglers and boaters all along the Outer Banks from Hatteras to Cedar Island off the North Carolina coast as they move southward in the fall and attack anything in the water not too large to swallow. Often they are so intent on chasing food fish at Hatteras that they swim right out on the beach and out of the water on the strand.

Thee black fin tuna has been in abundance in recent falls and the style 4000 Baltic Minnow has become a popular nemesis of these desirable edibles.

For years the giant channel bass or red drum of the Outer Banks have been plentiful and they move right on down the coast past Murrells Inlet. Pawley's Island and on to the Georgetown and Charleston harbors where they viciously attack both artificial lures and a variety of live and cut baits. There are not as many of the giants of the species caught now a sa decade ago, but every year someone comes in with a lunker or two long enough to fill a pickup truck. The smaller members of this family are known along the Carolinas Coasts as "spot-tailed bass" and often these are landed in wholesale numbers both in the estuaries and few miles out to sea. It is a real fighter, usually caught on cut mullet and it makes a fine fillet. By the time it gets to Florida it has changed names to "redfish" and is a delicacy for the gourmets.

Not as abundant as in yesteryear, and today talked about more as freshwater transplant than a native of the Atlantic, the striped bass or rockfish is still a huge species to be reckoned with. Stripers move out of the ocean to freshwater to spawn in many of the rivers and creeks of the Carolinas where the tide brings in an abundance of food. They are fished for with live shiners and a variety of minnow-shaped lures as well as jigs and spinner baits. But coming to the front now is an old live bait used ages ago, then forsaken by this generation—the runts of the American eel family.

With experimental eel farms researched along the Tar Heel coast as a result of the Sea Grant College Program designed to improve the resources of the sea, elvers are now being grown out from horsehair-sized wrigglers to near 1-pound edibles for export to Europe, Japan and China. But in an effort to find a market for the runts of the species, those eight to thirteen inches long, Sea Grant has been encouraging the use of these eels for striper and bluefish baits. It is a great bait that will live for hours and hours if unmolested while being trolled or cast. It is catching stripers as it did years ago when old timers recall having hunted these snakelike critters that rockfish and even largemouth bass in fresh water cannot resist.

Then there are the bottom fish taken in great numbers, groupers, triggerfish, black bass, snapper, and porgies.

Other species of large fish lurk off the Carolinas coasts, but these are the primary objectives of most anglers in the Atlantic.

But there are even more people after the smaller varieties of tasty fish that congregate just offshore and around the breakers, docks, bridges, piers, buoys and stickups. A favorite of these close-in anglers is the flounder, served in more seafood houses than any other variety along the coasts.

While a few flounders succumb to pier fishermen, the bulk of them are caught by boaters beginning in Oregon Inlet and on own the coast to Buxton, Beaufort, Morehead City, Southport and Calabash in North Carolina and in Cherry Grove Inlet, Murrells Inlet, Pawleys Island, Georgetown and Charleston. Perhaps the best catches of flounder in the fall in the Carolinas is around the Outer Banks shallows, although many are caught further south and in quantity from Myrtle Beach to Georgia.

Avid flounder fishermen drift baited hooks over sandy bottoms. Saltwater minnows make great baits as do live shrimp, but when the species is anxious to strike, most Outer Banks anglers simply snip off a little belly meat from a baby flounder, pig fish or other small species, and impale it on a hook. It will have results comparable to the live bait. Many small flounder are caught in the lets in the spring, but by fall they have grown enough to reach the Tar Heel legal limit. Smaller flounder than that must be released. You catch a few "saddle blanket" flounder in the 7-pound class, but they are not plentiful.

Charter boats carry flounder parties after this delicacy from border to border of the Carolinas, but by far the majority of these fishermen have their own boats, usually 16 to 20-footers with powerful outboards that can combat strong rip tides and winds that are common obstacles to fall floundering.

Drum, speckled trout and Spanish mackerel anglers make up a sizeable number of fall fishermen as to those who seek croakers and sheepshead, but meat hunters from all over flock to the Carolinas coasts in the fall to fish for spots—the most sought after species of all, despite its usual weight of less than a pound and no bigger than a lady's hand, it is sought by half the native and tourist fishermen.

PULL THE TRIGGER ON TRIGGERFISH

For hours we had trolled six-inch-long cigar mullet minnows through the choppy waters just off Carolina Beach near Wilmington in search of a kingfish strike and the thrill of fighting a giant of the species. But the water was too warm and the mackerel elected to hide in deeper water miles further out in the Atlantic.

"It's no use to keep soaking those mullet on the lines out there. We are not going to catch any king mackerel today," opined our veteran guide. "They simply are not here. But if you want to have some fun despite this trolling failure, let's give the bottom fish a try over the reefs that have been made here to attract all kinds of fish. Even the novices have fun on the reefs when everything else fails."

There was no objection from the half-dozen customers who had enough of the futile mackerel search hours ago. And such is how many fishing parties in this angling Mecca end up with a cooler full of the unglamorous, yet spirited bottom species known as "triggerfish" because of a curved fin on the back that looks exactly like a firearms trigger. Ironically, it performs somewhat like a trigger, too. The dorsal fin of a triggerfish locks upright and offers some protection from predators. But a slight pull on the trigger immediately releases the fin and it folds onto the fish's back.

Few anglers go out expressly to catch trigger fish off the Carolina coast, but you may go for them when it looks like you are striking out. That's why this little-respected species often spells the difference between success and failure, meat on the table or none.

One of the manmade reefs popped up on the depthfinder where tires, cars, appliances and other assorted junk has been piled in 60 feet of water.

"There should be some bottom fish right here," the guide said, as he idled the motor and handed each of us a 7 1/2-foot custom rod with a Penn 66 reel. A No. 5 hook was covered with a glob of squid and eight ounces of slip sinker took the 30-pound monofilament line off the reel quickly. It bumped the bottom and I reeled a few feet to tighten the line.

Bump, bump, bump and you knew a creature down there among the discarded debris had gulped down a morsel of food without knowing an above-the-surface predator was expecting just such a mistake. I didn't need to set the hook. There was a wild critter trying to escape and the tug was vicious enough to sink the barb into even the tough, bony mouth of an 8-pound triggerfish. I struggled with the reel and slowly out-dueled the worthy adversary that used all the power of its muscular, flat, perch-shaped body to try to shake loose and escape. This one did not, and minutes later it was pulled over the gunnels and lay flopping on the deck. It was a giant of the species weighing more than 8-pounds. Few Atlantic triggerfish are caught that reach such size. Here in the Carolinas, these giants are unique.

"What do you do with such a leathery-looking fish?" I asked.

"It is one of the finest eating fish in the ocean. Years ago people considered it a trash fish and tossed them overboard like you would a toad or a stingray. But no more. Triggerfish meat is delicious."

And so it was. Mixed with the blue crabs of the shallows, or the meat from the claws of a rock crab that inhabit these same waters, you concoct a protein dish that tastes as if it were all crab meat instead of a 50-50 mixture. While only 21 percent of the triggerfish carcass is edible, that is a much higher percentage than the ten percent weight of the blue crab that makes the dinner table. Commercial fishermen once believed that any sea creature that did not yield 30 percent of its weight as edible meat was not worth catching, but with a declining number of choice species in the oceans today, even the ten-percent crab and the 21-percent triggerfish is profitable to harvest.

"And while restaurateurs will deny it, most West Indies salads are made exclusively from triggerfish, not crabs," volunteered a seafood authority, Roy Martin, holder of 37 salt and freshwater fishing records.

Triggerfish are almost armor plated, with a hide that closely resembles shoe leather. When it is dry, you can sharpen a knife on the hide and in the dark, sparks actually fly when the blade is pushed across the hide. But once that tough skin is removed, the beautiful, fine-grain white meat that is filleted from the bones is a delicacy to remember.

Perhaps the next best thing to be said for the rather ugly species is its total ignorance of the danger that lies in hooks, lines, rods and reels. They will bite almost any kind of meat you put on a hook, day or night, summer or winter, deep water or shallow. They seem to have no preference for season, no fear of boats or man and this trait is what makes it the answer to the fishermen's prayers when efforts to catch other species have failed. They are reluctant to bite when baits are not near the bottom, but you can catch them around pilings in ten feet of water, or in more than 60 feet of water around the reefs where forage fish school. They are found at much greater depths in various other areas of the Carolinas coast. And while there are many fish, namely grouper, among others, that cannot stand the rapid change of pressure when hooked and reeled to the surface without having their eyes pop out, the ride from the depths to the deck has no deforming effect on the triggerfish. That leathery armor withstands the fast emergence from the depths without taking away the fish's fight or his life. He'll flounce and fight on the deck with few apparent ill effects from his struggling ascension from the distant bottom.

That morning off Carolina Beach, after having struck out in our search for kingfish, the party put 22 triggerfish in the boat in a little more than an hour. Black sea bass and other species were landed too, but none had the spunk of this little-known bottom feeder that uses every centimeter of its broad tail, pectoral, anal and dorsal fins to scrap with the fisherman all the way from the bottom to the deck. It compares in strength ounce for ounce with the freshwater shellcracker (redear) that never gives up and fights gallantly from the moment it feels the sharp steel in its mouth.

Triggerfish do not succumb to the pull on the line by coming straightway out of their habitat head-first to the surface. They come up in a spiral, circling in a two-foot diameter that gives them power enough to thrill the angler and often make him suspect a much larger creature than the stubby-nosed critter that eventually succumbs to the reel and flounces into view.

Some wag has said that fishing for triggerfish is like entering the Indianapolis 500 race on roller skates, intimating that there are so many larger, more glamorous species that no one in his right mind would deliberately fish for them. That could be true of the regular, near-professional sports fishermen who dream of marlin, sailfish, giant blues and tournament-winning kingfish or channel bass. But for that fisherman who has only a few days of vacation each year to make his mark, have fun and put meat in the freezer, the triggerfish is often his salvation. After all, if all the sleek, sophisticated cars at Indianapolis broke down, the humble man on the roller skates might come in a winner, like the tortoise that won a classic race.

Be it ever so ugly, be it ever so humble, there's a place for the triggerfish in the sportsman's schedule—and on his dinner table, too. Some of the veteran saltwater fishermen with acumen from decades of experience snicker at a cooler full of triggerfish and whisper to each other that they are "tourist pompano." So be it! If this creature's strike made the novice feel like minnows were jumping in his veins, a pompano could have done no better.

COBIA MARAUD OFF HATTERAS

Wade Martin's heart seemed to skip a beat and his breathing stopped for a moment. There was a four-foot shadow lurking just beneath the surface on the west side of the tripod channel marker and that could mean only one thing—the giant cobia off Hatteras were at home. He cut the motor on his Ranger bass boat, eased out the anchor in the 12-foot water and quietly nodded to his companion to start fishing.

Nick Ward and Wade were largemouth bass guides in the Carolinas, talented fishermen, and both saw the ominous figure of the big cobia. Nick quickly impaled a live five-inch pinfish under the dorsal fin on his hook and flipped the enticing morsel in the face of the fish a dozen yards away. For a moment it seemed the cobia wasn't interested and then, like a cat, he dashed after the hooked bait, gulped it down and dived.

Nick was no amateur angler. He had handled monster-size largemouths all over the South for years, and he had the expertise to set drags properly on No. 9 Penn reels. He knew when to bow to the surge of the fish and when to reel like mad if there was dangerous slack in the line. He didn't set the hook on the cobia. There was no need. The fast run and surge of the powerful fish had sunk the big No. 8 hook. It was now a case of hanging on, pitting his strength and stamina against the giant's. He would get his adversary to the gunnels or else the monster on the line would win.

Cobia are not easy to land, even by experts, and Nick's fish was no exception. With the line tight as a bowstring, the fish circled the channel marker and sawed the 40-pound monofilament against the razor-sharp edges of the barnacles that encrusted every piling. No fishing line could stand that abuse. It parted! Nick sat down panting. This cobia fishing was challenging. He looked at his partner and grinned at the misfortune.

"I lost him, but he will be back. Cobia don't hit once and leave the country. They come back for more," Nick said, still excited from his novel saltwater experience.

A slightly smaller dark shadow quickly glided near the surface and surveyed the food possibilities of this tripod channel marker. Then it stopped all movement except the gentle, graceful tail wagging.

"That's another cobia! Wade, flip your bait to him!" Nick instructed.

Wade tossed the wriggling pinfish within inches of the quiet shadow. It barely fluttered below the surface before chaos disrupted the peacefulness of the October dawn within eyesight of the historic old lighthouse.

Instinctively, Wade yanked the 7-foot Berkley rod and it bent as the tip fluttered under the strain. He had the hook set and the monster was fighting to disgorge it. He couldn't and then he made a fatal mistake. He headed seaward instead of dashing for the barnacled pilings. It took time, but eventually Wade wrestled the cobia to boatside.

Nick dragged the cobia into the small boat. The fish was still green and dangerous. It flopped and flounced, turning over tackle boxes, bait buckets and everything else that wasn't tied down. In the melee, Wade lost all the skin from the shins of both legs and was complaining of the pain when the fish finally succumbed to a blow across its flat head with a fungo bat brought along for the purpose.

Wade looked down upon a 38-pound fish that would make a lot of fillets for the family once they got it dressed and back home.

Nick moved the boat to the next marker. There had been little traffic out the channel. That made him hopeful of finding more cobia. Once a lot of boats ply these waters, the cobia generally disappear. The wakes seem to offend the feeding giants more than getting hooked by anglers. That's the primary reason for getting your boat in the water and going after the species at dawn. Shrimp boats, pleasure craft and sports fishermen often leave the docks later. When you are in the channel early in the morning, from April to late fall you are almost assured of finding cobia, also known as crab eaters or ling, which stalk panfish, shrimp and other forage meals around these man-made obstacles that are dinner tables for predators.

Even the veteran cobia anglers with tried, tested and proven tackle will lose more cobia than they land, but the exciting tussle with this elongated, toothy critter, said to be the meanest and toughest fish in the inshore Atlantic, makes every hang-up memorable and a conversation topic.

When Nick stopped at the next buoy, there were two distinct shadows lurking quietly on the lee side as the current trickled past. It was his time to fish. He flipped his bait near the closest cobia and expectantly, intensely fingered his line. The shadow approached the squirming pinfish, nosed it around and gulped it down.

Nick set the hook like he had on thousands of largemouth bass. The battle was on, but the veteran angler bested the fish in almost record time. He had it at the gunnels. Wade gaffed it. The cobia had lost its fight. It came quietly into the boat. Not as large as the first one, it still topped 30 pounds.

"Well, Wade, it's your time. The twin to this fish is out there waiting for breakfast. Flip him a bait," Nick commanded.

After the bouts with the other cobia, Wade wasn't sure he wanted to tackle the monster and be assured of a blue belly tomorrow from the pounding in the tummy by the rod butt. But he obeyed and soon had another cobia devil on the line. He yelled, grimaced and laughed, but won the struggle. The cobia bellied-up and was near lifeless when lifted into the boat. This fish was indeed a twin to Nick's.

Nick remembered he had lost the monster at the first buoy.

"Let's go back and see if Mr. Mean has come back to the buoy," Nick suggested, and soon Wade was anchoring the boat at the same spot where they first encountered Nick's nemesis.

"He's back! You see him in between the pilings? He can cut you off in either direction if you hook him in there. Maybe you better wait until he moves out," Wade advised.

"No, I'll try him where he is. He might spook if we wait around for him to move," Nick said, and he flipped his hand-size pinfish in front of the shadow. Again the cobia was fearless, without caution, even though previously hooked. He jumped on the bait and fiercely shook his head as the pinfish went down. Nick yanked, reeled and groaned. The cobia won again. He cut the line over the barnacles and was home free.

This time he didn't even leave his man-made haven. He just surfaced outside the tripod and wagged his tail as he had previously. Nick quickly tied on a big No. 8 steel hook and impaled another bait. He was motivated and determined. This fish could not outsmart and outfight him forever.

Without hesitation, the cobia struck again. Nick maneuvered the monster with his long stiff rod and this time kept him away from the pilings. He fought for 15 minutes, then gave up the ghost. He came to Wade's gaff and the courageous cobia at last had lost the battle.

With the green gone, Nick dragged the fish over the side. He was tired but happy. He won the war while losing two battles. His trophy weighed 68 pounds. Unbelievably, the gallant but stupid cobia had Nick's two hooks with 40-pound monofilament line hanging from his mouth. The same critter had taken Nick's enticing morsel three times that morning.

The bass guides headed for home with a boat full of cobia, a gourmet seafood species everywhere. It was a day to remember. They experienced great freshwater adventures almost daily, but never had they encountered monsters of this size and tenacity. They would continue to make a living guiding for bass, but for sheer excitement, they would return to Hatteras on off days to challenge this mean critter that marauds around the buoys, challenging the best laid plans and tackle of adventuresome sportsmen.

CAROLINA SWAMPLAND SQUIRRELS

Rustling rackets in the dead palmetto fronds along the Waccamaw River shoreline in the pristine swamplands of eastern Carolina relayed an unintentional message . . . squirrels were having a reunion in the treetops. That was music to an old-time hunter with ideas of taking home a bag full of the cagey critters for a squirrel bog supper, cooked just like chicken bog, long a Southern delicacy.

Still hunting for squirrels in these dense forests a foot or two above the water line is a misnomer in the late fall and winter. There's no way you can move about without making a noise in the leaves that cover the wilderness floor. But you can move cautiously and often get a shot at the squirrels that may be too busy chasing each other or eating the berries in the treetops to hide from a hunter among the foliage. The pressure isn't great on these squirrels and they are not as apt to disappear as those in woodlands with skimpier cover.

A few devout squirrel hunters still go after these little rodents with fice dogs that bark and chase the critters up a tree, then lean back on their haunches, bay or tree them and the hunter comes a-runnin' to try to find the hiding squirrel and bring him down with a rifle or a shotgun. While it isn't impossible to shake a limb, beat the tree trunk with a switch or even throw a lightwood knot and make the squirrel slide around to your side of the tree and into your gun sight, it is almost impossible to outsmart a squirrel hiding in the top of a palmetto with half the limbs dead from hurricane winds. Embedded in the leaves after being frightened by even a tiny dog, his instinct is to remain immobile.

Natives of the area who have hunted in these palmetto groves for a generation often use patience to outfox the squirrels. They don't stalk them, they just go to where the rustling in the fronds is heard, lean up against a tree and wait. Within a quarter of an hour, the squirrel will start his activity again, thinking he is alone, and the astute hunter will get his quarry within range. It's the surest way to put squirrels in the bog pot.

A few old-timers have novel ways of hunting squirrels. They use their house cat for squirrel hunting. They entice the cat to go with them when they pick up a gun and the cat obliges. The feline will play along in front of the hunter until it sights a squirrel. Then the squirrel will often just hop up on a bush or a tree trunk and playfully look at the cat. If the hunter isn't too far behind his cat, he can usually get a good shot off before the squirrel hides out in the dead fronds. Some hunters say a cat is much better for hunting palmetto squirrels than a dog, even a small one.

One old hunter who has harvested these plentiful animals for half a century recalls a time when he parked his boat among the cypress trees and knees on the west bank of the Waccamaw and turned his golden retriever loose. The dog was a pretty good squirrel chaser and would tree the animals if he saw them run up a palmetto. He wasn't much for tracking.

One early morning when he was after a mess of squirrels for the table, his dog went along and quickly chased a squirrel up a tree. The squirrel didn't bark, but the hunter was close by and started circling the palmetto looking for the invisible quarry. He spotted no ear or tail, the two most common squirrel giveaways. As a last resort, he cut off a branch from a sweetgum tree, stripped the leaves, and began whipping the palmetto trunk. This often makes a squirrel move when all other rackets fail. He apparently thinks someone is coming up the tree after him. This old squirrel couldn't stand the whipping noise and exploded out of hiding in the fork of the tree, ran to the upper frond of the palmetto and jumped for the ground. The retriever was baying like a coyote as he watched the squirrel scamper to the end of the uppermost frond. The squirrel spread its legs and jumped for the ground. The timing was poor for the squirrel and the hunter. The squirrel landed head first in the retriever's big mouth and scarcely stopped. He went right on down the dog's throat, choking a muffled bark. That dog must have been in considerable pain as the squirrel scratched and clawed in his stomach.

The dog rolled over and over, yelping and groaning. In a few minutes his stomach was still and so was the retriever. He looked around as if to ask what had happened. The hunter lost his squirrel that morning.

There are not many den trees for squirrels along the river shorelines any more. Many have been cut by vandals who went after 'coons and squirrels wherever they were, not hesitating to destroy their natural homes. Most of the nests that squirrels use now as nurseries are made of leaves and twigs and are constructed in the forks of trees, often tall pines where they can feed off the burrs while looking after their offspring.

If you are hunting squirrels at a time when they are not raising a litter of young and if the squirrel hides in one of these leafy nests, you can often shoot a load of number four shot into the nest and get your squirrel. Almost every time that you kill a grown squirrel in this kind of nest, it will kick and roll enough to tear up the structure and then tumble to the ground. It's a bad idea to shoot into one of these nests during nesting seasons as it may be filled with little squirrels that will be destroyed.

In an era of a generation ago when squirrel populations were in no way endangered and wildlife was an important part of the family diet in virtually every rural household, I shot into a nest one day when I was having trouble getting a mess of squirrels. It's easy today to say that was a mistake, but it was not unusual then. Anyhow, when those shot hit that bundle of leaves and twigs, the nest shook violently.

Moments later a dead old mother squirrel tumbled to the ground and three tiny babies soon followed, plunging through the tree limbs to the ground. One was dead. Two were uninjured, but so small that I had to take them home and feed them with a medicine dropper filled with milk for a month before they were strong enough to be released into the wild again. I felt bad about killing the mother and one of the offspring, but I knew instantly that I had not harmed the squirrel population. The little dead male had been castrated, possibly that same morning. The evidence was there and I knew that some old male had realized there were too many squirrels in the territory for the habitat to support. Male squirrels instinctively hold down the population by castrating their young. That had happened to this offspring.

Opossums will often take up residence in these squirrel beds and root the owners out. Shooting the nest will bring disaster to the 'possum and you will have taken a life without getting anything in return. While 'possums are edible, most lovers of this meat will eat it only after the creature has been cooped up for at least two weeks and fed sweet potatoes and milk so that the scavenged substances in its stomach have had time to clear out of the critter's system.

While the 'possum isn't considered much of a harvestable animal, I felt bad one fall morning when I shot into a squirrel nest and ended the life of one of the ugly grinning beasts that often feint death as a defense when cornered, thus coining the phrase "playing 'possum." It was an accidental, but useless, death.

Another factor to consider when hunting squirrels along the river shorelines is poisonous snakes. There are many rattlers still making homes in the leaves, stumps and fallen trees. There are even some canebrake rattlesnakes around as big as your leg. Cottonmouth moccasins are fairly plentiful, as are copperheads and none of these reptiles is especially friendly. They will get out of your way if they can, but slipping along in the swamplands, you might be so quiet that a snake gets under foot because you are so adept at stalking squirrels you surprise the snake. There are a few coral snakes in the wild today. Unless you sit down on one, it usually doesn't pose much of a threat, in that this little snake must get a bite of skin and hang on for some time before it can put its nerve poison into its prey. The coral snake has no fangs, unlike other venomous reptiles. It and all other such creatures, should be respected and cautiously avoided when squirrel hunting the swamplands among the desolate junges of the Carolinas.

That memorable morning when I tied my boat to a cypress knee, picked up my rifle and headed into that wilderness where the rustle of fronds relayed the message of plenty of squirrels in the area, I ran into no snakes, no unfriendly alligators, just plenty of full-grown, healthy gray squirrels. I stuffed my hunting jacket pouch with half a dozen, cranked the outboard and high-tailed it back home.

Skinned, gutted and washed, then boiled slowly for an hour before I dumped in a cup of white rice and simmered them for about 30 additional minutes, they made what the locals call a "squirrel bog." And that's fine eating in the fall and winter when the squirrels hold a reunion in the palmettos along the river shorelines. Anyone can make chicken bog. Only hunters can enjoy the luxury of this wildlife delicacy that shows no signs of running out. There are plenty of squirrels in the palmetto fronds and probably will be for a generation or two. There's enough food and cover to keep them plentiful for a long time.

You see, on that particular morning along the Waccamaw, I was the old-timer who heard the rustling in the palmetto fronds.

Shrimp—Trash or Treasure

Carolina fishermen know the shrimp crop is one of the most important seafood harvests that they bring to market. But it has not always been so. As recently as 70 years ago, these spiny crustaceans could hardly be given away. They were considered pests that littered commercial fishermen's nets.

Shrimp then were so abundant that acres of black-looking water were observed in the sounds where they meandered unmolested, except for the diving birds that feasted on them.

Inadequate refrigeration facilities and poor transportation methods were devastating obstacles for fisheries in the early days when the perishable shrimp began to show demand. Boats were too small and gear too simple, with gill, cast, dip, fyke and pound nets in use. The development of the otter trawl greatly expanded the fishermen's capabilities and new and better boat design enhanced the productivity of the shrimpers.

Shrimping is now a multimillion dollar operation on the Carolinas coasts and shrimp is the most popular seafood sold in the South.

TRIPLETAILS FOR THE TABLE

Miles of spherical floats bob on the surface from south to north along the Carolinas coast and mark traps baited for crabs by commercial crabbers who harvest thousands of pounds of this delicacy daily for the local seafood markets. But the buoys serve another purpose—they gather barnacles and other small crustaceans that attract the tripletails, a gourmet species of fish seldom sought by sportsmen, but never forgotten once you hang a mature adult on lightweight tackle. They are powerful flatfish that veterans compare to the freshwater shellcrackers when it comes to stamina and strength. Tripletails look somewhat like giant bluegills.

"They strike like a coiled steel spring and run and pull like a trophy-size jack crevalle," one native angler who has landed several off the Carolina coastline says:

"Tripletails, also known as 'buoy fish,' gnaw the crustaceans off the buoys on the surface and that's its uniqueness. You fish for the tripletail by sight like you do cobia. The feeding tripletails come to the surface, turn over on their sides and scrape off the shells from the buoys for hours. Anglers motoring through the area can easily spot the flat monsters as they lie on their sides and eat. Often the tripletail is mistaken for a leaf lodged on the crab marker, but once you draw close, the fish spooks and dives. You may still be able to catch the fish by dropping a live natural bait near the buoy—a sand fiddler, barnacle attached to your hook with a rubber band, shrimp, pinfish or other live critter that tripletails devour. They occasionally will strike a Tiny Trap, Mister-Twister or Cotee white jig, Culprit crawfish and even a silver spoon or floating bucktail.

"Tripletails reach weights at times up to 50-pounds, but normally along the Carolina Coast they are more likely to weigh 3-pounds or less.

"Best fishing equipment for tripletails is an open-face reel, 8- to 10-pound test line, with a 6 1/2-foot limber rod. If you are trying to catch the fish on the surface where he is gnawing on a buoy, presentation is ultra-important. You must put the bait right in his face. They will almost never turn around to hit a bait that is behind them. They want to eyeball it while in their lolling position from which their small teeth slowly grind off the growth from the bobbers.

"While most often tripletails are sighted feeding off the man-made floats, they also eat crustaceans that grow on the rocks in the tidal waters of the coast. Anglers occasionally catch a tripletail while fishing the shallows for redfish and trout. And in the summer months when there is a lot of drift grass on the surface, tripletails often can be spotted in the middle of these hay fields feeding on tiny organisms.

"It's a unique species that gets little ink, notoriety or conversation at the 19th hole, but it is a thrilling fish to fight on a line and a tasty seafood entree on the dinner table.

"It's a Carolinas coast gamefish that is destined to be more popular in the years ahead."

BASS AND BREAM PETS

Cat-eating-canary grins sweep across the faces of most listeners when Sarah Wideman talks about her direct communication with a bluegill and a largemouth bass. Sarah, who lives on the Waccamaw River near Conway, kept pet fish for years in her 920-gallon aquarium in her den..

"I talked with Freddie and George just like I would to a cat or a dog and they began to respond in the same way as those other creatures. I quickly found that they would respond to the same tender loving care as other pets and, in their own way, talked back to me every day of their lives," says this pretty 35-year-old housewife who learned to love these fish while she helped her fisherman husband.

Freddie was a full-grown bluegill that Sarah raised from a small three-finger size fish. She says, "Bream are smart. I would go into the den in the morning and ask Freddie if he would like to have something to eat. He would immediately come to the side of the aquarium as close to me as possible and then frantically wriggle his pectoral fins back and forth as rapidly as he could, all the time smacking his lips. I knew he was saying he wanted something to eat.

"I would then hold a cricket, grasshopper or worm on or just above the surface and Freddie would rise and take the food happily. I have fed him as many as 27 crickets at one time as he gorged himself. But providing an adequate food supply for this hungry little rascal almost sent me into bankruptcy. He wanted to eat all the time, and I found I was so busy catching insects and other edibles, putting them in my purse for Freddie, that I was neglecting my housework. I even had the children of the community out looking for worms and crickets for this bluegill.

"Then Freddie almost caused my divorce. I heard that one of the bait shops had a big supply of fishing worms that were getting old, many of them dying in the cups. I went to them and said I would go through those hundreds of worm cups and pick out those that they could sell if they would let me have the dead and dying ones for my pet bream. They agreed, and I took the whole bunch home, sat down with them on the floor and began sorting those stinking, decaying worms. It put a terrible scent in the whole house, I had dirt up to my elbows, and right in the middle of this, my husband came home. He wanted to know what I was doing, and I explained, at the same time telling him I had supper on the stove. He was upset and made it clear he didn't know whether he wanted anything to eat that I had prepared under such circumstances. It was the closest we have come to divorce during our 20 years of marriage," Sarah says, only half in jest.

Eventually she began hatching and raising worms and crickets for Freddie's healthy appetite. "I even got into raising maggots and flies for my pet," she says.

All this effort was rewarding for the petite little lady who talked to her fish and felt they talked back.

"All the children in the neighborhood came by regularly to talk to Freddie. They eventually watched him mate with a female I had put in the tank and then watched the babies grow up. It was a real educational process to observe and the children dearly loved to feed Freddie. I actually loved that fish. I wouldn't have given him all that TLC if I hadn't. He had personality that drew me to him. Others that I raised had bad tempers and were mean, but Freddie was always lovable. He knew the feeding times and would scold me if I wasn't prompt, by fluttering and getting in a frenzy as he bumped his nose against the glass nearest me. Several times when I ignored him, he would splash water on me by flipping his tail on the surface.

"And then came the tragedy. I was on vacation for several days. When I returned, Freddie was dead and dry on the floor. I suppose he tried time after time to attract someone's attention at feeding time and when he got no attention, he just jumped over the side and committed suicide.

The lady had other experiences with bass, catfish and crappie in that aquarium. The most noteworthy memory focuses on

George, a largemouth bass that she got from a local fisherman.

"I noticed that the fish was still breathing and the fisherman didn't really want the bass anyway. I put some dissolved aspirin in its mouth and began working the fish back and forth in the water. Soon he showed signs of life and began swimming upright. He was scared and not friendly. He wouldn't eat for weeks and shied away from me when I tried to pat his head. He lost a lot weight. Then he began to accept me as a friend and soon he would gulp down all the minnows and insects I turned loose in the water. Like my bream Freddie, George began to expect regular meals and we became almost as intimate. I loved George and he loved me.

"Tragedy struck that relationship too. I knew that chlorine in the water in excessive amounts would kill fish, but we had never had to worry about that, always using the water from our well. But one day I put a few drops of Clorox in the water to help purify it. George was dead the next morning and I cried just like I had lost a loved one, which I had," said Mrs. Wideman.

"I could go up to the aquarium any time and George would rise to the surface and stay perfectly still while I rubbed his head and patted him. We were very close," she says.

Sarah has raised some other bass in that tank and learned a great deal about largemouth bass behavior. She rigged some hookless lures and experimented with those, dragging them past her captive pet fish.

"There were some interesting revelations," she says, "It was a proven fact that the flippin' system was the most successful with George. He would pay more attention to a worm being flipped in his territory than he would anything else being retrieved and dragged in front of his nose. I kept him as a friend for two years and it was a real learning experience," says the little lady who fishes, hunts and admits she was a leather and lace child from the age of five—a tomboy if you will.

Fishing with her father and brother all along the Waccamaw where she was raised, she was a proficient angler even as a little girl.

Among her most memorable incidents was the time she and her brother decided to raid a wasp nest on the river to get the unhatched larvae, a fine bluegill bait all over the South then and now.

"The nest was on an old piling that once marked the channel when there was commerce in lumber and other goods on this scenic river. We decided that I would spray some insecticide on the nest, while covering myself with a blanket. When the wasps all left the nest, we would grab it and rush down the river. Well, it didn't work. Those wasps came right after me and stung me good. I soon found out that wasps can fly faster than a 3 1/2 horsepower motor can run. I couldn't stand the stings any more and jumped out of the boat to get away from them. After awhile they went back to the nest and my brother put tobacco juice on the stings. We never did get those larvae for bream baits from that particular nest," Sarah laughs as she recalls this childhood disaster.

This young lady also notes that her husband is an accomplished bass fisherman. But he is quick to point out that his lovely little lady is also an expert basser, having won a tournament with both the most poundage and the largest bass.

"I have never caught any real trophy bass, but have landed my share of the 5- and 6-pounders. I like to fish and we have a lot of fun on the rivers and lakes. I also do a lot of deer hunting, and I'm a pretty fair bow and arrow hunter. I prefer that to hunting with a gun, and I can field dress my own deer. I think archery is a fine sporting way to get your buck.

"I am not much of a beach person even though we live close to the saltwater. I do like to spear fish on the reefs or in the river near here. The tide pushes the water up three or four feet in some places. Our water isn't brackish here, but it is just a few miles down the river to the ocean.

"This low country area is glamorous for outdoor people and I love this section where I have lived all my life. It has good fresh and saltwater fishing as well as fine deer, quail, squirrel and dove hunting," the lady angler says with sincerity.

"This small boat that my husband and I use goes anywhere in the river. We can maneuver it more easily in some of the narrow coves and shallows than we can the larger, more expensive boats. It will make up to 30 miles per hour. We fish way down the river and catch a fine string of bass. We like spinner baits particularly and bring in our share of the largemouths," Sarah says.

It's not often that you encounter a pretty lady who goes from keeping house to sorting live worms from the rotting ones on the living room floor, to simultaneously cooking supper for a tired and hungry husband. It's especially unusual to find one who does all those things and communicates with bass and bream.

SC WATERWAY RAMPS

There are good public boat launching ramps from one end of the Inland Waterway to the other as it flows through South Carolina. You can put your boat in the water across the North Carolina line at the end of Highway 904 at Ocean Isle or just a mile down the Waterway at Sunset Beach. You can move still further south and find good launching facilities at Calabash. From that point you enter South Carolina, where there are ramps at Little River, just off Highway 17. More ramps are public when you reach the Grand Strand beach area where the Waterway flows only a crow-flying mile from the Atlantic through Horry County. All these launching areas could be used if you choose to fish for saltwater species like spots, speckled trout, flounder and other saltwater species. You can even use these ramps to fish for the freshwater species. There are many miles of water between Socastee and Bucksport, beginning three miles from Myrtle Beach, where the best freshwater fishing is available.

To fish the Socastee to Bucksport stretch of the Waterway and the estuaries of the Waccamaw River, the best place to launch and get to fishing fast is Bucksport. It is about ten miles south of the Socastee bridge.

There are ramps at Socastee, mostly private and you should have permission before launching your boat at these ramps.

Asa Heath–Deer Hunting Legend

Nearly 75 years ago, when Asa Heath was only ten, he swapped a homemade batteau to his brother-in-law for a Black-and-Tan deer hound. That bit of bartering launched a career of chasing bucks in he flatlands of eastern North Carolina that has spanned a lifetime. This Pollocksville, NC senior citizen was among the craftiest, most knowledgeable deer hunters in the Tar Heel state for years. The white tails were so thick in the '70s and '80s that they were being killed by cars regularly on the highways and shot by farmers in the field in numbers so consequential that this devout outdoorsman was concerned.

"I really think that instead of the wildlife commission issuing permits to farmers to shoot does and bucks that eat their beans and corn in the fields, they should devise a system of simply paying the growers for the crop losses they suffer from the wildlife. Let the game live. It would preserve the deer that are now so plentiful, and wouldn't be as costly as many other state and federal projects," Heath said. "Shooting hundreds of them when they are pregnant and often when they are being followed by tiny fawns that dies from bobcats and starvation when the mother is killed is tragic."

Heath and members of his family were farmers near Pollocksville, a tiny Tar Heel village on Highway 17, a short hop from the Atlantic Ocean, just south of New Bern. They were aware that the abundant deer damaged their crops, but they placed more emphasis on the survival of the species than the few dollars lost to the grazing white tails.

Hunting has changed dramatically over the many decades since this near-legendary sportsman has began hunting as a boy with his original Black-and-Tan hound from a home site less than two miles from where he lived his adult life. He never moved out of his home township.

"The land back then was grazed over by stock, and the

owners burned the woods in the fall or spring to keep the undergrowth down so the grass would grow. This kept the land open and hunting was easier. There are more deer here now than there were then, but now that paper and pulpwood companies own most of the forest, thick undergrowth covers the woodlands. You've got to be alert and work hard to get your deer, although I killed my four deer limit for a long time," said this master woodsman, once president of the "We Boys Hunting Club," and organization of 60 hunters who leased 8000 acres for deer hunting. He guided the members of the club daily in season and always got the jump on the deer.

"The companies came in and cut the big timber and the turpentine drippers that were everywhere around here then. They put out new trees that have grown to harvestable size, but the undergrowth is allowed to grow. It is not burned out any more. It makes great cover for the deer, but it challenges the patience and expertise of the hunters.

"I have always been the 'dog man' with the deer hunters of this area. I go in the cover with the dogs and I prefer just one or two with me. If you go in with a whole pack of dogs, they scatter everywhere, and if you jump a deer, there is so much barking and confusion you don't know where the buck is headed. I stay with the dogs and most of the deer that I kill personally, I get on the jump when the dogs first flush the animal," he said.

"I always have people on stand when I go in with the dogs. When I jump a deer, I shoot even if I know I'm not going to hit the deer in the thicket. I want the others to know a deer is on the way. They can hear my shot many times when the wind is in a direction that keeps them from hearing the dog bark. This gives the hunters a chance to move toward the flushed deer's path, cut him off and perhaps get a shot. If I kill the buck on the jump, I fire three more shots. That lets my hunting partners know I have made a kill and they need not be alert for that deer. I used to carry a cow horn that I learned to blow. You could hear it for a mile or so. Three blasts on that meant I had killed the deer too," confides this robust hunter who lived past his threescore and ten years. "Sometimes I would signal by blowing blasts with my gun barrel."

He recalls a hunt years ago when many of the best hunters of Pollocksville had been thwarted repeatedly in their effort to shoot an unusually big and smart buck that they had seen several times every season, but never managed to get in their gun sights. Even when they put standers out by the dozen, he managed to evade them.

"One morning, I took two old men with me just to hunt this special buck. I had been after him enough to know that he always ran east or west, never north or south. I told these two standers that I would go in with the dogs and when the buck was jumped, I would fire three shots if he headed east and two shots if he headed west. This would give them time to move quickly with their pickup truck and get in the path of the deer. Before long, the dogs jumped the buck and I blew three times for the easterly direction he was traveling. The old men hurried to the firebreak in their pickups, but the deer and dogs had already crossed. They went to the second one and were just seconds late as the buck bounced over the roadway before they got out of the truck. Again they rushed to the next opening and scampered to a stump stand before the deer reached the opening. He came leaping out of the pocosin and one of my old timers shot him.

"I had already walked home. They were a long way from where I had jumped that smart buck. They came by my house at 12:30 with the deer. Hunters for miles around heard about it and came by. They couldn't believe that a jumper and two old men could get the smartest buck this section had ever produced when others had made a project out of getting him for years.

"That buck would hear a car door slam a half mile away and head for the thickets and safety. He was really spooky and smart, but that day we outsmarted him. He had six points and weight 175 pounds," said Asa.

Heath knew he needed to stay in good health at his age to keep up with the dogs in the thick undergrowth of the woodlands, and made a point to preserve his stamina. He farmed for a while and then put in 25 years with a paper company before retiring in 1979. Sometimes he took a stand and waited for the deer to come to him, but that was never his forte. He would sit, wait and listen to the music sometimes. He painted a lawn chair

Carolina blue in order to blend in with his truck when he parked in the lanes.

The old veteran told of another targeted buck that he managed to shoot after trailing him with his dogs for nearly a half a day in the woodlands.

"I put some standers out that morning after I had found some big deer tracks in the dust of the road. I had two silent trailing dogs then. They would trail a deer, but never open (bark) until the deer was actually jumped. I stayed right with my dogs as they trailed along, stopping at a stream where the deer got water. I could see where he had eaten shoots of bushes and weeds. It was just 7:00 a.m. when I started trailing that buck. At 11:30, the dogs and I came out of that swampy area onto a wire grass ridge. The grass was waist high or more. The dogs still hadn't barked. We went into the grass, and that buck came up almost under my feet. He was hard to see in the tall grass, but I fired my Western Field Pump, 12 gauge Montgomery Ward Special four times. None of those No. 1 buck shot touched the weaving deer in the grass. He then turned to the left, and I decided to lead him by about three feet this time. Again the deer kept bouncing and weaving, turning right. I had just one more shot. I aimed at his head and fired. The deer didn't even flinch, just kept right on running.

"As I came out of the wire grass, I met a man driving a two wheel mule cart. He yelled at me, `Asa, why didn't you get that deer? He could hardly make it when he crossed the road.' I told him I was sure after that buck, but it didn't look like I could hit him. The dogs had opened up by now, and 100 yards off the road lay that big eight pointer. He had two shots in the right side of his head, four inches apart. I had killed him on my sixth and last shot. The standers were so far away that they never heard the dogs bark, nor my gun shots. I managed to blow my three level blasts on the cow horn to tell them where I was and that the deer was dead. When they showed up, one of them was really grouchy. He complained that they had been waiting all day and had not heard a dog bark or a gun fire. When I told them I had killed a deer, they didn't believe it because they had not heard any gun shots. I went with them into the woods and showed them the big buck. That changed their tune," Asa said with a grin as he recalled how they had to carry that buck about three miles to get him back to the parked cars. "We named that old buck 'Sherman.'"

Heath began his deer hunting career using buckshot in a shotgun, but shifted to a 44 caliber Winchester rifle about 30 years ago. He was getting too many shots of 80 yards or more and the pellets from his shotgun were causing too many flesh wounds to deer without killing them.

"When I got that rifle, all my friends began knocking it. 'You'll not be able to hit a deer with a rifle bullet. You won't kill anything from now on,' was the general comment. Well, I took it on a hunt right after they were making fun of me, and went into the woods with the dogs to try and jump a deer. We did flush one, and the deer headed for a nearby roadway. I ran back into the road with that deer coming straight for me at full speed. When he got within about 40 yards, he came to a sudden stop. I fired my 44 magnum just as he pulled up, aiming for his chest. He fell without so much as a kick. I went up to the buck, rolled him over, and couldn't find any hole in him or any blood anywhere. My standers gathered around and looked him over," Asa smiled.

"Asa, you didn't kill this deer, he doesn't have a scratch on him. This buck died of heart failure," one of the hunters said.

"I have to admit it was puzzling," Heath said, "but I didn't see how I could have missed him in such an opening and at such close range. I told them to string the buck up and let's dress him to see what killed him. Would you believe it? That deer had opened his mouth when he came to that quick stop. I fired at the same time, and my bullet went down his throat and mutilated his internal organs. It had been an instant death with not a drop of blood on the outside. At least my experience with the rifle had been a success, even though a strange one."

"Young hunters today don't know much about the old times. We had the smart deer back then. The three big ones on my wall are Luther, Sherman, and George. We named them after the landowners where these bucks ranged before I shot them. We had to outsmart deer back then, but there is a lot of hunting now with four wheel drives, CB radios, walkie-talkies and such that really makes deer hunting modern and sophisticated. They now turn loose a whole pack of dogs, and when a deer heads in some direction, the pickups and other vehicles converge on that place. Everyone leaves their stand to try and get a shot at the deer. I call it 'truck hunting.' It's dangerous. The young people do not have patience to hunt like we did. They are too restless and anxious. They won't just sit and wait like we used to, " Heath noted.

"I'm a great believer in dogs. I killed ten deer with my little Plott hound in two and a half years. She was a great dog. I have had as many as 16 deer dogs at a time, and I don't really know how many I've had over the past 50 years," Asa said. His wife, listening, quipped that they would be rich had they not spent so much on dog food over those five decades, though confidentially she admires her husband's astute hunting skills.

"Smokey (the Plott hound) and I get our share of whitetails every season. The largest deer I ever killed weighed 200 pounds, and I've killed about 350 in my lifetime. Deer today are fat and healthy. We hunt them right here in Jones and Craven counties from Pollocksville to Rhems. I hunt every day of the season except Sundays," says this member of the local Mormon Church who took a great interest in young people. He coached the Babe Ruth baseball league in nearby New Bern for 22 years, carrying his team to the top three in the nation in 1983. He also served as a Scoutmaster for eight years.

"I've never been without dogs since I had that Black and Tan when I was ten. I like hearing dogs run. It's not as much fun hunting without the dogs. I like hearing when they jump a deer. Then the sound of someone shooting. That caps it all. If it's a single shot, that's good. If it's two or three shots, real fast, that's bad. If you hear one shot followed a minute or two later by another single shot, that's really good. The hunter has finished off the deer and he's ready to drag it out to the truck to carry it home."

Asa Heath was a legend in Eastern North Carolina's deer hunting annals. A sportsman, a family man, and a master of woodcraft and hunting lore possessed of a sense of humor and the kind of character that is so rare as to be precious.

YESTERYEAR'S RABBIT HUNTERS

Robert Almond was a country boy who grew up in the swamplands of Horry County's river wilderness along the Little Pee Dee. A teenager during the Great Depression years, he never made a lot of money, or held any public office, but for those who knew him, this quiet and unassuming youngster was remarkable, a Phi Beta Kappa in the woods and fields. Indeed, he was to the locals of that generation what Dan'l Boone was in the last century. He didn't have to contend with hostile Indians, but the struggle for food and survival was just as challenging. Robert used his talents and ingenuity to put food on the table at little or no cost.

Lacking even the pocket change to buy shotgun shells or rifle cartridges, Almond used a pocket knife, a pair of scissors, some cast-off manmade materials and a limb fork from a red maple to make unsophisticated slingshots that were deadly cottontail rabbit harvesters when in his hands.

Long before there were any store-bought toy slingshots in the stores, Robert was making his own for hunting. He began by cutting a forked limb ten inches long, peeling off the bark, smoothing it, notching each prong, and then baking his creation in the kitchen stove oven until it was dry and hard.

With his mother's sewing scissors he cut two half-inch wide strips of rubber from a discarded T-model tire inner tube a foot long. With strong thread, he tied the rubber strips to the forked stick. Rummaging in the attic, he found a pair of worn-out high-top brogan shoes. He cut out the leather tongue, punched a hole in each end and tied the rubber bands to the leather pocket. He had a slingshot, not comparable to the sling that David used to kill Goliath, but a formidable cottontail harvester.

Free ammunition, marble-size slate and flint pebbles he gathered when he visited in the Piedmont, were all over the ground upstate. If he hadn't been lucky enough to find a few steel ball bearings from wheels in the junk yard, the ideal sling-shot ammo, he always had a pocket full of the smooth, round rocks. Released from the shoe tongue pocket after the rubber bands were stretched to the limit, a properly aimed stone would bring an early demise to any cottontail.

Not even Robert with his pioneer-like hunting gadget could hit many scampering rabbits that bounced from the hedgerows and ditch banks and scooted away at 20 miles an hour, miraculously keeping broom straw and other high weeds between him and the hunter. But that's where Almond's un-canny expertise paid off. He didn't have to shoot the bunnies on the run. He was one of those unique people who could see rab-bits in their daytime nests, "rabbits setting" as the rural resi-dents said. Always they were backed into the ditch banks and hedgerows where perfect camouflage protected them from predators, including hunters. Only a few could catch the flash in the rabbit's eye that gave them away. The bright glint would stop a hunter in his tracks and often it took seconds to realize what had startled him. Then, focusing carefully, he could dis-tinguish the eyes and ears of the rabbit, often with half its body buried in the dirt. Slingshot shooting setting rabbits was Almond's specialty and for years he put meat on the table of that family when few people had the dime to buy a pound of steak or 15 cents for a gallon of gas for the car.

Rabbits were plentiful in the 30s and 40s, but they began to disappear following World War II when DDT and other agri-cultural poisons used against the cotton boll weevil decimated the population. Late in the 70s the cottontails began to reappear as careless crop poisoning was outlawed.

It was an area and an era of small, family-size farms then and land owners were not persnickety about who hunted their land. Some expected the courtesy of being asked before you hunted, but almost no one refused permission. Few parcels were posted then.

Today there are not many wildlife refuges in the Caroli-nas, but almost all rabbit hunting is on private lands. The sling-shot has disappeared with prosperity and shotguns have taken their place. Beagles jump the bunnies and chase them in a circle until they return to their original hideout. Hunters wait with sophisticated weaponry that easily puts tasty protein on the table.

Few bring home more meat than Robert Almond, whose special talents and crude weapon made him an outdoorsman worth remembering and writing about.

SWAMP RABBIT TRICKS

Staccato barks from my pair of beagles a couple of football fields away in the dense wilderness of the Lumber River rain forest relayed the message—the hounds had rediscovered the trail of the cagey rabbit we had jumped 15 minutes earlier. The old swamp rabbit was apparently headed in my direction. I slinked even closer to the trunk of a huge cypress tree on the shoreline of the narrow creek in this dark jungle of trees, vines and gallberry bushes, my shotgun snuggled in the crook of my arm. I was ready to blast this tiptoeing swamp critter the moment he hopped within range.

The unbelievable episode that followed froze me against that tree. I never fired a shot, although the huge, dark-colored rodent, larger and darker than a cottontail, sneaked out of the thick ground cover a dozen yards from my stand and lingered long enough for me to have easily drawn a bead and pulled the trigger.

Furtively, the astute swamper momentarily eyed the blackgum tree that had fallen across the stream. Then, as if he had practiced this maneuver many times before, he leaped on the log, rushed across to the other side, and jumped to the ground. Hurriedly, the rabbit scampered out of sight for a few seconds, then reappeared, back-tracking to the tree crossing.

From a distance of four or five feet, he leaped on the tree, and headed towards the creek bank that he had originally come from. But instead of jumping to the ground, he dived into the water. A good swimmer, the swamp critter dog-paddled downstream 30 or 40 feet, then turned toward the hill, struggled up the low bank and trotted off into the dense jungle.

Mouth agape, I hadn't taken my gun out of its cradle. I had simply observed with astonishment as this critter of the Carolina low country performed an escape tactic that would have been a credit to a man being tracked by bloodhounds.

Moments later, my beagles came yelping into sight, smelled the tracks on the fallen tree, and quickly ran to the other bank, jumping off and barking with enthusiasm as they headed into the jungle. A minute later they stopped barking, and began milling around. They were frustrated. The trail ended abruptly as if the rabbit had disappeared into the proverbial thin air.

I called them back to me, and we headed upstream, hoping to jump another swamp rabbit. That crafty old hare deserved to escape.

I have never been sorry I didn't shoot him.

CAGEY SWAMP RABBITS

Cottontail rabbits try to avoid the wetlands of the Carolinas, but their cousins, the swamp rabbits, choose the low country jungles in which to live and thrive. These critters, darker colored than the cottontails, use the marshlands to evade dogs and hunters, and their wily ways in the habitat are nothing short of remarkable.

In the eastern Carolinas these larger rabbits, known as marsh rabbits, rather than swamp rabbits, do not have the puff of white hair on their behinds that denotes the cottontail species. Rather, the hair on the tail is the same dark color as the rest of the rabbit. They all have shorter ears, and are larger than their cottontail cousins.

Carolina marsh rabbits are found around tidal water rivers and streams where there is flora that the creatures can feed upon when the tide is low. They hide out in tufts of saltgrass or cattails when the tide is high. These tidal wetlands belong to the state, and in that fact lies an advantage for the marsh rabbit hunter. You do not have to get anyone's permission to hunt these tidal water marshes. However, if you stray off the tidal land, you may step onto private property that joins the stream's high water mark. When you get off the tidal land, you need the landlord's permission to hunt on his property. That isn't normally a chore if you convince the landowner that you are not a slob, and that you will not destroy his fences, leave his gates unlocked or damage his hogs or cattle that may be pastured adjoining the state's marshland.

Almost every land owner resents hunters helping themselves to his land without at least asking for permission. But rabbits are not the favorite wild animal of most farmers, and permission to hunt them is usually forthcoming.

Indeed, rabbits are in such low esteem in some states that it is legal to hunt them the years 'round. There is no closed season. But the intelligent rabbit hunters of Carolina respect the rattlesnakes, cottonmouth moccasins and coral snakes enough to stay out of the savannas and jungle habitat until a frost or two falls over the land. This puts most of the snakes to hibernating and the hunting is not as dangerous to men and dogs. In the tropical South, snakes may be stepped on the year 'round. The cold does not drive them underground.

Most of the Carolina marsh rabbits are found around areas where cypress trees abound along shorelines of tidal rivers. Cypress trees grow only in wet, jungle-like areas. But small game biologists say that so much of the Carolinas in the east is low and marshy that some of this cunning species of hares are found over a wide area. Avid rabbit hunters have little trouble jumping the swampers, but often they have a great deal of trouble shooting the wily creatures once they have been routed from their nests by hunters and beagles.

A veteran says, "You would be surprised to learn how smart these creatures are, or if not smart, at least well-versed in the particular habitat that they choose to live in.

"Almost always a marsh rabbit will circle a lake or pond two or three times or more when dogs are after him. You keep hoping that he will pass your way or get tired and quit going around and around the lake. But if he does decide not to go around again, shooting the marsh rabbit becomes even more of a problem. He may decide to swim across and confuse the trackers. Swamp rabbits can swim like otters. Sometimes one will swim only halfway across the lake, decide he has tricked the beagles enough and come back.

"I had my dogs chasing a rabbit in the tidal marshlands along a pond in Horry County one fall. The rabbit had circled a small pond three times. The dogs seemed to lose the track, but one alert beagle detected the scent at the water's edge. He jumped in to investigate. In the middle of the pond was a small tussock of grass with an old, well-hidden stump. That rabbit was sitting on top of the stump and taking it easy. The dog scared him off his perch and the hunt was on again," chuckled the old hunter as he remembered that particular hunt.

The salt land where the tide rises and falls is the best place for the swampers. They like that kind of habitat and they are safer from predators than in the woodlands and fields where cottontails reside. The cottontails live off the grasses and farm crops of the fields while the swampers depend almost entirely upon the wild shoots that sprout in the jungle lowlands.

There are not as many swamp rabbits or any other kind now as there were a quarter century ago, but they are hunted so infrequently and by such a small band of hunters that a real handle on their population is difficult for Carolina wildlife authorities.

Generally, it is conceded that the rabbit population declined after World War II when DDT poisoned many of them. It was used on farms and pasture lands. Also, many campgrounds and housing developments were built on river banks and in marshlands. The swampers were routed out. The clearing of ditch banks and hedgerows that once made good habitat for cottontails and even swampers around salt land further diminished the population of rabbits. The drainage of jungle lands for farming and cattle pasture reduced the abundance of habitat once enjoyed by the swampers.

But there are signs that swampers and cottontails have made a recovery. They may be more plentiful than they were a decade or two ago. More and more of the creatures are being run over on the highways and quail and 'coon hunters report seeing more rabbits than they did a few years ago. That's good news for the rabbit hunters.

Keep in mind that you have to be careful during warm months when snakes are around. You can also expect to see a few alligators in the tidal water areas. They are not usually a threat, but it's best not to tempt an old reptile that every now and then decides he has seen enough of these two-legged critters that are traipsing in his play house.

Then keep in mind that the marsh rabbit is no ordinary bunny. You can't just jump him, put the beagles on the scent and wait for him to trot slowly into your cross-hairs. Once in a great while one may do that, but most often he will hide in the cover so deep you have a hard time seeing him when he reruns his course. More frequently, he will use the water to outfox you and your dogs. That's one reason there are still plenty of swamp rabbits in all of the Carolina low country counties. They give man and other predators the slip.

But it's fun to try to outsmart these fuzzy, dark rabbits that almost seem to play cat and mouse with those who stalk them in the marshlands.

Swamp Rabbits Survival

Surviving in the marshy lowlands of the coastal Carolinas despite the advent of dangerous agricultural chemicals that wiped them out in many states after World War II, the unique swamp rabbit once provided protein dinners for families living near the lakes and swampland streams. Ironically, when man's intrusion into their habitat forced them to exit their conventional territory, they went deeper into the marshes where few hunters guessed their whereabouts.

Man and unpenned dogs have harassed the rabbits in the swamps and made life difficult for generations. Using instinct perhaps more than brains, the swamp rabbits fled the harassers and took up permanent residence on some of the larger islands. There was plenty of flora, their food, and a livelihood on the deserted islands was easy. Also, they had ample habitat for nesting and reproduction.   Rabbits reproduce like . . . well, like rabbits. A single healthy pair left unmolested and with plenty of food can have as many as 30-50 offspring in a single season in the Carolinas.

In time, the islands became thriving rabbit-producing incubators. The vegetation was thick, but hordes of rabbits marooned on these floating mini-farms began to eat themselves out of house and home. As the undergrowth was reduced, fishermen discovered the swamp bunnies that no longer had undisturbed hiding places. The time approached when their overpopulation would have led to their demise, but with their discovery by fishermen, some of whom were hunters too, the survival problem took on a new aspect. Hunters carried their beagle hounds to the islands, turned them loose to chase the swamp rabbits, and harvested them by the dozens as they swam for shore, often using broom handles instead of guns. Rabbits that remained in sight along the island fringes succumbed to shotgun hunters. Swamp rabbits were a delicacy on the dinner tables of Carolina outdoorsmen for years.

Swamp rabbits are a darker color than the cottontail that is more popular in virtually all Southern states. It is also about one-third larger than the cottontail and much smarter. Veteran rabbit hunters reminisce about their adventures chasing these crafty swampers.

Swamp rabbits are always around water and they use this natural obstacle to confuse hunting dogs and to escape. Often they will criss-cross branches and creeks repeatedly until trailing beagles give up the chase. Cottontails, when trailed, will always circle and return to within a few yards of the spot where they were jumped. Gun hunters staying put where the rabbit left its hideout, will almost always get a shot at the bunny when it returns ahead of the dogs. The rabbit's stupidity leads to its demise.

Not so with swamp rabbits. They seem to rejoice in tricking dogs and hunters by back-tracking and losing even dogs with the best of noses. They have been known to swim down creeks for hundreds of feet and then jump out on the same side of the waterway and high-tail it. Dogs smelling the rabbit's trail to the water, instinctively cross the stream and search for the scent on the opposite shore where often they find nothing from a cagey swamper. He outfoxes the dogs.

One swamp rabbit hunter recalls a day when he watched a swamp rabbit approach a stream with the trailing dogs barking in the distance. The rabbit leaped up on a leaning tree that spanned the stream, ran to the other side and jumped to the ground. Moments later it jumped back on the tree, went to midstream and leaped for a grassy tussock the size of a bathtub in the middle of the creek two feet below. It quickly nosed out a nest in the grass and buried itself there. Soon the dogs reached the tree, bayed and yelped as they found their quarry had crossed on the tree. They carefully maneuvered over the stream on the leaning tree, hit the ground on the other side and immediately lost the track. It never occurred to the dogs that the swamp rabbit went back to the tussock and the hunter was so impressed with what he saw, he just grinned and called the dogs off. That swamper deserved another chance to survive. And it did.

There are hunting season restrictions on swamp rabbits

and cottontails in the Carolinas. It is open season and you can kill them without any legal limit any time of the year in some states. This perhaps dates back to Scotland where rabbits at one time were so plentiful that they ruined farm crops and killed themselves by piling on top of each other at rock fences that they sought to cross and could not. It became a much-despised critter in Scotland and it is still remembered as a nuisance species there.

In the United States during the dust bowl era, the larger jack rabbits of the West were so plentiful and hungry that they gnawed all the newly-planted trees down to the hard, dry ground and caused them to die. The U.S. government hired the late Dr. John N. Hamlet, then with the Biological Survey, the forerunner of the U.S. Fish and Wildlife Service, to recruit teams of hunters. They walked the prairies in a "V" with shotguns for more than a year, killing hundreds of thousands of jack rabbits that were hauled in trucks to Chicago and given to the hungry people during the Depression. They killed enough of the rabbits that other seedlings survived, stopping the topsoil from blowing away, and the adult forests still stand there today, protecting the land from wind and erosion. The jack rabbits almost destroyed that effort, but their abundance fed many Chicagoans at a time when food and money were scarce.

Little has been done by wildlife agencies to preserve or enhance the rabbit population, either cottontail, jack, or the odd-looking swamp rabbit. With chemicals taking a terrible toll over the last three decades, along with the clearing of woodlands, ditch banks and other rabbit-hiding habitat, these little rodents may soon disappear. But the uncanny fortitude and instincts of the swamper may keep it around for a few more generations, particularly in the Carolinas where rabbit hunting is not as popular as it once was. The swamp rabbit is a survivor.

CAROLINA DUCK SWAMPERS

Duck hunting the dismal swamps of Southeastern North Carolina where your only shot is through a peephole among cypress, gum and oak branches entangled with vines and Spanish moss that the woodies explode past, demands fast reflexes, good eyesight and excellent hearing that can alert the hunter to his quarry's approach. In the Old West lingo, these swampers would have needed a fast draw and a quick trigger.

Dr. James R. Rabon, DVM, of Whiteville, NC in Columbus County, is one of those swamp duck hunters who began adventures along the Lumber River near Fair Bluff as a youngster when his father, an agriculture teacher in the local high school, introduced him to hunting wood ducks in the swamps. With a hearing deficiency, the elder Rabon carried Jimmy along so that he might tip him off a fraction of a second earlier when the wing beats of the approaching ducks penetrated the jungle along the riverbank.

"Dad often carried me on his shoulders up the river, and I would try to warn him that ducks were whistling over before he heard them. The hunting was much different then from what it is now. Trees were thicker, and at some places, they lapped across the river. The wood ducks generally flew up and down the river. This was the only water of consequence when Dad started taking me hunting. In that the ducks flew along the river, you had more openings to track the ducks and get a bead on them," the astute veterinarian Rabon says today.

"When I was eight years old, I began hunting without Dad. David Scott and I had been born and raised along this fast-running Lumber River, and we did little else other than hunt and fish together for years. We knew every river oxbow and cove and those never to be forgotten places like Big Hog Lake, Piney Lake, Black Lake, Deep Lake and Little Hog Lake. We always hunted up the river, just in case our old outboard motor failed.

We would be able to float and paddle back home more easily. When we got an infrequent shot at a mallard back then, it was like a Canada goose had come by—they were so much larger than the wood ducks we usually saw," Jim says.

"The change in hunting on the Lumber has resulted from several things. First, timber has been clean cut along the shore-line of much of the stream, leading to canals and drainage ditches being cut across the land to the river. Secondly, the beavers have come in in greater numbers than ever. Although there have always been some of these animals active on the river, the beavers have begun damming up the canals and making bigger and bigger lakes and ponds which have attracted more and more ducks. We have more wood ducks and mallards now than we did when I was a youngster on the river, but I think they are harder to shoot. When the river was the only opening through the swamps, the ducks always flew up and down the river where they fed. Now, with the ponds made by the beavers and the irrigation and drainage canals, the ducks no longer have the river as a flyway. They criss cross the river, coming in at right angles. This means the openings you have to shoot through are just little patches between the thick tree tops. You have to track your ducks as they zoom over the cypress and gum tops and hope you have him in your sights when he passes a hole in the cover, before he gets out of range. It's quite a trick to shoot a fast waterfowl in the Lumber River swamp or the Waccamaw swamp that is also in this county. There are a lot more man-made ponds along the river now than ever before that help bring in ducks, but the beavers deserve most of the credit," this articulate young animal doctor says.

When Rabon began hunting in the Lumber River swamps, he said he simply found a sandbar that he could stand on and waited for the woodies to fly over. The river is not their feeding ground now, and you have to pick a spot along the bank that you hope they will pass over when feeding in the surrounding ponds. Coming in at right angles to the river makes your stand important.

Rabon now usually hunts with Bill Williamson, a Whiteville attorney, and his old childhood companion, David

Scott. The two Fair Bluff wood duck veterans introduced Williamson to swamp duck hunting, and now they go together.

"We now go up or down the river in a three man canoe. Our motor is more trustworthy now, and we aren't so concerned that we can't get back to the landing. We spread out about a half a mile apart on the river bank and hope that we have chosen a place where the ducks will cross within range. We do not build duck stands. We hunt miles of the river bank and simply keep moving from place to place until we find a flyway where the ducks cross over and we can get a few shots. Sometimes we see them cross over above or below where we are and the next day we will move that direction and hope the ducks fly the same pattern," Rabon reveals. "We have had retriever, but they make the canoe kind of tipsy, and we don't really need a dog because most of our ducks are shot at close range or not at all. You can't see that far in this jungle.

Scott and Rabon learned early how to make the squeal sound of a wood duck, and they use that skill today to try to entice the woodies to their hiding places. When they succeed in getting a return squeal of an approaching duck, it is a big help in being ready for that brief instant in which the bird is in sight.

The most frequently hunted place for this threesome is the Ashepole Swamp on the Lumber between Fairmont, NC and the South Carolina border. "This is wood duck country," Rabon says, "and there are more mallards than we have had before. The last 20 years have seen a big comeback of the mallards that were scarce before."

"The way we hunt ducks in the swamps appeals to just a few people. We get up long before daylight, and we are in the swamps waiting for the ducks when it is dark as pitch. Our hunt then lasts about 20 minutes. At sunrise, the ducks either fly over or they don't. If we kill a few, that's fine. If not, we enjoyed the outing anyway and are usually back home and on our jobs by 8:30 in the morning. It is illegal to hunt in the afternoon.

"We usually hunt three or four mornings a week during the season, from December 7 through January 20. We do not hunt during the so-called teal season, the first weekend in October. It's still warm weather and the cottonmouth moccasins are too thick to get in the swamp then. There's also a Thanksgiving weekend duck hunt authorized, but we don't hunt that either. That's the time to take my wife to se her folks. We concentrate on the December—January hunting days, although we have the triple season.

"Most duck hunters think the swampers are disgusting. They are used to hunting the sounds and the marshes where there is open shooting and you can hunt all during the day, not 20 minutes at sunrise. But that's OK with us. We like it. We probably don't kill more than 80 ducks among the three of us during an average season, but we have a great time. You become bat-blind in those jungles where there is not open shooting, and you learn to concentrate on the bird coming into your little opening. You hear his wing beat and maybe a squeal that tips you off as to his direction. In a flash, he is upon you, and you track him down the gun barrel, hoping he will cross that opening just ahead. You can't always wait for a clean shot, though. You fire through the trees and hope. That experience gained since we were eight or nine helps us put some ducks in the bag under these adverse and challenging conditions.," Rabon says, with the look of a man in love with his sport.

Rabon and his companions have no lead or steel shot problem. The swamps they hunt are not filled with hunters that concentrate lead pellets in one place, and the shooting is often over water too deep for ducks to feed on the bottom. "It's places where there are duck blinds that hunters use day in and day out, like Currituck Sound, that the saturation of lead shot becomes a problem.," Rabon points out.

Rabon attended NC State University in Raleigh and went on to veterinary school at the University of Georgia. His love for duck hunting in the swamps moved with him to Georgia where he got some county maps and soon was trudging through swampy jungles around Athens during duck season, awaiting the wood duck squeal and wing beats at daylight. "there were some beaver ponds down there like we have here with wood ducks on them. I hunted right through college," he remembers.

The beavers have done these wood duck hunters a lot of

favors by building ponds, and Rabon feels badly about the $10,000 appropriation by the NC General Assembly to pay trappers to rid swamps of beavers in Columbus County. They have trapped hundreds of beavers, but Rabon is satisfied that this rodent will not be destroyed by trappers and will survive to keep gnawing trees and building dams. "While beavers may not be friends to some farmers along the swamps, they are doing a great deal for other wildlife," Rabon says, "As long as there are river basins in desolate places, and more drainage canals than ever before along the swamp lines, many almost inaccessible to man, there are going to be beavers. The farmers will just have to learn to live with them."

Rabon and Williamson are raising another generation of swamp duck hunters. Both have boys and, like Jim's father, these two avid hunters are carrying their offspring into the swamps before daylight to listen for the wing beats. Camouflaged and riding the canoe, the boys enjoy the novelty of such a hunt, albeit they are not so enthusiastic about getting up at 4:00 in the morning.

"There are other wood duck swampers taking to the river around Fair Bluff now too. Some have learned to whistle like the wood ducks that we imitate, and they have dependable motors that let them go up and down the river with confidence. We didn't have that as youngsters in the 60's. They are learning about the thrills of the outdoors before sunrise in remote turns of the river, when the wild waterfowl give your heart an extra beat as they swish across the treetops.

"We don't kill a lot of ducks. We don't have to. We often don't fire a shot, but still enjoy the opportunity to stand on the edge of Ashepole in the dark and hear the swamp come alive. We feel better if we at least see some waterfowl, but we don't have to see 'em to make the day a success."

Dr. Rabon expresses the philosophy of all the devout outdoor people and makes you want to get up early some cold morning this winter and stand with him and his companions in the dark along the meandering Lumber River.

THE QUAIL RESURRECTION

When the mules disappeared from eastern farms in the Carolinas, about midway through the century, the lifestyles of quail changed dramatically, and for a time, the game bird population was so sparse that only a few of the more dedicated hunters bothered to keep trained dogs. The hunters who once thrilled to the thunder of flushed coveys had mostly memories of the good old days prior to World War II when the counties jutting down to the Atlantic along the border once attracted quail hunters from New York and all over each fall. Some of those visiting sportsmen built crude clubhouses and spent weeks each season hunting the native bobwhite quail on the small farms of the lowland wildlife paradise. Others reserved rooms by the month from one bird season to the next in boarding houses and private homes before the advent of motels in the villages of this rural area.

While hunting for the wild quail today cannot compare to the bonanza of 40 and 50 years ago, there is still fine habitat and good bird hunting territory in the area. Happily, the veteran hunters who stayed with their sport during the famine years tell of more and bigger coveys now than have been seen in a decade. They are making a comeback, a remarkable recovery from near extinction, and the lean years prompted many changes in quail hunting from the sandhills of Pinehurst in North Carolina to the South Carolina low country counties.

What did the mules have to do with it? They were innocent bystanders, but these animals had to eat, and lespedeza hay was the crop grown most extensively for these creatures used in the tobacco fields long before much mechanization was introduced to leaf farmers. This hay crop had plentiful seeds palatable to quail, and where you found a hayfield, you flushed coveys of quail that fed early and late in the open and darted back to the dense cover of swampland woods in the middle of the day. There were savannas, briar thickets and gallberry patches near these cleared feeding grounds that offered protection from wild predators and hunters. Getting a craw full of hay seed was easy.

Lespedeza disappeared in the Carolinas with the advent of small, easily controlled tractors, plows, cultivators and harvesters. Machines didn't eat, and the changing face of America drastically altered the lifestyles of quail and the men who chased them. Soybeans and corn replaced a lot of hay fields. The beans are good quail feed, but so high in protein and oil that they cannot provide the only food for quail. The birds can eat a full craw of soybeans every other day and thrive. They can spend the rest of the time foraging for weed and grass seeds in the dense, lush savannas without exposing themselves to hunters in the open. That changed the hunting styles of bird hunters all over the Carolinas.

Had it not been for other breakthroughs that made life easier for farmers, quail might have enjoyed their biggest heyday with the coming of soybeans. DDT, Endrin and other dangerous insecticides followed close behind the exodus of the mule, however. These chemicals wiped out millions of creatures from quail to sparrows, bluebirds and rabbits as they were used on tobacco, corn, soybeans and family garden vegetables. Both native and visiting bird hunters were almost nonexistent for a time, and the lean years of the late '50's and the '60's saw the introduction of the first quail hunting preserves in the area where pen-raised birds were grown and released by the thousands for hunters and their dogs to find and harvest.

There are some veteran quail hunters today who where young men in the '40's and who marched off to war, leaving farms dotted with many coveys of game birds. They returned to find their quail resource surprisingly reduced during the war despite little hunting for lack of shells, guns and the induction of the hunters into the armed forces. Yet there were enough coveys left to keep the sport interesting for a few well into the '50's as mechanical farming grew, lespedeza and mules disappeared and chemicals and tractors were in every barn.

Two of those early hunters who have pursued the sport during much of their three score years and more in North Carolina are Wilbur Smith and Bennet White. These veterans come from different sections of southeastern North Carolina where tourist bird hunters once flocked to kill limits day after day from

Thanksgiving until February. Some were arrested for shipping crates filled with dressed birds back to New York and elsewhere. Smith and White often hunted together and they experienced the vast changes in the birds and in the hunting, finding both some good and some bad in the changes.

Smith says, "I began hunting quail when I was about ten years old. I had an old single barrel, hammer gun and I learned to kill quail with it. I started raising bird dogs way back there before I went in the Army, and later I had 14, some setters and some pointers. I have had some fine dogs. I hunted them and I also sold and trained them." You look over his dog pens with jumping, barking canines of many shapes and colors and you know that few bird hunters remain like this veteran who was seriously wounded at Normandy, suffering injuries in the legs and hips such that it seems like a miracle that he could have returned to romp the swamplands for Carolina quail.

Smith and White enjoyed watching their dogs point these pen-raised quail. They enjoyed the same thing on their own 267 acre quail preserve in Columbus County. They liked to shoot these domesticated birds, but are quick to point out that it is not like shooting fish in a barrel when the birds are trained to fly in huge wire impoundments before they are released.

"We hunt both wild and pen-raised quail. I think it is harder to kill the best-bred pen quail than it is the wild, native ones. You never know where a pen-raised bird will fly. He just might come right at your face, but the wild one is predictable. You pretty well know what direction he is going. But both kinds know where the thickest cover is. They'll find the bushes," Smith said.

"The best pen-raised quail are mix bred with the Northern bobwhite crossed with the Tennessee Red species, plus about 25 percent Mexican quail. This is the ideal combination. They can fly and they are a challenge to hit. If you bred the old original bobwhite quail that once flourished on every hedgerow around here, they wouldn't be any good on a preserve. They won't fly much, and when they do, they are slow. It's the smaller, faster half-breeds that make the best hunting preserve stock," this cagey old hunter and dog trainer remarks. You know he is a man with expertise.

"When the Mexican quail sub-species was introduced into this country about 30 years ago, many people were upset about

426

it and criticized the wildlife people for bringing in this bird that was smaller, often perched in trees and was far different from the native bobwhite. But the Mexican species saved quail hunting for all of us. If we had depended solely on the very edible and slow native partridge, there wouldn't be any now," he observes. "This bird is fast and knows how to get away."

While there are more quail now than a few years ago and there is a revival of interest in bird hunting, some tourists are returning to hunt birds. Smith says there would be many more coveys if farmers would stop using Azdrion 5 to poison tobacco and other crops. DDT and Endrin are no longer permitted, but the newer insecticide is even more deadly to wildlife than those outlawed chemicals. Smith says you can spray Azdrion 5 in a field and by the time your tractor turns around and gets to the other end of the row, the fast-working poison has mockingbirds, sparrows and anything else that feeds there dying. It's fast and deadly.

"There are other insecticides that are just as good like Orthane that is totally safe for wildlife. You can even use it on cabbage. But Azidron is deadly and it destroys quail and any other wildlife that feeds on the insects or grasses in treated fields." Smith says.

Smith and White have hunted some of the large quail preserves like Pinewood Lakes Hunting Preserve, near West End in Moore County, where hundreds of thousands of birds have been released for harvesting and learned from their experience there and elsewhere how to get the best results from their own smaller preserve. Theirs is largely for their families and close friends. They built a spacious wire enclosure in which they put their grown, pen-raised quail that are bought on contract, and spook them regularly before their release so that they learn to fly and know how to challenge hunters when they are unfettered in the wooded preserve.

"We want a good percentage of our released birds to escape and reproduce on the preserve, and they will if handled properly before the release. If they are de-billed, as some raisers do to the young birds by clipping a piece of their beaks so they won't peck each other, they cannot live long in the wild. Taking this bit off their beaks keeps them from being able to tear the husks off of peas and soybeans, the primary crop. If they cannot do that, they will starve. They also must be taught to fly before the release," Smith says.

But by far the greatest hazards to quail reproduction and growth are the weather and the hawks. If there is a lot of cold, rainy weather during the nesting season, it virtually destroys a generation of quail. Many released quail will die from bad weather if it hits a week or two after they are released and before they learn to cope with it. Hawks, once shot on sight by every farmer, are now protected by federal laws and the increased population of these predators takes a toll of Carolina released and wild birds. Foxes, stray cats and bobcats prey on the quail here too.

"When the weather is good, we start hunting our released birds a day or two after we have turned them loose. They stay near the feeders we provide and they will remain in coveys. If you shoot one covey down to five or six birds, they will take up with another covey. This is true of all quail whether pen-raised or wild natives.

"There is a lot of difference in hunting released birds here in this lowland corner of the Carolinas and hunting them in the sandhill communities. Up there they drop down around black-jack and turkey oaks in some grass and weeds and are easy to flush. here they have heavy cover and it is hard to get them up once they are settled down." Smith reveals. "There are some of those areas, like the military reservation at Fort Bragg, where you need to have high-powered dogs and a jeep to hunt quail and you must cover a lot of territory. Some of the places we hunt in South Carolina and Georgia are spread out and you need something to ride there too.

"Here in the Carolina Coastal area, we still have a country of small landowners and very little posted land. Hunters who will ask permission of the farmer and agree not to vandalize his fences or shoot the covey down to extinction, are almost always permitted to hunt on these private and often productive quail lands. Slob hunters who trespass without asking permission are generally unwanted and ordered off the property. About the only land that is posted now is that which hunting clubs have leased. Most farmers no longer put up no trespassing signs. And there is some good hunting of wild, native quail over much of the low country," Smith says.

These old veterans like to hunt the wild coveys on the farms and detest the slob who does not respect the property rights of landowners.

Smith started bird hunting seriously when he was in high school and the late Judge Ernest Harrelson hunted the area around his old home place. He tagged along as a youngster and liked it. At 15, he had his first bird dog and has never been without dogs since. He went from his old single barrel gun to a 26" double barrel during that era. He then went to an automatic. He knows how to shoot, as does White.

"But I am against all these sawed-off guns that are on the market. I think any shotgun with a barrel less than 26 inches should be outlawed because it cripples too many birds.

"I have bird dogs named after all colleges in the North Carolina Big Four—Duke, State, Wake and the University of North Carolina at Chapel Hill. The setter I had for Carolina I called "Choo Choo" after Charlie Justice, the big football star of the '40's. Choo Choo was the best dog I ever owned. He knew just where to look for birds. He was conceived in the woods on a hunt and born two days before the close of the season. He started off hunting like a veteran the very first year and required little training. It was while hunting with Choo Choo that I recorded my most memorable quail experience. That dog could make the coveys fly the direction I wanted them to fly and three times in the SAME afternoon, I killed five birds on the covey rise. The dog ran the birds toward me. I shot two on the way to where I was standing, and three as they were going away each time. You don't forget that kind of afternoon and I don't forget that fine dog," Wilbur smiles.

"Training bird dogs is a lot easier now than it once was. We have beepers to keep them in range. That saves a lot of yelling, and the remote control shock collars give the trainer a big advantage over the dog. These collars have some dogs still working the woods that would have gone to the pound a generation ago. I trained the offspring of Choo Choo for about 20 years and had some great bird dogs from that strain. I trained most of them the hard way.

"When I came back from the war and was without dogs, I heard that a neighbor, Jim Long, had an old setter that no one could breed. I had a leg in a brace, and couldn't do much of anything except drive to a field, put the dog out and stand around hoping a covey was close that I could maybe get a shot at. That old dog absolutely realized that I was a cripple that couldn't follow her around and certainly couldn't beat her up like she was accustomed to. She understood my plight. She sympathized and quickly became a great dog. I named her Bess. I taught her to back and she was the mother of my college dogs— State, Duke and Wake. State wouldn't retrieve until one day when he pointed on a log over water. I shot the bird and down it fell in the pond. State jumped right in, swam to the bird, picked it up like a lab and brought it back to me. From that day on she retrieved every bird that went down, often staying behind to look for a bird that we gave up on, later bringing it to me and looking happy," Smith recalls. Wilbur is no longer a cripple, but still carries some serious scars from WW2.

Like all bird hunters, Smith is proud of his dogs and his ability to shoot down quail. "My friend Bennett here has a pretty good dog that would be a real good dog if he were mine," Smith grins.

"I absolutely will not hunt with people who have better bird dogs than mine and who can kill more birds than I can," Smith says, and you get the impression that there would be few companions if you took this statement literally and hunters' talk about themselves and their dogs seriously.

Back in the bonanza days of wild quail hunting in the Carolinas, when Smith was a young man, he set himself a quota one season of 500 birds. Two weeks before Christmas he tabulated his harvest. He had downed 485 quail already, and there were still six weeks of the season. When the season ended, he had brought home more than 1000 birds, twice as many as he had nonchalantly predicted. He loves the outdoors but bringing home some birds is the difference between success and failure.

"It's a lot of work and expense to maintain 14 bird dogs. I carry all of them to the vet every two weeks for heart worm shots and that's trouble. They know how to eat, too," he acknowledges.

Like all bird hunters, these old pros have tales to laugh about, particularly when they are designed to embarrass one of the fraternity. The late Ed Prince, another native who used to hunt quail with Smith, White and others, told the story of a hunt in the sandhill area some years ago when a quail lit in a tree. Prince had a young dog that he was training and he told Smith to shoot the bird off the limb for his dog to nuzzle. Maybe it would help train the pup.

"Wilbur pulled down on that bird and missed it a mile. Then he killed it on the second shot," Ed joked.

"It's not so!" Smith counters, "The bird lit in the tree and I told Ed to shake a bush or something to make it fly so I could shoot it on the wing, a legal kill, not a sitting duck. He wouldn't shake anything, so I shot a few feet away from the bird in the thick tree, the shot cutting a hole through the leaves so that the bird could fly out. When it flew through the hole, I knocked it down on the wing."

Take your choice as to who was telling the truth.

There are not many young men interested in quail hunting today. It's the older generations. Smith has an answer to that:

"The birds are in the thickets, the bushes today. It takes a lot of work and hustle to get them out. The young hunters just won't beat the bushes for a shot like we did years ago," he says.

There is a definite resurrection of wild quail hunting in the Carolinas. There are more birds now than have been available in several years and some hunters are raising and training bird dogs to take advantage of the expanded game population. Harvesting them won't be easy. It's a challenge to kill fast-flying quail darting through holes in the swamp underbrush and thick tree cover. But for those sportsmen with patience, ability and well-trained canines, some great thrills are waiting.

When Day Is Done . . . .

A biting wind out of the east demanded attention and I wriggled down a little deeper in my old flotation jacket and snuggled the hood tighter around my ears. The Spanish moss that draped the cypress trees lacing the Black River shoreline was standing out at 45 degree angles toward the setting sun. An old bald eagle and several noisy ospreys circled above the acres of nervous weeds where the wind was rooting its way across the surface of the river.

I watched a single hyacinth bulb cork patiently as it maneuvered near the marshy grassline with the gust of wind above and my tied-out shiner on the hook below making this best of nature's bobbers move and look alive. It kept me expectant, tense, ever hopeful of just one more thrill before the day was done.

Clumps of billowing white clouds rushed along overhead and looked for the all the world like scoops of vanilla ice cream with a touch of chocolate syrup oozing down the outer edges. They promised worsening weather once the sun was down. That would be soon, but for now, the rays of fading light from the reddening sun glinted, ricocheted off the tiny waves of rolling water in gold and blue hues that seemed splashed on by an artist's brush.

Fishing here was not just for the elusive largemouth that I knew lurked somewhere nearby, perhaps watching my cavorting shiner at that very moment and wondering why it didn't escape from the imminent threat of predation that would end its life. Just being here is a frame of mind for the outdoorsman who marvels at God's masterpiece of nature that surrounds him and he falls in love with this Carolina coast artistry. Only a few ever comprehend this relationship to the wilderness.

Patiently, I watched and waited for the hyacinth-bulb cork to go down, my apparent purpose in being here. But was that really paramount? There was joy in watching an old mama 'coon sneak along among the cypress knees with two tiny offspring wading just behind, stopping, slapping at a school of gambusia minnows that were too careless in these shallows. Some made a meal for the alert little masked marauders. An old fox squirrel barked in the tree overhead and flitted close to a well-honed hole in the trunk where she had nursed a family a few months earlier. A blue heron flapped gracefully, slowly, just above the bulrushes and headed into the sundown. I could hear the ghostly squawks of a flock of sandhill cranes in the distance. A quartet of seldom-quiet crows settled in the cedars along the edge of the marshland. While some creatures were just beginning to stir and look for food and fun, others were bedding down for the night.

I shivered a little more as the sun disappeared and a full moon peeked through the tree line across the river, which was beginning to whitecap.

I would wait a few more minutes as day died and the last shades of dusk settled amid the croaking of the leopard frogs. I had been here for hours hoping, hunting for a big bass. It is man's natural instinct to hunt and fish, to prey upon those other creatures of the world. It was just as natural as the raccoons and the gambusia, the osprey and the shad and the bass that was hopefully eyeing my fluttering bait that was now struggling against a clump of rock grass. I was here to hunt and to try to outwit another of nature's creations that I was sure hovered out of sight in the darkness in the grass and weeds. I was sitting here competing with my prey. We waited to see which would win this silent game, played with a set of unwritten rules, but clearly understood. I would never spear or shoot one of this great species. I wouldn't dare set a trap or cast a net over the trophy I sought. I loved this challenge. Could I out-duel this gallant fish? Could I entice a stalking, hungry lunker to make a mistake? I would dearly love to see that cork go down.

A brighter than normal star popped out of the heavens. That must be Venus. A purplish hue moved across the heavens and I knew it was time to head for home, supper and the blessings of a happy family relationship. I would wait just a moment more and I flicked the tip of my fishing rod just enough to encourage that shiner to renew its movement.

Unbelievable! That old hyacinth bulb popped like an explosion and pieces drifted apart on the surface. I could see a fast-moving wake where my line was screaming along the grassline. It tightened. I lowered the rod tip for an instant, then yanked it overhead with all my strength, ignoring the cold tiredness in my muscles, the tears seeping from my eyes where the wind was taking a toll. I was suddenly as nervous as a pregnant fox in a forest fire.

Then came that strong surge of something alive on the line. Slowly I pulled the darting weight nearer and nearer. Now it was alongside. Gently I grasped its lower jaw between my thumb and forefinger and lifted a beautiful glistening largemouth bass over the gunnels. I smiled admiringly at what must have been at least a 10-pound beauty. For one last long moment, my eyes lingered on this great trophy. This was success, victory, a perfect day. Then with a pang of sadness, but also with thanks, I eased the big bass back into the river and watched her paddle slowly, deeper and out of sight. I had won!

I reeled in the rest of my line. There was the sound of a barking dog that echoed across the water. It was time to call it a day. The sunlight had disappeared even before my lunker hit. I cranked the motor and slowly, calmly headed for home. Tomorrow was another day. I would again feel, see, enjoy the loneliness of this wonderful region. I would seek out another of these great fish and play the waiting game. All good things must come to an end. Day was done.

Coastal Carolinas
Tales and Truths

Places To Go
& Things To See
In The Coastal Carolinas

PATRIOTS POINT

The world's largest naval and maritime museum, Patriots Point, is home to four historically important vessels—the *Savannah*, the *Laffey*, the *Clamagore*, and the *Yorktown*.

The *Savannah* is the world's first nuclear-powered merchant ship. Built as part of Eisenhower's Atoms-for-Peace program, the *Savannah* sailed as an experiment in nuclear fuel from 1961-1970. In these eight years, the ship burned only 163 pounds of uranium, equaling 28,800,000 gallons of fuel oil.

The destroyer *Laffey* (DD-744) was commissioned on February 8, 1944, and after participating in the D-Day landings of Allied troops at Normandy, was transferred to the Pacific. Here, on April 16, 1945, she was hit by three bombs and five Japanese Kamikaze suicide planes in one hour. The *Laffey* was not to be defeated, however. Her crew kept her afloat, gunning down 11 planes during the process.

Commissioned June 28, 1945, the submarine *Clamagore* (SS-343) operated in the Atlantic and Mediterranean during World War II. She patrolled Cuban waters during 1962 and was one of the Navy's last operating diesel-powered submarines.

The flagship of the Patriots Point fleet, the aircraft carrier *Yorktown* (CV-10) is also known as the "Fighting Lady" of World War II. Commissioned on April 15, 1943, the *Yorktown* fought in many historic World War II battles, patrolled the western Pacific during the Cold War, and fought in Vietnam. In 1968, she recovered the crew of Apollo VIII, the first manned spacecraft to circle the moon. Now, the *Yorktown* displays such national memorials on board as the "Carrier Aviation hall of Fame."

Each of these vessels is unique, and all can be toured at their berthing place just across the Cooper River Bridge at Patriots Point in Mt. Pleasant.

EDISTO ISLAND

Some 40 minutes south of Charleston on the Atlantic coast is the picturesque and unique Edisto Island. Not only are the waters near Edisto prolific saltwater fishing havens that attract visitors, the old-fashioned atmosphere of the land and the people where time stands still set it aside as early American. There are few one-time tourists to Edisto. You get caught up in its remoteness and the casual living of the natives and they draw visitors back again and again.

Once reached only by the creaking, rusty Dawhoo Bridge on State Road 174, modern engineering has replaced the Dawhoo with a high bridge across the Intracoastal Waterway that separates Edisto from the South Carolina mainland. It now is much quicker and easier to reach this Shangri-la that many feel is only a mite short of Utopian. The old bridge now is a manmade reef a mile and a half offshore where anglers celebrate one successful fishing trip after another, as spadefish, sheepshead, black bass, mackerel and other desirable dinner table species congregate and forage for food.

Invariably, easy access to remoteness launches a renaissance and such is the case at Edisto today, as its popularity as a tourist spot is on the rise as are real estate and property prices. Many despise the change, but like everything and everywhere else, "one man's trash is another man's treasure."

There's plenty of charm and solitude remaining on Edisto Island where a simple chat with an old-timer may bring tears to your eyes as conversation swings back to past generations contrasted to the late 20th century.

There are still many shady dirt road walks where ancient Spanish live oaks lap across the sandy pig paths. Strange seashells wash onto the desolate beaches and a myriad of various songbirds sing and search for food in the acres of island marshlands that remain despite the influx of people and development.

Still attracting sightseers are the old country churches and well-kept cemeteries with names of earlier natives etched in wood and stone. Others love the beachfront cottages and camp-sites where American Indians once lived peacefully with nature. There is still bed and breakfast lodging and a smattering of simple seafood restaurants.

Some locals proudly but quietly have roots on Edisto dating back before the Civil War and many are not happy with the new bridge that has revolutionized economic growth but led to a congestion once believed impossible.

Some of those in business, like Weldon Bell and his Bell Buoy Seafood House, realize that more dollars will cross their counters with the influx of people and this means more sales and more profits. But that alone is not always what makes these island folk happy.

Mead's Landing attracts newcomers who never before have seen oysters hosed down by Bernie Flowers as he washes away the mud and sand from his morning's harvest. Like his predecessors, Flowers gathers his tasty mollusks the hard way—tearing the oysters loose from the bottom of tidal inlets with humble tongs. You know you have freshly-caught oysters when you bargain with Bernie Flowers.

Crabbers corral blue crabs along the creeks of Edisto and make a living selling the ugly seafood with dangerous-looking claws to natives and tourists. Ron Elliott is such a crabber, but he adds to his income by repairing cast nets used by the local commercial fishermen. You have to be a weaver to do this kind of repair service. Elliott's skiff eases along the waters of Frampton Creek near isolated Edingsville Beach. He likes the solitude there and the unbelievable shell hunting success. Inclined to be critical of the creeping society called "progress" that has changed Edisto in this decade, Elliott's words may not be acceptable in high society. He hates to see nature's naturalness destroyed by man's greed.

There's a fossil hunter of note along these island beaches. He is a retired architect, Don Marvin. With spade in hand, he walks the dunes along the beaches overturning old earth where he finds bones and teeth from long-extinct creatures that once roamed these shores, even prehistoric mastodon remains.

An Edisto tour with Marie Elliott introduces first-time tourists to the ancient cemeteries, churches, landings and homes on the island. Marie's ancestors have been here for five generations and she has personal knowledge of the era when rice, indigo and cotton crops were grown here. She points out the present bountiful crops of garden vegetables grown in the fertile black muck soil.

Bruce Earnshaw and his wife Tecla have restored Cassina Point Plantation. The 1840 mansion is four stories high and they have turned it into a bed and breakfast inn. Among the pecan trees and oaks overloaded with Spanish moss, horses graze peacefully as visitors admire Nature's beauty along a slow-flowing tidal creek.

Mike Spivey supervises the Edisto Beach State Park. Because park supervisors are regularly shifted from one location to another, Mike will never be a true Edistonian. But he greets vistors like he was a native. He often even walks a dark wooded trail and searches an ancient shell mound for bones and Indian artifacts. He likes the place and thrills at the boats that slowly move along the grass-lined banks of Big Bay Creek.

David and Doris Lybrand live in a house along Big Bay Creek. They boat the estuaries along the South Edisto River and into St. Helena Sound when they get a good view of Edisto Beach. The Lybrands are realtors and the new bridge has brought them business. But they don't want to see the uniqueness and isolation of Edisto destroyed. View corridors and areas reserved for wildlife are in their minds as a trust has been developed with preservation of the charm the focus.

Most old acquaintances of Edisto Island pray that it will never be loaded down with shopping malls, hotels, traffic and stoplights. We'll see!

EDISTO BUOY

South of Charleston South Carolina, and north of Savannah, Georgia, is a neat little coastal island that juts out into the Atlantic. It's separated from the mainland by the Intracoastal Waterway. That long canal with its tributaries in the South Carolina Low Country, along with offshore reefs planted by promotion-minded sportsmen, have created a real bonanza fishing ground for brackish, salt and even freshwater fish.

Buoy 6HI was built by the Beaufort-Jasper Outdoorsmen in 1971. It consists of eight barge sections (10 by 10 feet), two 57-foot landing crafts, three 120-foot barges and a 30-foot dredge. Properly marked by the South Carolina Marine Resources Department, this large reef off the Palmetto State coast has become a veritable mecca for mackerel, spadefish, sheepshead, grouper and snapper, among other species. It has drawn fishermen from everywhere for the last decade.

Congregating around these bottom hideouts, the Atlantic spadefish has found a new home. They feed on blue ball jellyfish that float on or near the surface off the South Carolina coast. Once considered a small species, since 1988 spadefish giants have risen from the reefs to hit quartered jellyfish on anglers' hooks. Many reach weights above 11 pounds. One was a giant 13-pounder!

You can even catch them with golf-ball-sized homemade lures made from household plastic wrap. The blue ball jellyfish are almost transparent and the plastic wrap closely mimics the real thing.

CHARLES TOWNE LANDING

Home of the first permanent English settlement in South Carolina, Charles Towne Landing still preserves the history of its colonial past.

Persuaded by a Kiawah Indian to settle on the west bank of the Ashley River, colonists established Charles Towne Landing in 1670. The experiences and daily activities of these first settlers are today represented on the nature preserve and historic site.

Because trade was such an important part of colonial life, the full-scale reproduction of the 17th century trading vessel, *Adventure* is an excellent addition to the site. After touring the ship, one can step into the Settler's Life Area and view the 1670 Experimental Crop Garden which allows visitors to see the kinds of crops grown for export and use by the settlers. These include rice, indigo, and cotton.

While experiencing the colonists' daily life, visitors are also given a glimpse of the wilderness with the 20-acre natural habitat zoo. Such animals as wolves, bears, pumas, and bison as would have been seen by the settlers can be seen in this animal forest.

You can enjoy the 80 acres of gardens which Charles Towne Landing has to offer. Whether you are walking along the marsh or bicycling past the tranquil lagoons which reflect blossoming camellias and azaleas, the gardens are a thing of beauty.

Boone Hall Plantation

Originally a prosperous cotton plantation, Boone Hall was established by Major John Boone, one of the original settlers of South Carolina. The plantation manor house was rebuilt in 1935 by Thomas A. Stone, Canadian Ambassador to the United States. The now 738-acre estate is rich in the history of South Carolina's Low Country.

In the 18th and 19th centuries, Boone Hall covered more than 17,000 acres. The plantation was an important source of the state's main colonial-era export—cotton. In the Boone Hall gin-house, the cotton fibers were separated from the seed by the cotton gin and the cotton was pressed into bales. The bales were then loaded onto barges at the old boat house and sent to Charleston for export.

Not only was Boone Hall an important cotton plantation, it was also an important producer of handmade bricks and tiles. The plantation's mansion, slave quarters, cotton gin house, and circular smokehouse, as well as its garden walls and walks were constructed of the bricks originally produced on the Boone Hall Plantation. These same bricks may still be seen in the plantation's structures even today.

While Boone Hall Plantation no longer exports cotton or produces bricks and tiles, its pecan groves are still productive. By 1904, the plantation's pecan groves were the largest in the world.

Adding to Boone Hall's beauty is its famous avenue of oaks, a three-quarter mile drive lined with massive Spanish moss-draped oaks. The first of these oaks were planted in 1743 by Captain Thomas Boone who is believed to be buried beside the avenue, his grave indicated by an unmarked tombstone.

Bordering the avenue of oaks are nine original slave cabins which housed the plantation's house servants and skilled craftsmen. This cluster of cabins, known as Slave Street, is one of the few remaining intact in the Southeast.

KIAWAH ISLAND

Located 21 miles south of Charleston, Kiawah Island is a lush 10,000-acre resort covered with dense vegetation and offering a wide variety of activities in a relaxing setting.

Kiawah Island was named for the Kiawah Indians who inhabited the island in the 1600's. The Island was deeded to George Raynor in 1699 by the Lords Proprietors, and was later acquired by Charleston's prominent Vanderhorst family, who finally sold the island in 1952, after 180 years of ownership.

The first Vanderhorst to own the island, Arnoldus II, built a three-story mansion which looks over a bend in the Kiawah River. Built in 1772, the mansion has been host to George Washington and residence of the governor of South Carolina, Arnoldus II. The Vanderhorst Mansion weathered the vandalism and destruction caused by Union troops during the Civil War and has been the subject of much conversation for its tale of the ghost of Major Arnoldus IV, who died in 1881. Today visitors can tour the outside of the mansion on a Kiawah Jeep Safari, but inside tours are banned because they are unsafe.

In addition to the historic elements of Kiawah Island, Kiawah boasts a number of beautiful and challenging golf courses, one designed by Jack Nicklaus. Nicklaus' course, Turtle Point, has been called one of the top resort courses by *Golf Digest* and rates among the top 10 South Carolina golf courses.

In addition to Kiawah Island's excellent golfing amenities, the tennis facilities are equally as exceptional. *Tennis* magazine ranks Kiawah among the nation's top tennis resorts with its 28 hard-surface or Har-tru clay courts, fully staffed pro shops, and instructional programs.

Not to be forgotten, the ocean presents opportunities for sport. For the avid fisherman, spring and fall are the seasons to fish at Kiawah. During these times, giant 15 to 20-pound channel bass near the beach at high tide, providing exciting chances to battle the waves and reel in that huge red bass that fishermen dream of.

The adventurous Kiawah Jeep Safari explores the dense sea island forest, points out natural features of beach and dunes, and pauses at the Vanderhorst mansion. The well-known Straw Market offers avid shoppers an array of boutiques to browse.

Whether sporting, adventuring, shopping or relaxing, visitors to Kiawah Island can expect to discover something new every time on this island.

FORT MOULTRIE

In its primitive beginnings as a palmetto log fortification during the American Revolution, Fort Moultrie's artillery, commanded by General William Moultrie, held back the British fleet under Sir Peter Parker. Hastily constructed to protect Charleston from the attack, Fort Moultrie's two walls made of palmetto logs and sand proved to be effective. The spongy palmetto and yielding sand easily absorbed shot and shell from the British ships. In the June 28, 1776, battle, Fort Moultrie's flag was shot down, but Sergeant Jasper leaped onto the beach, recovered the flag, and restored it to its ramparts, exclaiming, "Don't let us fight without a flag."

After the Revolution, Fort Moultrie was enlarged into a five-sided structure with earth and timber walls 17 feet high. After completion in 1798, it was not long before the fort was destroyed in the hurricane of 1804. Since then, Fort Moultrie has undergone modification and has seen action in the War of 1812. Later, Osceola, the great leader of the Seminole Indians of Florida, was incarcerated at the fort and died there. His grave stands just outside the main portal. In the 1830s, one soldier to serve at the fort was Edgar Allen Poe. During his service, Poe wrote his famous short story, "The Gold Bug," which is set on Sullivans' Island.

During the April 12, 1861, siege of Fort Sumter, Fort Moultrie played a vital role. The two-day siege on Fort Sumter resulted not only in the surrender of Major Anderson's troops, but also in the start of the Civil War.

Fort Moultrie also participated in the Mexican War, the Spanish American War, and both world wars. The fort is administered by the National Park Service and is located at West Middle Street on Sullivan's Island, ten miles east of Charleston.

DRAYTON HALL

Settling in Carolina in 1679, the Draytons became one of South Carolina's most distinguished families. In 1738, John Drayton, a young planter, purchased a plantation next to his father's plantation, now known as Magnolia Gardens.

Completed in 1742, after four years of construction by European and African-American craftsmen, elegant Drayton Hall now stands as the oldest and finest example of Georgian Palladian architecture built in America before the Revolution. The house's striking, two-story portico is the first of its kind in America, with its Doric and Ionic columns of Portland stone imported from England.

Symmetry, order, and bold classical detail distinguish the architectural style of Drayton Hall. Although the actual architect is still unknown, the design of the house can be traced to a style popular in Britain after 1715.

Lasting through seven generations of Drayton ownership, until 1974, Drayton Hall's original construction remains intact today. In fact, Drayton Hall is the only Ashley River plantation house that survived the Civil War fully intact. Today , the National Trust for Historic Preservation owns the house and has preserved its beauty and authenticity.

In spite of changing tastes, periods of disuse, and occasional repairs, the house has hardly been altered, and approaches the close of the 20th century without running water, electricity, gas lights or central heating. Also, the National Trust has elected not to furnish the house, but rather to leave the interior open for interpretation.

MIDDLETON PLACE

The 18th-century rice plantation of Henry Middleton, president of the First Continental Congress, and his son, Arthur, a signer of the Declaration of Independence, Middleton Place, still preserves a significant slice of the Low Country past.

Built in 1755, the Middleton Place House was originally a gentleman's guest wing. Federal troops burned most of the house during the Civil War, but because this wing survived, it became the family residence. Guided tours reveal the Middleton family lifestyles from 1741 to 1865 and include the original Middleton silver, paintings, furniture, and documents.

Farm life goes on at the Plantation Stableyards. Here visitors experience the workings of a self-sustaining 18th-century Low Country plantation. A blacksmith, potter, carpenter, and weaver, dressed in clothing of the period, recreate the daily activities which were once vital to Middleton Place. Visitors are encouraged to help dip candles, grind corn and milk cows. Horses, mules, hogs, cows, sheep, goats and guinea hens populate the stableyard.

As well as experiencing plantation life, visitors can enjoy Middleton's extensive gardens, laid out in 1741. They encompass 110 acres of overwhelming symmetry and elegance that reflect the landscaped gardens with terraces and ornamental lakes of the English and French styles.

Contributing to the beauty of Middleton Place is the camellia, first introduced to America at Middleton Place by Andre Michaux during the 18th century. Paths lead to the finely sculpted terraces of grass which end at the magnificent Butterfly Lakes below.

Located on Highway 61, 14 miles northwest of Charleston, Middleton Place is open from 9 a.m. to 5 p.m. daily.

Provost Dungeon

For the residents of early Charles Towne, the Exchange building was a place where town meetings were held and imprisoned pirates and Indians were kept.

Completed in 1771, the Exchange was an important part of the 18th-century port, central to social, political, and economic life. The election of South Carolina delegates to the First Continental Congress was held here in 1774 and in March of 1776 the independent Colony of South Carolina was declared from the Exchange steps.

During the American Revolution, the building was converted to a British prison, the Provost, where signers of the Declaration of Independence were held. In 1788 the state convention to ratify the U.S. Constitution met at the Exchange. Also, George Washington was entertained several times here during his Southern tour in 1791.

Charleston's post office from 1818-1896, the building served both federal and confederate governments. In 1917, the U.S. Congress deeded the Exchange to the South Carolina Daughters of the American Revolution, and today the old Exchange is open for tours.

Central to Charleston life since its establishment, the Old Exchange Building still preserves its history. The Exchange's Provost Dungeon of 1780 still stands as a monument to the past with its lifelike representations of prisoners. Held in the confines below the elegant colonial halls of the Old Exchange, these imprisoned figures offer a chance to experience history to the fullest.

Located at 122 East Bay Street, the Exchange is open as a museum Monday through Saturday, 9:30 a.m.–5:00 p.m. Visitors are welcomed with special tours, educational events and group activities offered by the Old Exchange staff year round.

THE SWEETGRASS BASKET

Sweetgrass basket making has been a part of the Mount Pleasant community near Charleston for more than 300 years. Brought to the area by slaves who came from West Africa, basket making is a traditional art form which has been passed on from generation to generation. Today it is one of the oldest art forms of African origin in the United States. Mount Pleasant enjoys the distinction of being the only place where this particular type of basketry is practiced. Here the descendants of slaves from West Africa continue the tradition.

During the days of slavery, rice cultivation and the flourishing plantations of the Old South, these baskets were in great demand for agricultural purposes. They also brought extra income to slave owners who often sold baskets to other plantation owners.

During this era, large work baskets were popular. For the most part, they were used to collect and store vegetables, staples, etc. Men made these large baskets from marsh grasses called bulrush. A common form to evolve during this era was the winnowing basket (rice basket) called the "fanner." Other agricultural baskets were for grain storage, cotton, fish and shellfish.

Functional baskets for everyday living in the home were made by women. Some of these were made for bread, fruits, sewing, clothes, storage, etc. They were made from the softer, pliable grass commonly called sweetgrass (*Muhlenbergia filipes*), because of its pleasant fragrance, similar to the smell of fresh hay.

With the decline of the plantation system, black families acquired land and started a new way of life. Because they felt that this basket making tradition was an important part of their cultural heritage, and that future generations would be able to retain an identity with Africa through the baskets, they kept the tradition alive. The tradition remains very much alive today. For generations, it has been passed from mother to daughter to granddaughter. Around the beginning of the 20th century, the Lowcountry nearly lost this valuable art. However, in the 1930s, basketmakers saw a new surge of interest from gift shop owners, museums and handcraft collectors. The paving of Highway 17 North and the construction of the Cooper River Bridge made the route through Mount Pleasant a major north-south artery. Basketmakers then started marketing their wares from a new invention, the roadside basket stand, which was directly accessible to tourists.

Today most basket stands are still built along the shoulder of Highway 17 North. Once a small residential community outside of Charleston, Mount Pleasant has become the sixth largest city in South Carolina. This, for the most part, is due to large-scale planned development. With this massive growth, basket stands—a part of the community for over half a century—have dwindled tremendously in number. Within the past ten years, development has forced many basket stands to relocate farther north. Others have been totally displaced, as there was no other space in which to relocate.

Another serious problem confronting the basketmakers of Mount Pleasant is the dramatic decline in sweetgrass materials due to private development of coastal islands and marshlands. Constant search for these materials has taken basketmakers to other areas outside the community from North Carolina to Florida. Mount Pleasant basketmakers depend on open access to these materials if their art is to continue.

Basket making has always involved the entire family. As was the custom, men and boys gathered the materials, while women and girls "sewed" the baskets. This custom continues today; however, in some instances, all members of the family are engaged in both the gathering of the materials and the making of the baskets. Rigorous craftsmanship and long hours of work are involved in making these baskets. Even for the most experienced basketmaker, a simple design can take as long as 12 hours. A larger and more complex design can take as long as two to three months.

Family members have always enjoyed close cooperation in marketing their work. It is quite common to find work belonging to several members of a family on the same basket stand. It is usually these stands that display a wide selection of baskets.

In continuous production since the 18th century, Lowcountry coil basketry is one of the oldest crafts of African origin in America. Today baskets are purchased by museums and art collectors through out the world, such as the Museum of American History at the Smithsonian Institution. Each basket reflects the artist's skill as both designer and technician. A basket's value increases with age and with proper care it will last indefinitely. Examples of Lowcountry coil basketry exist that are well over a century old.

ANGEL OAK

The Angel Oak in Charleston is a live oak (*Quercus virginiana*), a native tree species found throughout the low country, but especially on the sea islands. Live oaks are not particularly tall trees, but have wide spreading canopies. Only in the very oldest specimens do you find massive limbs resting on the ground, as do the limbs of the Angel Oak. Many people believe that the "Angel" in Angel Oak refers to a species or type of live oak that has limbs arching down to the ground, but this is not true.

In the eighteenth and nineteenth century lumber from the live oak forests of the sea islands was highly valued for ship building.

The age of the Angel Oak has long been reported to be in excess of 1,400 years. This age has never been substantiated scientifically and determining the exact age will be extremely difficult, if not impossible, because the tendency of live oaks toward heart rot makes core samples unusable. The huge size and age of the Angel Oak has been recognized locally for at least a century.

The property on which the Angel Oak stands was originally part of a land grant to Abraham Waight in 1717. Waight became a prosperous planter owning several plantations, including The Point where the Angel Oak stood. The property passed from generation to generation of Waights, acquiring the Angel name when Martha Waight married Justis Angel in 1810. The property was sold to the Mutual Land and Development Corporation in 1959, but the Angel Oak itself was leased for $1 per year by the S.C. Agricultural Society, who cared for the tree.

In 1964 W. E. Felkel purchased the tree and surrounding site. The Magnolia Garden Club cared for the tree and grounds until the late 1970s when vandalism and other problems forced the owner to fence the tree. It then became a tourist attraction and a small fee was charged to view the tree.

The City of Charleston acquired the Angel Oak and surrounding property in 1991. Angel Oak Park was opened to the public on September 23, 1991.

Height–65 feet   Circumference–25.5 feet

Area of Shade–17,000 sq. ft.   Largest Limb Circumference–11.25 feet

Length–89 feet

THE BEST FRIEND OF CHARLESTON

In the 1820's, the bustling seaport of Charleston experienced an alarming economic recession as settlements expanded inland and westward. With the decrease in commerce, Charleston merchants began aggressively investigating avenues to revitalize the floundering economy.

At this time, Europeans were just beginning to experiment with the concept of a "Rail Road," a new means of transportation that employed a "locomotive" propelled along rails by steam power.

In 1827, Charleston merchants persuaded the state legislature to charter the "South Carolina Canal and Rail Road Company" to investigate the feasibility of a rail road system connecting Charleston with inland markets, and a canal between the Ashley and Savannah rivers to divert trade from the Savannah River to Charleston.

Although a canal was never built, funds *were* raised for the rail road, and Horatio Allen was employed as the project's chief construction engineer. Allen was responsible for charting the rail route and selecting the best mans of propulsion. The rails ran a total of 136 miles from Charleston to Hamburg, passing through Summerville, Branchville and Aiken. Both sail power and horsepower were considered before a steam engine was chosen.

In October 1830, the engine arrived by packet ship from the West Point Foundry in New York. It was assembled and tested. Dubbed "Best Friend of Charleston" by eager merchants, the train made its premier trip on Christmas Day, 1830, becoming the first steam locomotive in the US to establish regularly scheduled passenger service. It ran along six miles of wood and metal rails terminating near the junction of State and Dorchester roads. This first trip was described by the "Charleston Courier" on December 29:

"The one hundred and forty-one persons flew on the wings of the wind at the speed of fifteen to twenty-five miles per hour, annihilating time and space . . . leaving all the world behind. On the return we reached Sans-Souci in quick and double quick time, stopped to take up a recruiting party—darted froth like a live rocket, scattering sparks and flames on either side—passed over three salt creeks hop, step and jump, and landed us all safe at the Lines before any of us had time to determine whether or not it was prudent to be scared."

Until this time, travel had been limited to road conditions and river navigability. More times than not, roads were dry and dusty or wet and sloggy, undependable whether being traveled by coach, horseback, or foot. Waterway navigation was severely limited to the course, water flow, depth and tides of the river systems. Both means of transportation were totally dependent upon weather and temperature conditions.

The rail road transcended these obstacles and brought economic prosperity back to Charleston. Within five months of the "Best Friend's" debut, a second locomotive arrived in Charleston. One month later, the rail line reached "Woodstock," a point between Charleston and Summerville. Then tragedy struck. A careless fireman unwittingly caused an explosion. It killed him, scalded the engineer, and destroyed the "Best Friend."

The accident proved only a minor setback to the railway transportation system. Within three years, the rail road boasted six steam locomotives, including the "Phoenix," an engine constructed from the "Best Friend's" remains.

The "Best Friend" did much in its short life. It returned economic prosperity to Charleston, and it instituted regularly scheduled steam passenger service. In doing so, it completely revolutionized America's transportation. The "Best Friend" was indeed "The little engine that die!"

The "Best Friend" Museum features a full-size antique replica of the "Best Friend" and many railroad artifacts. The engine was constructed from the original plans in 1928 to commemorate the 100th anniversary of the "South Carolina Canal and Rail Road Company." It was donated to the City of Charleston by Norfolk Southern in 1993. The Museum gift shop offers a variety of railroad merchandise. The Museum is made available to the public by a join venture of the Charleston Chapter of the National Railway Historical Society and the City of Charleston. There is no admission charge.

Charleston Firsts & Oldests

Charleston built America's first golf course, Harleston Green, and organized the first club, the South Carolina Golf Club, in 1786 • The world's first successful submarine attack occurred in Charleston harbor in 1864 when the Confederate submarine *Hunley* sank the Union warship *Housatonic*. A replica of the *Hunley* can be seen at the Charleston Museum. • The first fire insurance company in America, the "Friendly Society for Mutual Insurance of Houses against Fire," was founded in Charleston in 1736. It was bankrupted in 1740 by the great fire which destroyed more than 300 buildings. • The Best Friend of Charleston, the nation's first regularly scheduled train offering passenger service, originated from Charleston in 1830. It was the world's largest when the 140-mile rail line was completed to Hamburg, S.C. • America's first recognized woman artist, Charleston's own Henrietta Johnson began painting portraits in 1707. • Middleton Place, c. 1741, is America's oldest formally landscaped gardens. • The first prescription drug store began operation in 1780 in Charleston. • Organized in 1773, the Charleston Museum Society was the first in America. • Chartered in 1785, the College of Charleston is the oldest municipal college in America. • The Charleston Metro Chamber of Commerce, organized in 1773, is the oldest continuously running municipal Chamber in the U.S. • The first decisive American victory of the American Revolution was the Battle of Fort Sullivan on Sullivan's Island. • Formed in 1749, Congregation Beth Elohim is the second oldest synagogue in the U.S. and the oldest in continuous use. • Old St. Andrew's Parish Church, founded and built in 1706, is the oldest surviving church in the Carolinas. • Charlestonian Joel R. Poinsett first introduced the popular poinsettia plant to the U.S. in 1820. • Completed in 1742, Drayton Hall now stands as one of the oldest and finest examples of Georgian Palladian architecture built before the American Revolution.

WHERE THE CIVIL WAR BEGAN

Fort Sumter at the entrance to Charleston harbor was occupied by Union forces at the beginning of the Civil War. It was in a strategic location and the seceded South demanded that the fort be vacated. The Union refused and that set in motion the first shot of the tragic War Between the States, as some Southerners still prefer to call that war that claimed the lives of more Americans than any other war in history.

On April 12, 1861, South Carolina troops on nearby Fort Johnson, a Confederate bastion, fired on Fort Sumter. A vicious two-day bombardment followed before the Union troops surrendered.

The Confederacy held the fort until the war was lost, and it was evacuated February 17, 1865. The fort endured one of the longest sieges in history. The Confederate forces held on for almost two years while 46,000 shells weighing over seven million pounds were fired into the besieged fort.

Today, Fort Sumter is a national monument and museum housing priceless exhibits. The fort is America's most historic landmark. It is administered by the National Park Service and is located on a man-made island at the mouth of the picturesque Charleston harbor.

Tour boats have been built specifically to carry visitors to the historic fort. They are equipped with modern conveniences and every seat affords passengers a panoramic view of Charleston's unique waterfront.

ISLE OF PALMS

The Isle of Palms is a unique vacation and residential community located just ten miles north of Charleston. bordered by the Atlantic Ocean, Intracoastal Waterway, and pristine saltwater marshes abounding with wildlife, this inviting sea island is quickly and easily accessible via I-526 and the award-winning Isle of Palms Connector. Visitors discover sun-drenched beaches, a wide array of accommodations, and a diverse business district which makes it unnecessary to leave the Isle of Palms for dining, shopping, groceries or banking!

Among the island's special features are several marinas for boating travelers. Wild Dunes Resort is situated at the northern end of the island and offers two Tom Fazio golf courses, the Harbor and world-ranked Links with breath-taking views of the island's lush surroundings. This world-class golf and beach resort includes an oceanfront Grand Pavilion, a conference center and Top 50 tennis.

Seabrook Island

Seabrook Island is an exclusive, private, residential sea island located just 22 miles south of Historic Charleston. The island combines the amenities of a fine resort and the attributes of a residential community, making it attractive as a vacation home, investment property or for retirement. Seabrook is distinctive in that it is totally controlled by its property owners, who own and control a private equity club. The Club at Seabrook Island offers an impressive oceanfront Executive Conference Center, two 18-hole championship golf courses, an outstanding tennis complex and a marina offering deep-sea fishing charters. A distinctive feature of The Club is an equestrian center which provides boarding facilities and features horseback riding along trails and through the surf. While there are no hotels on the Island, privately owned homes and villas are readily available through rental programs.

PRESERVATION SOCIETY OF CHARLESTON

Founded in 1920 by Susan Frost, the Preservation Society of Charleston is a major force for the preservation of buildings, structures and sites of historical and aesthetic significance. The Society is a non-profit organization which has dedicated itself to maintaining the heritage of Charleston and the Low Country for 70 years.

The Preservation Society is a permanent institution in the community. It is the oldest community-based preservation organization in the nation and boasts over 1,500 members in the Charleston area alone.

The many important accomplishments of the Preservation Society include saving the Joseph Manigault House and the Heyward-Washington House from destruction. The Preservation Society is also responsible for the 1931 enactment of the first historic district ordinance in the United States.

From September 27–October 27 the Society hosts its Annual Fall House and Garden Tours. A tradition for the past 14 years, the Candlelight Tour of Homes and Gardens gives a glimpse into the Charleston legacy. This tour is unique because Charlestonians open their homes and gardens for those who wish to participate in the Candlelight Tour.

The Historic Charleston Foundation also concerns itself with the preservation and physical conservation of architecture representing the American heritage. Organized and incorporated in 1947, the Historic Charleston Foundation is a non-profit educational organization. The Foundation focuses on property conservation, neighborhood and commercial/business zone revitalization and stabilization of Charleston's architecturally significant urban environment.

For more than 40 years, the Foundation's primary efforts have involved Charleston's Historic District. The Foundation's house museums include the Nathaniel Russell House and the

Edmondson-Alston House. Each year the Historic Charleston Foundation hosts its Festival of Houses and Gardens. Since 1947, the tour has explored the private dwellings and gardens of Charleston's Historic District which traces its origins to the 1670s. The tour provides participants with a view of Charleston's history and architectural development.

The Historic Charleston Foundation and the Preservation Society's preservation efforts also extend to the outlying tri-county area. Most recently, the organizations saved Snee Farm as a National Historic Site. For about 200 years Snee Farm was a working plantation, beginning in the late 1600s. Snee Farm was purchased in 1754 by Col. Charles Pinckney and was later inherited by his son, Charles Pinckney, III, governor of South Carolina for four terms. During his Southern tour in the spring of 1791, George Washington visited Snee Farm before crossing the Cooper River to Charleston.

The Preservation Society is located at 147 King Street and is open daily 9 a.m.–5 p.m. For more information write the Preservation society of Charleston, Box 251, Charleston, South Carolina 29402; or call (803) 722-4630.

The Historic Charleston foundation is located at 51 Meeting Street and is open daily 10 a.m.–5 p.m For more information write the Historic Charleston Foundation, 51 Meeting Street, Charleston, South Carolina 29401; or call (803) 723-1623.

CHARLESTON—LOVINGLY PRESERVED

The story is told of a wealthy Charlestonian who was once asked why she so seldom traveled. When asked, she replied, "My dear, why should I travel when I'm already here?"

Those who have visited the beautiful area can understand her complacence. Few places on earth can rival the blend of grace, beauty, history and tradition. Charleston is a place that can satisfy the mind, body and spirit—America's most beautifully preserved architectural and historic treasure, Charleston is more than a place in the imagination, it is a dream.

Charleston is an "old world" region, lovingly preserved and unique in the American experience. You can step back to a time in the 18th century, before the revolution when Charleston was the seat of British rule and a cultural capital of British America. A seaport city rivaling the great northern colonial maritime cities of Boston and Philadelphia, but more importantly, providing a crossroads for the new thinking of a world that was only just beginning to understand the meaning of the Renaissance.

In this grand holy city, church bells still toll the hours and as the rhythmic sound of horse drawn carriages joins in, the melody fills the air. Feel and smell the salty sea breeze blowing onto the beaches of the resort islands. You can taste the delicious fresh-caught seafood, or dine in one of Charleston's restaurants. There are *Ante Bellum* homes and the plantations that echo a lifestyle of the Old South. Symbolic as monuments to the men and women who helped to mold a great nation, Charleston's plantations and gardens are elegant, stately, and are a reminder of the wars and suffering that Charlestonians saw for freedom. Not to be missed are the pew in St. Michael's Church designed for President George Washington or the hand-crafted iron gates that are handsome and utilitarian.

America's oldest gardens explode with vibrant colors and the scents of the flowers are like no others. The vision of the azaleas, roses, and camellias is too exquisite to capture on film. Charleston is beautiful and aristocratic—where century-old houses peek at you from behind gates that are alive with Carolina jessamine, the state flower of South Carolina.

You'll find a mode of transportation to show you the intimate alleys, the private gardens, and the romantic parks of a place that can never be known completely. Mystery and allure draw visitors from all over the world.

You can visit Charles Towne Landing, site of the original settlement; the Charleston Museum, America's oldest; or the world's largest naval and maritime museum at Patriots Point, home of the aircraft carrier *Yorktown*, as well as a submarine, nuclear merchant ship, a destroyer, and a Vietnam Museum. You can take a boat cruise and see Charleston as the first settlers did in 1670, from the water. Cruises start at the Charleston Marina and go up the harbor to the Charleston Naval Base or to Fort Sumter, where the Civil War began. You can drive to Fort Moultrie, scene of the first decisive American victory in the Revolution or simply stroll along the historic battery, which served as a strong defense point for the peninsula.

Charleston is a living museum and has been the setting for novels, films and operas for years. From Edgar Allen Poe's "Gold Bug" to Gershwin's *Porgy and Bess*, to Conroy's *Prince of Tides*, Charleston continues to make history.

Lush island resorts and public beaches are wide and quiet, almost as pristine as when the first settlers waded ashore from longboats, muskets at the ready. On the Isle of Palms is the Wild Dunes resort. Former host of the US Men's Clay Court Championship, this island resort boasts luxurious villas, a marina for sport and deep sea fishing, and two spectacular golf courses that skirt either the ocean or the Intracoastal Waterway.

Kiawah Island Resort is a 10,000-acre island offering ten miles of broad beach, deluxe accommodations, and abundant wildlife. The Ocean Course at Kiawah, designed by Pete Dye, hosted the 1991 Ryder Cup. Each resort is close enough to Charleston to experience all it has to offer, and yet far enough away for an unforgettable resort vacation.

Charleston is a Mecca for culture. You can visit art galleries, magnificent churches, historic homes, and public buildings and America's only tea plantation. You can charter fishing boats to the Gulf Stream, kayaks for the rivers, and sailboats for the harbor.

The City of Manners and Grace celebrates like no other can. Charleston, where pubs line the market and live music fills the night air with the feeling that, in Charleston, the party is never over. Where a seven-course meal is accompanied by music and song, turning what could be a simple supper into a dining delight. Where world-famous restaurants are as varied as the cultures that meld in this old city and charm is their common denominator. Charleston is gracious, cordial in everything she does.

Charleston is full of life, vitality, hope and celebration. These ideals are most apparent during the world-famous Spoleto Festival USA when all eyes in the arts world turn towards Charleston. This 18-day festival, founded in 1977, has been called "the number-one festival of the arts" by the *Washington Post*. Over 125 performances of opera, chamber music, symphonic and choral works, jazz theater, classical ballet, modern dance and the visual arts fill historic Charleston.

In February, thousands of people flock to the area for the Southeastern Wildlife Expo, the nation's largest wildlife art show. This festival showcases wildlife artists, sculptors and carvers from North America, Europe and Africa.

In the spring and early fall the Festival of Homes and Gardens will take you into some of the oldest and grandest homes in the South. These private residences, once taboo to "commoners," are now proudly shared with the public. The manicured private gardens spotlight the area's most beautiful flowers and trees. To visit a home once lived in by famous Americans is to go back in history, an experience you won't soon forget.

Charleston offers native hospitality finely tuned by 300 years of making visitors welcome. For more information contact the Convention & Visitors Bureau, P.O. Box 975, Charleston, SC 29402 or call (803) 853-8000.

CHARLESTON—WHERE HISTORY BEGAN

Charleston is America's most beautifully preserved architectural and historic treasure, with a rich, 300-year history just waiting to be discovered. Hundreds of significant and lovingly preserved structures from the colonial and antebellum periods grace the Historic District's narrow streets. Church bells toll the hour as history unfolds around each and every corner. In no other place are the past and present more intertwined!

The entire Charleston area is a never-ending feast for the senses, with history serving as the main course. Charles Towne Landing is the site where the original settlement was established in 1670. Patriots Point is the world's largest naval and maritime museum and home of World War II's "Fighting Lady," the aircraft carrier Yorktown. Fort Moultrie is the scene of the first decisive American victory of the Revolution and a mainstay of shore defense until 1947. Fort Sumter is the man-made island fortress where the Civil War began. World-famous plantations and gardens give you a fascinating glimpse into life during the antebellum era.

The area's lush sea islands and sun-drenched beaches offer as much recreation or relaxation as your heart desires. Golf is on a world-class level, with challenging courses reflecting the natural beauty of the South Carolina low country. Charter fishing to the Gulf Stream or inshore waters is readily available. The native sweetgrass baskets and handmade crafts found in Charleston's famous open-air market are unique.

CHARLESTON SURVIVORS

The birth of a new decade brings a certain freshness which invigorates the human spirit as does the birth of a new colony, one which 148 foreigners in 1670, would proudly call home within a century. The marshy shores, the lush forests, and the abundant wildlife welcomed the weary wanderers, captivated them and changed not only their destinies, but their children's lineage from English to Charlestonian.

In 1669, under the leadership of Joseph West, the three vessels, the *Carolina*, the *Port Royal*, and the *Albemarle* (which was replaced by the *Three Brothers* after suffering heavy damage) set their sights on the new land—America. A severe storm separated the three vessels, wrecked the *Port Royal*, and forced the *Carolina* to Bermuda. In Bermuda, Colonel William Sayle joined the party as governor.

The first view of Carolina came in March at Bull's Island. The weary travelers were entreated by the Kiawah Indians to settle at a more promising location further up the coast. The colonists landed on a tract of land they christened Albemarle Point in April 1670. They later changed the name to Charles Town, after King Charles II of England.

The ten-acre plot of land protected by the marsh, a creek and the Ashley River, proved a wise location for the young colony. Additional settlers arrived from Barbados in February 1671. By 1672 the expanding settlement recognized the advantages of relocation across the river on the peninsula of land then known as Oyster Point, between the Ashley and Cooper rivers. The classical continental plan was used, with the "great streets," now Meeting and Broad, intersecting at the market square. In fact, it was here that city planning was first tried in America.

With its many wharves along East Bay Street, Charleston became a busy seaport. Ships with raw materials: deer skins, hemp, rice, indigo, and eventually cotton, returned to England and commerce was born. They returned heavy with the staples and luxuries of Europe, which lent a cosmopolitan air to the growing community. Even in its infancy, Charleston won the reputation of being "Little London" in the semi-tropical wilds of the New World.

Colonists found out early that the New World had its share of troubles and danger. The temperament of their adopted land revealed a smallpox epidemic, a fire which destroyed one-third of the colony, a plague among the cattle, yellow fever and hurricanes that thrashed the Charles Town coast.

An archaic form of government stifled local political freedom, while a liberal provision in the second charter guaranteed religious freedom. The latter was a landmark for its day and attracted diverse groups to the Carolina province. This religious toleration was responsible for great growth during the first years. French Huguenots came over in great numbers after the revocation of the Edict of Nantes; the Baptists had built a church by 1701, and the Congregationalists and the Presbyterians were united in 1690. Early in the next century, however, twelve Scottish families withdrew to form the Scots Kirk, now the First (Scots) Presbyterian Church. A Jewish congregation had formed by 1750, followed shortly by a Lutheran Church and Methodist assembly. Roman Catholic mass was held first in 1786.

"Free schools" were established in 1710 by the prosperous colony, growing wealthy from the mounting exports of rice from the surrounding plantations.

In 1715 Charles Town learned of a massive Indian conspiracy to overrun the English in the South. In fact, 190 settlers around Pocotaligo were murdered by the Yemassee Indians. Reinforcements came in from Virginia and North Carolina to help the Carolina province militia restore the peace.

Pirates were the "Indians" of the sea. Looting, murdering, and pillaging were a way of life that endangered ships and crews leaving the safety of Charleston harbor. Finally, with the Indians silenced and the pirates humbled, the colonists took stock of their condition. They decided to repudiate the rule of the Lords

Proprietors and pledged themselves to the King of England. Charles Town entered the 1720's as a Royal Colony.

The colony settled down to the pleasant task of cultural pursuits, and in mid-century the already thriving economy was reinforced by the advent of indigo which made possible the elegant mansions and urban dwellings for which Charles Town became noted. In 1740 the tranquility of the prosperous period was marred. In the month of November a fire destroyed 300 houses and a great number of stores in four hours.

In 1776 a fleet of ships with 270 guns failed to take Colonel William Moultrie's palmetto fort. In 1778 the British attacked again, this time coming overland from Savannah. The city held, but much of the surrounding countryside was put to the torch. The British took control and Charles Town was an occupied city until the autumn of December 1781, when the British returned to England and Charleston was born.

Having established a city government, the state capital was moved to the center of the state, and Columbia was founded. Prosperity returned and plantations began to thrive once again. Slaves were used in making the system feasible. By the middle of the 19th century prosperity from an agrarian society was interlaced with great interest in cultural affairs. In 1791 President George Washington made a tour of states and was received in Charleston with the pomp and display once reserved for royal governors.

In April 1861 Fort Sumter was under siege and General Beauregard prepared the city for the bloody war. Following the war, Charlestonians were too poor to remodel their magnificent old homes to conform to the Victorian period. Charleston simply adapted her old buildings which had charm, distinction and tradition. The adaptation has been molded, strengthened, and guided by preservation groups that have beaten the dust of deterioration out of once proud neighborhoods and renewed the city with vigor and determination.

CONCLUSION

Many have said that man is a disease upon the earth and his bulldozers and draglines have raped the marshes, estuaries and forests of the wilderness areas. Poisons have been spread upon the land and in the air that have made survival impossible for many creatures. Some wildlife has adapted to change to accommodate man's demands, but other have succumbed to people's progress.

Regardless of one's affection for ecology, there must be some destruction of wildlife, some change in the life style of creatures. Animals can no longer move deeper into the plains of the West or the swamps of the Southland as man steadily creeps into every nook and corner of the land where he lives, breeds and faces the task of providing more and more food and fiber for a world of humans now numbering almost four billion. The real tragedy is that man waited so long before trying to maintain the ecological and environmental balance of the flora and fauna in this beautiful New World. Man has been wasteful and inconsiderate as he looked upon North America as a land flowing with an inexhaustible supply of milk and honey.

I am thankful that all over our country today the movement is to preserve some of the natural habitat of wildlife with which America is still blessed, so that lower life will not perish from this earth.

People ensnared in the concrete jungles of big cities yearn for an opportunity to live close to nature in Gardens of Eden like the Carolina coastal counties. They want to live near the sea, the sun and the sand. They want to escape the cold of the North and enjoy this warm Paradise. Even with man's intrusion looking for prettier, warmer places to live and enjoy, this Carolina coast can accommodate mankind and still remain a refuge for the birds, mammals, reptiles and fish that attracted the itinerant Indians thousands of years ago.

It is with that hope, that prayer, that this, my favorite spot on earth, will be preserved forever.

W.H.C.

I would like to have additional copies of this book.

Coastal Carolinas Tales and Truths

Please mail me _____ copies to the address below:

Name _____

Address _____

_____

Enclosed please find check or money order in the amount of $16.95 that includes postage and handling for each book.

Plase mail to: W. Hoarace Carter

Atlantic Publishing Company

P.O. Box 67

Tabor City, NC 28463

Phone 910-653-3153

(Tear out & mail this sheet to publisher.)

Please ship me one copy of Atlantic Book checked below:

Hannon's Field Guide for Bass Fishing	$ 9.95
Creatures & Chronicles from Cross Creek	9.30
Land That I Love (Hard-bound)	14.50
Wild & Wonderful Santee-Cooper Country	8.30
Return to Cross Creek	9.30
Nature's Masterpiece at Homosassa	9.30
Catch Bass	8.30
Hannon's Big Bass Magic	13.50
A Man Called Raleigh	9.50
Damn the Allegators	10.95
Bird Hunters Handbook	11.50
Lures for Lunker Bass	12.95
Best Bass Pros, Vol. I & Vol. II	10.95
Deer & Fixings	9.95
Hunting Hogs, Boar & Javelina	10.95
Trophy Stripers	12.95
Forty Years in the Everglades	9.95
Headstart Fishing Handbook	16.95
Florida Nature Coast Tales & Truths	14.95
Tremblin' Earth	12.95